Adobe® Photoshop® CS

CLASSROOM
IN A BOOK®

www.adobepress.com

Adobe Press books are published by Peachpit Press, Berkeley, CA. To report errors, please send a note to errata@peachpit.com.

Printed in the U.S.A.

ISBN # 0-321-19375-X

9 8 7 6 5 4

Contents

Getting Started

Adobe® Photoshop® CS delivers powerful, industry-standard, image-editing tools for professional designers who want to produce sophisticated graphics for the Web and for print. Included with Photoshop CS is ImageReady™ CS and its versatile set of Web tools for optimizing and previewing images, batch-processing images with droplets in the Actions palette, and creating rollovers and GIF animations. Photoshop and ImageReady combined offer a comprehensive environment for designing graphics for the Web.

About Classroom in a Book

Adobe Photoshop CS Classroom in a Book® is part of the official training series for Adobe graphics and publishing software developed by experts at Adobe Systems. The lessons are designed to let you learn at your own pace. If you're new to Adobe Photoshop or ImageReady, you'll learn the fundamental concepts and features you'll need to master the programs. And, if you've been using Adobe Photoshop or ImageReady for a while, you'll find that Classroom in a Book teaches many advanced features, including tips and techniques for using the latest version of these applications and for preparing images for the Web.

The lessons in this edition include information on many new features, such as a new chapter on using Smart Guides to arrange layer objects in ImageReady and new sections on creating and using layer comps. Other lessons incorporate other new features.

Although each lesson provides step-by-step instructions for creating a specific project, there's room for exploration and experimentation. You can follow the book from start to finish or do only the lessons that match your interests and needs. Each lesson concludes with a review section summarizing what you've covered.

Prerequisites

Before beginning to use *Adobe Photoshop CS Classroom in a Book*, you should have a working knowledge of your computer and its operating system. Make sure that you know how to use the mouse and standard menus and commands, and also how to open, save, and close files. If you need to review these techniques, see the documentation included with your Microsoft® Windows® or Apple® Mac® OS 10 documentation.

Installing Adobe Photoshop and Adobe ImageReady

Before you begin using *Adobe Photoshop CS Classroom in a Book*, make sure that your system is set up correctly and that you've installed the required software and hardware. You must purchase the Adobe Photoshop CS software separately. For system requirements and complete instructions on installing the software, see the *InstallReadMe* file on the application CD.

Photoshop and ImageReady use the same installer. You must install the applications from the Adobe Photoshop CS application CD onto your hard disk; you cannot run the program from the CD. Follow the on-screen instructions.

Make sure that your serial number is accessible before installing the application; you can find the serial number on the registration card or CD sleeve.

Starting Adobe Photoshop and Adobe ImageReady

You start Photoshop and ImageReady just as you would most software applications.

To start Adobe Photoshop or ImageReady in Windows:

1 Choose Start > Programs > Adobe > Photoshop CS or choose Start > Programs > Adobe > ImageReady CS.

If you have deleted the preferences file, a message appears asking if you want to edit your color settings.

2 Click No to close the message without editing your color settings.

You'll learn more about calibrating a monitor, later. (See Lesson 19, "Setting Up Your Monitor for Color Management," in this book.)

3 In the Welcome Screen, select Close.

To start Adobe Photoshop or Adobe ImageReady in Mac OS:

1 Open the Application/Adobe/Adobe Photoshop CS folder, and double-click the Adobe Photoshop or Adobe ImageReady program icon. (If you installed the program in a folder other than Adobe Photoshop, open that folder.)

If you have deleted the preferences file, a message appears asking if you want to edit your color settings.

2 Click No to close the message without editing your color settings.

You'll learn more about calibrating a monitor, later. (See Lesson 19, "Setting Up Your Monitor for Color Management," in this book.)

3 In the Welcome Screen, select Close.

Installing the Classroom in a Book fonts

To ensure that the lesson files appear on your system with the correct fonts, you may need to install the Classroom in a Book font files. The fonts are in the Fonts folder on the *Adobe Photoshop CS Classroom in a Book* CD. If you already have these on your system, you do not need to install them.

Installing fonts from the Adobe Photoshop CS Classroom in a Book CD

Use the following procedure to install the fonts on your hard drive.

1 Insert the *Adobe Photoshop CS Classroom in a Book* CD into your CD-ROM drive.

2 Install the font files using the procedure for the version of your operating system:

• Windows. Drag the fonts from the CD to your hard disk and place them in your Adobe common fonts folder (typically in C:\Program Files\Common Files\Adobe\Fonts).

• Mac OS. Open the Fonts folder on the CD. Select all of the fonts in the Fonts folder and drag them into the Library/Fonts folder on your hard disk. You can select and drag multiple fonts to install them, but you cannot drag the entire folder to install the fonts.

Copying the Classroom in a Book files

The *Adobe Photoshop CS Classroom in a Book* CD includes folders containing all the electronic files for the lessons. Each lesson has its own folder, and you must copy the folders to your hard disk to do the lessons. To save room on your disk, you can install only the folder necessary for each lesson as you need it, and remove it when you're done.

To install the Classroom in a Book lesson files:

1 Insert the *Adobe Photoshop CS Classroom in a Book* CD into your CD-ROM drive.

2 Browse the CD contents and locate the Lessons folder.

3 Do one of the following:

• To copy all of the lessons, drag the Lessons folder from the CD onto your hard disk.

• To copy only individual lessons, first create a new folder on your hard disk and name it **Lessons**. Then, drag the lesson folder or folders that you want to copy from the CD into the Lessons folder on your hard disk.

If you are installing the files in Windows 2000, you need to unlock them before using them. You don't need to unlock the files if you are installing them in Windows XP or Mac OS.

4 (Windows 2000 only) Unlock the files you copied:

• If you copied all of the lessons, double-click the unlock.bat file in the Lessons folder.

• If you copied a single lesson, drag the unlock.bat file from the Lessons folder on the CD into the Lessons folder on your hard disk. Then, double-click the unlock.bat file in the Lessons folder on your hard disk.

This final step is not necessary for Windows XP or Mac OS.

Note: As you work through each lesson, you will overwrite the start files. If you want to restore the original files, recopy the corresponding Lesson folder from the Adobe Photoshop CS Classroom in a Book *CD to the Lessons folder on your hard drive.*

Restoring default preferences

The preferences files store palette and command settings and color-calibration information. Each time you quit Adobe Photoshop or Adobe ImageReady, the positions of the palettes and certain command settings are recorded in the respective preferences file. When you use the Adobe Color Management Assistant, monitor-calibration and color-space information is stored in the Photoshop preferences files as well. Any selections you make in the Preferences dialog box are also part of this type of application file.

At the beginning of each lesson in this book, you will be told to reset the default preferences, using a three-key combination. This deletes any custom color-calibration information that you may have configured earlier in the session. It also deletes any options you may have selected in the Preferences dialog box.

You can ignore the instructions to reset your preferences. If you do so, be aware that the tools, palettes, and other settings in your Photoshop CS application may not match those described in this book, so you'll have to be slightly more resourceful in finding things. With that in mind, you should be able to do the lesson without other difficulties.

Saving your monitor-calibration settings is a simple procedure that you should perform before you start work on this book. (See "To save your current color settings:" on page 5.) If you have not yet custom-calibrated your color monitor; this procedure is unnecessary.

Saving the options you've selected in the Preferences dialog box is more complicated on the newer Windows and Macintosh operating systems and beyond the scope of this book. If you are not sure how to do this yourself, get help from your group's Network Administrator. Otherwise, you could simply keep a record of preferences that you've customized and then restore them manually after you finish these lessons.

To save your current color settings:

1 Start Adobe Photoshop.

2 Choose Edit > Color Settings.

3 In the Color Settings dialog box, examine the Settings option.

• If the Settings option is Custom, go on to Step 4 of this procedure.

• If the Settings option is anything other than Custom, click OK to close the dialog box. You do not need to do any more of this procedure.

4 Select the Save button. (Be careful to select Save, *not* OK.)

The Save dialog box opens to the Settings folder, which contains various files with the .csf extension.

5 In File Name, type a descriptive name for your color settings. Then click Save.

6 In the Color Settings Comment dialog box, type any descriptive text that will help you identify the color settings later, such as the date, specific settings, or your workgroup.

7 Click OK to close the Color Settings Comment dialog box, and again to close the Save dialog box.

To restore your color settings:

1 Start Adobe Photoshop.

2 Choose Edit > Color Settings.

3 In the Settings pop-up menu in the Color Settings dialog box, select the color-settings file you defined in the previous procedure.

4 Click OK.

Additional resources

Adobe Photoshop CS Classroom in a Book is not meant to replace documentation that comes with the program or to be a comprehensive reference for every feature in Photoshop CS or ImageReady CS. Only the commands and options used in the lessons are explained in this book. For comprehensive information about program features, refer to any of these resources:

• Photoshop Help, which is the complete version of the user guide built into the Adobe Photoshop CS application. You can view by choosing Help > Contents (Windows) or Help > Help Contents (Mac OS). For more information, see Lesson 1, "Getting to Know the Work Area."

• The Adobe Web site (www.adobe.com), which you can view by choosing Help > Adobe Online if you have a connection to the World Wide Web.

• The *Adobe Photoshop CS User Guide*, which contains most of the material included in the Help system. If the user guide book is not included in your Photoshop CS package, it is available for purchase at the Adobe Web site: www.adobe.com. The Help system that is already built into the application contains all the information in the User Guide, plus additional information not included in the printed version.

Adobe Certification

The Adobe Training and Certification Programs are designed to help Adobe customers improve and promote their product-proficiency skills. The Adobe Certified Expert (ACE) program is designed to recognize the high-level skills of expert users. Adobe Certified Training Providers (ACTP) use only Adobe Certified Experts to teach Adobe software classes. Available in either ACTP classrooms or on-site, the ACE program is the best way to master Adobe products. For Adobe Certified Training Programs information, visit the Partnering with Adobe Web site at http://partners.adobe.com.

Lesson 1

1 Getting to Know the Work Area

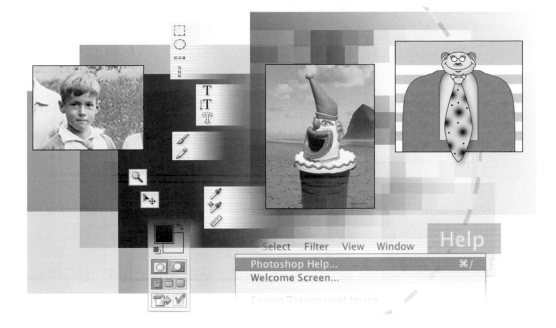

As you work with Adobe Photoshop and Adobe ImageReady, you'll discover that there is often more than one way to accomplish the same task. To make the best use of the extensive editing capabilities in these programs, you first must learn to navigate the work area.

In this lesson, you'll learn how to do the following:

- Open Adobe Photoshop files.
- Open, close, and use the File Browser to preview and select files.
- Select and use some of the tools in the toolbox.
- Set options for a selected tool, using the tool options bar.
- Use various methods of zooming in and out on an image.
- Select, rearrange, and use palettes.
- Select commands on palette menus and context menus.
- Open and use a palette docked in the palette well.
- Undo actions to correct mistakes or to make different choices.
- Jump from Photoshop to ImageReady.
- Find topics in Photoshop Help.
- Prepare your own How To topics and list them on the Photoshop Help menu.

This lesson will take about an hour to complete. The lesson is designed to be done in Adobe Photoshop. Most of this lesson could be done in Adobe ImageReady, but the File Browser is not available in ImageReady, so it's best to do this lesson in Photoshop.

Before starting Adobe Photoshop, locate the Lesson01 folder on the *Adobe Photoshop CS Classroom in a Book* CD, and copy the folder into the Lessons folder that you created on your hard disk for these projects (or create it now). As you work on this lesson, you'll overwrite the start files. If you need to restore the start files, copy them again from the *Adobe Photoshop CS Classroom in a Book* CD.

Note: Windows 2000 users need to unlock the lesson files before using them. For more information, see "Copying the Classroom in a Book files" on page 3.

Starting to work in Adobe Photoshop

The Adobe Photoshop and Adobe ImageReady work areas include the command menus at the top of your screen and a variety of tools and palettes for editing and adding elements to your image. You can also add commands and filters to the menus by installing third-party software known as *plug-in modules*.

Both Photoshop and ImageReady work with bitmapped, digitized images (that is, continuous-tone images that have been converted into a series of small squares, or picture elements, called *pixels*). In Photoshop, you can also work with vector graphics, which are drawings made up of smooth lines that retain their crispness when scaled. In ImageReady, you can create moving elements, such as animations and rollovers, for on-screen viewing.

You can create original artwork in both Photoshop and ImageReady, or you can import images into the program from many sources, such as:

- Photographs from a digital camera.
- Commercial CDs of previously digitized images.
- Scans of photographs, transparencies, negatives, graphics, or other documents.
- Captured video images.
- Artwork created in drawing programs.

For information on the kinds of files you can use with Adobe Photoshop CS, see "About file formats" in Photoshop Help.

Starting Photoshop and opening a file

To begin, you'll start Adobe Photoshop and reset the default preferences.

Note: Usually, you won't reset the defaults when you're on your own. However, while you're working in this book, you'll reset them each time, so that what you see on screen matches the descriptions in the lessons. See "Restoring default preferences" on page 4.

1 On the desktop, double-click the Adobe Photoshop icon to start Adobe Photoshop and then immediately hold down Ctrl+Alt+Shift (Windows) or Command+Option+Shift (Mac OS) to reset the default settings.

If you don't see the Photoshop icon on your desktop, look in the Start/Programs/Adobe menu (Windows) or in either the Applications folder or the dock (Mac OS).

2 As the following three messages appear:

- Click Yes to confirm that you want to delete the Adobe Photoshop Settings File.
- Click No to close the message about configuring your color monitor settings.
- Click Close to close the Welcome Screen.

The Photoshop work area appears in the configuration shown in the illustration below.

Note: The illustration below shows the Mac OS version of Photoshop. On Windows, the arrangement is the same but some of the operating system styles are different.

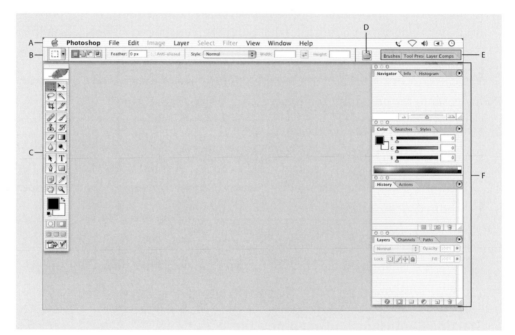

A. Menu bar B. Tool options bar C. Toolbox D. File Browser button E. Palette well F. Palettes

The default work areas of Photoshop and ImageReady consist of a menu bar at the top of the work area, a tool options bar below the menu bar, a floating toolbox on the left, floating palettes, and one or more image windows, which you open separately.

Note: Photoshop and ImageReady have many palettes in common, but some palettes are unique to one application or the other. You'll learn more about the different palettes in virtually every lesson in this book.

3 Choose File > Open, and navigate to the Lessons/Lesson01/Project1 folder that you copied to your hard drive from the *Adobe Photoshop CS Classroom in a Book* CD.

4 Select the 01End1.psd file and click Open.

The 01End1.psd file opens in its own window, called the *image window*. The End files in this book show you what you are aiming for in the different projects. In this End file, an old school photograph has been enhanced so that one student in the class appears spotlighted while the rest of the picture appears to be in shadow.

5 Choose File > Close, or click the close button on the title bar of the window in which the photograph appears. (Do not click the close button for Photoshop.)

Opening a file with the File Browser

You'll do your work in different start files within each lesson. You can make additional copies of these files and save them under different names or locations. Or, you can work in your original start files and then copy them again from the CD again if you want a fresh start. There are four different start files for this lesson, each of which is in its own Project folder.

In the previous procedure, you used the classic method of opening a file. Now you'll open another file using the File Browser, one of the Photoshop features that takes the guesswork out of finding the image file you need.

1 Click the File Browser button ( ) on the tool options bar.

The File Browser opens, displaying a collection of palettes, menus, buttons, and panes.

Note: You can also open the File Browser by choosing File > Browse.

2 In the Folders palette within the File Browser, navigate to the Lessons/Lesson01 folder on your hard drive and select the Project1 folder nested within it.

When you select the Project1 folder, thumbnails of the folder contents appear in the right pane of the File Browser.

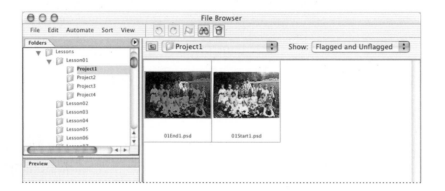

3 Select the 01Start1.psd file and open it in either of the following ways:

• Double-click the thumbnail for the 01Start1.psd file.

• Select the thumbnail for the 01Start1 file, and then, using the menu bar that is inside the File Browser, choose File > Open.

The image window for the 01Start1 file now appears in front of the File Browser.

4 Close the File Browser in any of the following ways:

• Click the close button on the File Browser title bar.

• Select the File Browser button on the tool options bar once to bring the File Browser forward and a second time to close it.

• Click the File Browser to bring it forward, and then choose File > Close on the main Photoshop menu bar.

The File Browser is much more than a convenient visual interface for opening files. You'll have the chance to learn more about the many features and functions of the File Browser in Lesson 2, "Using the File Browser."

Using the tools

Together, Photoshop and ImageReady provide a consistent and integrated set of tools for producing sophisticated graphics for print and online viewing. ImageReady includes many tools that are familiar to Photoshop users and some that are unique. Lessons 14–18 focus on ImageReady tools and features.

It could easily require an entire book to catalog details for the wealth of tools and tool configurations that are possible in Photoshop. While that would certainly be a useful reference, it's not the goal of this book. Instead, you'll start gaining experience by configuring and using a few tools on a sample project. Every lesson will introduce you to more tools and ways to use them. By the time you finish all the lessons in this book, you'll have a solid foundation for further explorations of the Photoshop tool set.

Selecting and using a tool from the toolbox

The toolbox—the long, narrow palette on the far left side of the work area—contains selection tools, painting and editing tools, foreground- and background-color selection boxes, and viewing tools.

You'll start by using the Zoom tool, which appears in many other applications, including Adobe products such as Acrobat, Illustrator, PageMaker, and InDesign.

1 Examine the status bar at the bottom of the work area (Windows) or image window (Mac OS) and notice the percentage listed on the far left end. This represents the current enlargement view of the image, or zoom level.

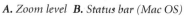

A. *Zoom level* **B.** *Status bar (Mac OS)*

Note: *In Windows, look for the status bar across the bottom of the Photoshop work area.*

2 Move the pointer over the toolbox and let it hover over the small magnifying-glass button until a tooltip appears, identifying the tool by name and providing the keyboard shortcut for the tool.

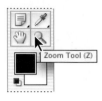

3 Select the Zoom tool to make it active by doing either of the following:

• Click the Zoom tool button ($\mathcal{Q}$) in the toolbox

• Press Z, which is the keyboard shortcut for the Zoom tool.

4 Move the pointer over the image window. Notice that the pointer now looks like a tiny magnifying glass with a plus sign (+) in the center of the glass.

5 Click anywhere in the image window.

The image enlarges to a preset percentage level, which replaces the previous value in the status bar. The location you clicked when you used the Zoom tool becomes the center of the enlarged view. If you click again, the zoom advances to the next preset level, up to a maximum of 1600%.

6 Hold down the Alt key (Windows) or Option key (Mac OS) so that the Zoom tool pointer appears with a minus sign (-) in the center of the magnifying glass, and then click anywhere in the image. Then release the Alt or Option key.

Now the view zooms out to a lower preset magnification. Examine the photograph and decide which child you want to spotlight.

Note: There are other ways to zoom out. You can select the Zoom In ($\mathcal{Q}$) or Zoom Out ($\mathcal{Q}$) tool mode on the tool options bar for the Zoom tool. You can choose View > Zoom In or View > Zoom Out. Or, you can type a lower percentage in the status bar.

7 Using the Zoom tool, drag a rectangle to enclose the area of the image that includes the child you want to spotlight.

The image enlarges so that the area you enclosed in your rectangle fills the image window.

You have now tried out three different ways of using the Zoom tool to change the magnification in the image window: clicking, holding down a keyboard shortcut while clicking, and dragging to define a magnification area. Many of the other tools in the toolbox can be used with keyboard combinations. You'll have opportunities to use these techniques in various lessons in this book.

Selecting and using a hidden tool

Photoshop has many tools you can use to edit image files, but you will probably work with only a few of them at a time. The toolbox arranges some of the tools in groups, with only one tool shown for each group. The other tools in the group are hidden behind that tool.

A small triangle in the lower right corner of a button is your clue that other tools are available but hidden under that tool.

1 Position the pointer over the tool at the top of the left toolbox column until the tooltip appears, identifying it as the Rectangular Marquee tool (⬚) with the keyboard shortcut M. Then select that tool.

2 Select the Elliptical Marquee tool (◯), which is hidden behind the Rectangular Marquee tool, using one of the following methods:

• Hold down the mouse button over the Rectangular Marquee tool to open the pop-up list of hidden tools, and select the Elliptical Marquee tool.

• Alt-click (Windows) or Option-click (Mac OS) the tool button in the toolbox to cycle through the hidden marquee tools until the Elliptical Marquee tool is selected.

• Press Shift+M, which switches back and forth between the Rectangular and Elliptical Marquee tools.

3 Move the pointer over the image window, so that the pointer appears as crosshairs (-¦-) and move it to the upper left side of the child's head.

4 Drag the pointer down and to the right to draw an ellipse around the child and then release the mouse button.

An animated dashed line indicates that the area inside it is *selected*. When you select an area, it becomes the only editable area of the image. The area outside the selection is protected.

5 Move the pointer inside the elliptical selection you created, so that the pointer appears as an arrow with a small rectangle (▶₍₎).

6 Drag the selection so that it is accurately centered over the child.

When you drag the selection, only the selection border moves, not pixels in the image. When you want to move the pixels that make up the image, you'll need to use a different technique, which you'll learn a little later. There's more about making different kinds of selections and moving the selection contents in Lesson 4, "Working with Selections."

Using keyboard combinations with tool actions

Many tools can operate under certain constraints. You usually activate these modes by holding down specific keyboard keys as you move the tool with the mouse. Some tools have modes that you choose in the tool options bar.

The next task is to make a fresh start at selecting the child. This time, you'll use a keyboard combination that constrains the elliptical selection to a perfect circle that you'll draw from the center outward instead of from the outside inward.

1 Make sure that the Elliptical Marquee tool (⬭) is still selected in the toolbox, and deactivate the current selection by doing one of the following:

• In the image window, click anywhere in that is outside of the selected area.

• Choose Select > Deselect.

• Use the keyboard shortcut, Ctrl+D (Windows) or Command+D (Mac OS).

2 Position the pointer in the center of the child's face.

3 Hold down Alt+Shift (Windows) or Option+Shift (Mac OS) and drag outward from the center of the face until the circle completely encloses the child's face.

4 Carefully release first the mouse button and then the keyboard keys.

If you are not satisfied with the selection circle, you can move it: Place the pointer inside the circle and drag. Or, you can click outside the selection circle to deselect it, and then try again.

Note: *If you accidentally release one or both of the keys prematurely, the tool reverts to its normal behavior (unconstrained and drawing from the edge). However, if you haven't yet released the mouse button, you can just press the keys down again, and the selection changes back. If you have released the mouse button, simply start again at Step 1.*

5 In the toolbox, double-click the Zoom tool (🔍) to return to 100% view. If the entire image doesn't fit in the image window, select the Fit In Screen button on the tool options bar.

Notice that the selection remains active, even after you use the Zoom tool.

Applying a change to a selected area

In order to spotlight the selected child, you'll want to darken the rest of the image, not the area inside the current selection. Since the area within the selection is protected from change, you'll reverse the selection, making the rest of the image active and preventing the change from affecting the one child's face.

1 Choose Select > Inverse.

Although the animated selection border around the child looks the same as it did before, notice that a similar border appears all around the edges of the image. Now the rest of the image is selected and can be edited, while the area within the circle is not selected and cannot be changed while the selection is active.

A. *Selected area (editable)* **B.** *Unselected area (protected)*

2 Choose Image > Adjustments > Curves.

💡 *The keyboard shortcut for this command, Ctrl+M (Windows) or Command+M (Mac OS) appears by the command name on the Adjustments submenu. In the future, you could just press that keyboard combination to open the Curves dialog box.*

3 In the Curves dialog box, make sure that the Preview option is selected. If necessary, drag the Curves dialog box to one side so that you can see most of the image window.

The Preview option shows the effect of your selections in the image window, so the picture changes as you adjust settings. This makes it unnecessary to repeatedly open and close a dialog box as you try out different options and refine them.

4 Drag the control point in the upper right corner of the graph straight down until the value shown in the Output option is approximately 150. (The Input value should remain unchanged.)

As you drag, the highlights are reduced in the selected area of the image.

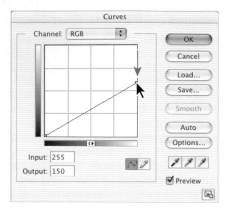

💡 *As soon as you click the control point, the Output value at the bottom of the page can be edited directly, so you can set the level by typing, or you can* scrub *to set it. To scrub, move the pointer over the label* Output, *so that it appears as a pointing finger with two tiny, horizontal arrows. Drag left over the label to reduce the value, or right to increase it. Scrubbing is now available for many numeric options in Photoshop and ImageReady, whether in the tool options bar, a palette, or a dialog box.*

5 Examine the results in the image window, and then adjust the Output value up or down until you are satisfied with the results.

6 Click OK to close the Curves dialog box.

7 Do one of the following:

• If you want to save your changes, choose File > Save and then choose File > Close.

• If you want to revert to the unaltered version of the file, choose File > Close, and select No when you are asked if you want to save your changes

• If you want to do both of the above, choose File > Save As, and then either rename the file or save it to a different folder on your computer, and click OK. Then choose File > Close.

It's not necessary to deselect, because closing the file cancels the selection.

Congratulations! You've just finished your first Photoshop project. Although the Curves dialog box is actually one of the more sophisticated methods of altering an image, it isn't that difficult to use, as you have seen. You will learn more about making adjustments to images in many other lessons in this book. Lessons 3 and 7 especially address techniques that are comparable to those used in classic darkroom work, such as adjusting for exposure, retouching, and correcting colors.

Try this: another way to zoom and scroll in the image window

The Navigator palette is another speedy method of making large changes in the zoom level, especially when the exact percentage of magnification is unimportant to you. It's also a great way to scroll around in an image, because the thumbnail shows you the context so you can tell exactly what part of the image appears in the image window.

The slider underneath the image thumbnail in the Navigator palette enlarges the image when you drag it to the right (toward the large mountain icon) and reduces it when you drag to the left.

The heavy red rectangle outline represents the area of the image that appears in the image window. When you are zoomed in far enough so that the image window shows only part of the image, you can drag the red outline around the thumbnail area to see other areas of the image. This also is an excellent way to verify which part of an image you're working on when you work at very high zoom levels.

Using the tool options bar and other palettes

Did you notice that you've already had some experience with the tool options bar? In the previous project, you saw that there are options on the tool options bar for the Zoom tool that change the view of the current image window. You also used the File Browser button that always appears on the tool options bar, regardless of which tool might be active.

Previewing and opening another file

The next project involves a promotional postcard for a community project. You'll use the File Browser again to preview the end file—which shows you what you're aiming to do—and to open the start file.

1 Select the File Browser button ( ) on the tool options bar to open the File Browser.

2 In the File Browser Folders palette, select the Lessons/Lesson01/Project2 folder.

3 Select the 01End2.psd file in the thumbnails pane so that it appears in the Preview palette.

Examine the image and notice the text that is set against the cloud-like area across the lower part of the image.

💡 *You can drag the vertical bar that is between the thumbnails pane and the three palettes on the left to resize the areas. Drag it to the right to enlarge the image in the Preview palette to get a better look at the finished image. You can also drag the horizontal bars above and below the Preview palette to make it taller or shorter.*

4 Select the thumbnail for the 01Start2.psd file and open it in Photoshop, either by double-clicking the thumbnail or by choosing File > Open on the File Browser menu bar.

5 Click the File Browser to bring it forward and then close it.

Setting tool properties on the tool options bar

With the 01Start2.psd file open in Photoshop, you're now ready to select the characteristics for the text and then to type your message.

1 In the toolbox, select the Type tool (**T**).

The buttons and menu in the tool options bar now relate to the Type tool.

2 In the tool options bar, do the following:

• Select a font you like from the first pop-up menu. (We used Adobe Garamond, but you can use another font if you prefer.)

• Select **12 pt** as the font size. (You can select using the pop-up menu illustrated below, by typing directly in the font-size text box, or by scrubbing the font-size option label.)

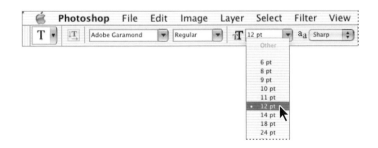

3 Click once anywhere on the left side of the image and type **Monday is Beach Cleanup Day**.

The text appears with the font and font-size formatting that you selected.

4 In the toolbox, select the Move tool (⊹) at the top of the column on the right.

5 Position the Move tool pointer over the text you typed and drag the text into the misty white rectangle near the bottom of the image, centering the text inside it.

Using palettes and palette menus

The text color in your image is the same as the Foreground Color swatch in the toolbox, which is black by default. The text in the End file example was colored a dark blue that coordinates nicely with the rest of the image. You'll color the text by selecting it and then selecting another color.

1 In the toolbox, select the Type tool (T).

2 Drag the Type tool from one end of the text to the other to select all the words.

3 In the Color palette group, select the Swatches palette tab to bring it forward.

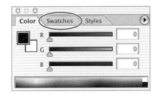

4 Select any swatch, so that the color appears in three places: in the Foreground Color in the toolbox, in the text color swatch on the tool options bar, and in the text you typed in the image window. (Select any other tool in the toolbox to deselect the text so that you can see the color applied to it.)

Note: When you move the pointer over the swatches, it temporarily changes into an eyedropper. Set the tip of the eyedropper on the swatch you want, and click to select it.

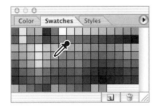

That's how easy it is to select a different color, although there are many other methods in Photoshop. However, you'll use a specific color for this project, and it's easier to find it if you change the Swatches palette display.

5 Make sure that the Type tool is not still selected. Click the arrow (⊙) on the Swatches palette to open the palette menu, and choose the Small List command.

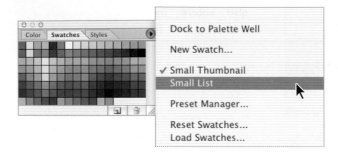

6 Select the Type tool and reselect the text, as you did in Steps 1 and 2.

7 In the Swatches palette, scroll down to near the bottom of the list of swatch colors to find the Darker Cyan swatch, and then select it.

Now the text appears in the Darker Cyan color.

8 Select the Hand tool (✋) to deselect the text. Then, click the Default Foreground And Background Colors icon (◼) on the toolbox to make Black the active foreground color.

Resetting the default colors does not change the color of the text, because the text is no longer selected.

You can now close the file because you've finished the task. You can either save the file, close it without saving it, or save it under a different name or location, as you did for your Project1 file.

It's as simple as that—you've completed another project. Nice job!

Undoing actions in Photoshop

In a perfect world, you'd never make a mistake. You'd never click the wrong item. You'd always anticipate perfectly how specific actions would bring your design ideas to life exactly as you imagined them. In a perfect world, you'd never have to backtrack.

For the real world, Photoshop and ImageReady give you the power to step back and undo actions so that you can try other options. The next project for this lesson provides you with an opportunity to experiment freely, knowing that you can reverse the process.

This project also introduces you to layering, which is one of the most fundamental and powerful features in Photoshop. There are many kinds of Photoshop layers, some of which contain images, text, or solid colors, and others that simply interact with layers below them. The file for this project has both kinds of layers. You don't really have to understand layers to complete this project successfully, so don't worry about that aspect of the project. You'll learn more about layers in Lesson 5, "Layer Basics," and Lesson 11, "Advanced Layer Techniques," with more about how to use one layer to control another one in Lesson 10, "Vector Masks, Paths, and Shapes."

Undoing a single action

Even beginning computer users quickly learn to use and appreciate the familiar Undo command.

1 Select the File Browser button ( ) on the tool options bar, and use the Folders palette to find and select the Lessons/Lesson01/Project3 folder.

2 In the thumbnails pane, select the 01End3.psd file so that you can see the results you'll achieve in this lesson. Then, select and double-click the 01Start3.psd file to open it in Photoshop. Close the File Browser.

Notice the listings in the Layers palette. The layers structure includes a clipping mask, which works somewhat like a selection, restricting the area of the image that can be altered. With the clipping mask in place, you can paint a design over the man's tie without worrying about any stray brush strokes disturbing the rest of the image. The Tie Designs layer is selected, because it's the layer you'll be altering in this project.

3 In the toolbox, select the Brush tool (✐), or press B to select it by its keyboard shortcut.

4 On the tool options bar, select the Brushes tab in the palette well to temporarily open the Brushes palette.

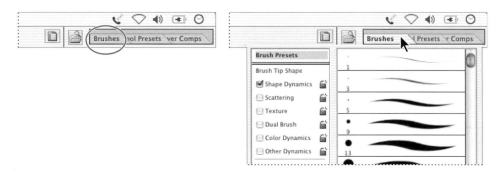

5 Scroll down the list of brushes and select the Soft Round 35-pixels brush. (The name will appear as a tooltip if you let the pointer hover over a brush.)

If you want to try a different brush, that's OK, but for this task select a brush that's reasonably close to 35 pixels—preferably in the range between 20 and 50 pixels.

6 Move the pointer over the image so that it appears as a circle with the diameter you selected in Step 5. Then draw a stripe anywhere in the yellow tie. You don't have to worry about staying within the lines because the brush won't paint anything outside of the tie clipping mask.

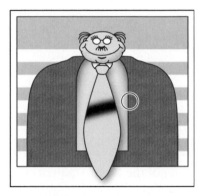

Oops! Your stripe may be very nice, but the design calls for dots, so you'll need to remove the painted stripe.

7 Choose Edit > Undo Brush Tool, or press Ctrl+Z (Windows) or Command+Z (Mac OS) to undo the Brush tool action.

The tie is again a solid yellow color, with no stripe.

You'll get more experience with clipping masks when you do the project in Lesson 10, "Vector Masks, Paths, and Shapes" and Lesson 11, "Advanced Layer Techniques."

Undoing multiple actions (Photoshop)

The Photoshop Undo command reverses only one step. This is a practicality because Photoshop files can be very large, and maintaining multiple Undo steps can tie up a lot of memory, which tends to degrade performance.

However, you can still step back through multiple actions, thanks to the History palette.

1 Using the same Brush tool settings, click once over the (unstriped) yellow tie to create a soft dot.

2 Click several more times in different areas on the tie to create a pattern of dots.

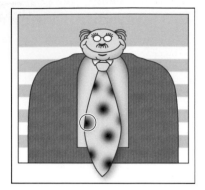

3 Using the History palette tab, drag it from its palette group to a position next to the other palettes. Then, drag down the lower right corner of the History palette to expand it so that you can see more steps. (This isolating and resizing is only for convenience.)

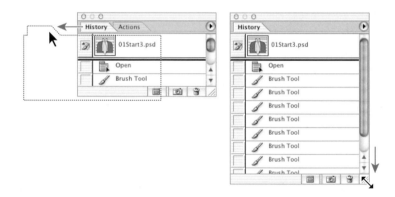

○ *You can also expand the History palette by clicking the minimize/maximize button (Windows) or the green zoom button (Mac OS) on the palette title bar. This resizes the palette so that all the current history states are in view.*

The History palette records the recent actions you've performed in the image. The current state is selected, at the bottom of the list.

4 Click one of the earlier actions in the History palette, and examine the changes this causes in the image window: Several previous actions are undone.

5 In the image window, create a new dot on the tie with the brush tool.

Notice that the History palette has removed the dimmed actions that had been listed after the selected history state and added a new one.

6 Choose Edit > Undo Brush Tool or press Ctrl+Z (Windows) or Command+Z (Mac OS) to undo the dot you created in Step 5.

Now the History palette fills in with the earlier listing of dimmed actions.

7 Select the state at the bottom of the History palette list.

Now the image is restored to the condition it was in when you finished Step 2 of this procedure.

By default, the Photoshop History palette retains only the last 20 actions. This is also a compromise, striking a balance between flexibility and performance. You can change the number of levels in the History palette by choosing Edit > Preferences > General (Windows) or Photoshop > Preferences > General (Mac OS) and typing a different number in the History States option.

You'll explore the History palette more in Lesson 7, "Retouching and Repairing."

About the ImageReady Undo command

ImageReady has multiple levels of Undo. You can reverse your most recent actions by selecting the Undo command or pressing Ctrl+Z (Windows) or Command+Z (Mac OS) repeatedly. You reinstate actions that you've undone by choosing Edit > Redo <*tool*>, or pressing Ctrl+Shift+Z (Windows) or Command+Shift+Z (Mac OS).

The default number of Undo steps available in ImageReady is 32. You can change that number by choosing Edit > Preferences > General (Windows) or Photoshop > Preferences > General (Mac OS) and typing a different number in the Undo Levels option. Type a higher number to make it possible to step back more than 32 actions, or type a lower number for better performance.

Using a context menu

Context menus are short menus that are appropriate to specific elements in the work area. They are sometimes referred to as "right-click" or "shortcut" menus. Usually, the commands on a context menu are also available in some other area of the user interface, but using the context menu can save time.

1 If the Brush tool ( ) is not still selected in the toolbox, select it now.

2 In the image window, right-click (Windows) or Control-click (Mac OS) anywhere in the image to open the Brush tool context menu.

Context menus vary with their context, of course, so what appears can be a menu of commands or a palette-like set of options, which is what happens in this case.

3 Select a finer brush, such as the Hard Round 5 pixels brush. You may need to scroll up or down the list in the context menu to find the right brush.

4 In the image window, use the selected brush to create smaller dots on the tie.

Note: *Clicking anywhere in the work area closes the context menu. If the tie area is hidden behind the Brush tool context menu, click another area or double-click your selection in the context menu to close it.*

5 Place additional dots on the tie.

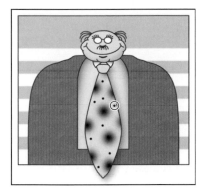

6 As it suits you, use the Undo command and the History palette to backtrack through your painting actions to correct mistakes or make different choices.

When you finish making changes to your tie design, give yourself a pat on the back because you've finished another project. You can choose File > Save if you want to save your results, or File > Save As if you want to save it in another location or with a different name, or you can close the file without saving.

More about palettes and palette locations

The Photoshop and ImageReady palettes are powerful and varied. You rarely would have a project in which you needed to see all palettes simultaneously. That's why they're in palette groups and why the default configurations leave some palettes unopened.

The complete list of palettes appears on the Window menu, with check marks appearing by the names of the palettes that are currently open at the front of their palette groups. You can open a closed palette or close an open one by selecting the palette name on the Window menu.

You can hide all palettes at once—including the tool options bar and toolbox—by pressing the Tab key. To reopen them, press Tab again.

You've already used the palette well when you opened the Brushes palette for Project3. You can drag palettes to or from the palette well. This is especially handy for bulky palettes or ones that you use only occasionally but want to keep handy.

Other actions that you can use to arrange palettes include the following:

• To move an entire palette group, drag the title bar to another location in the work area.

• To move a palette to another group, drag the palette tab into that palette group so that a black highlight appears inside the group, and then release the mouse button.

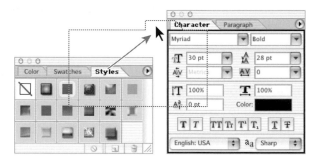

• To dock a palette in the palette well on the Photoshop tool options bar, drag the palette tab into the palette well so that the palette well is highlighted.

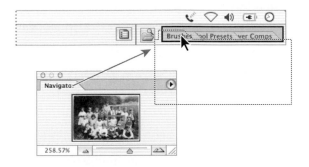

Note: *In Photoshop CS, the File Browser is a full-fledged window, not a palette, and cannot be docked in the palette well.*

Expanding and collapsing palettes

You can also resize a palette to see more or fewer of the available options it contains, either by dragging or clicking to toggle between preset sizes.

• To change the height of a palette, drag its lower right corner.

• To expand a palette to show as much as possible of its contents, click the minimize/maximize button (Windows) or the zoom button (Mac OS). (A second click collapses the palette group.)

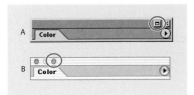

A. *Windows* **B.** *Mac OS*

• To collapse a palette group so that only the title bar and tabs are visible, double-click a palette tab or the palette title bar. Double-click again to restore it to the expanded view.

• (ImageReady) To toggle through expansions of palettes with a double-arrow icon (⬍) on the tab, click that icon.

Notice that the tabs for the various palettes in the palette group and the button for the palette menu remain visible after you collapse a palette.

Note: You cannot resize the individual Info, Color, Character, and Paragraph palettes in Photoshop, or the Optimize, Info, Color, Layer Options, Character, Paragraph, Slice, and Image Map palettes in ImageReady.

Special notes about the toolbox and tool options bar

The toolbox and the tool options bar share some characteristics with the other palettes:

• You can drag the toolbox by its title bar to a different location in the work area. You can move the tool options bar to another location by dragging the grab bar at the far left end of the palette.

• You can hide the toolbox and tool options bar.

However, there are other palette features that are not available or do not apply to the toolbox or tool options bar:

• You cannot group the toolbox or tool options bar with other palettes.

• You cannot resize the toolbox or tool options bar.

• You cannot dock the toolbox in the palette well. (Obviously, the same is true for the tool options bar because the palette well appears within the tool options bar.)

• The toolbox and tool options bar do not have palette menus.

Jumping to ImageReady

Now you'll switch to ImageReady. Jumping between the applications is an easy way to access the unique features of each application—especially when you're preparing Web graphics—yet still maintain a streamlined workflow.

Note: ImageReady is Web-oriented, so it automatically reduces high resolution images to 72 dpi. If you need to maintain a higher resolution, always use Photoshop.

1 Switch to ImageReady by doing one of the following:

• To open ImageReady without resetting its preferences, select the Jump To ImageReady button ( ) in the Photoshop toolbox. If the ImageReady Welcome Screen appears, click Close.

• To reset the preferences and open ImageReady, hold down Ctrl+Alt+Shift (Windows) or Command+Option+Shift (Mac OS), and then select the Jump To ImageReady button ( ) in the Photoshop toolbox. When asked if you want to delete the preferences, select Yes. When the ImageReady Welcome Screen appears, select Close.

You can jump between Photoshop and ImageReady to transfer an image between the two applications for editing, without closing or exiting the originating application. Also, you can jump from ImageReady to other graphics-editing applications and HTML-editing applications you may have installed on your system. For more information on jumping to other applications in ImageReady, see Photoshop Help.

2 In ImageReady, click the Jump To Photoshop button ( ) in the toolbox to return to Photoshop.

Each time an image in Photoshop or ImageReady is updated with changes made in a jumped-to application, a single history state is added to the Photoshop or ImageReady History palette. You'll learn more about how to use the History palette later; see "About snapshots and History palette states" on page 231 of this book.

Note: You can do all the projects in this lesson again in ImageReady instead of Photoshop, but if so you should be aware of a few differences. The most important of these is that the File Browser is available only in Photoshop. Other differences between Photoshop and ImageReady that affect this lesson are: (Project1) you must use the Hue/Saturation command and reduce the Lightness slider to darken the image instead of the Curves command; (Project 2) the Small List option is not available on the Swatches palette menu; (Project 3) you must use the pop-up palette on the tool options bar to select a brush size (there is no Brushes palette in ImageReady).

Using Photoshop Help

For complete information about using palettes, tools, and other application features, refer to Photoshop Help. Help includes all the topics in the printed *Adobe Photoshop CS User Guide* and more information that is not in the print version.

Adobe Photoshop Help (which contains all ImageReady Help topics, and vice versa) includes the complete list of keyboard shortcuts, how-to tips, tutorials, explanations of Photoshop and ImageReady concepts, feature descriptions, and more.

Photoshop Help is easy to use, because you can look for topics in several ways:

• Scanning the table of contents.

• Searching for keywords.

• Using the index.

• Jumping from topic to topic using related topic links.

First, you'll try looking for a topic using the Contents screen.

1   Choose Help > Photoshop Help (Photoshop) or Help > ImageReady Help
(ImageReady).

Note: *In Windows, you can also open Photoshop Help by pressing F1.*

Your default Web browser opens. The topics for the Help system appear in the left frame
of the Web browser window.

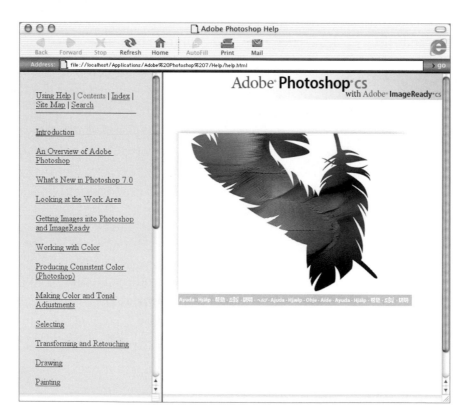

2 In the left frame of the Help window, scroll down to skim through the Help contents. The contents are organized in topics, like the chapters of a book.

3 Near the top of the list of topics in the left pane, click *Looking at the Work Area*. The "Looking at the Work Area" Help topic appears in the right pane, which consists of a list of specific topics.

4 In the right pane, click *Using the toolbox* to open that topic.

5 Near the bottom of the "Using the toolbox" topic, click *Toolbox overview (1 of 3)* to open that topic. An illustration of various tools appears with brief descriptions of each tool.

6 On the left side of the topic, either at the top or the bottom, click the word Next to advance to the next topic: *Toolbox overview (2 of 3)*.

The Help topics are interactive. You can click any text link to jump to another topic. Whenever you move the mouse pointer over a link or a hotspot, the mouse pointer changes to a pointing-finger icon (👆).

7 Click the name of one of the tools to open the linked topic about that tool. (The name of the tool appears in color and underlined in the Toolbox overview topic, indicating that it is linked to another page.)

Using the Help system keywords, links, and index

If you can't find the topic you're interested in by skimming the Contents page, you can try searching for a keyword.

1 At the top of the left pane, click the word *Search*.

A search text box appears in the left pane.

2 Type a keyword in the text box, such as **lasso**, and click the Search button. After a brief pause, a list of topics appears below the text box in the left pane. To see any of these topics, click the topic name.

You can also search for a topic using the index.

3 At the top of the left pane, click the word *Index*. An alphabetical list of letters appears across the top of the left pane, followed by the listings for the letter A.

4 Click another letter, such as T, to display index entries for that letter.

These entries appear alphabetically by topic and subtopic, like the index of a book. You can scroll down the list to see more entries that begin with the letter "T."

5 Click the number [1] next to an entry to open the first topic about that entry. (If there is more than one number, clicking the number [2] or [3] opens a second or third topic about the same entry.)

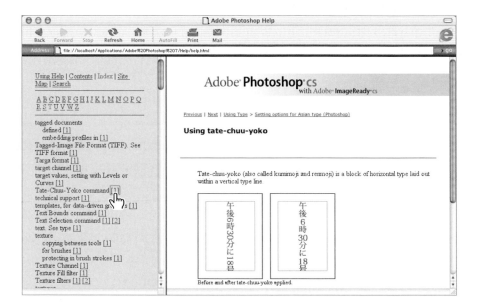

6 When you have finished browsing, quit the browser to close Photoshop Help.

Creating custom Help topics

You can create your own Help topics for Adobe Photoshop CS and ImageReady CS. Your custom topics appear at the bottom of the Photoshop and ImageReady Help menus. This offers an easy solution for sharing information with your work group about department procedures, standards, policies, references, or techniques, because you can distribute your custom Help topics for others to add to their Photoshop CS application. If you customize your Photoshop or ImageReady keyboard shortcuts, a special Help topic listing those key combinations might be a perfect use for this feature.

Your custom Help topics can be any HTML page, either on your own computer, on your local network, or on the Internet. To create your own pages, you need a Web authoring application. such as Adobe GoLive, or a knowledge of HTML code. For this lesson, you don't need to concern yourself with that because a topic has been created for you.

1 On the desktop for your operating system, open the Lessons/Lesson01/Project4 folder and select the MyHelp01.html file.

2 Drag the MyHelp01.html file into the Additional How To Content folder, which is located in the Programs/Adobe/Photoshop CS/Help folder (Windows) or the Applications/Adobe/Photoshop CS/Help folder (Mac OS). (Scroll down to find it.)

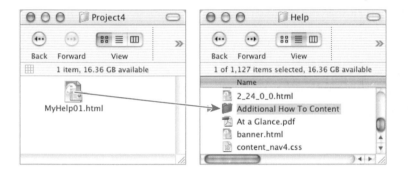

3 Start any text-editing application, such as NotePad or WordPad (Windows), TextEdit (Mac OS), or another word-processing application.

4 Choose File > Open,.

5 In the Open dialog box, do the following:

• Go to the Additional How To Content folder (located as described in Step 2).

• (Windows only) In the Files Of Type pop-up menu, select All Files.

• Select the Add_001.howto file.

• Click Open.

6 Place the cursor at the end of the existing text, press Enter (Windows) or Return (Mac OS) to start a new paragraph and type (including the quotation marks, as shown): **"Department Policies" "Handoff Procedures" MyHelp01.html**

7 Choose File > Save, and then quit your text-editing application.

When you restart Photoshop, your custom category (submenu) and topic appear on the Help menu. You can choose the Handoff Procedures topic to open the file in your Web browser.

The text that you added to the Add_001.howto file determines the submenu (the Department Policies category) that appears on the Help menu. The topic title (Handoff Procedures) appears on the Department Policies submenu.

You can define more categories and add more topics to them by typing new entries in the Add_001.howto file. You can also customize your Help menu with commands that point to an Internet Web page or an HTML page on your local network, as long as you include the complete path to the page in the .howto file.

When you create new topics, you can use the template provided in the Additional How To Content folder. This template uses graphic elements included in Photoshop Help that give your topics a consistent look. See Photoshop Help for more information.

Using Adobe online services

Another way to get information about Adobe Photoshop or other Adobe products is to use the Adobe online services. If you have an Internet connection and a Web browser installed on your system, you can access the U.S. Adobe Systems Web site (www.adobe.com) for information on services, products, and tips pertaining to Photoshop.

1 In Photoshop or ImageReady, choose Help > Adobe Online, or click the icon (◼) (Photoshop) or (◼) (ImageReady) at the top of the toolbox.

2 Choose Edit > Preferences > Adobe Online (Windows) or Photoshop > Preferences > Adobe Online (Mac OS) and enter the preferences you want to use, including settings in the Update Options pop-up menu for updating Adobe Online.

When you set up Adobe Online to connect to your Web browser, Adobe can either notify you whenever new information is available or automatically download that information to your hard disk. If you choose not to use the Adobe automatic download feature, you can still view and download new files whenever they are available from within the Adobe Online window.

3 If you use Netscape as your Web browser, click the bookmark button (▲) in the Adobe Online dialog box to view Web pages related to Photoshop and Adobe. These bookmarks are automatically updated as new Web pages become available.

4 Click Close to return to Photoshop or ImageReady.

Using Adobe Online, you can find information specifically on Photoshop and ImageReady, including tips and techniques, galleries of artwork by Adobe designers and artists around the world, the latest product information, and troubleshooting and technical information. Or, you can learn about other Adobe products and news.

Congratulations again; you've finished Lesson 1.

Now that you're acquainted with the basics of the Photoshop CS work area, you're ready to explore more about the File Browser feature or to jump ahead and begin learning how to create and edit images. Once you know the basics, you can do the *Adobe Photoshop CS Classroom in a Book* lessons either in sequential order or according to the subject matter that most interests you.

Review questions

1 Describe two ways to change your view of an image.

2 How do you select tools in Photoshop or ImageReady?

3 What are two ways to get more information about Photoshop and ImageReady?

4 Describe two ways to create images in Photoshop and ImageReady.

5 How do you switch between Photoshop and ImageReady?

Review answers

1 You can choose commands from the View menu to zoom in or out of an image, or to fit it to your screen; you can also use the zoom tools and click or drag over an image to enlarge or reduce the view. In addition, you can use keyboard shortcuts to magnify or reduce the display of an image. You can also use the Navigator palette to scroll an image or change its magnification without using the image window.

2 To select a tool, you can select the tool in the toolbox, or you can press the tool's keyboard shortcut. A selected tool remains active until you select a different tool. To select a hidden tool, you can use either a combination keyboard shortcut to toggle through the tools, or you can hold down the mouse button on the tool in the toolbox to open a pop-up menu of the hidden tools.

3 Adobe Photoshop contains Help, with all the information in the *Adobe Photoshop CS User Guide*, plus keyboard shortcuts and some additional information and full-color illustrations. Photoshop also includes a link to the Adobe Systems home page for additional information on services, products, and tips pertaining to Photoshop. ImageReady CS also contains Help and a link to the Adobe home page.

4 You can create original artwork in Adobe Photoshop or ImageReady, or you can get images into the program by scanning a photograph, a transparency, a negative, or a graphic; by capturing a video image; or by importing artwork created in drawing programs. You can also import previously digitized images—such as those produced by a digital camera or by the Kodak Photo CD process.

5 You can click the Jump To button in the toolbox or choose File > Jump To to switch between Photoshop and ImageReady.

2 | Using the File Browser

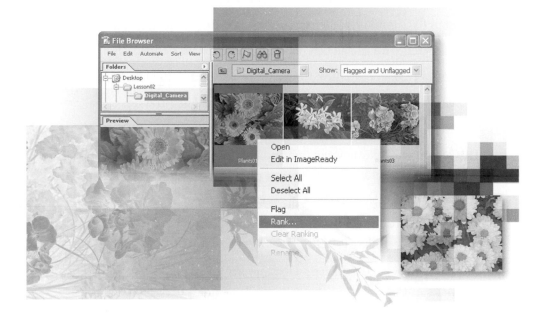

When you're hunting for specific pictures in your stash of image files, the File Browser is your new best friend. It helps you save time with features that organize files so that you can both see and search for exactly the files you need—without even opening the files in Photoshop.

In this lesson, you'll learn how to do the following:

- Identify and resize the File Browser palettes and panes.

- Rotate, resize, and view thumbnail and preview image files without opening them.

- Sort and manually rearrange thumbnails in the File Browser.

- Delete, rename, and batch-rename files from the File Browser.

- Assign flags, rankings, metadata, and keywords to image files.

- Run searches for image files, based on criteria you define.

- Create a PDF Presentation from images selected in the File Browser.

- Create a Web Gallery of images selected in the File Browser.

- Prepare a customized Picture Package of the image selected in the File Browser.

This lesson will take between one and two hours to complete. The File Browser is not available in ImageReady, so you must do this lesson in Photoshop.

Copy the Lesson02 folder from the *Adobe Photoshop CS Classroom in a Book* CD into the Lessons folder on your hard drive that you set up earlier. As you work, you'll overwrite some of the start files. To restore these original files, recopy them from the CD.

Note: Windows 2000 users need to unlock the lesson files before using them. For more information, see "Copying the Classroom in a Book files" on page 3.

Getting Started

You've already had a brief introduction to the File Browser in Lesson 1, "Getting to Know the Work Area." If you've completed that lesson, you know that the permanent File Browser button (🗁) on the Photoshop tool options bar opens, closes, or brings the File Browser forward. In this lesson, you'll explore the File Browser in greater depth. The aim of the first project for the lesson is to organize and annotate a motley collection of photographs.

The File Browser shares some functionality with your desktop regarding files and folders. The changes you apply to files in the File Browser change the files themselves, not merely the File Browser view of them. At the end of the lesson, you'll experience how easy it can be to find specific images on your computer. Unlike other Photoshop palettes, the updated File Browser has a menu bar instead of a palette menu.

1 Start Photoshop and then immediately hold down Ctrl+Alt+Shift (Windows) or Command+Option+Shift (Mac OS) to restore the default preferences. (See "Restoring default preferences" on page 4.)

As messages appear, select Yes to confirm that you want to reset preferences, No to defer setting up your color monitor, and Close to close the Welcome Screen.

2 Click the File Browser button ( ) in the tool options bar to open the File Browser.

3 (Optional) Press Tab to hide the toolbox and all the palettes, leaving the File Browser open.

This optional step merely tidies up the work area by closing palettes you won't use in the next several tasks. If you want to reopen those palettes now, press Tab again.

You can also click the maximize button (Windows) or the zoom button (Mac OS) on the title bar to expand the File Browser so that it fills all of the space made available by closing the palettes. (This takes two clicks in Mac OS.)

Note: *The Photoshop CS File Browser does not dock to the palette well.*

Viewing and editing files in the File Browser

The left side of the File Browser holds palettes that you can rearrange, collapse, and group within the File Browser, using the same techniques as with regular Photoshop palettes. The File Browser palettes help you navigate, preview, search, and manage information for your image files and folders.

Customizing the File Browser views and spaces

The ideal arrangement and relative sizes of items and areas of the File Browser depend on your work style and preferences. Depending on the tasks you're doing, it may be important to see what images are in files; at other times, viewing information about the file may take priority. You can customize the File Browser to increase your efficiency in these different situations.

In this procedure, you'll try out some of the custom views you can use in the File Browser. The default configuration of the File Browser areas appears in the following illustration.

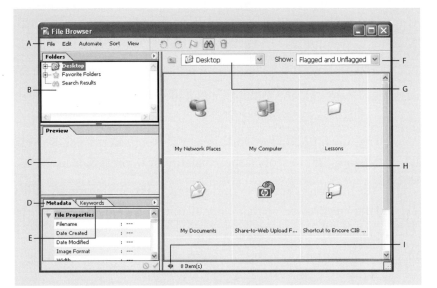

*A. File Browser menu bar and buttons **B.** Folders palette **C.** Preview palette*
*D. Metadata palette **E.** Keywords palette **F.** Show option **G.** Location option*
*H. Thumbnails pane **I.** Toggle Expanded View button*

Note: *If you do not see the tabbed palettes on the left side of the File Browser window, click the Toggle Expanded View button (◀▶) at the bottom of the File Browser.*

1 In the Folders palette in the File Browser, navigate to the Lessons/Lesson02 folder file you copied from the *Adobe Photoshop CS Classroom in a Book* CD, and select the Digital_Camera folder.

On the right side of the File Browser, thumbnails appear, showing the contents of the Digital_Camera folder.

2 In the File Browser, choose View > Medium Thumbnail. Then, choose some of the other size options on the File Browser View menu, such as Small Thumbnail, Custom Thumbnail, or Details. When you finish experimenting, choose the view you prefer.

Note: If you do not see the Medium Thumbnail command, make sure that you are looking at the View menu in the File Browser, not the View menu in the main Photoshop work area.

3 Select any thumbnail by clicking it once.

An enlargement of the image appears in the Preview palette, filling the available area.

4 Double-click the Folders tab to collapse the Folders palette. The Preview palette expands to fill the space.

5 Move the pointer over the vertical bar separating the left and right panes of the File Browser until the pointer appears as double lines with arrows (⊹⊱), and then drag the bar to the right so that the left pane is wider.

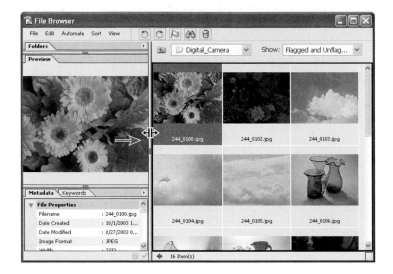

6 Continue to adjust the spaces and palettes within the File Browser until the arrangement suits you.

Note: You can also drag the horizontal bars between the File Browser palettes up and down to resize the space vertically.

Rotating and opening images

In Lesson 1, you've already seen how you can open files directly from the File Browser instead of using the Open command on the Photoshop File menu.

You can also change the orientation of selected images using a one-click technique. Rotating the thumbnails and previews in the File Browser does not affect the resolution or quality of the files. However, the rotation is not permanent until you actively apply it, either by using the Edit menu in the File Browser window or by opening and saving the image in Photoshop.

1 Select the 244_0107.jpg thumbnail in the Digital_Camera folder.

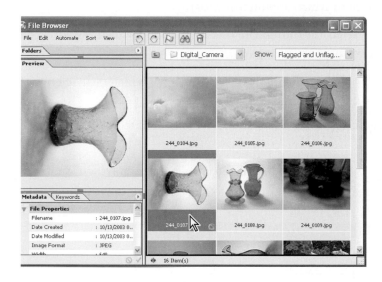

2 Click the Rotate Counterclockwise button (↶) on the File Browser menu bar. If a message appears, click OK to close it.

3 Using the File Browser menu bar, choose Edit > Apply Rotation.

4 In the thumbnails pane, select the 244_0111.jpg thumbnail.

5 Click the Rotate Clockwise button (↷).

6 In the File Browser, choose Edit > Apply Rotation.

💡 *You can select multiple thumbnails in the File Browser and then open or rotate them together. Select the files by using the usual methods for your operating system: Click and then Shift-click to select contiguous files, or select them by dragging the cursor across the image thumbnails you want to select; Ctrl-click (Windows) or Command-click (Mac OS) to select discontiguous images.*

Deleting images from the File Browser

You can use the File Browser to remove files or folders from your system, exactly like removing them from folders on your desktop. Deleting images in the File Browser sends the files to the Recycle Bin (Windows) or Trash (Mac OS). When you empty the Recycle Bin or Trash, the file is permanently erased from your computer.

Using the File Browser to examine your images, you can confidently select and delete files that you no longer need or which are unsatisfactory.

1 In the File Browser, select the thumbnail for 244_0109.jpg, which is poorly composed, out of focus, and underexposed—a real loser.

2 Click the Delete File button (🗑) on the File Browser menu bar. When a message appears asking you to confirm this action, click OK.

3 Review the other images in the folder and select another mediocre photograph, but don't delete it yet.

4 Click the Flag File button (🚩) on the File Browser menu bar. Now a similar flag icon appears with the image thumbnail. Continue to flag any other low-quality photographs.

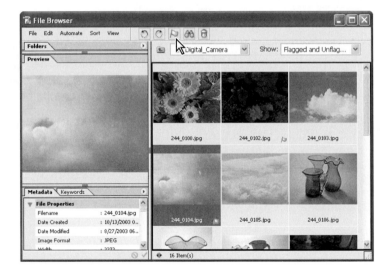

5 Select Flagged Files from the Show pop-up menu to hide thumbnails of all the unflagged files, and then reexamine each flagged image to make sure that you don't want to keep it.

Note: *If you accidentally flagged a good image, select the file and click the Flag button again to remove the flag.*

6 In the File Browser menu bar, choose Edit > Select All to select all of the flagged files, and click the Delete File button (🗑) in the File Browser to delete the selected files. When a message appears, select Yes to confirm that you want to delete these files.

7 Select Flagged And Unflagged on the Show pop-up menu so that you can see the remaining image files.

💡 *Instead of showing only flagged files and using the Select All command, you could choose Edit > Select All Flagged from the File Browser menu bar.*

At this point, the deleted files are not yet removed from your computer, although they are not visible in the File Browser. You can find and retrieve the deleted files by switching to the desktop and dragging them back out of the Recycle Bin (Windows) or Trash (Mac OS). When you empty your desktop trash container, remember that the files will be permanently deleted from your computer.

Rearranging and renaming image files

You can rearrange thumbnails in the File Browser as freely as you might move negatives or slides on a light table. You can use a batch-renaming process to give image files friendlier but well-organized file names. In this task, you'll rearrange the thumbnails according to subject matter—colored glass containers, flowers, and cloudy skies—and then rename them.

1 In the thumbnails pane, drag the thumbnails of cloudy-sky photographs one by one until they are next to each other.

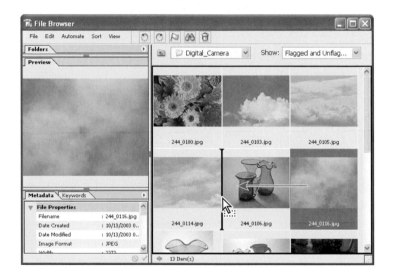

2 Select the first sky thumbnail in the group and then Shift-click the last sky thumbnail to select the entire group.

3 In the File Browser, choose Automate > Batch Rename.

4 Under File Naming in the Batch Rename dialog box, specify the following:

• In the first blank, type **Clouds** to replace "Document Name," the default entry.

• In the second blank, select 2 Digit Serial Number from the pop-up menu.

• In the third blank, select extension. (Do not select the capitalized EXTENSION option.)

• In the Starting Serial # option, make sure that 1 is selected, or type **1** now.

• For Compatibility, select the check boxes for other operating systems: Windows, Mac OS, and Unix. (The operating system you are using will be dimmed but already checked.)

5 Review the sample shown in the Example area to make sure that it reads "Clouds01.gif," and then click OK.

Note: The "gif" extension is merely the default example of an extension in the dialog box. It does not change the file format of the selected files.

6 In the File Browser, choose Sort > Filename to arrange the thumbnails in alpha-numeric order.

7 Using the techniques described in Steps 1-6, select and batch-rename the remaining photographs in according to the subject matter pictured: flowers and ornamental glassware. When you set options in the Batch Rename dialog box, type **Plants** instead of *Clouds* to name the flowers images, and **Glass** for the remaining set of images. Other than that, use the same File Naming options as in Step 4.

Embedding information for easy identification

The File Browser puts numerous tools in your hands for retrieving the images you need to find. This is critical when you have a large number of stored images and no time to waste on browsing through hundreds or thousands of files.

You've already seen two of these features: the different viewing sizes for thumbnails and previews, and the flags you can apply for selective viewing. In this section, you'll work with three more ways to embed information in files so that you can quickly find them later: rankings, metadata, and keywords.

Ranking and sorting image files in the File Browser

The File Browser has a ranking feature that you can use to group and sort image thumbnails. This gives you an alternate way to sort images in the File Browser thumbnails pane. You can invent your own alphanumeric code to assign rankings, such as numbers, one or more letters, words, or combinations of these.

In this exercise, you'll let "A" stand for the best and most usable images, and "C" for the poorest quality or least desirable photographs, with "B" for medium quality. Which letter you assign to which image is a personal judgment, so there are no right or wrong answers for letter designations, and—unlike the real world, perhaps—no one will take offense at your choices.

1 In the File Browser, choose View > Large Thumbnails (if it is not already selected), and then choose View > Show Rank.

A line of text appears below each file name with a hyphen indicating that the files are unranked.

2 Using the thumbnail of one of the more successful photographs (such as the red glass pitcher), click the Rank hyphen to make it active, and then type **A**.

3 Select several files, including one or two of the other better-quality images in each category (glass, flowers, and skies).

Note: Use Ctrl-click (Windows) or Command-click (Mac OS) to select discontiguous thumbnails, if needed.

4 On the File Browser menu bar, choose Edit > Rank, and type **A** in the Rank Files dialog box, if it is not already entered. Then click OK.

The rank-designation A appears in the thumbnails of all the files you selected.

Note: You can also open the Rank Files dialog box by right-clicking (Windows) or Control-clicking (Mac OS) one of the selected files and choosing Rank on the context menu.

5 Choose Sort > Rank to rearrange the thumbnails so that the best images are listed first.

6 Continue to assign rankings to all the files in the folder, either by ranking them individually (as in Step 2) or in multiples (as in Steps 3 and 4) until all images are ranked A, B, or C.

7 Choose Sort > Rank again to arrange the files in alphabetical order of their rankings.

Note: Quality is not the only thing the rank might indicate. In your own work, you can use rankings to indicate anything—subject matter, client, project name, or time of day, for example. The key concept to remember is that you can use the rankings to sort images quickly in the File Browser.

Advanced Topic: About the Camera Raw plug-in

Camera raw image file formats are like digital negatives created by some digital cameras. Camera raw formatting contains all the information the camera has about the image. The image information is captured directly from the camera's Charged Coupled Device (CCD) or Complementary Metal-Oxide Semiconductor (CMOS) without filters and adjustments applied by the camera. Photographers can use this to interpret the image data rather than letting the camera make the adjustments and conversions.

Unlike the standard JPEG format which actually throws out data as it processes and compresses an image, camera raw compression does not destroy any image information to generate a file-—it uses lossless compression—but camera raw image files have the advantage of being smaller than uncompressed TIFFs.

Although different cameras use unique formats to save the camera raw image data, the Photoshop Camera Raw feature can open many camera raw file formats. Workflow is improved because the camera raw image files are opened directly in Photoshop, where you can edit them immediately. The adjustments available within the Photoshop Camera Raw plug-in provide flexibility to produce the best image possible from a camera raw image file.

Opening a camera raw file in Photoshop or ImageReady opens the Camera Raw dialog box. You can save the settings in the Camera Raw dialog box for a specific camera or a specific lighting condition, and then reuse the settings to open another camera raw image file or even a batch of camera raw image files. By default, the Camera Raw dialog box opens in Basic mode. Selecting the advanced mode allows access to the Camera Raw Preferences, and to controls for correcting chromatic aberration, color cast, and more.

For more information about camera raw and the Camera Raw plug-in, refer to Photoshop Help.

Reviewing and editing metadata

You can quickly see file information in two ways: using the Details view for the File Browser thumbnails pane or using the Metadata palette. But there are differences in their content; you'll compare the two information displays next.

The information on the Metadata palette is nested under headings that you can expand or collapse by clicking the arrow next to a heading. The three headings are File Properties, IPTC, and Camera Data (exif). In the File Browser, you can directly edit only some of the IPTC metadata.

1 In the File Browser, choose View > Details, and select the thumbnail of one of the A-ranked glassware images.

When you work with large amounts of metadata, double-click the tabs for the Folders and Preview palettes to collapse them. This reduces the amount of scrolling needed to review and edit the information. (The Folders palette is already collapsed in this case.)

2 If necessary, click the Metadata tab to bring that palette forward in the lower left pane of the File Browser. If any of the major headings are collapsed, click the arrows (▶) to expand them so that you can compare the amount of information here with that listed in the Details view of the thumbnails.

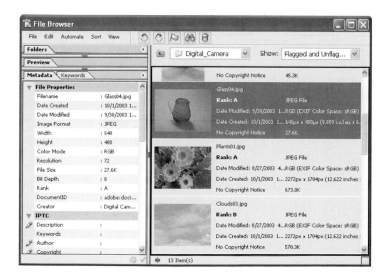

3 If necessary, scroll down the Metadata palette to the IPTC heading, so that you can see the items listed under it. The pencil icons (✎) on the left indicate items that you can edit.

4 Click the blank space for Description and type a few words describing the image, such as **red pitcher**.

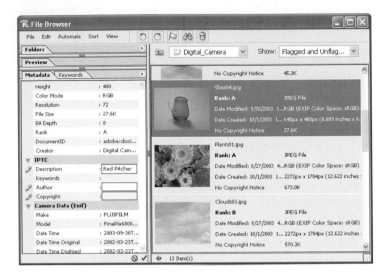

5 At the bottom of the Metadata palette, click the Apply button (✓) to enter the information you typed.

Note: *One of the important metadata fields is the copyright, which is an editable field under the IPTC heading. Although you can type or change what appears in this field for the* Classroom in a Book *lesson files, please remember that the copyright for these images still belongs to Adobe Systems, Inc.*

Creating and applying keywords

Keywords can streamline your searches for images. If you have a large collection of images, the few seconds required to enter some well-chosen keywords can save you hours later as you try to locate specific pictures or images.

The Keywords palette organizes your keywords in categories that you can expand and collapse as you did with on the Metadata palette. The Keywords palette standardizes your keywords so that you can apply identical terms to specific types of images. This greatly reduces the risks of occasional typographical errors or inconsistencies that can turn keyword searches from a dream-come-true into a nightmare.

Note: *There is also a Keywords item on the Metadata palette, under the IPTC heading. However, it is not directly editable in the File Browser.*

1 Select the Keywords tab to bring that palette forward from behind the Metadata palette.

2 Click the arrow in the upper right area to open the Keywords palette menu, and choose New Keyword Set. Or, you can simply click the New Keyword Set button (▣) at the bottom of the palette.

3 Type **Glass Project** in the new blank to name the keyword set, and press Enter (Windows) or Return (Mac OS). Leave the Glass Project keyword set selected, or reselect it if necessary.

4 Click the New Keyword button (⬚) to create a keyword under the Glass Project category, type **Red**, and press Enter (Windows) or Return (Mac OS). Then, select the Glass Project category again and repeat the process until you have created five more new keywords, naming them **Green**, **Blue**, **Orange**, **Purple**, and **Yellow**.

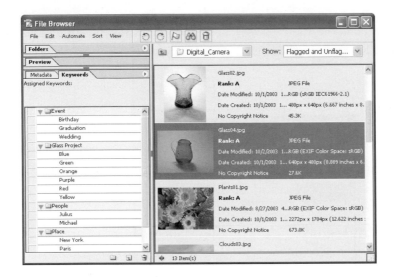

5 Select the thumbnail for the photograph of the green vase and red pitcher.

6 In the Keywords palette, click the boxes for both the Red and Green keywords to apply them to the image metadata. Or, double-click each of those keywords.

A check mark appears next to the applied keywords. The bold hyphen symbol next to the Glass Project category indicates that some but not all of the keywords in that set apply to the selected file.

7 One by one, select each of the other glassware images and apply the appropriate keywords for the glass colors in those photographs. Or, you can select multiple files—such as all the images with blue glassware, if there were several—and simultaneously apply the keyword Blue to each of them.

You can apply all the keywords in a category to the selected files by double-clicking the category name. This places check marks in the boxes for the category and all the keywords in it. By organizing your custom keywords into well-planned sets, this can save time when you deal with large numbers of similar images. However, you don't want to do that in this case because not all the color keywords are appropriate for any of the individual images.

Editing keyword terms and categories

Photoshop automatically populates the keywords section with some sample information. You could simply delete these sample keywords, or you can rename them.

Renaming keywords is easy, but there's a little trick to it. Since double-clicking a keyword applies it to the currently selected files, that technique won't work for editing keyword text. Instead, you use the Keywords palette menu or context menu to make keywords or keyword category names active.

1 In the Keywords palette under the People category, select the keyword "Julius" (one of the sample keywords available to all files by default).

2 Click the palette menu button (⊙) to open the Keywords palette menu, and then choose Rename. Or, right-click (Windows) or Control-click (Mac OS) to open the context menu, and choose Rename. Click OK to close the message that appears.

The keyword text is now active in the Keywords palette.

3 Type **Mark Antony** (or your name) and press Enter (Windows) or Return (Mac OS).

You can use the same technique to rename keyword categories.

Deleting keywords

The lists on the Keywords palette are application-wide, so that the same keyword choices are available regardless of what folder you're browsing. Many of the preset keywords may not be useful to you. Fortunately, you can rename or delete keywords you won't need. Since there is no orange glass in the images, you can delete it.

You don't have to worry about deleting a keyword that is currently applied to some files. In those cases, the keyword is deleted from the heading but shows up under a new heading named *Other Keywords*. You'll prove that to yourself in this procedure.

1 In the Keywords palette, select the "Orange" keyword, and then click the Delete Keyword button (🗑) at the bottom of the palette. Click OK to dismiss the warning that appears.

2 Repeat Step 1, but this time delete the "Red" keyword.

3 Select one of the thumbnails showing a red glass item. (You assigned "Red" to this file in an earlier task.)

4 In the Keywords palette, find the Other Keywords category and locate the "Red" keyword. Drag the keyword back into the Glass Project category to group it with the other color keywords.

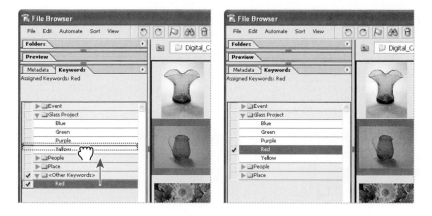

Note: *You can also use the Trash button on the File Browser menu bar to delete an entire keyword category and all the keywords in that set. Any keywords in the category that are still in use reappear under the Other Keywords category, but the deleted category itself does not.*

Searching with the File Browser

Now that you've taken the time to associate information with the images in the Lesson02 folder, you're ready to see how much easier this makes searching.

1 On the File Browser menu bar, choose File > Search or click the Search button ( ).

2 In the Search dialog box, make sure that the Digital_Camera folder appears in the Look In option, or click Browse and navigate to that folder.

3 Under Criteria, enter the following in the three blanks that appear:

• In the first blank, choose File Name, if it is not already selected.

• In the second blank, select Contains from the pop-up menu.

- In the third blank, type **Glass**.

4 Click the plus-sign button to open another set of blanks.

5 Enter the following information in the second row: Keywords, Contains, and type **Red**.

6 Click the plus-sign button to open a third row, and select Rank, Is, and type **A**.

7 Click Search.

Any files that match all three sets of criteria—that is, "A"-quality images of red glassware, if you've done the previous tasks as described—appear in the thumbnails pane. Expand the Folders palette (double-click the tab) if it is minimized, and notice that the current location is a new folder named Search Results. To return to the view of all the images, locate and reselect the Digital_Camera folder in the Folders palette.

Using automated features for output

The File Browser Automate menu includes a number of automated features that also appear on the File > Automate submenu of the main Photoshop menu bar. You'll try out three of these before you finish this File Browser lesson.

The advantage of the automated commands in the File Browser is that you can use them without even opening the files in Photoshop. You can apply these commands to all the files in a selected folder or to individual files in the folder that you select—it's your choice.

Creating a PDF Presentation from the File Browser

You can create an Adobe Acrobat PDF slide show or a multipage PDF document from a set of Photoshop files just by applying the PDF Presentation command and setting the options you want. You can select which files within the folder you want to include or simply select the folder to include all the files stored inside it.

The order in which the files appear in the PDF document follows the order in which you arrange the thumbnails in the File Browser, so the process is practically foolproof.

1 In the Folders palette, find and select the Lessons/Lesson02/Presentation folder.

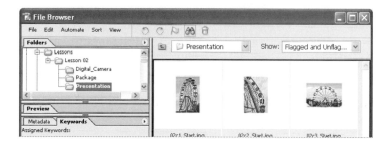

2 Choose View > Large Thumbnail on the File Browser menu bar, and then drag the thumbnails in the thumbnail pane to place them in the following order:

- 02c3_Start.jpg

- 02c1_Start.jpg

- 02c4_Start.jpg

- 02c2_Start.jpg

- 02c5_Start.jpg

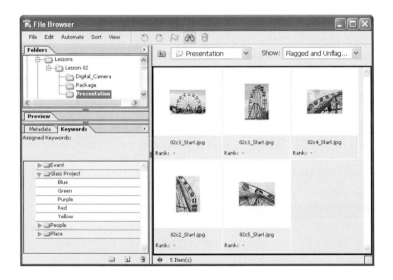

3 On the File Browser menu bar, choose Edit > Deselect All, and then choose Automate > PDF Presentation.

The PDF Presentation dialog box opens. Notice that the five files from the Presentation folder already appear in the Source Files area.

4 In the dialog box, do the following:

• Under Output Options, select both Presentation and View PDF After Saving.

• Under Presentation Options, use the Transitions pop-up menu to select Wipe Right.

• Click Save.

5 In the Save dialog box, type **Ferris_wheel.pdf** as the presentation filename and set the location to the Lesson02 folder. (Do *not* select the Presentation folder.) Click Save.

6 In the PDF Options dialog box, click OK to accept the default settings.

If you have a version of Adobe Acrobat or Acrobat Reader installed on your computer, it starts automatically and starts the slide show of the PDF Presentation.

7 When the slide show finishes, press Esc to return to the standard Acrobat window. You can then quit your Acrobat application and return to Photoshop.

Creating a Web Photo Gallery

The Web Photo Gallery command generates an entire Web site for you, with thumbnails, images, text, and even an area for review feedback that the user fills out on the site and e-mails to the alias you designate. You can choose from a generous assortment of predefined layouts and styles that you can customize further to suit your purposes.

In this project, you'll use the same files you used in the previous task for the PDF presentation.

1 In the Folders palette in the File Browser, open the Lessons/Lesson02/Presentation folder if necessary, and make sure that only the five ferris-wheel photographs are in that folder but none of them are currently selected.

Note: If you saved the Ferris_wheel.pdf in the Presentation folder instead of saving it in the Lesson02 folder, select the PDF icon in the thumbnails pane and drag it into the Lesson02 folder in the Folders palette.

2 Choose Automate > Web Photo Gallery from the File Browser menu bar.

3 In the upper area of the Web Photo Gallery dialog box, do the following:

• Use the Styles pop-up menu to select Centered Frame 1- Feedback.

• Type your own e-mail address as the address at which you want to receive any feedback from the people who will view the images online.

4 Under Source Images, do the following, if they are not already done:

• For the Use option, select Folder.

• Click the Browse button (Windows) or Choose button (Mac OS), and then verify that the Presentation folder is selected. Or, select it now.

• Create a destination folder for your Web gallery: Click the Destination button, browse to the Lesson02 folder, and click the Make New Folder button. Type **Wheel Web Site** to name the folder. Make sure that Wheel Web Site appears in the Folder option before you click OK (Windows) or Close (Mac OS) to close the Browse For Folder (Windows) or Select A Destination Location (Mac OS) dialog box. (Don't close the Web Photo Gallery dialog box yet.)

5 Under Options, use the pop-up menu to select each of the following categories in turn (General, Banner, Large Images, Thumbnails, and Custom Colors), and then select options for each, as indicated here:

• General: Select .html on the Extension pop-up menu, and deselect all three check boxes.

• Banner: Type **Ferris Wheel Photos** for Site Name, **Adobe Systems** for photographer, and today's date (if necessary) or another date. You can leave the Contact Info option blank or type any phone number or street address.

• Large Images: Select the Resize Images check box (if necessary), choose Large from the pop-up menu, and leave the other options at the default settings.

• Thumbnails: Select Custom from the pop-up menu, and type **70** pixels. Leave the other options at the default settings.

Because you'll accept the default settings for Custom Colors and Security, you don't need to select those options.

6 Click OK.

After a short delay, during which Photoshop automatically opens the files and creates the resources for the Web gallery, the gallery opens in your default Web browser application.

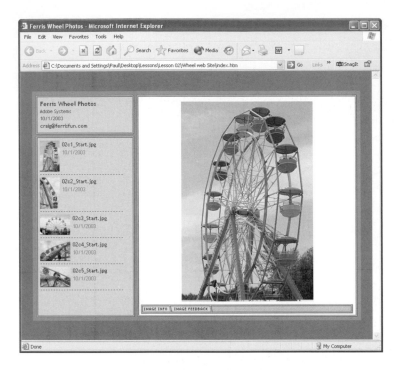

Viewing your Web Photo Gallery

This procedure is done entirely in your Web browser, such as Microsoft Internet Explorer, Safari, or Netscape Communicator.

1 If the Web page you created in the previous procedure is not already open in your Web browser, use the desktop to go to the Lessons/Lesson02/Wheel Web Site folder, and double-click the index.html file to open it.

2 If necessary, select the 02c1_Start.jpg thumbnail, so that the image of the entire ferris wheel appears on the right side of the page. (It should appear by default when the page opens.)

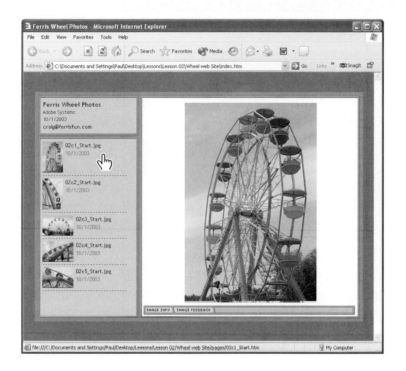

3 Click Image Info tab at the bottom of the Web page on the right to open the information display about the selected image.

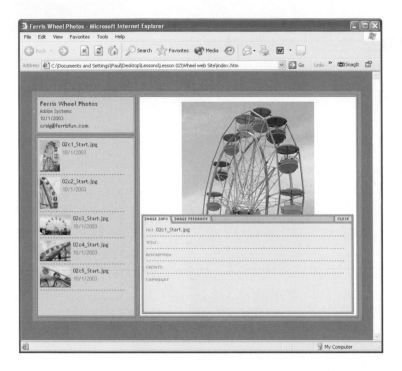

4 Click the Image Feedback tab, and do the following actions, as if you were one of your own clients reviewing the files:

• Select Approved.

• Type **Good angle shot** in the comment area of the Feedback tab**.**

Note: *You do not need to save your feedback yet. These Feedback options are not lost if you switch to another image or close the Feedback tab. However, if you close your Web browser or open another HTML page, your feedback entries will be discarded.*

5 Select the 02c2_Start.jpg thumbnail. On the Feedback tab, select Other and then type **Sky is too cloudy** in the comment area.

6 Select E-Mail Feedback, and then type your name in the dialog box that opens.

7 Review the e-mail message that opens in your default e-mail application. Notice that the subject line includes the name you typed in Step 6 and that your approval selections and comments appear for each of the images your reviewed. Then close the e-mail message without sending it.

Creating a Picture Package for printing

When you want to print multiple copies of an individual picture with maximum efficiency, the Picture Package feature can save you lots of time and paper. The Picture Package automatically arranges the layout so that you waste the least amount of paper printing the size of pictures that you want.

1 In the File Browser, select the Lessons/Lesson02/Pict_Package folder, and then select—but don't open—the Boat.jpg thumbnail in the thumbnails pane.

2 Choose Automate > Picture Package in the File Browser menu bar.

3 In the Picture Package dialog box under Document, select (1)5x7 (2)3.5x5 as the Layout option. Leave the dialog box open.

4 Under Label, select Custom Text in the Content pop-up menu.

5 Type **Summer Vacation, 2004** in the Custom Text option.

6 Select the following font options:

• For Font, select a sans serif font, such as Arial or Helvetica.

• For Font Size, select 10 pt.

• For Color, select White from the pop-up menu, so that the text will show up well against the deep colors in the foreground of the photograph.

• For Position, select Bottom Right.

- Leave None selected for Rotation.

Note: *You cannot preview the custom text. It may require some trial-and-error testing to give the custom text the appearance you want in the Picture Package output file.*

7 Click OK. After a pause for Photoshop to copy, resize, and arrange images, Picture Package 1 opens in an image window, showing the copies of the picture with the custom text in each copy. You can now print this image or save the file to print later.

If the palettes are still hidden, you can press Tab to show them again. Then, you can zoom in on the images as needed to examine the text and other details.

⚲ *You are not limited to the predefined Layout options. You can define custom picture sizes and arrangements. To do this, click the Edit Layout button in the lower right corner of the Picture Package dialog box. For more information, see Photoshop Help.*

Congratulations—you've finished this lesson on the File Browser. As you work through this book, you'll have many more opportunities to use the File Browser and discover what a time-saver it can be.

Review questions

1 Describe two ways to open the File Browser as a window.

2 What are some of the similarities between working with folders and files on the desktop and working with them in the Photoshop File Browser?

3 Why doesn't the File Browser have a palette menu?

4 Can you add or move palettes on the File Browser?

5 What are the advantages of using the File Browser instead of a desktop folder?

6 Describe two ways to rotate an image from the File Browser.

Review answers

1 You can open the File Browser by selecting the File Browser button on the tool options bar or by choosing File > Browse.

2 You can use either the File Browser or a desktop folder—such as the Explorer (Windows) or the Finder (Mac OS)—to rename files, move files into the Recycle Bin (Windows) or Trash (Mac OS), move files and folders from one location to another, rename files and folders, and create new folders.

3 The File Browser is a window, not a palette. Instead of a palette menu, it has a menu bar with five menus. Each menu within the File Browser contains an average of about 10 items. The menu bar also has five buttons that you can apply to files.

4 You can rearrange the palettes on the left side of the File Browser by dragging them by their tabs. You can minimize the File Browser palettes and resize them. However, you cannot close them entirely or move them into the work area outside the File Browser, nor can you place palettes from the work area in the File Browser.

5 The File Browser shows a thumbnail of each image file or folder within a folder, a scalable, high-resolution preview of the selected item, and information (*metadata*) about the selected item, including EXIF information for images captured by a digital camera and Camera Raw data—all at the same time. You can apply a number of Photoshop changes to files in the File Browser without first opening them in Photoshop. You can also use the File Browser for a number of file-management procedures, such as assigning rankings to files, sorting files by various criteria, manually rearranging the order in which the files are listed or shown, and batch-naming files with a consistent naming scheme. You can perform certain automated functions from the File Browser, such as creating Web galleries and Adobe PDF presentations. You can rotate images so that they open in Photoshop with the orientation you assigned in the File Browser.

6 You click the rotation buttons on the File Browser menu bar to rotate selected images two ways: clockwise ( ) or counterclockwise ( ). Each click rotates the image 90º.

3 | Basic Photo Corrections

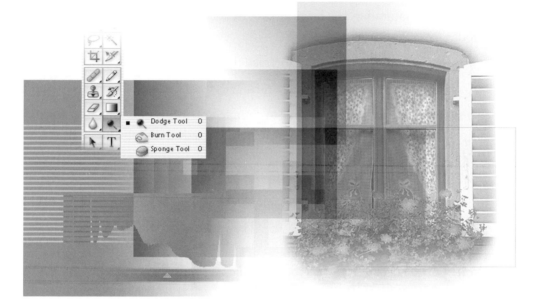

Adobe Photoshop and Adobe ImageReady include a variety of tools and commands for improving the quality of a photographic image. This lesson steps you through the process of acquiring, resizing, and retouching a photo intended for a print layout. The same workflow applies to Web images.

In this lesson, you'll learn how to do the following:

• Choose the correct resolution for a scanned photograph.

• Crop an image to final size.

• Adjust the tonal range of an image.

• Remove a color cast from an image Auto Color correction.

• Adjust the saturation and brightness of isolated areas of an image using the Sponge and Dodge tools.

• Apply the Unsharp Mask filter to finish the photo-retouching process.

• Save an Adobe Photoshop file in a format that can be used by a page-layout program.

This lesson will take about an hour to complete. The lesson is intended for Adobe Photoshop, but information on how to perform tasks in Adobe ImageReady is included where appropriate. Because ImageReady permanently converts 16-bit files into 8-bit files when you open them, it's recommended that you do this lesson in Photoshop.

If needed, remove the previous lesson folder from your hard drive, and copy the Lesson03 folder onto it. As you work on this lesson, you'll overwrite the start files. If you need to restore the start files, copy them from the *Adobe Photoshop CS Classroom in a Book* CD.

Note: *Windows 2000 users need to unlock the lesson files before using them. For more information, see "Copying the Classroom in a Book files" on page 3.*

Strategy for retouching

You can retouch photographic images in ways once available only to highly trained specialists. You can correct problems in color quality and tonal range created during the original photography or during image scanning. You can also correct problems in composition and sharpen the overall focus of the image.

Photoshop provides a comprehensive set of color-correction tools for adjusting the color and tone of individual images. ImageReady has a more basic set of color-correction tools, including Levels, Auto Levels, Brightness/Contrast, Hue/Saturation, Desaturation, Invert, Variations, and the Unsharp Mask filter.

Organizing an efficient sequence of tasks

Most retouching follows these eight general steps:

• Duplicating the original image or scan. (Always work in a copy of the image file, so that you can recover the original later if necessary.)

• Checking the scan quality and making sure that the resolution is appropriate for the way you will use the image.

• Cropping the image to final size and orientation.

• Repairing flaws in scans of damaged photographs (such as rips, dust, or stains)

• Adjusting the overall contrast or tonal range of the image.

• Removing any color casts.

• Adjusting the color and tone in specific parts of the image to bring out highlights, midtones, shadows, and desaturated colors.

• Sharpening the overall focus of the image.

Usually, you should complete these processes in the order listed above. Otherwise, the results of one process may cause unintended changes to other aspects of the image, making it necessary for you to redo some of your work.

Later in this book, you'll get experience using adjustment layers, which is another technique that gives you great flexibility to try out different correction settings without risking damage to the original image.

Adjusting your process for intended uses

The retouching techniques you apply to an image depend in part on how you will use the image. Whether an image is intended for black-and-white publication on newsprint or for full-color Internet distribution affects everything from the resolution of the initial scan to the type of tonal range and color correction that the image requires. Photoshop supports the CMYK color mode for preparing an image to be printed using process colors, as well as RGB and other color modes. ImageReady supports only RGB mode, used for on-screen display.

To illustrate one application of retouching techniques, this lesson takes you through the steps of correcting a photograph intended for four-color print publication.

For more information about CMYK and RGB color modes, see Lesson 20, "Producing and Printing Consistent Color."

Original image

Image cropped and retouched

Image placed into page layout

Resolution and image size

The first step in retouching a photograph in Photoshop is to make sure that the image is the correct resolution. The term *resolution* refers to the number of small squares known as *pixels* that describe an image and establish its detail. Resolution is determined by *pixel dimensions*, or the number of pixels along the width and height of an image.

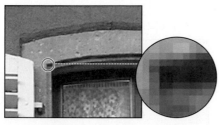

Pixels in a photographic image

Types of resolution

In computer graphics, there are different types of resolution:

The number of pixels per unit of length in an image is called the *image resolution*, usually measured in pixels per inch (ppi). An image with a high resolution has more pixels (and therefore a larger file size) than an image of the same dimensions with a low resolution. Images in Photoshop can vary from high resolution (300 ppi or higher) to low resolution (72 ppi or 96 ppi), whereas images in ImageReady are fixed at 72 ppi.

The number of pixels per unit of length on a monitor is the *monitor resolution*, usually measured in pixels per inch (ppi). Image pixels are translated directly into monitor pixels. In Photoshop, if the image resolution is higher than the monitor resolution, the image appears larger on-screen than its specified print dimensions. For example, when you display a 1-inch-by-1-inch, 144-ppi image on a 72-ppi monitor, the image fills a 2-inch-by-2-inch area of the screen. ImageReady images have a consistent image resolution of 72 ppi and display at the monitor resolution.

4 in. x 6 in. at 72 ppi; *100% on-screen view* 4 in. x 6 in. at 200 ppi; *100% on-screen view*
file size 342K   file size 2.48 MB

Note: *It is important to understand what "100% view" means when you work on-screen. At 100%, 1 image pixel = 1 monitor pixel. Unless the resolution of your image is exactly the same as the resolution of the monitor, the image size (in inches, for example) on-screen may be larger or smaller than the image size will be when printed.*

The number of ink dots per inch produced by an imagesetter or laser printer is the *printer* or *output resolution*. Of course, higher-resolution printers combined with higher-resolution images generally produce the best quality. The appropriate resolution for a printed image is determined both by the printer resolution and by the *screen frequency* or lines per inch (lpi) of the halftone screens used to reproduce images.

Keep in mind that the higher the image resolution, the larger the file size and the longer the file takes to download from the Web.

Resolution for this lesson

To determine the image resolution for the photograph in this lesson, we followed the computer-graphics rule of thumb for color or grayscale images that are intended for print on large commercial printers: Scan at a resolution 1.5 to 2 times the screen frequency used by the printer. Because the magazine in which the image will be printed uses a screen frequency of 133 lpi, the image was scanned at 200 ppi (133 x 1.5).

🔲 For complete information on resolution and image size, see Adobe Photoshop Help.

Getting started

The image you'll work on in this lesson is a scanned photograph. In this scenario, you'll prepare the image to be placed in an Adobe InDesign® layout for a fictitious magazine. The final image size in the print layout will be 2 inches by 3 inches.

You'll start the lesson by viewing the finished image. The picture you'll work on shows an interesting window with a window box that is overflowing with blooming red geraniums.

1 Start Photoshop and then immediately hold down Ctrl+Alt+Shift (Windows) or Command+Option+Shift (Mac OS) to restore the default preferences. (See "Restoring default preferences" on page 4.)

As messages appear, select Yes to confirm that you want to reset preferences, No to defer setting up your color monitor, and Close to close the Welcome Screen.

2 On the tool options bar, select the File Browser button, and use the Folders palette to navigate to and select the Lessons/Lesson03 folder on your hard disk.

3 In the thumbnails palette, select the 03End.psd file, so that it appears in the Preview palette in the File Browser.

4 Select the 03Start.psd thumbnail and compare it to the 03End file. Then double-click the 03Start.psd thumbnail or preview to open the file in Photoshop. Close the File Browser.

⬤ For some color illustrations of the artwork for this lesson, see the color section.

The colors in the 03Start.psd file are relatively dull, the scan is crooked, and the dimensions are larger than needed for the requirements of the magazine. These are the qualities that you'll fix in this lesson using Photoshop retouching techniques.

5 Choose File > Save As, and save the file in the same location as before, but rename it 03Work.psd.

Remember, when you're making permanent corrections to an image file, it's always wise to work on a copy rather than in the original. Then, if something goes horribly wrong, at least you'll be able to start over on a fresh copy of the original image.

Straightening and cropping an image

You'll use the Crop tool to trim and scale the photograph for this lesson so that it fits the space designed for it. You can use either the Crop tool or the Crop command to crop an image, which permanently deletes all the pixels outside of the crop selection area.

You can decide whether to delete the area outside of a rectangular selection, or whether to hide the area outside of the selection. In ImageReady, the Hide option is useful when creating animations with elements that move from off-screen into the live image area.

1 In the toolbox, select the Crop tool ( ). Then, in the tool options bar (at the top of the work area), enter the dimensions (in inches) of the finished image: For Width, type **2 in** and for Height, type **3 in**.

Note: If you are working in ImageReady, select the Fixed Size option in the tool options bar before entering the dimensions.

2 Draw a crop marquee around the image. Don't worry about whether or not the entire image is included, because you'll adjust the marquee size later.

As you drag, the marquee retains the same proportion as the dimensions you specified for the target size (2 x 3).

When you release the mouse button, a *cropping shield* covers the area outside the cropping selection, and the tool options bar now displays choices about the cropping shield.

3 In the tool options bar, make sure that the Perspective check box is *not* selected.

4 In the image window, move the pointer outside the crop marquee, so that it appears as a curved double arrow (↱). Drag clockwise to rotate the marquee until it is parallel with the edges of the window frame in the picture.

5 Place the pointer inside the crop marquee, and drag the marquee until it contains all the parts of the picture you want shown to produce an artistically pleasing result. If you also want to adjust the size of the marquee, drag one of the corner handles.

Initial crop marquee *Marquee rotated* *Marquee moved* *Marquee resized*

6 Press Enter (Windows) or Return (Mac OS). The image is now cropped, and the cropped image now fills the image window, straightened, sized, and cropped according to your specifications.

Image cropped

◯ *In Photoshop and ImageReady, you can use the Image > Trim command to discard a border area around the edge of the image, based on transparency or edge color.*

7 Choose File > Save to save your work.

💡 *Try choosing File > Automate > Crop And Straighten Photos when you work with your own scan of multiple photographs. Photoshop recognizes the rectangular edges of images that contrast with their background and makes individual straightened image files for each area. Then, you can crop within those images as needed for aesthetic reasons. For more information, see Photoshop Help.*

Using automatic adjustments

Photoshop CS contains a number of highly effective automatic features that fix pictures with very little effort on your part. These are all you need for certain kinds of jobs you might face. However, when you want more control, you can dig down into some of the more technical features and controls available in Photoshop.

Just to be a good sport about it, you'll try the automatic adjustments first. A little later, you'll make adjustments using manual controls on another copy of the lesson image.

1 Make sure that you remembered to save your work after you finished cropping the image in the previous procedure, or choose File > Save now.

2 Choose File > Save As, type **03Auto.psd** to rename the cropped file, and click Save.

3 Choose Image > Adjustments > Auto Color.

4 Choose Image > Adjustments > Shadow/Highlight.

5 In the Shadow/Highlight dialog box, drag the Highlight and Shadow sliders as needed until you think the image looks good. Make sure that Preview is selected so that you can see the changes applied to the image window as you work.

6 Click OK to close the dialog box, and then choose File > Save.

7 Close the 03Auto.psd file. Then choose File > Open Recent, and select the 03Work.psd on the submenu of recently opened files.

Adjusting the tonal range

The tonal range of an image represents the amount of *contrast*, or detail, in the image and is determined by the image's distribution of pixels, ranging from the darkest pixels (black) to the lightest pixels (white). You'll now correct the photograph's contrast using the Levels command.

In this task, you'll use a graph in the Levels dialog box that represents the range of values (dark and light). This graph has controls that adjust the shadows, highlights, and midtones or gamma of the image. You'll also refer to the Histogram palette, which simply displays the information for you. Unless you're aiming for a special effect, the ideal histogram extends across the full width of the graph, and the middle portion has fairly uniform peaks and valleys, representing adequate pixel data in the midtones.

1 Choose Window > Histogram, or click the Histogram tab in the Navigator palette group to make it visible. Then choose Expanded View on the palette menu.

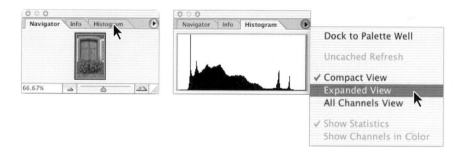

2 Choose Image > Adjustments > Levels, to open the Levels dialog box.

3 Make sure that the Preview check box is selected, and then move the dialog box, if necessary, so that you can also see the image window and Histogram palette.

Three triangles below the histogram represent the shadows (black triangle), highlights (white triangle), and midtones or *gamma* (gray triangle). If your image had colors across the entire brightness range, the graph would extend across the full width of the histogram. Notice that at this point, the graphs in the Levels dialog box and the Histogram palette are identical.

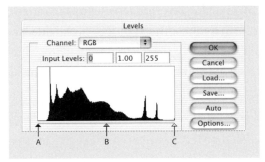

A. *Shadows* **B.** *Midtones or gamma* **C.** *Highlights*

4 Drag the left triangle to the right to the point where the histogram indicates that the darkest colors begin.

As you drag, the first Input Levels value (above the histogram) changes and so does the image itself. In the Histogram palette, the left portion of the graph now stretches to the edge of the frame. This indicates that the darkest shadow values have shifted closer to black.

Note: *You can also scrub to change the Input Levels value: First click in the text box for the value you want to change, and then drag the pointer over the words "Input Levels."*

5 Drag the right triangle to the left to the point where the histogram indicates that the lightest colors begin. Again, notice the changes in the third Input Levels value and in the image and the changed shape of the Histogram palette graph.

6 Drag the middle triangle a short distance toward the left side to lighten the midtones.

Watch the image updates in the image window and the changes in the Histogram palette graph to determine how far to drag the middle triangle.

7 When the image looks good to you (the sample uses Input Levels values of 18, 1.30, and 232), click OK to apply the changes. Then save your work.

Note: *The Levels command is also available in ImageReady, but the Histogram palette is not.*

About Auto Contrast

You can also adjust the contrast (highlights and shadows) and the overall mix of colors in an image automatically using the Image > Adjustments > Auto Contrast command. Adjusting the contrast maps the darkest and lightest pixels in the image to black and white.

This remapping causes the highlights to appear lighter and the shadows to appear darker and can improve the appearance of many photographic or continuous-tone images. (The Auto Contrast command does not improve flat-color images.)

The Auto Contrast command clips white and black pixels by 0.5%—that is, it ignores the first 0.5% of either extreme when identifying the lightest and darkest pixels in the image. This clipping of color values ensures that white and black values are representative areas of the image content rather than extreme pixel values.

For this project, you won't use the Auto Contrast feature, but it's a feature you should know about so that you can use it in your own projects.

Removing a color cast

Some images contain color casts (imbalanced colors), which may occur during scanning or which may have existed in the original image. This photograph of the window has a blue cast. You'll use the Auto Color feature in Photoshop CS to correct this. (ImageReady does not include the Auto Color command, so this task must be done in Photoshop.)

Note: To see a color cast in an image on your monitor, you need a 24-bit monitor (one that can display millions of colors). On monitors that can display only 256 colors (8 bits), a color cast is difficult, if not impossible, to detect.

For an illustration of color casting, see figure 3-1 in the color section.

1 Choose Image > Adjustments > Auto Color.

Notice that the blue color cast is gone.

2 Choose File > Save.

> ### Using the Auto Color command (Photoshop)
>
> *The Auto Color command adjusts the contrast and color of an image by searching the actual image rather than the channel histograms for shadows, midtones, and highlights. It neutralizes the midtones and clips the white and black pixels based on the values set in the Auto Correction Options dialog box.*
>
> ### Setting Auto Correction options (Photoshop)
>
> *The Auto Correction Options dialog box lets you automatically adjust the overall tonal range of an image, specify clipping percentages, and assign color values to shadows, midtones, and highlights. You can apply the settings during a single use of the Levels dialog box or Curves dialog box, or you can save the settings for future use with the Levels, AutoLevels, Auto Contrast, Auto Color, and Curves commands.*
>
> *To open the Auto Correction Options dialog box, click Options in the Levels dialog box or Curves dialog box.*

Replacing colors in an image

With the Replace Color command, you can create temporary *masks* based on specific colors and then replace these colors. (A mask isolates an area of an image, so that changes affect just the selected area and not the rest of the image.) The Replace Color dialog box contains options for adjusting the hue, saturation, and lightness components of the selection: *Hue* is color, *saturation* is the purity of the color, and *lightness* is how much white or black is in the image.

You'll use the Replace Color command to change the color of the wall at the top of the image. The Replace Color command is not available in ImageReady.

1 Select the Rectangular Marquee tool (⬚), and draw a selection border around the blue wall at the top of the image. Don't worry about making a perfect selection, but be sure to include all of the blue wall.

2 Choose Image > Adjustments > Replace Color to open the Replace Color dialog box.

By default, the Selection area of the Replace Color dialog box displays a black rectangle, representing the current selection.

Notice the three Eyedropper tools in the Replace Color dialog box. One selects a single color; another selects additional colors and adds them to the color selection; the third selects colors and removes them from a color selection.

A. Single-color Eyedropper tool
B. Eyedropper Plus tool
C. Eyedropper Minus tool

3 Using the first (single-color) Eyedropper tool (✐) in the Replace Color dialog box, click anywhere in the blue-wall area of the image window to select all of the area with that color.

4 In the Replace Color dialog box, select the Eyedropper Plus tool (✐+), and use it to select other areas of the blue wall until the entire wall shape is highlighted in white in the dialog box.

5 Adjust the tolerance level by scrubbing, dragging the Fuzziness slider, or typing **80**.

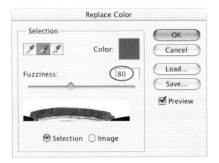

Fuzziness controls the degree to which related colors are included in the mask.

6 If there are any white areas of the mask display in the dialog box that are not part of the wall and therefore should not be included, fix those now: Select the Eyedropper Minus tool (✎) and click those areas in either the image window or the Replace Color dialog box to remove most of the white. (It's OK if a few pixels in the shadowed window inset remain in the selection.)

7 In the Replacement area of the Replace Color dialog box, drag the Hue slider to **–40**, the Saturation slider to **–45**, and leave the Lightness slider at **0**.

As you change the values, the color of the wall changes in hue, saturation, and lightness, so that the wall is now a slaty green color.

8 Click OK to apply the changes.

9 Choose Select > Deselect, and then choose File > Save.

Adjusting lightness with the Dodge tool

You'll use the Dodge tool to lighten the highlights and bring out the details of the curtains behind the window. The Dodge tool is based on a traditional photographer's method of holding back light during an exposure to lighten an area of the image.

1 In the toolbox, select the Dodge tool (🔍).

In ImageReady, the Dodge tool is hidden under the Clone Stamp tool (🗻).

2 In the tool options bar, select the following settings:

• For Brush, select a fairly large feathered brush on the Brush pop-up palette, such as 27. Then, click outside the palette to close it.

• In the Range pop-up menu, select Highlights.

• For Exposure, type, scrub, or use the pop-up slider to enter **15%**.

| 🔍 ▾ | Brush: 27 ▾ | Range: Highlights ▾ | Exposure: 15% ▸ | 🖊 |

3 Using vertical strokes, drag the Dodge tool over the window curtains to bring out the details and remove the dinginess from the lace.

You don't always need to use vertical strokes with the Dodge tool, but they work well with this particular image. If you make a mistake or don't like the results, choose Edit > Undo and try again until you are satisfied with the results.

Original   *Result*

4 Choose File > Save.

Adjusting saturation with the Sponge tool

Next, you'll use the Sponge tool to saturate the color of the geraniums. When you change the saturation of a color, you adjust its strength or purity. The Sponge tool is useful for making subtle saturation changes to specific areas of an image.

For an illustration of saturating with the Sponge tool, see figure 3-2 in the color section.

1 Select the Sponge tool (   ), hidden under the Dodge tool (   ).

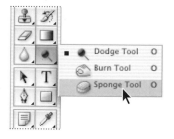

ImageReady also has a Sponge tool hidden under the Clone Stamp tool (   ).

2 In the tool options bar, select the following settings:

• In the Brush pop-up palette, again select a large, feathered brush, such as 27.

• In the Mode pop-up menu, select Saturate.

• In Flow, drag the slider or type **90%** to set the intensity of the saturation effect.

3 Drag the sponge back and forth over the blossoms and leaves to saturate their color. The more you drag over an area, the more saturated the color becomes.

Original   *Result*

4 Save your work.

Applying the Unsharp Mask filter

The last step you take when retouching a photo is to apply the Unsharp Mask filter, which adjusts the contrast of the edge detail and creates the illusion of a more focused image.

1 Choose Filter > Sharpen > Unsharp Mask.

2 In the Unsharp Mask dialog box, make sure that the Preview option is selected so that you can see the results in the image window.

You can drag inside the preview window in the dialog box to see different parts of the image or use the plus (+) and minus (−) buttons below the thumbnail to zoom in and out.

3 Drag the Amount slider until the image is as sharp as you want (we used 75%).

💡 *As you try different settings, toggle the Preview check box off and on to see how your changes affect the image in the image window. Or, you can just click-hold the image in the dialog box to toggle the filter off and on. If your image is large, using the display in the dialog box can be more efficient because only a small area is redrawn.*

4 Drag the Radius slider to determine the number of pixels surrounding the edge pixels that will affect the sharpening. The higher the resolution, the higher the Radius setting should be. (We used the default value, 1.0 pixel.)

5 (Optional) You can adjust the Threshold slider. This determines how different the sharpened pixels must be from the surrounding area before they are considered edge pixels and subsequently sharpened by the Unsharp Mask filter. The default Threshold value of 0 sharpens all pixels in the image. Try a different value, such as 4 or 5.

6 When you are satisfied with the results, click OK to apply the Unsharp Mask filter.

Sharpening the image

Unsharp masking, or USM, is a traditional film compositing technique used to sharpen edges in an image. The Unsharp Mask filter corrects blurring introduced during photographing, scanning, resampling, or printing. It is useful for images intended for both print and online viewing.

The Unsharp Mask locates pixels that differ from surrounding pixels by the threshold you specify and increases the pixels' contrast by the amount you specify. In addition, you specify the radius of the region to which each pixel is compared.

The effects of the Unsharp Mask filter are far more pronounced on-screen than in high-resolution output. If your final destination is print, experiment to determine what dialog box settings work best for your image.

Compare the manual and automatic results

Near the beginning of this lesson, you adjusted the lesson image using only automatic color and value controls. For the rest of the lesson, you painstakingly applied manual adjustments to get specific results. Now it's time to compare the two.

1 Choose File > Open Recent, and select the 03Auto.psd file on the submenu list, if it is available. Otherwise, use the File Browser or choose File > Open to locate and open the file.

2 Choose Window > Arrange > Tile, to arrange the 03Auto.psd image window and the 03Work.psd image window side by side.

3 Visually compare the two results.

4 Close the 03Auto.psd file.

For some people, the automatic commands may be all they'll ever need. For others with more sensitive visual requirements, the manual adjustments are the way to go. The best of both worlds is when you understand the tradeoffs of the two methods and can choose one or the other according to your requirements for the specific project and image.

Saving the image for four-color printing

Before you save a Photoshop file for use in a four-color publication, you must change the image to CMYK color mode in order to print your publication correctly in four-color process inks. You'll use the Mode command to change the image color mode.

[?] For more information on color modes, see "Converting between color modes" in Photoshop Help.

You can perform these tasks only in Photoshop. ImageReady does not have printing capability and uses only one color mode, RGB, for on-screen display.

1 Choose Image > Mode > CMYK Color.

• If you are using Adobe InDesign to create your publication, you can skip the rest of this process and just choose File > Save. InDesign can import native Photoshop files, so there is no need to convert the image to TIFF format.

• If you are using another layout application, you must save the photo as a TIFF file.

2 Choose File > Save As.

3 In the Save As dialog box, choose TIFF from the Format menu.

4 Click Save.

5 In the TIFF Options dialog box, select the correct Byte Order for your operating system and click OK.

The image is now fully retouched, saved, and ready for placement in a publication layout.

Review questions

1 What does resolution mean?

2 How can you use the Crop tool in photo retouching?

3 How can you adjust the tonal range of an image?

4 What is saturation, and how can you adjust it?

5 Why would you use the Unsharp Mask filter on a photo?

Review answers

1 The term *resolution* refers to the number of pixels that describe an image and establish its detail. The three different types are *image resolution, monitor resolution*—both of which are measured in pixels per inch (ppi)—and *printer* or *output resolution*, measured in ink dots per inch (dpi).

2 You can use the Crop tool to trim, scale, and straighten an image.

3 You can use the black, white, and gray triangles below the Levels command histogram to control the midpoint and where the darkest and lightest points in the image begin, thus extending its tonal range.

4 Saturation is the strength or purity of color in an image. You can use the Sponge tool to increase the saturation in a specific area of an image.

5 The Unsharp Mask filter adjusts the contrast of the edge detail and creates the illusion of a more focused image.

Lesson 4

4 Working with Selections

Learning how to select areas of an image is of primary importance—you must first select what you want to affect. Once you've made a selection, only the area within the selection can be edited. Areas outside the selection are protected from change.

In this lesson, you'll learn how to do the following:

• Make specific areas of an image active, using various tools.

• Reposition a selection marquee.

• Move and duplicate the contents of a selection.

• Use several keyboard-mouse combinations that save time and hand motions.

• Deselect a selection.

• Constrain the movement of a selected area.

• Adjust the position of a selected area, using the arrow keys.

• Add to and subtract from a selection.

• Rotate a selection.

• Use multiple selection tools to make a complex selection.

• Erase pixels within a selection.

This lesson will take less than an hour to complete. The lesson is designed to be done in Adobe Photoshop, but information on using similar functionality in Adobe ImageReady is included where appropriate.

If needed, remove the previous lesson folder from your hard drive, and copy the Lesson04 folder onto it. As you work on this lesson, you'll overwrite the start files. If you need to restore the start files, copy them from the *Adobe Photoshop CS Classroom in a Book* CD.

Note: *Windows 2000 users need to unlock the lesson files before using them. For more information, see "Copying the Classroom in a Book files" on page 3.*

Getting started

You'll start the lesson by viewing the finished lesson file to see the image that you'll create as you explore the selection tools in Photoshop.

1 Start Adobe Photoshop, holding down Ctrl+Alt+Shift (Windows) or Command+Option+Shift (Mac OS) to restore the default preferences. (See "Restoring default preferences" on page 4.)

As messages appear, select Yes to confirm that you want to reset preferences, No to defer setting up your color monitor, and Close to close the Welcome Screen.

2 On the tool options bar, select the File Browser button, and use the Folders palette to navigate to and select the Lessons/Lesson04 folder on your hard disk.

3 In the thumbnails palette, select the 04End.psd file, so that it appears in the Preview palette in the File Browser.

The project is a collage of objects, including a writing journal, a pen, globes, a number, a flower, and a padlock. The challenge in this lesson is to arrange these elements, each of which is part of a multi-image scan. The "ideal" composition is a judgment call, so this lesson won't describe precise locations. There are no "right" or "wrong" placements of the objects.

4 Select the 04Start.psd file in the thumbnails pane, and double-click to open it.

About selecting and selection tools

Selecting and making changes to an area within an image is a two-step process. In Photoshop, you first select the part of an image you want to change with one of the selection tools. Then, you can use another tool to make changes, such as moving the selected pixels to another location or erasing pixels within the selection. You can make selections based on size, shape, and color, using four basic sets of tools—the Marquee, Lasso, Magic Wand, and Pen tools. The selection process limits changes to within the selected area. Other areas are unaffected.

Note: In this lesson, you'll use only the marquee tools, lasso tools, and Magic Wand tool to make your selections. You'll learn about the pen tools in a lesson entirely devoted to them (Lesson 9, "Basic Pen Tool Techniques"). You'll also use the Move tool.

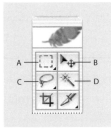

A. Rectangular Marquee tool
B. Move tool
C. Lasso tool
D. Magic Wand tool

The best selection tool for a specific area often depends on the characteristics of that area, such as shape or color. There are three categories of selections:

Geometric selections You use the *Rectangular Marquee tool* (⬚) to select a rectangular area in an image. The *Elliptical Marquee tool* (◯), which is hidden behind the Rectangular Marquee tool, selects elliptical areas. Use the *Single Row Marquee tool* (⋯) and *Single Column Marquee tool* (⁝) to select either a 1-pixel-high row or a 1-pixel-wide column, respectively.

Freehand selections You can drag the *Lasso tool* (𝒫) around an area to trace a freehand selection. Using the *Polygonal Lasso tool* (⊱), you can click to set anchor points in straight-line segments around an area. The *Magnetic Lasso tool* (⊱) in Photoshop works something like a combination of the other two lasso tools, and is best when there is good contrast between the area you want to select and its surroundings.

Color-based selections The *Magic Wand tool* (✎) selects parts of an image based on the similarity in color of adjacent pixels. This tool is useful for selecting odd-shaped areas that share a specific range of colors.

ImageReady includes the basic marquee selection tools, the Lasso and Polygonal Lasso tools, and the Magic Wand tool. For more convenience in working with common Web shapes, ImageReady adds an extra marquee selection tool, the Rounded Rectangle Marquee tool (⬭).

Selecting with the Magic Wand tool

The Magic Wand tool is one of the easiest ways to make a selection. You simply click a particular colored point in the image to select areas of that color. This method is most successful for selecting an area of closely similar colors that is surrounded by areas of different color. After you make the initial selection, you can add or subtract areas by using specific keyboard combinations with the Magic Wand tool.

The Tolerance option sets the sensitivity of the Magic Wand tool. This limits or extends the range of pixel similarity, so that 32—the default tolerance—selects the color you click plus 32 lighter and 32 darker tones of that color. The ideal tolerance level depends on the color ranges and variations in the image.

Using the Magic Wand tool to select a colored area

The large number "5" in the 04Start file (which should be open now) is a good candidate for using the Magic Wand tool because the entire "5" is blue and the surrounding area is a light gray shadow. For the collage you're creating in this lesson, you'll select and move just the number, not the shadow or background behind it.

1 Select the Magic Wand tool (✎).

2 In the tool options bar, scrub the Tolerance label or type **70** in the Tolerance text box to increase the number of similar tones that will be selected.

3 Using the Magic Wand tool, click what looks like the surface of the large number "5" image. Most of it will be selected.

4 To select the remaining area of the number "5," hold down Shift, so that a plus sign appears with the Magic Wand tool pointer, indicating that whatever you click will be added to the current selection. Then, click one of the unselected areas of the blue number "5."

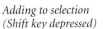

Initial selection   *Adding to selection*   *Complete selection*
                              (Shift key depressed)

Note: *When you use other selection tools, such as a marquee tool or a lasso tool, you can also use the Shift key to add to a selection. Later in this lesson, you'll learn how to subtract from a selection.*

5 Continue adding to the selection until all the blue areas are selected. If you accidentally select an area outside the blue number, choose Edit > Undo, and try again.

Leave the selection active so that you can use it in the next procedure.

Moving a selected area

Once you've selected an area of an image, any changes you make apply exclusively to the pixels within the selection marquee. The rest of the image is not affected by those changes.

When you want to move the selected image area to another part of the composition, you'll use the Move tool. On a single-layer image like this one, the moved pixels replace the pixels beneath them. This change is not permanent until you deselect the moved pixels, so you can try different locations for the moved selection before you make a commitment.

1 If the blue "5" is not still selected, repeat the previous procedure to select it. (See "Using the Magic Wand tool to select a colored area" on page 123.)

2 Select the Move tool (![move tool icon]). Notice that the blue "5" remains selected.

3 Drag the selected part of the image (the "5") to the upper left area of the collage, so that a small area of the number overlaps the border of the book.

4 Choose Select > Deselect, and then choose File > Save.

In Photoshop, it's not easy to accidentally deselect. Unless a selection tool is active, stray clicks in the image will not deselect the active area. To deliberately deselect, you can use one of three methods: You can choose Select > Deselect, you can press Ctrl+D (Windows) or Command+D (Mac OS), or you can click outside the selection with one of the selection tools to start a different selection.

Using the Magic Wand with other selection tools

If a multicolored area that you want to select is set against a differently colored background, it can be much easier to select the background than the area itself. In this procedure, you'll try out this neat little technique.

1 Select the Rectangular Marquee tool ([ ]).

2 Drag a selection around the water lily. Make sure that your selection marquee is set back from the tips of the flower so that a margin of white appears between the petals and the edges of the marquee.

At this point, the water lily and the white background area are selected. You'll subtract the white area from the selection, so that only the water lily remains in the selection.

3 Select the Magic Wand tool; then in the tool options bar, set the Tolerance to **32**, to reduce the range of colors the wand will select.

4 Hold down Alt (Windows) or Option (Mac OS), so that a minus sign appears with the magic wand pointer, and then click in the white background area within the selection marquee.

Now all the white pixels are deselected, leaving the water lily perfectly selected.

5 Select the Move tool (⯐) and drag the water lily beside the book, placing it so that a few petals overlap the lower right edge of the book.

6 Choose Select > Deselect, and then save your work.

Working with oval and circular selections

You've already had experience with the Rectangular Marquee tool, which you used to select the area surrounding the water lily image. Now you'll use a different marquee tool.

The best part about this section is the introduction of some more keyboard shortcuts that can save you time and arm motions. The repositioning techniques that you'll try here work equally well with the other marquee shapes.

Repositioning a selection marquee while creating it

Selecting ovals and circles can be tricky. It's not always obvious where you should start dragging, so sometimes the selection will be off-center or the ratio of width to height won't match what you need. In this procedure, you'll try out techniques for managing those problems, including two important keyboard-mouse combinations that can make your Photoshop work much easier.

As you do this procedure, be very careful to follow the directions about keeping the mouse button or specific keyboard keys pressed down. If you accidentally release the mouse button at the wrong time, simply start the procedure again from Step 1.

1 Select the Zoom tool (🔍), and click the black oval on the right side of the image window as needed to zoom in to at least 100% view (use 200% view if the entire oval will fit in the image window on your screen).

2 Select the Elliptical Marquee tool (○) hidden under the Rectangular Marquee tool.

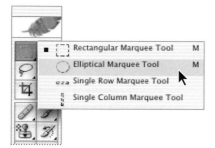

3 Move the pointer over the oval, and drag diagonally across the oval to create a selection, but do not release the mouse button. It's OK if your selection does not match the oval shape yet.

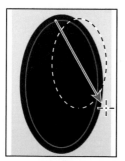

If you accidently release the mouse button, draw the selection again. In most cases—including this one—the new selection replaces the previous one.

4 Still holding down the mouse button, hold down the spacebar on your keyboard and drag the selection. The border moves as you drag.

5 Carefully release the spacebar (but not the mouse button), and continue to drag, trying to make the size and shape of the selection match the oval as closely as possible. If necessary, hold down the spacebar and drag to move the selection marquee into position around the black oval.

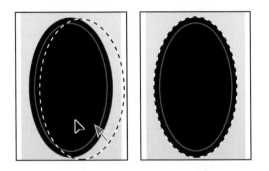

Note: *You do not have to include absolutely all of the black oval, but make sure that the shape of your selection has the same proportions as the oval and that the thin yellow line is contained symmetrically within the selection. As long as the selection marquee is between the yellow line and the outer edge, you're fine.*

6 When the selection border is positioned and sized correctly, release the mouse button.

7 Choose View > Zoom Out or use the slider in the Navigator palette to reduce the zoom view so that you can see all of the image.

Leave the Elliptical Marquee tool (○) and the selection active for the next procedure.

Moving selected pixels with a keyboard shortcut

Next, you'll move the black oval to the center of the book, using a keyboard shortcut. The shortcut enables you to temporarily access the Move tool instead of selecting it from the toolbox.

1 If the black oval is not still selected, repeat the previous procedure ("Repositioning a selection marquee while creating it" on page 127) to select it.

Leave the Elliptical Marquee tool (◯) selected in the toolbox.

2 Hold down Ctrl (Windows) or Command (Mac OS), and move the Elliptical Marquee tool pointer within the selection. The pointer icon now includes a pair of scissors (✂) to indicate that the selection will be cut from its current location.

Note: When you use the Ctrl (Windows) or Command (Mac OS) keyboard shortcut to temporarily switch to the Move tool, you don't need to keep the keyboard key down after you start to drag. The Move tool remains active even after you release the mouse button. Photoshop reverts back to the previously selected tool when you deselect, either by clicking outside of the selection or using the Deselect command.

3 Drag the oval onto the book so that it is only roughly centered. (You'll use another technique to nudge the oval into the exact position wanted.) Release the mouse button but do not deselect the black oval.

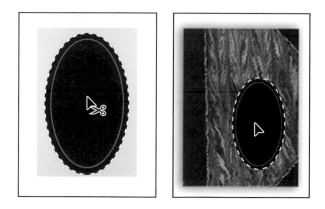

Moving with the arrow keys

You can make minor adjustments to the position of selected pixels, using the arrow keys to nudge the oval in increments of either 1 pixel or 10 pixels.

When a selection tool is active in the toolbox, the arrow keys nudge the selection border, but not the contents. When the Move tool is active, the arrow keys move the selection border and its contents.

Before you begin, make sure that the black oval shape is still selected in the image window.

1 In the toolbox, select the Move tool (▸⊕) and press the Up Arrow key (▯) on your keyboard a few times to move the oval upward.

Notice that each time you press the arrow key, the oval moves in a 1-pixel increment. Experiment by pressing the other arrow keys to see how they affect the selection.

2 Hold down Shift, and press an arrow key.

Notice that the selection now moves in 10-pixel increments.

Sometimes the border around a selected area can distract you as you make adjustments. You can hide the edges of a selection temporarily without actually deselecting and then display the selection border once you've completed the adjustments.

3 Choose View > Show > Selection Edges or View > Extras.

Either command makes the selection border around the oval disappear.

4 Use the arrow keys to nudge the oval until it is positioned where you want it. Then choose View > Show > Selection Edges.

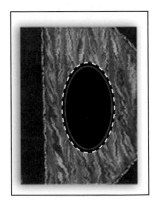

5 Choose Select > Deselect, or press Ctrl+D (Windows) or Command+D (Mac OS).

Selecting from a center point

In some cases it's easier to make elliptical or rectangular selections by drawing a selection from the center point. You'll use this technique to select the globe.

1 If necessary, scroll to the lower left area of the image where the globe appears.

2 Select the Zoom tool (🔍) and click the globe as needed to increase the magnification to about 300%. Make sure that you can see the entire globe in your image window.

3 In the toolbox, select the Elliptical Marquee tool (◯).

4 Move the pointer to the approximate center of the globe. You can use the pivot points holding the globe and line of the equator as visual guides to help you locate the center.

5 Click and begin dragging. Then, without releasing the mouse button, hold down Alt (Windows) or Option (Mac OS) and continue dragging the selection to the outer edge of the globe.

Notice that the selection is centered over its starting point.

💡 *To ensure that your selection is a perfect circle, you can also hold down Shift as you drag. If you held down Shift while using the Rectangular Marquee tool, you'd constrain the marquee shape to a perfect square.*

6 When you have the entire globe selected, release the mouse button first and then release Alt or Option (and the Shift key if you used it). Do not deselect, because you'll use this selection in the next topic.

If necessary, adjust the selection border using one of the methods you learned earlier. If you accidentally released the Alt or Option key before you released the mouse button, try selecting the globe again.

Moving and changing the pixels in a selection

Now you'll move the globe to the upper right area of the book image. Then, you'll do a completely different kind of change by altering the color of the globe for a dramatic effect.

Before you begin, make sure that the globe is still selected. If it is not, reselect it, following the procedure in the previous topic. (See "Selecting from a center point" on page 131.)

1 Choose View > Fit On Screen to adjust the magnification so that the entire image fits within the image window.

2 In the toolbox, select the Move tool (✥).

3 Position the pointer within the globe selection. The pointer becomes an arrow with a pair of scissors (✂), to indicate that dragging the selection will cut it from its present location and move it to the new location.

4 Drag the globe over the book image to the right of center. If you want to adjust the position after you stop dragging, simply start dragging again. The globe remains selected throughout the process.

5 Choose Image > Adjustments > Invert.

The colors making up the globe are inverted, so that now it is effectively a color negative of itself.

6 Leaving the globe selected, choose File > Save to save your work.

Moving and duplicating simultaneously

Next, you'll move and duplicate a selection simultaneously. If your globe image is no longer selected, reselect it now, using the techniques you learned earlier.

1 With the Move tool (⊹) selected, hold down Alt (Windows) or Option (Mac OS) as you position the pointer inside the globe selection. The pointer becomes a double arrow, which indicates that a duplicate will be made when you move the selection.

2 Continue holding down Alt or Option, and drag a duplicate of the globe down and to the right, so that it is near the upper right corner of the book image. You can allow the duplicate globe to partially overlap the original one. Release the mouse button and Alt or Option, but do not deselect the duplicate globe.

3 Choose Edit > Transform > Scale to activate a bounding box around the selection.

4 Hold down Shift and drag one of the corner points to enlarge the globe so that it is larger than the original by about half. Then, press Enter (Windows) or Return (Mac OS) to commit the change and remove the transformation bounding box.

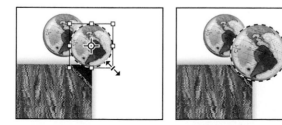

Notice that the selection marquee also resizes and that the resized, copied globe remains selected. The Shift key constrains the proportions so that the enlarged globe is not distorted.

5 Hold down Shift+Alt (Windows) or Shift+Option (Mac OS), and drag a new copy of the second globe down and to the right.

Holding down Shift when you move a selection constrains the movement horizontally or vertically in 45° increments.

6 Repeat Steps 3 and 4 for the third globe, making it about twice the size of the first one.

7 When you are satisfied with the size and position of the third globe, choose Select > Deselect, and then choose File > Save.

For information on working with the center point in a transformation, see "Transforming objects in two dimensions" in Adobe Photoshop Help.

Copying selections or layers

You can use the Move tool to copy selections as you drag them within or between images, or you can copy and move selections using the Copy, Copy Merged, Cut, and Paste commands. Dragging with the Move tool saves memory because the Clipboard is not used as it is with the Copy, Copy Merged, Cut, and Paste commands.

Photoshop and ImageReady contain several copy and paste commands:

• *The Copy command copies the selected area on the active layer.*

• *The Copy Merged command makes a merged copy of all the visible layers in the selected area.*

• *The Paste command pastes a cut or copied selection into another part of the image or into another image as a new layer.*

• *(Photoshop) The Paste Into command pastes a cut or copied selection inside another selection in the same image or different image. The source selection is pasted onto a new layer, and the destination selection border is converted into a layer mask.*

Keep in mind that when a selection or layer is pasted between images with different resolutions, the pasted data retains its pixel dimensions. This can make the pasted portion appear out of proportion to the new image. Use the Image Size command to make the source and destination images the same resolution before copying and pasting.

Selecting with the lasso tools

You can use the lasso tools to make selections that require both freehand and straight lines. You'll select the fountain pen for the collage using the lasso tools in this way. It takes a bit of practice to use the lasso tools to alternate between straight-line and freehand selections—if you make a mistake while you're selecting the fountain pen, simply deselect and start again.

1 Select the Zoom tool (🔍), and click the fountain-pen image as needed until the view enlarges to 100%. Make sure that you can see the entire pen image in the window.

2 Select the Lasso tool (🔎). Starting at the lower left of the image, drag around the rounded end of the fountain pen, tracing the shape as accurately as possible. Do not release the mouse button.

3 Hold down Alt (Windows) or Option (Mac OS), and then release the mouse button so that the lasso pointer changes to the polygonal lasso shape (🔾). Do not release the Alt or Option key.

4 Begin clicking along the top side of the cap and barrel of the pen to place anchor points, following the contours of the fountain pen. Be sure to keep the Alt or Option key held down throughout this process.

The selection border automatically stretches like a rubber band between anchor points.

5 When you reach the curved edge of the nib, keep the mouse button held down and then release the Alt or Option key. The pointer again appears as the lasso icon.

6 Carefully drag around the nib of the pen, keeping the mouse button down.

7 When you finish tracing the nib and reach the lower side of the barrel, first hold down Alt or Option again, and then release the mouse button and start clicking along the lower side of the pen. Continue to trace the pen until you arrive back at the starting point of your selection near the left end of the image.

8 Make sure that the last straight line crosses the start of the selection, release Alt or Option, and then release the mouse button. The pen is now entirely selected. Go on to the next procedure without deselecting the fountain pen.

Rotating a selection

So far, you've moved selected images and inverted the color of a selected area. But there are many more things that you can do with a selection. In the following steps, you'll see how easy it is to rotate a selected object.

Before you begin, make sure that the fountain pen is selected.

1 Choose View > Fit on Screen to resize the image window to fit on your screen.

2 Hold down Ctrl (Windows) or Command (Mac OS), and drag the fountain-pen selection to the area just below and off-center to the left of the book.

3 Choose Edit > Transform > Rotate. The pen and selection marquee are enclosed in a bounding box and the pointer appears as a curved double-headed arrow (↻).

4 Move the pointer outside the bounding box and drag to rotate the pen to a jaunty angle. Then, press Enter (Windows) or Return (Mac OS) to commit the transformation changes.

5 If necessary, select the Move tool (▶₊) and drag to change the position of the pen. When you're satisfied with the pen position, choose Select > Deselect.

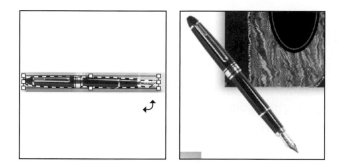

6 Choose File > Save.

Selecting with the Magnetic Lasso tool

You can use the Magnetic Lasso tool in Photoshop to make freehand selections of areas with high-contrast edges. When you draw with the Magnetic Lasso tool, the border automatically snaps to the borders between areas of contrast. You can also control the selection path by occasionally clicking the mouse to place anchor points in the selection border. (There is no Magnetic Lasso tool in ImageReady.)

You'll now move the padlock to the center of the black oval you placed on the book cover earlier in this lesson, using the Magnetic Lasso tool to select the padlock.

1 Select the Zoom tool (🔍), and click the padlock to zoom in to a 300% view.

2 Select the Magnetic Lasso tool (➿), hidden under the Lasso tool (◯).

3 Click once along the left edge of the padlock, and begin tracing the outline of the padlock by moving the magnetic lasso pointer around the outline of the padlock, staying fairly close to the edge of the padlock as you move.

Even though you're not holding down the mouse button, the tool snaps to the edge of the padlock and automatically adds fastening points.

💡 *If you think that the tool is not following the edge closely enough (such as in low-contrast areas), you can place your own fastening points in the border by clicking the mouse button. You can add as many fastening points as you feel are necessary. You can also remove the most recent fastening points by pressing Delete for each anchor point you want to remove. Then, move the mouse back to the last remaining fastening point and continue selecting.*

4 When you reach the left side of the padlock again, double-click the mouse button to make the Magnetic Lasso tool return to the starting point, closing the selection. Or, move the Magnetic Lasso over the starting point and click once.

5 Double-click the Hand tool (🖑) to fit the image on-screen.

6 Select the Move tool (▸⊕), and drag the padlock to the middle of the black oval in the center of the notebook.

7 Choose Select > Deselect, and then choose File > Save.

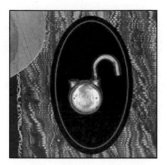

Softening the edges of a selection

You can smooth the hard edges of a selection by anti-aliasing and by feathering.

***Anti-aliasing** Smooths the jagged edges of a selection by softening the color transition between edge pixels and background pixels. Since only the edge pixels change, no detail is lost. Anti-aliasing is useful when cutting, copying, and pasting selections to create composite images.*

Anti-aliasing is available for the Lasso, Polygonal Lasso, Magnetic Lasso tool, Rounded Rectangle Marquee (ImageReady), Elliptical Marquee, and Magic Wand tools. (Select the tool to display its tool options bar.) You must specify the anti-aliasing option before using these tools. Once a selection is made, you cannot add anti-aliasing.

***Feathering** Blurs edges by building a transition boundary between the selection and its surrounding pixels. This blurring can cause some loss of detail at the edge of the selection.*

You can define feathering for the marquee, Lasso, Polygonal Lasso, and Magnetic Lasso tools as you use them, or you can add feathering to an existing selection. Feathering effects become apparent when you move, cut, or copy the selection.

• To use anti-aliasing, select the Lasso, Polygonal Lasso, Magnetic Lasso, Rounded Rectangle Marquee (ImageReady), Elliptical Marquee, or Magic Wand tool, and select Anti-aliased in the tool options bar.

• To define a feathered edge for a selection tool, select any of the lasso or marquee tools. Enter a Feather value in the options bar. This value defines the width of the feathered edge and can range from 1 to 250 pixels.

• To define a feathered edge for an existing selection, choose Select > Feather. Enter a value for the Feather Radius, and click OK.

Cropping an image and erasing within a selection

To complete the artwork, you'll crop the image to a final size and clean up some of the background scraps left behind when you moved selections. In both Photoshop and ImageReady, you can use either the Crop tool or the Crop command to crop an image.

In ImageReady, use the Crop command or the Crop tool set to Hide when creating animated elements that move from off-screen into the live image area.

1 Select the Crop tool (⌷), or press C to switch from the current tool to the Crop tool. Then, drag diagonally across the collage composition to prepare for cropping.

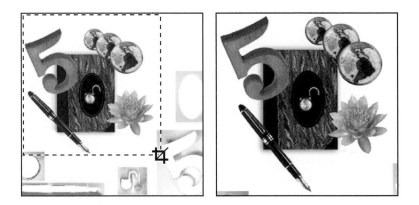

2 Adjust the crop area, as necessary:

• If you need to reposition the crop border, position the pointer anywhere inside the cropping area and drag.

• If you want to resize the crop area, drag a handle.

3 When you are satisfied with the position of the crop area, press Enter (Windows) or Return (Mac OS) to crop the image.

The cropped image may include some scraps of the gray background from which you selected and removed shapes. You'll fix that next.

4 Use a selection marquee tool or the Lasso tool (⌷) to drag a selection marquee around a scrap of unwanted gray background. Be careful not to include any of the image that you want to keep.

5 In the toolbox, select the Eraser tool ( ), and then make sure that the foreground and background color swatches in the toolbox are set to the defaults: black in the foreground and white in the background.

If the default colors are not black and white, click the Default Colors icon ( ) in the lower left area beside the foreground and background swatches.

6 Drag the eraser over the gray in the selection area. The gray pixels are erased and replaced by the background color, white. If your erasing strays outside the selection border, nothing happens because the unselected area is protected from being changed.

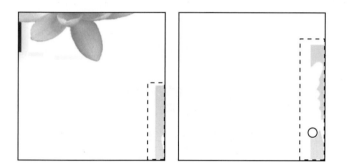

To erase in large strokes, select a larger brush size in the tool options bar.

7 Select another area with only unwanted pixels, and then press Delete.

Continue selecting and erasing or deleting until you finish removing all the unwanted scraps of background. When you finish, choose File > Save to save your work.

Note: You don't absolutely have to select an area in order to erase. However, it's often a good idea, especially when the area that you want to erase is close to another area that you want to protect.

The collage is complete.

Review questions

1 Once you've made a selection, what area of the image can be edited?

2 How do you add to and subtract from a selection?

3 How can you move a selection while you're drawing it?

4 When drawing a selection with the Lasso tool, how should you finish drawing the selection to ensure that it is the shape you want?

5 How does the Magic Wand tool determine which areas of an image to select? What is tolerance, and how does it affect a selection?

Review answers

1 Only the area within the selection can be edited.

2 To add to a selection, hold down Shift, and then drag or click the active selection tool on the area you want to add to the selection. To subtract from a selection, hold down Alt (Windows) or Option (Mac OS), and then drag or click the active selection tool on the area you want to remove from the selection.

3 Without releasing the mouse button, hold down the spacebar, and drag to reposition the selection.

4 To make sure that the selection is the shape you want, end the selection by dragging across the starting point of the selection. If you start and stop the selection at different points, Photoshop or ImageReady draws a straight line between the start point of the selection and the end point of the selection.

5 The Magic Wand tool selects adjacent pixels based on their similarity in color. The Tolerance setting determines how many color tones the Magic Wand tool will select. The higher the tolerance setting, the more tones the Magic Wand tool selects.

Lesson 5

5 | Layer Basics

Both Adobe Photoshop and
Adobe ImageReady let you isolate
different parts of an image on layers.
Each layer can then be edited as discrete
artwork, allowing unlimited flexibility in
composing and revising an image. Layer
comps you define for combinations of
layer settings give you easy flexibility for
reviewing various designs.

In this lesson, you'll learn how to do the following:

• Organize artwork on layers.

• Create new layers.

• View and hide layers.

• Select layers.

• Remove artwork from layers.

• Rearrange layers to change the stacking order of artwork in the image.

• Apply blending modes to layers.

• Link layers to work on them simultaneously.

• Apply a gradient to a layer.

• Add text and layer effects to a layer.

• Save a copy of the file with the layers flattened.

• Create layer comps with differences in visibility, position, and effects.

• Duplicate, update, and display layer comps.

This lesson will take about two hours to complete. If you want to break the lesson into more than one work session, there are natural break points before beginning "Creating a layer set and adding a layer" on page 168 and before starting "Using layer comps" on page 172. The lesson is designed to be done in Adobe Photoshop, but information on using similar functionality in Adobe ImageReady is included where appropriate.

If needed, remove the previous lesson folder from your hard drive, and copy the Lesson05 folder onto it. As you work on this lesson, you'll overwrite the start files. If you need to restore the start files, copy them from the *Adobe Photoshop CS Classroom in a Book* CD.

Note: *Windows 2000 users need to unlock the lesson files before using them. For more information, see "Copying the Classroom in a Book files" on page 3.*

Getting started

You'll start the lesson by viewing an image of the finished lesson file.

1 Start Photoshop and then immediately hold down Ctrl+Alt+Shift (Windows) or Command+Option+Shift (Mac OS) to restore the default preferences. (See "Restoring default preferences" on page 4.)

As messages appear, select Yes to confirm that you want to reset preferences, No to defer setting up your color monitor, and Close to close the Welcome Screen.

2 On the tool options bar, select the File Browser button, and use the Folders palette to navigate to and select the Lessons/Lesson05 folder on your hard disk.

3 In the thumbnails palette, select the 05End.psd file, so that it appears in the Preview palette in the File Browser.

4 Select the 05Start.psd file and compare it to the 05End file.

About layers

Every Photoshop file contains one or more *layers*. New files are generally created with a *background layer,* which contains a color or an image that shows through the transparent areas of subsequent layers. You can view and manipulate layers using the Layers palette.

All new layers in an image are transparent until you add text or artwork (pixel values).

Working with layers is analogous to placing portions of a drawing on sheets of acetate: Individual sheets of acetate may be edited, repositioned, and deleted without affecting the other sheets. When the sheets are stacked, the entire composition is visible.

Viewing information in the Layers palette

The Layers palette displays all layers with the layer names and thumbnails of the images on each layer. You can use the Layers palette to hide, view, reposition, delete, rename, and merge layers. The palette thumbnails are automatically updated as you edit the layers.

1 In the File Browser thumbnails pane, double-click the 05Start.psd file to open it in Photoshop. (Do not close the File Browser yet.)

2 If the Layers palette is not visible in the work area, choose Window > Layers.

There are three items listed in the Layers palette for the 05Start.psd file: first Statue, then Doorway, and finally Background. The Background layer is highlighted, indicating that it is the active layer. Notice the layer thumbnails and the icons on the Background layer level.

💡 *Use the context menu to hide or resize the layer thumbnail. Right-click (Windows) or Control-click (Mac OS) an empty area of the Layers palette to open the context menu, and then select None, Small, Medium, or Large*

3 Use the File Browser again (or choose File > Open) to open the Door.psd file in the Lesson05 folder. Then close the File Browser.

The Layers palette changes to display the layer information and a thumbnail for the Door.psd file. There is only one layer in the Door.psd image: Layer 1.

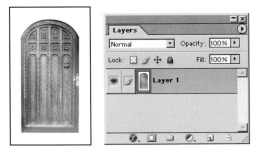

In the Layers palette for the 05Start file, you saw three icons on the Background layer: a lock icon at the right side of the layer name, an eye icon, and a paintbrush icon. None of these appeared on the other two layers.

• The lock icon (🔒) indicates that the Background layer is protected.

• The eye icon (👁) indicates that the layer is visible in the image window. If you click the eye, the image window no longer displays that layer.

• The paintbrush icon (🖌) reminds you that the layer is active; that is, that the changes you make will affect that layer only.

For more information, see the "About the background layer" inset, below.

About the background layer

When you create a new image with a white background or a colored background, the bottommost image in the Layers palette is named Background. An image can have only one background. You cannot change the stacking order of a background, its blending mode, or its opacity. However, you can convert a background to a regular layer.

When you create a new image with transparent content, the image does not have a background layer. The bottommost layer is not constrained like the background layer; you can move it anywhere in the Layers palette, and change its opacity and blending mode.

To convert a background into a layer:

1. Double-click Background in the Layers palette, or choose Layer > New > Layer From Background.

2. Set layer options as desired.

3. Click OK.

To convert a layer into a background:

1. Select a layer in the Layers palette.

2. Choose Layer > New > Background From Layer.

Note: You cannot create a background by renaming a regular layer Background—you must use the Background From Layer command.

Renaming a layer and copying it to another image file

Creating a new layer can be as simple as dragging from one file into the image window of another file. Whether you drag from the image window of the original file or from its Layers palette, only the active layer is reproduced in the destination file. Before you begin, make sure that both the 05Start.psd and Door.psd files are open and that the Door.psd file is active.

First, you will rename Layer 1 with a more descriptive name.

1 In the Layers palette, double-click the name *Layer 1*, type **Door**, and then press Enter (Windows) or Return (Mac OS).

2 If necessary, drag the Door.psd and 05Start.psd image windows so that you can see at least part of both images. Then, select the Door.psd image so that it is the active file.

3 In the toolbox, select the Move tool (▶⊕) and move it over the Door.psd image window.

4 Drag the door image and drop it into your 05Start.psd image window. The Door layer now appears in the 05Start file image window and its Layers palette.

5 Close the Door.psd file, and do not save your changes to that file.

💡 *If you hold down Shift when you drag an image from one file into another, the dragged image automatically centers itself in the target image window.*

Viewing individual layers

The Layers palette shows that the 05Start file contains three layers in addition to the Door layer, some of which are visible and some of which are hidden. The eye icon (👁) to the far left of a layer name in the palette indicates that that layer is visible. You can hide or show a layer by clicking this icon.

1 Click the eye icon next to the Door layer to hide the door.

2 Click again to redisplay it.

Leave the other layers at their original visibility settings, whether hidden or shown.

Selecting and removing some pixels from a layer

Notice that when you moved the door image onto the garden image in the start file, you also moved the white area surrounding the door. This opaque area blocks out part of the garden image, since the door layer sits on top of the garden background layer.

Now, you'll use an Eraser tool to remove the white area around the door.

1 Make sure that the Door layer is selected. (To select the layer, click the layer name in the Layers palette.)

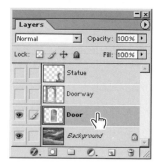

The layer is highlighted, and a paintbrush icon (🖌) appears to the left of the layer name, both of which indicate that the layer is active.

2 To make the opaque areas on this layer more obvious, hide all layers except the Door layer by holding down Alt (Windows) or Option (Mac OS) and clicking the eye icon (👁) for the Door layer.

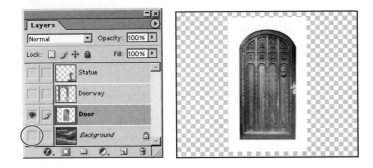

The garden image disappears, and the door appears against a checkerboard backdrop. The checkerboard indicates transparent areas of the active layer.

3 Select the Magic Eraser tool (🪄), hidden under the Eraser tool (🩹).

You can set the tolerance for the Magic Eraser tool. If the tolerance is too low, the Magic Eraser tool leaves some white remaining around the door. If the tolerance setting is too high, the Magic Eraser tool removes some of the door image.

4 In the tool options bar, set the Tolerance value either by scrubbing the Tolerance label or by typing **22** in the text box.

5 Click the white area surrounding the door image in the image window.

Notice that the checkerboard fills in where the white area had been, indicating that this area is now transparent also.

6 Turn the background back on by clicking the eye-icon box next to its name. The garden image now shows through where the white area on the Door layer was removed.

Rearranging layers

The order in which the layers of an image are organized is called the *stacking order.* The stacking order of layers determines how the image is viewed—you can change the order to make certain parts of the image appear in front of or behind other layers.

Now, you'll rearrange layers so that the door image moves in front of another image in the file that is currently hidden.

1 Make the Statue and Doorway layers visible by clicking the eye-icon boxes next to their layer names.

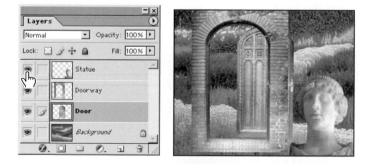

Notice that the door image is partially blocked by the image of the brick doorway.

2 In the Layers palette, drag the Door layer up above the Doorway layer—look for a wider white line between the Doorway layer and the Statue layer—and then release the mouse button.

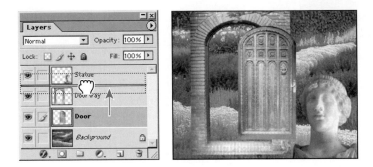

The Door layer moves up one level in the stacking order, and the door image appears in front of the doorway image.

Changing the opacity and mode of a layer

The door image now blocks any images that lie on layers below it. You can reduce the opacity of the door layer to allow other layers to show through it. You can also apply different *blending modes* to the layer, which affects how the color pixels in the door image blend with pixels in the layers below them. (Currently, the blending mode is Normal.)

1 With the Door layer selected, click the arrow next to the Opacity text box in the Layers palette, and drag the slider to **50%**. Or, you can scrub the Opacity label to set the value.

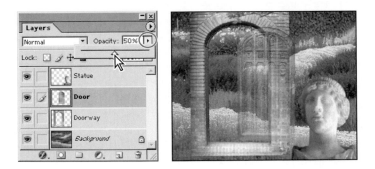

The door becomes partially transparent, and you can see the layers underneath. Notice that the change in opacity affects only the image area of the Door layer. The statue and doorway images remain completely opaque.

2 To the left of the Opacity option in the Layers palette, open the blending modes pop-up menu, and select Luminosity. (You may need to scroll down to find it.)

3 Readjust the Opacity value, changing it to **90%**.

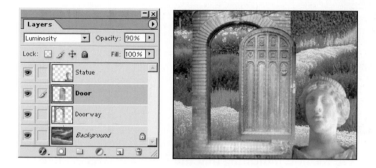

4 Choose File > Save to save your work.

You'll do more work with blending modes in later lessons. For an explanation of the key terms, see "Blending an image with the background" on page 249.

Linking layers

Sometimes an efficient way to work with layers is to link two or more related layers. By linking layers together, you can move and transform them simultaneously, thereby maintaining their alignment to each other.

You'll now link the Door and Doorway layers, and then move and transform them as a unit.

1 Select the Move tool ( ), and drag the door to the left so that the left edge of the door aligns with the right side of the doorway arch.

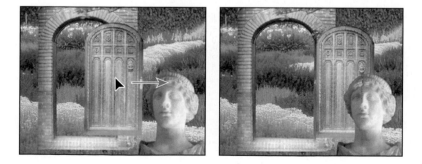

2 Locate the Doorway layer in the Layers palette. Then, without selecting that layer, click the small box next to the eye icon for that layer.

A link icon (⊛) appears in the box, indicating that the Doorway layer is linked to the Door layer. The active (selected) layer does not display a link icon when you create linked layers.

3 Still using the Move tool, drag the doorway to the left side of the image window so that the bricks touch the left margin of the image. The door and doorway images move together.

Now, you'll simultaneously resize both linked layers.

4 Select the Doorway layer in the Layers palette, and choose Edit > Free Transform. A transformation bounding box appears around the images in the linked layers.

5 Hold down Shift and drag the handle in the right bottom corner box down, to scale the door and doorway to a slightly larger size. (You may need to drag down the bottom right corner of the image window to enlarge it enough to see the complete transformation bounding box.)

6 If necessary, position the pointer inside the bounding box, and drag to reposition the door and doorway images.

7 Press Enter (Windows) or Return (Mac OS) to apply the transformation changes.

8 Choose File > Save.

Adding a gradient layer

Next, you'll create a new layer with no artwork on it. (Adding empty layers to a file is comparable to adding blank sheets of acetate to a stack of images.) You'll use this layer to add a semi-transparent gradient effect that influences the layers stacked below it.

In ImageReady, which does not have a Gradient tool, you can apply a Gradient/Pattern layer style from the Layers palette. You'll get some experience applying layer styles in Photoshop later in this lesson; see "Applying a layer style" on page 162.

1 In the Layers palette, select the Background layer to make it active, and then click the New Layer button (▣) at the bottom of the Layers palette.

A new layer, named Layer 1, appears between the Background and the Doorway layer.

Note: You can also create a new layer by choosing New Layer on the Layers palette menu or Layers > New > Layer on the Photoshop menu bar.

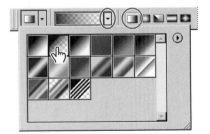

2 Double-click the name Layer 1, type **Gradient**, and press Enter (Windows) or Return (Mac OS) to rename the layer.

3 In the toolbox, select the Gradient tool (▣).

4 In the tool options bar, make sure that the Linear Gradient button (▣) is selected, and then click the small arrow to expand the gradient picker.

5 Select the Foreground To Transparent swatch, and then click anywhere outside the gradient picker to close it.

💡 *You can list the gradient options by name rather than by sample. Just click the palette menu button (◉) on the gradient picker and select either Small List or Large List. Or, you can let the pointer hover over a thumbnail until a tooltip appears, showing the gradient name.*

6 Click the Swatches palette tab to bring it to the front of its palette group, and select any shade of purple that appeals to you.

7 With the Gradient layer active in the Layers palette, drag the Gradient tool from the right margin of the image to the left margin. (You can hold down Shift as you drag to constrain the gradient horizontally.)

The gradient extends over the width of the layer, starting with purple on the right and gradually blending to transparent on the left. The gradient partially obscures the garden image—the layer below the gradient layer. You'll lighten the effect by changing the Gradient layer's opacity so that the garden is only veiled by the gradient.

8 In the Layers palette, change the Opacity for the Gradient layer to **60%**. The full garden shows through the gradient.

Note: In ImageReady, the gradient attributes appear as an effect, nested under the layer to which you applied it as a layer style. A gradient is still visible in the ImageReady image window.

Adding text

Now, you're ready to create and customize some type. You'll create text with the Type tool, which places the text on its own type layer. You'll then edit the text and apply a special effect to that layer. (ImageReady also has features for creating and manipulating type, but it uses a palette to display type options, rather than a dialog box.)

1 In the Layers palette, click the Statue layer to make it active.

2 Set the foreground color to black by clicking the small Default Foreground And Background Color box (▣) near the swatches in the toolbox.

Note: If you decide to change a text color later, you can do this by selecting the text with the Type tool and using the color swatch in the tool options bar.

3 In the toolbox, select the Type tool (T). Then, in the tool options bar, select the following options for the Type tool:

- Select a font from the Font pop-up menu (we used Adobe Garamond).

- Select a font style (we used Regular).

- Enter a large point size in the Size text box (we used **60** point).

- Select Crisp from the Anti-Aliasing pop-up menu (ᵃₐ).

- Select the Center Text (≡) alignment option.

4 Click somewhere in the upper middle area of the image window.

Notice that the Layers palette now includes a layer named Layer 1 with a "T" thumbnail icon, indicating that it is a type layer.

5 Type **Jardin,** press Enter or Return, and then type **2000**.

The text appears in the upper left area of the image where you clicked. This appears in the Layers palette as Layer 1, but the layer name will automatically change to "Jardin 2000" as soon as you select another layer or another tool. You'll see that next when you reposition the text in the image.

6 Select the Move tool (➤₊), and drag the "Jardin 2000" text to center it under the arch of the doorway. The text may be a little difficult to read against the dark shrubbery in the background, but you'll make adjustments for that shortly.

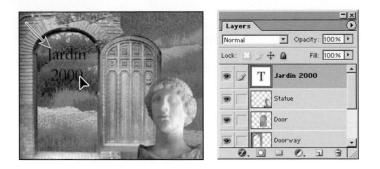

Notice that the layer name in the Layers palette is now *Jardin 2000* instead of *Layer 1*.

Applying a layer style

You can enhance a layer by adding a shadow, glow, bevel, emboss, or other special effect from a collection of automated and editable layer styles. These styles are easy to apply and link directly to the layer you specify.

Photoshop Layer Style dialog box

Like layers, individual layer styles can be hidden by clicking eye icons (👁) in the Layers palette. You can apply a copy of a layer style to a different layer by dragging the effect onto the destination layer.

Now, you'll make the text stand out by adding a glowing, yellow stroke around the type, and filling the type with a pattern.

1 With the Jardin 2000 type layer still active, choose Layer > Layer Style > Outer Glow. (There may be a slight pause as the Layer Style dialog box opens.)

You can also open the Layer Style dialog box by clicking the Add A Layer Style button (⊘) at the bottom of the Layers palette and then choosing a layer style, such as Outer Glow, in the pop-up menu.

2 In the Layer Style dialog box, make sure that the Preview option is selected, and then move the dialog box aside as needed so that you can see the Jardin 2000 text in the image window.

3 In the Elements area of the dialog box, enter **10** for Spread and **10** for Size in pixels.

4 In the left pane of the Layer Style dialog box, select the Stroke check box, and notice that the right pane of the dialog box still shows the options for the Outer Glow effect. Click the name *Stroke* to change the display so that the Stroke layer style options appear on the right side of the dialog box, and then select the following options:

• In the Structure area, enter **1** for Size to create a 1-pixel-wide stroke.

• Under Fill Type, click the Color swatch to open the color picker. Then, choose a yellow color (we used R=**255**, G=**255**, and B=**0**). Click OK to close the color picker but leave the Layer Style dialog box open.

5 On the left pane of the dialog box, click the name *Pattern Overlay*. Notice that by clicking the name, you automatically select the Pattern Overlay check box and change the available options on the right side of the dialog box. Select the following options:

• Click the arrow beside the pattern thumbnail to open a pop-up display of available patterns, and select Wood. Click a blank area of the dialog box to close the pop-up.

💡 *You can identify the Wood pattern thumbnail by waiting for a tooltip to appear or by choosing Small List or Large List on the palette list for the pattern picker.*

• In the Scale option, enter **200**%.

6 Examine the Jardin 2000 text in the image window. Then click OK to accept all the settings and close the Layer Style dialog box.

7 If necessary, scroll or resize the Layers palette so that you can see the changes in the palette listings.

Now, there are four rows of information nested under the Jardin 2000 text layer. The first of these rows identifies them as Effects. The other three rows are named by the three styles that you applied to the layer: Outer Glow, Pattern Overlay, and Stroke. There is also an icon for layer styles (𝅘) next to each of the three style names. You can turn off an individual effect by clicking its eye icon (👁) to make it disappear. Clicking this visibility box again restores both the eye icon and the effect. You can hide all three layer styles by clicking to remove the Effects eye icon. Before you continue, make sure that eye icons appear for all four items nested under the Jardin 2000 layer.

To hide the layer styles listings, click the arrow by the layer styles icon (⬤) on the right side of the Jardin 2000 layer to collapse the Effects list.

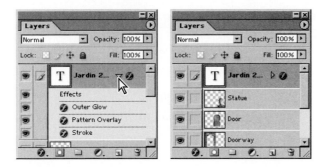

Editing text

Layer effects are automatically applied to changes you make to a layer. You can edit the text and watch how the layer effect tracks the change.

1 In the Layers palette, select the Jardin 2000 text layer, if it is not already selected.

2 In the toolbox, select the Type tool (T) but do not click in the image window yet.

3 In the tool options bar, change the Font Size option from 60 pts to **72 pts**.

Although you didn't select the text by dragging the Type tool (as you would have to do in a word-processing program), all the text on the layer now appears in 72-point type.

4 Using the Type tool, select the last zero in "2000."

5 Type **4** so that the text block now reads "Jardin 2004."

Notice that the text formatting and layer styles remain applied to all the text.

6 Do one of the following to commit your typing changes on the text layer:

- On the tool options bar, click the Commit Any Current Edits button (✔).

- Select another layer or tool.

Note: You cannot commit type by pressing Enter or Return because this merely applies a carriage return, creating a new line for typing.

7 Choose File > Save.

💡 *One of the other interesting things you can do in Photoshop CS is to place text on a path. The words or numbers can radiate out from a circle or follow a squiggly line, for example. For more information, see Photoshop Help.*

Flattening and saving files

When you finish editing all the layers in your image, you can merge or flatten layers to shrink the file size. Flattening reduces all the layers into a single background. However, you shouldn't flatten an image until you are certain that you're satisfied with all your design decisions. Rather than flattening your original .psd files, it's a good idea to save a copy of the file with its layers intact, in case you need to edit a layer later.

To appreciate what flattening does, notice the two numbers for the file size in the bar at the bottom of the application window (Windows) or image window (Mac OS).

The first number represents what the file size would be if you flattened the image. The second number represents the file size without flattening. In the lesson file, the flattened file would be about 900K but the current file is much larger—about 4 or 5 MB—so flattening is well worth doing in this case.

1 If the Type tool (T) is currently selected in the toolbox, select any other tool, to be sure that you're no longer in type-editing mode. Choose File > Save (if it is available), to be sure that all your changes have been saved in the file.

2 Choose Image > Duplicate.

3 In the Duplicate Image dialog box, type **05Flat.psd** to name the file and click OK.

4 Close the 05Start.psd file, but leave the 05Flat.psd file open.

5 On the Layers palette menu, choose Flatten Image.

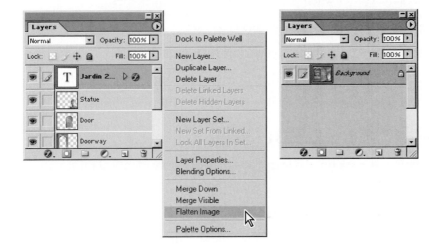

6 Choose File > Save. Even though you selected Save rather than Save As, the Save As dialog box appears.

7 Make sure that the location is set to the Lessons/Lesson05 folder, and then click Save to accept the default settings and save the flattened file.

You have saved two versions of the file: a one-layered flattened copy and the original file, in which all the layers remain intact. You will continue to work in the flattened file and add layers above the flattened Background layer. You'll use the original version again later in this lesson.

 If you want to flatten only some of the layers in a file, you can click the eye icons to hide the layers you don't want to flatten, and then choose Merge Visible on the Layers palette menu.

Creating a layer set and adding a layer

You can nest layers within the Layers palette. This makes it easier to manage your work and minimizes the clutter when you work on large, complex files.

1 In the Layers palette menu, choose New Layer Set.

2 In the New Layer Set dialog box, type **Conf Info**, and click OK.

In the Layers palette, a Conf Info folder appears above the Background layer. You'll use this layer set to hold layers that display information about the Jardin 2004 conference.

Adding type layers to a flattened background

You're now going to work on two text layers that will have identical information but in different languages.

1 In the toolbox, select the Type tool (T).

2 In the tool options bar, set the following type specifications:

• For Font family, select Adobe Garamond (or another serif font).

• For Font Style, select Italic.

• For Font Size, enter **24** pts.

• Click the color swatch to open the color picker and select the same yellow color you used for Outer Glow earlier in this lesson (R=**255**, G=**255**, B=**0**); then click OK to close the color picker.

• Make sure that the Crisp option and the Center Text icon (≡) are selected.

3 Make sure that the Conf Info layer set is selected in the Layers palette. Then, click the Type tool (T) in the upper right area of the image window and type **Mai 18** (the date in the French language), press Enter or Return to create a line break, and type **Montreal**.

4 In the tool options bar, select the Commit Any Current Edits button (✔).

In the Layers palette, a new type layer appears, nested under the Conf Info layer set. The name of the layer in the Layers palette is now "Mai 18."

5 Select the Move tool (▸₊) and drag the text to the upper right side of the image so that the design is balanced and the text is readable against the foliage behind it.

6 Select the "Mai 18" layer in the Layers palette and drag it to the New Layer button at the bottom of the palette. When you release the mouse button, a duplicate of the text layer appears, also nested in the Conf Info layer set.

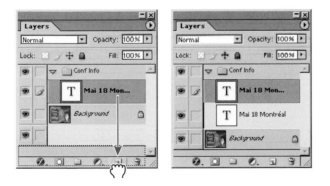

💡 *If you decide later that you want to reposition the two text layers, you can select the Conf Info layer set in the Layers palette, and then use the Move tool to drag both layers, as if they were linked.*

You now have an identically formatted and positioned text layer that you can edit to create an alternative version.

Creating alternate text and designating dictionaries

Photoshop includes a versatile spelling checker that can selectively reference dictionaries for various languages. You can designate entire text layers or individual words to be checked in different dictionaries. When you run the spelling checker, Photoshop automatically compares each word to the appropriate dictionary.

1 In the Layers palette, select the upper "Mai 18" layer, if it is not still selected.

2 Choose Window > Character to open the Character palette.

3 On the dictionary pop-up menu in the lower left corner of the Character palette, select Canadian French.

4 One after another, select the "Mai 18" layers in the Layers palette and verify that the Character palette indicates an English dictionary for the lower layer and a Canadian French dictionary for the upper layer.

5 Choose File > Save.

Using the multilingual spelling checker

Now that you've designated the dictionaries that Photoshop will use for different text within your file, you're ready to review the text for spelling errors.

1 In the Layers palette, make sure that the eye icons (👁) for the "Mai 18" layers so that both text layers appear in the image window. Since these are right on top of each other, you can't see any difference in the image window.

2 Choose Edit > Check Spelling. The Check Spelling dialog box appears, indicating that the word Montreal is misspelled in the Canadian French version because the word lacks an accent over the letter e.

3 Click the Change button to accept the suggested replacement, *Montréal*.

The text in the image changes, and the display in the dialog box also changes, now indicating that the word *Mai* is not in the English: USA dictionary. Notice that the Change To option is (probably) *Mail*—not the word you want.

4 Scroll down the Suggestions list if necessary, and select the word *May*. Now, *May* appears in the Change To option. Then, click Change.

Instead of scrolling and selecting, you can type **May** directly into the Change To option.

5 If a message appears indicating that the spell check is complete, click OK.

6 Alternately click the eye icons off and on for the two Conf Info text layers to see the two versions of the text.

7 Choose File > Save to save the image, which now has the original flattened layer plus two unflattened text layers. Leave the 05Flat.psd file open for the next procedure.

Notice the change in file size in the Status bar. Although your file size has grown slightly, it is still not nearly as large as the completely unflattened project would be.

Leave the 05Flat.psd file open, because you'll need it in an upcoming task.

Using layer comps

Layer comps is a new feature in Photoshop CS that provides one-click flexibility in switching back and forth between different views of a multilayered image file. A layer comp is simply a definition of the settings in the Layers palette. Once you've defined one layer comp, you can change as many settings as you please in the Layers palette and then create another layer comp to preserve that configuration of layer properties. Then, by switching from one layer comp to another, you can quickly review the two designs. The beauty of layer comps becomes apparent when you want to demonstrate a number of possible design arrangements to a client, for example.

In this section of the lesson, you'll continue working with your gardening conference project, but you'll use the version you saved earlier, not the flattened version. You'll create different comps for each of the two languages used. You'll also try out different visibility and layer styles, and then record layer comps for these possibilities. When you finish creating the layer comps, you can then review all the possible arrangements you've defined without having to select and deselect eye icons or change settings in the Layers palette. The layer comps are saved as part of the file, so they are not lost when you quit Photoshop.

Preparing a full-layered version of the Photoshop file

You won't work in the flattened version of your work for these tasks. Instead, you'll use the unflattened version of the 05Start.psd image that you saved earlier (see "Flattening and saving files" on page 166), because this gives you full access to all of the original layers that went into the composition. However, you will update the 05Start.psd file by copying the two text layers from the 05Flat.psd file.

1 Choose File > Open Recent > 05Start.psd.

2 Choose File > Open Recent > 05Flat.psd, if this file is not already open.

3 Arrange the image windows for the two files so that you can see at least part of both windows, and then select the image window for the flattened version to bring it forward and make it active (or choose Window > 05Flat.psd).

4 In the Layers palette, select the Conf Info layer set. Hold down Shift and drag it from the Layers palette to the 05Start.psd image window.

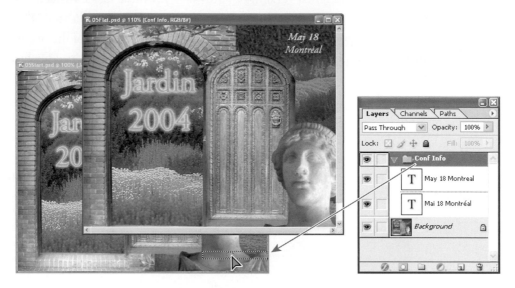

5 Close the 05Flat.psd file, but leave the 05Start.psd open.

6 Select the Move tool (⊹), and drag the text as needed to reposition it.

Because the Conf Info layer set is selected in the Layers palette, the two versions of the text move together when you drag. Holding down the Shift key as you drag places the layers in the same location they had in the original image window.

Create new layer comps based on layer visibility

The first two layer comps you create will simply show one or the other of the two language versions (French or English) for the conference information. This reduces the effort required to switch back and forth between the two versions from two clicks (resetting the eye icons) to one click (selecting a layer comp).

1 Open the Layer Comps palette by clicking its tab in the palette well.

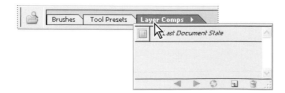

2 Drag the Layer Comps palette tab from the palette well to any convenient location on your screen, placing it so that you can see it, the entire image window, and the Layers palette as you work. (You can close the Navigator, Color, History, and Character palette groups to reduce clutter.)

3 Move and resize the Layers palette as needed so that you can see all levels with all items fully expanded.

4 In the Layers palette, click the eye icon (👁) for the "Mai 18" text layer to hide it. In the image window, make sure that the "May 18" text layer is visible.

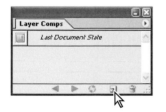

5 In the Layers Comp palette, click the Create New Layer Comp button (▣) at the bottom of the palette.

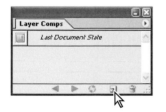

6 In the New Layer Comp dialog box, type **English** in the Name option and select all three check boxes under Apply To Layers: Visibility, Position, and Appearance. Then click OK.

7 Using the eye icons in the Layers palette, make the "Mai 18" layer visible and hide the "May 18" text layer.

8 Repeat Steps 5 and 6, but this time type **French** instead of English as the name for the new layer comp.

Although the switch between the French and English versions of the image involves only changes in visibility—that is, the state of the eye icons in the Layers palette—you'll be making other types of changes later in this section. That's why you selected all three check boxes under Apply To Layers when you defined these two layer comps.

What would happen if you had selected only the Visibility option? You'd need to backtrack later to select the other two options, reset the original layer conditions, and then update these layer comps—a lot of extra work that you can avoid by selecting all three options now.

Using layer comps to view document variations

Here's the fun part about layer comps: switching back and forth. Although your two layer states differ only in the visibility of two layers, with a little imagination you can appreciate how much of a time-saver this would be for more complex variations.

1 If the Apply Layer Comp icon (▣) does not already appear on the French layer comp, click the box to set it there now. The image window shows the "Mai 18" text layer and and hides the "May 18" text layer.

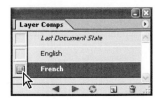

2 Click the box for the English layer comp. The Apply Layer Comp icon appears beside the English layer comp instead of by the French layer comp, and the visibility of the "Mai 18" and "May 18" text layers reverses.

3 In the Layers palette, click the "Jardin 2004" text layer eye icon to hide that layer.

In the Layer Comps palette, notice that the Apply Layer Comp icon now appears on the Last Document State level, indicating that the current layer settings are no longer based on a defined layer comp.

4 In the Layer Comps palette, click the box next to the French layer comp, so that the Apply Layer Comp icon appears there.

The image returns to its state when you defined this layer comp—with the "Jardin" and "Mai 18" text layers visible.

5 Click the box for Last Document State.

Now, the image appears as it did after Step 3, with the "Jardin" text layer hidden and the conference information in English.

Duplicating and editing layer comps

Like other items that appear on various palette lists in Photoshop, you can drag layer comps to icons at the bottom of the palette and use the Layer Comps palette menu to edit them. You do not need to set the Apply Layer Comp icon for a layer comp in order to duplicate, delete, or edit its options.

1 In the Layer Comps palette, click the box for the English layer comp to apply it to the image.

2 Drag the English layer comp to the Create New Layer Comp icon in the bottom of the Layer Comps palette.

3 Double-click the name of the new layer comp ("English copy") to make it active and type **English No Door**.

4 In the Layers palette, click the eye icon (👁) to make the Door layer invisible.

In the Layers Comp palette, the Apply Layer Comp icon (▥) now appears next to the Last Document State layer comp, but the English No Door layer comp is still selected.

5 Click the Update Layer Comp button (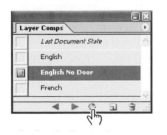) to update the English No Door layer comp. The Apply Layer Comp icon is back next to the English No Door layer comp and the Door layer is still hidden.

6 One by one, click the boxes in the Layer Comps palette to place the Apply Layer Comp icon beside each of the three defined layer comps. As you switch from one layer comp to the next, examine the results in the image window.

Creating layer comps for position changes

Now that you've seen how layer comps preserve various visibility settings, it's not much of a stretch to imagine how this could apply to different layer locations in the image window. This task gives you experience working with position changes and layer comps.

1 In the Layers Comp palette, click the box for the English layer comp (*not* the English No Door layer comp) to set the Apply Layer Comp icon.

2 Drag the English layer comp into the Create New Layer Comp icon, and then double-click and type **English Moved** to rename the layer comp copy.

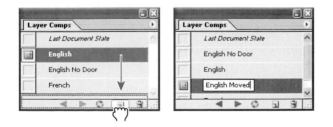

3 In the Layers palette, select the "May 18" text layer, and then select the Move tool (⊕) in the toolbox.

4 In the image window, drag the "May 18" text layer so that it centers under the "Jardin" text layer.

5 Click the Update Layer Comp button (⟳).

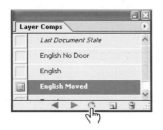

6 Review the results by clicking to set the Apply Layer Comp icon first in the English layer comp and then in the English Moved layer comp.

Creating layer comps for style changes

You've already had practice with two of the three categories you selected under Apply To Layer Comps when you defined each of your layer comps: Visibility and Position. Next, you'll work with changes to the third category: Appearance. Appearance includes changes in opacity as well as layer effects and layer styles. In this task, you'll define a layer comp that has layer-style settings that differ from the other layer comps that you've created.

1 In the Layer Comps palette, click the box next to the English Moved layer comp to set the Apply Layer Comp icon.

2 In the Layers palette, expand the "Jardin 2004" layer styles and click the eye icon to turn off the Outer Glow effect.

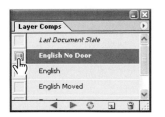

3 In the Layer Comps palette, click the Create New Layer Comp button ( ).

4 In the New Layer Comp dialog box, type **English Moved No Glow.** Make sure that all three Apply To Layers options are selected (checked), or select them now, before you click OK.

Leave the English Moved No Glow layer comp selected in the Layer Comps palette.

Reviewing layer comps

You've already switched from one layer-comp view to the next by resetting the Apply Layer Comp icon. (See "Using layer comps to view document variations" on page 177.) Now, you'll try another simple way to cycle through the entire set of layer comps.

1 Click to set the Apply Layer Comp icon for the defined layer comp at the top of the Layer Comps palette list.

2 Click the right-pointing arrow (▶)in the bottom of the Layer Comps palette. The Apply Layer Comp icon moves to the second layer comp on the list and the image window changes to show the layer settings for that layer comp

3 Click the left-pointing arrow (◀). The Apply Layer Comp icon moves back to the top layer comp on the list.

4 Click the right-pointing arrow repeatedly to review the five variations you've created so far.

5 Choose File > Save.

Imagine how much time it would take to show someone these different layer arrangements if you had to drag layers into position and select or deselect eye icons. Layer comps can be an especially valuable feature when the design is in flux or when you need to create multiple versions of the same image file.

Congratulations! Your work on the garden image is now complete. This lesson only begins to explore the vast possibilities and the flexibility you gain when you master the art of using Photoshop layers and layer comps. You'll get more experience and try out different techniques for layers in almost every chapter as you progress forward in the book. You'll also use layer comps in ImageReady, to streamline the animation process.

Review questions

1 What is the advantage of using layers?

2 When you create a new layer or layer set, where does it appear in the Layers palette stack?

3 How can you make artwork on one layer appear in front of artwork on another layer?

4 How can you manipulate multiple layers simultaneously?

5 When you've completed your artwork, what can you do to minimize the file size without changing the quality or dimensions?

6 How do you check spelling in more than one language?

7 What is the purpose of layer comps and how are they useful?

Review answers

1 Layers enable you to move and edit different parts of an image as discrete objects. You can also hide individual layers as you work on other layers by clicking to remove the eye icons (👁) for the layers you don't need to see.

2 The new layer or layer set always appears immediately above the active layer.

3 You can make artwork on one layer appear in front of artwork on another layer by dragging layers up or down the stacking order in the Layers palette, or by using the Layer > Arrange > commands: Bring to Front, Bring Forward, Send to Back, and Send Backward. Remember that you cannot change the layer position of a Background layer.

4 You can link the layers by first selecting one of the layers in the Layers palette. Then you click the box to the left of the Layer name of the layer to which you want to link it. Once linked, both layers can be moved, rotated, and resized together.

5 You can flatten the image, which merges all the layers onto a single background.

6 You designate the language dictionaries in the Character palette. You can set different language dictionaries to check different parts of the text in an image file, either by layer or by individual words:

• To designate a dictionary for an entire layer, first select that type layer in the Layers palette, and then select the Type tool (T) in the toolbox. Finally, select the dictionary you want to use from the pop-up menu in the Character palette. (You do not need to select the text with the Type tool.)

- To designate a language dictionary for individual words on a text layer, use the Type tool to select (highlight) those words, and then select the dictionary in the Character palette. Each word can be associated with only one language dictionary, but you can use as many different dictionaries as you need to check different words in your Photoshop files.

7 Layer comps make various combinations of layer settings available as a single-click action. These settings can include layer visibility, layer position, and layer effects, such as opacity and layer styles. In Photoshop, this is especially useful when you want to create alternate design choices for review or when the final output will include multiple versions of the file, each of which is directed to a different audience. In ImageReady, layer comps can be a tremendous time-saver for creating GIF animations, which you'll learn more about in Lesson 18, "Animating GIF Images for the Web."

6 | Masks and Channels

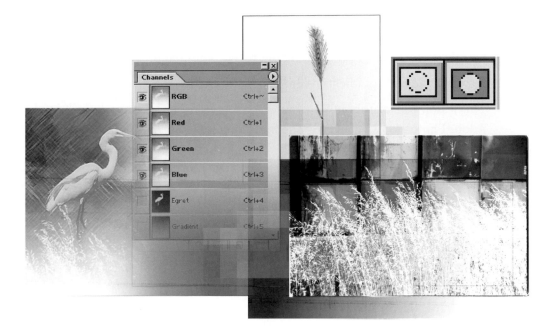

Adobe Photoshop uses masks to isolate
and manipulate specific parts of an
image. A mask is like a stencil. The cutout
portion of the mask can be altered,
but the area surrounding the cutout is
protected from change. You can create
a temporary mask for one-time use,
or you can save masks for repeated use.

In this lesson, you'll learn how to do the following:

- Refine a selection using a quick mask.

- Save a selection as a channel mask.

- View a mask using the Channels palette.

- Load a saved mask and apply effects.

- Paint in a mask to modify a selection.

- Make an intricate selection using the Extract command.

- Create and use a gradient mask.

This lesson will take about 70 minutes to complete. The lesson is designed to be done in Adobe Photoshop. ImageReady does not contain the advanced masking features available in Photoshop.

If needed, remove the previous lesson folder from your hard drive, and copy the Lesson06 folder onto it. As you work on this lesson, you'll overwrite the start files. If you need to restore the start files, copy them from the *Adobe Photoshop CS Classroom in a Book* CD.

Note: *Windows 2000 users need to unlock the lesson files before using them. For more information, see "Copying the Classroom in a Book files" on page 3.*

Working with masks and channels

Photoshop masks isolate and protect parts of an image, just like masking tape prevents a house painter from getting paint on the window glass or trim. When you create a mask based on a selection, the area not selected is *masked* or protected from editing. With masks, you can create and save time-consuming selections and then use them again. In addition, you can use masks for other complex editing tasks—for example, to apply color changes or filter effects to an image.

In Adobe Photoshop, you can make temporary masks, called *quick masks*, or you can create permanent masks and store them as special grayscale channels, called *alpha channels*. Photoshop also uses channels to store an image's color information and information about spot color. Unlike layers, channels do not print. You use the Channels palette to view and work with alpha channels. ImageReady does not support channels, except for alpha channels used for PNG transparency and weighted optimization.

Getting started

You'll start the lesson by viewing the finished image that you'll create using masks and channels.

1 Start Photoshop and then immediately hold down Ctrl+Alt+Shift (Windows) or Command+Option+Shift (Mac OS) to restore the default preferences. (See "Restoring default preferences" on page 4.)

As messages appear, select Yes to confirm that you want to reset preferences, No to defer setting up your color monitor, and Close to close the Welcome Screen.

2 On the tool options bar, select the File Browser button, and use the Folders palette to navigate to and select the Lessons/Lesson06 folder on your hard disk.

3 In the thumbnails palette, select the 06End.psd file, so that it appears in the Preview palette in the File Browser.

4 Select the 06Start.psd thumbnail and compare it to the 06End file.

5 Double-click the 06Start.psd thumbnail or preview to open it in Photoshop. Close the File Browser.

Your primary goal in this lesson is to take an ordinary photograph of an egret in the wild and make the landscape around the bird look as if it were hand-drawn in colored-pencil strokes. You'll also make intricate selections of the grasses from other photographs and place them in the foreground of the egret image. Your final touch will be to add a gradient, to soften the image.

Creating a quick mask

Now you'll open the start file and begin the lesson by using Quick Mask mode to convert a selection border into a temporary mask. Later, you will convert this temporary quick mask back into a selection border. Unless you save a quick mask as a more permanent alpha-channel mask, the temporary mask will be discarded once it is converted to a selection.

You'll begin by making a partial selection of the egret in the 06Start file, using the Magic Wand tool, and then you'll edit the selection using a quick mask.

1 Select the Magic Wand tool (✦).

2 In the tool options bar, enter **12** in the Tolerance text box.

3 Click anywhere in the white area of the egret to begin the selection process.

4 Hold down Shift (so that a plus sign appears next to the Magic Wand pointer) and click one of the unselected white areas of the egret to add to the selection.

5 Click a few more times with the Shift key down to add more areas to the selection, but don't try to make the selection perfect.

Magic Wand selection   *Selection extended*

6 Select the Quick Mask mode button (▣) in the toolbox. (By default, you have been working in Standard mode.)

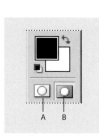 

A. *Standard mode*   *Quick mask selection*
B. *Quick Mask mode*   *showing red overlay*

In Quick Mask mode, a red overlay (resembling the *rubylith*, or red acetate, that traditional print shops used to mask an image) appears, to mask and protect the area outside the selection. You can apply changes only to the unprotected area that is visible and selected. (It's possible to change the color of the red overlay; the color is only a matter of display.)

Note: *A partial selection must exist to see the overlay color in Quick Mask mode.*

Editing a quick mask

Next, you will refine the selection of the egret by adding to or erasing parts of the masked area. You'll use the Brush tool to make changes to your quick mask. The advantage of editing your selection as a mask is that you can use almost any tool or filter to modify the mask. (You can even use selection tools.) In Quick Mask mode, you do all of your editing in the image window.

In Quick Mask mode, Photoshop automatically defaults to Grayscale mode. The foreground color defaults to black, and the background color defaults to white. When using a painting or editing tool in Quick Mask mode, keep these principles in mind:

• Painting with white erases the mask (the red overlay) and increases the selected area.

• Painting with black adds to the mask (the red overlay) and decreases the selected area.

Adding to a selection by erasing masked areas

You'll begin by painting with white to increase the selected area within the egret. This erases some of the mask.

1 To make the foreground color white, select the Switch Foreground And Background Colors icon (↰) above the foreground and background color-selection boxes.

2 Select the Zoom tool(🔍) and magnify your view of the image, if needed.

Zoom tool shortcuts

Many times when you are editing an image, you'll need to zoom in to work on a detail and then zoom out again to see the changes in context. You can use various keyboard shortcuts that make it easier than constantly switching between editing tools and the Zoom tool.

Switching to the Zoom tool

You can select the Zoom tool in two ways:

• *Click the Zoom tool in the toolbox to switch from the currently selected tool.*

• *Hold down Ctrl+spacebar (Windows) or Command+spacebar (Mac OS) to temporarily select the Zoom tool from the keyboard. When you finish zooming, release the keys to go back to the tool you were using.*

Zooming in

You can use the Zoom tool to zoom in (magnify the image view) in two ways:

• *Click the area you want to magnify. Each click magnifies the image by the next preset increment.*

• *Drag around the part of the image you want to magnify, creating a zoom marquee. When you release the mouse, the image portion within that marquee fills the image window.*

Zooming out

You can use the Zoom tool to zoom out (shrink the image view) in two ways:

• *In the toolbox, double-click the Zoom tool to return the image to 100% view.*

• *Hold down Alt (Windows) or Option (Mac OS) and click the area of the image you want to reduce. Each Alt/Option-click reduces the image by the next preset increment.*

3 Select the Brush tool (✎).

4 In the tool options bar, make sure that the mode is Normal. Then, click the arrow to display the Brushes pop-up palette, and select a medium-sized brush, such as one with a diameter of 13 pixels.

Note: You'll switch brushes several times as you do this lesson. For convenience, you can drag the Brushes palette from the palette well (on the right side of the tool options bar) so that it stays open, making your brush choices readily available.

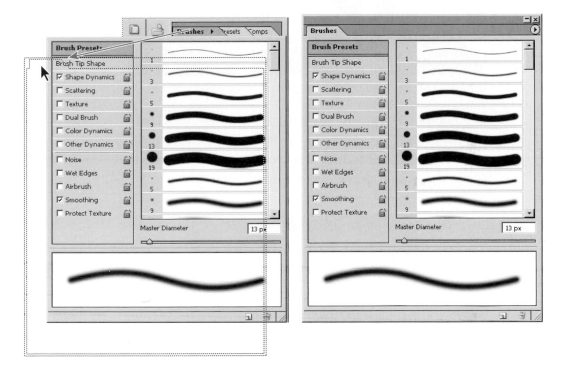

5 Using the Brush tool, begin painting over the red areas within the egret's body.

Although you are painting with white, what you see in the image window is the erasure of the red mask areas.

Don't worry if you paint outside the outline of the egret's body. You'll have a chance to make adjustments later by masking areas of the image as needed.

Unedited mask   *Painting with white*   *Result*

6 Continue painting with white to erase all of the mask (red) in the egret, including its beak and legs. As you work, you can easily switch back and forth between Quick Mask mode and Standard mode to see how painting in the mask alters the selected area.

Notice that the selection border has increased, selecting more of the egret's body.

Standard   *Edited mask in*   *Quick mask selection*
mode   *Standard mode*

For an illustration of the selection in Standard and Quick Mask modes, see figure 6-1 in the color section.

If any areas within the body of the egret still appear to be selected, it means that you haven't erased all of the mask.

Selection in Standard mode　　*Erasing in Quick Mask mode*

7 Once you've erased all of the red areas within the egret, click the Standard mode icon (☐) again to view your quick mask as a selection.

Subtracting from a selection by adding masked areas

You may have erased the mask beyond the edges of the egret. This means that part of the background is included in the selection. You'll fix these flaws by returning to Quick Mask mode and restoring the mask to those edge areas by painting with black.

1 Click the Quick Mask Mode button (☐) to return to Quick Mask mode.

2 To make the foreground color black, select the Switch Foreground And Background Colors icon (↕) above the foreground and background color-selection boxes. Make sure that the black color box now appears on top. Remember that in the image window, painting with black will add to the red overlay.

3 Choose a brush from the Brush pop-up palette. Select a small brush, such as a 1 px, 3 px, or 5 px brush size, for refining the edges of the selection.

4 Paint with black to restore the mask (the red overlay) to any of the background area that is still unprotected. Continue working until only the area inside the egret remains unmasked and you are completely satisfied with your mask selection.

Remember that you can zoom in and out as you work. You can also switch back and forth between Standard mode and Quick Mask mode.

Note: *In Quick Mask mode, you can also use the Eraser tool to remove any excess selection.*

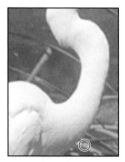

Painting with black to restore mask

For a color illustration of painting in Quick Mask mode, see figure 6-2 in the color section.

5 In the toolbox, switch to Standard mode to view your final egret selection.

6 Double-click the Hand tool ( ) to make the egret image fit in the window.

Saving a selection as a mask

Quick masks are temporary. They disappear as soon as you deselect. However, you can save a selection as an alpha-channel mask so that your time-consuming work won't be lost and you can reuse the selection in this or a later work session. You can even use alpha channels in other Photoshop image files.

When you save a selection as a mask, a new alpha channel is created in the Channels palette. (An image can contain up to 56 channels, including all color and alpha channels.)

Note: If you save and close your file while in Quick Mask mode, the quick mask will show in its own channel the next time you open your file. However, if you save and close your file while in Standard mode, the quick mask will be gone the next time you open your file.

1 In the Layers palette group, click the Channels tab to bring the Channels palette forward, or choose Window > Channels.

In the Channels palette, the default color-information channels are listed—a full-color preview channel for the RGB image and separate channels for red, green, and blue.

Note: You can click eye icons (☻) in the Channels palette to hide and display individual components of the color. When the RGB channel is visible, eye icons also appear for all three individual channels, and vice versa. If you hide one of the individual channels, the eye icon for the composite (the RGB channel) also disappears.

2 With the (Standard Mode) egret selection still active in the image window, click the Save Selection as Channel button () at the bottom of the Channels palette.

A new channel, Alpha 1, appears in the Channels palette. All new channels have the same dimensions and number of pixels as the original image.

Using alpha channels

In addition to the temporary masks of Quick Mask mode, you can create more permanent masks by storing and editing selections in alpha channels. This allows you to use the masks again in the same image or in a different image.

You can create an alpha channel in Photoshop and then add a mask to it. You can also save an existing selection in a Photoshop or ImageReady image as an alpha channel that will appear in the Channels palette.

An alpha channel has these properties:

• *Each image (except 16-bit images) can contain up to 24 channels, including all color and alpha channels.*

• *All channels are 8-bit grayscale images, capable of displaying 256 levels of gray.*

• *You can specify a name, color, mask option, and opacity for each channel. (The opacity affects the preview of the channel, not the image.)*

• *All new channels have the same dimensions and number of pixels as the original image.*

• *You can edit the mask in an alpha channel using the painting tools, editing tools, and filters.*

• *You can convert alpha channels to spot color channels.*

---

3 Double-click the Alpha 1 channel and type **Egret** to rename it.

4 Choose Select > Deselect to deselect everything.

Alpha channels can be added and deleted, and, like quick masks, can be edited using the painting and editing tools.

To avoid confusing channels and layers, think of channels as containing an image's color and selection information; think of layers as containing painting and effects.

Editing a mask

Your next job is to touch up your selection of the egret by editing the mask. It's easy to miss tiny areas when making a selection. You may not even see these imperfections until you view the saved selection as a channel mask.

You can use most painting and editing tools to edit a channel mask, just as you did when editing in Quick Mask mode. This time, you'll display and edit the mask as a grayscale image.

1 Make sure that the Egret channel is selected and that the RGB channels are all hidden, or select and hide them now, as appropriate.

When only the Egret channel has an eye icon (👁), the image window displays a black-and-white mask of the egret selection. (If you left all of the channels selected, the colored egret image would appear with a red overlay.)

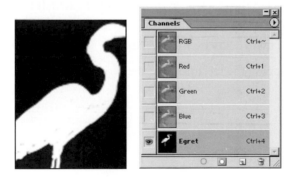

Look for any black or gray flecks within the body of the egret. You'll erase them by painting with white to increase the selected area. Remember these guidelines on editing a channel with a painting or editing tool:

• Painting with white erases the mask and increases the selected area.

• Painting with black adds to the mask and decreases the selected area.

• Painting with gray values adds to or subtracts from the mask in varying opacity, in proportion to the level of gray used to paint: The darker the gray is, the greater the opacity of the mask and the fewer number of pixels included in the selection.

2 In the toolbox, select the Brush tool ( ), and make sure that white appears in the Foreground Color swatch. If it does not, click the Switch Foreground And Background Colors icon ( ).

3 In the Brushes palette, select a small brush size, such as 3 px or 5 px, and use it to paint out any black or gray flecks.

Selection in channel　　*Painting out black or gray*

4 If any white or gray specks appear in the black area of the channel, switch to black as the foreground color and paint those spots. Remember that when you paint with black, you increase the masked area, which will decrease the selection.

5 Dock the Brushes palette by dragging the tab into the palette well.

6 Choose File > Save.

Loading a mask as a selection and applying an adjustment

Next, you'll load the Egret channel mask as a selection. The channel mask remains stored in the Channels palette even after you've loaded it as a selection. This means that you can reuse the mask whenever you want.

1 In the Channels palette, click the RGB preview channel to display the entire image, and then click the eye icon (👁) for the Egret channel to hide it.

2 Choose Select > Load Selection. Click OK.

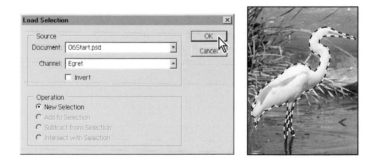

The egret selection appears in the image window.

3 Click the Layers palette tab to bring it forward again in the Channels palette group, and make sure that the Background layer is selected.

Now that you've corrected any flaws in the selection by painting in the channel, you'll adjust the tonal balance of the egret.

> ### *Loading a selection into an image using shortcuts*
>
> *You can reuse a previously saved selection by loading it into an image.*
>
> *To load a saved selection using shortcuts, do one of the following in the Channels palette:*
>
> • *Select the alpha channel, click the Load Selection button at the bottom of the palette, and then click the composite color channel near the top of the palette.*
>
> • *Drag the channel containing the selection you want to load onto the Load Selection button.*
>
> • *Ctrl-click (Windows) or Command-click (Mac OS) the channel containing the selection you want to load.*
>
> • *To add the mask to an existing selection, press Ctrl+Shift (Windows) or Command+Shift (Mac OS), and click the channel.*
>
> • *To subtract the mask from an existing selection, press Ctrl+Alt (Windows) or Command+Option (Mac OS), and click the channel.*
>
> • *To load the intersection of the saved selection and an existing selection, press Ctrl+Alt+Shift (Windows) or Command+Option+Shift (Mac OS), and select the channel.*

4 Choose Image > Adjustments > Auto Levels. This automatically adjusts the tonal balance of the colors within the selection.

Auto Levels defines the lightest and darkest pixels in each channel as white and black, and then redistributes the intermediate pixel values proportionately.

5 Choose Edit > Undo to compare the adjustment you just made. Then choose Edit > Redo to reapply the adjustment.

6 Choose Select > Deselect.

7 Choose File > Save.

Extracting an image

The next task involves another masking and selection tool, the Extract command. This command can make some difficult selections—in this case, some feathery marsh grasses and a spear of a foxtail plant.

The Extract command provides a sophisticated way to isolate a foreground object from its background. Even objects with wispy, intricate, or undefinable edges can be clipped from their backgrounds with a minimum of manual work.

You'll start with an image that consists of only one layer. You must be working in a layer to use the Extract command. If your original image has no layers (that is, it has only a Background), you can duplicate the image to a new layer.

For an illustration of extracting, see figure 6-3 in the color section.

The Foxtail grass image has the same resolution as the Egret image, 72 pixels per inch (ppi). To avoid unexpected results when combining elements from other files, you must either use files with the same image resolution or compensate for differing resolutions.

For example, if your original image is 72 ppi and you add an element from a 144-ppi image, the additional element will appear twice as large because it contains twice the number of pixels.

For complete information on differing resolutions, see "Understanding image size and resolution" in Photoshop Help.

Extracting an object from its background

Applying an extraction erases the background area to transparency, leaving just the extracted object. You'll use the Extract command on a foxtail grass image, which is set against a dark background. This command opens the Extract dialog box, where you'll highlight the edges of the object, define the object's interior, and preview the extraction. You can refine and preview the extraction as many times as you wish.

1 Use the File Browser or choose File > Open to open the Foxtail.psd file in the Lessons/Lesson06 folder.

2 Choose Filter > Extract.

The Extract dialog box appears with the Edge Highlighter tool ( ) selected in the upper left area of the dialog box.

If needed, you can resize the dialog box by dragging its bottom right corner.

3 On the right side of the dialog box, locate the Brush Size option, and then type or drag the slider to **20** pixels, if necessary.

You can select a brush size smaller than 20 pixels in the Brushes palette, but it's not necessary. The beauty of the Extract function is that it distinguishes between the light-colored stem and the dark background, so a few extra background pixels won't affect the results.

4 Using the Edge Highlighter tool, do both of the following:

• Drag to highlight the stem of the foxtail grass and the single leaf. (The highlighting will extend beyond the edges of the stem and leaf.)

• Drag all the way around the tip of the foxtail, covering the entire area around the fuzzy edges of the grass. Make sure that the outline forms a closed shape around the entire tip area.

Note: *It's OK if the highlight overlaps the edge. The Extract command makes its selection by finding the difference in contrast between pixels. You do not need to highlight areas where the object touches the image boundaries.*

If you make a mistake and highlight more than desired, select the Eraser tool ( ) in the dialog box and drag over the highlight in the preview.

5 Select the Fill tool ( ) in the Extract dialog box and click inside the outlined grass tip to fill its interior. (You must define the object's interior before you can preview the extraction.)

Highlighting edges of foxtail tip　　*Highlighting stem and leaves; then filling*

The default Fill color (bright blue) contrasts well with the highlight color (green). You can change either color if you need more contrast with the image colors, using the Highlight and Fill menus in the Extract dialog box.

6 Click the Preview button to view the extraction, and do one of the following:

• If you are satisfied with the results, click OK to apply the extraction.

• If you want to refine the extraction, select Original in the Show menu and select both the Show Highlight and Show Fill check boxes. Continue to work with the tools in the Extract dialog box to add to or erase areas of the selection until you create a satisfactory result. (You may need to redo Step 6 after you adjust the highlighting.) Then click OK.

The Extract dialog box closes and the image window displays the extracted area. (This may be difficult to see because the color is pale and does not stand out well against the checkerboard pattern indicating transparency.)

⭐ *To toggle quickly between the Edge Highlighter and Eraser tools when one of the tools is selected, press B (Edge Highlighter) or E (Eraser).*

Refining a selection in the Extract dialog box

To refine your selection, edit the extraction boundaries using these techniques:

• *Switch between the Original and Extracted views using the Show menu in the Extract dialog box.*

• *Click a filled area with the Fill tool to remove the fill.*

• *Select the Extract dialog box Eraser tool (▱) and drag to remove any undesired highlighting.*

• *Select the Show Highlight and Show Fill options in the Extract dialog box to view the highlight and fill colors; deselect the options to hide them.*

• *Zoom in on your selection using the Extract dialog box Zoom tool. You can then use a smaller brush size as you edit, switching between the Edge Highlighter tool and the Eraser tool as needed for more precise work.*

• *Switch to a smaller brush by entering a different size in the Brush Size option and continue to refine the selection border using the Edge Highlighter tool or to erase using the Eraser tool.*

Adding the extracted image as a layer

It's time to add the extracted image to the Egret image.

1 With the image window of the Foxtail image active, use the Move tool (▸₊) to drag the image to the right side of the Egret image. The foxtail is added as a new layer to the Egret image.

2 Close the Foxtail.psd image window without saving your changes. The 06Start.psd is now the active file, and the new layer with the foxtail is selected.

3 Zoom out so that the egret image covers only about half of the height of the image window.

4 Choose Edit > Transform > Scale. Drag the resize handles, holding down Shift to constrain the proportions, until the foxtail is about two-thirds the original image height. Press Enter (Windows) or Return (Mac OS) to apply the scaling.

Adding foxtail image *Scaling foxtail layer* *Result*

5 With the foxtail layer (Layer 1) selected, decrease the Opacity in the Layers palette to **70%**.

6 Choose File > Save.

Extracting by forcing the foreground

The Force Foreground option lets you make intricate selections when an object lacks a clear interior.

For an illustration of extracting the weeds image, see figure 6-4 in the color section.

1 Use the File Browser or choose File > Open to open the Weeds.psd image in the Lessons/Lesson06 folder.

2 Choose Filter > Extract.

3 On the right side of the dialog box, under Extraction, select the Force Foreground check box.

You'll start by selecting the color on which to base your selection. The Force Foreground technique works best with objects that are monochromatic or fairly uniform in color.

4 Select the Eyedropper tool (✐) in the Extract dialog box, and then click a light area of the weeds to sample the color to be treated as the foreground.

5 Select the Edge Highlighter tool (✎) and set the brush size at about 20 or 30, either by typing or dragging the slider for Brush Size on the right side of the dialog box.

6 Drag to highlight the wispy tops of the weeds where they overlap the dark background. When the weeds' edges are completely highlighted, highlight the top third of the weeds fully. The highlight should be solid.

Highlighting weed edges   *Selecting top third of weeds*

7 Find the Display option towards the bottom of the right side of the dialog box and choose Black Matte from the pop-up menu.

A black matte provides good contrast for a light-colored selection. For a dark selection, try the Gray or White Matte option. None previews a selection against a transparent background.

8 Click the Preview button to preview the extracted object.

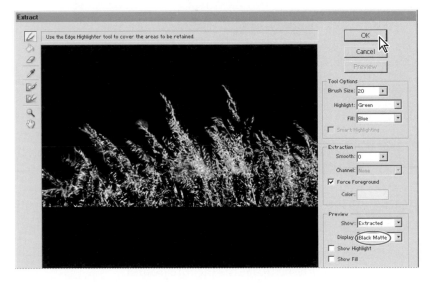

9 To view and refine the extraction, use one of the following techniques:

• Use the Show menu (on the right side of the dialog box under Preview options) to switch between Original and Extracted previews.

• Select the Show Highlight option to display the object's extraction boundaries.

10 When you are satisfied with the selection, click OK to apply the final extraction. All pixels on the layer outside the extracted object are erased to transparency.

Once you've extracted an image, you can also use the Background Eraser and History Brush tools to clean up any stray edges in the image.

An alternate method for making intricate selections is to select areas by color. To do so, choose Select > Color Range. Then, use the Eyedropper tools from the Color Range dialog box to sample the colors for your selection. You can sample from your image window or from the preview window.

Adding the forced-foreground extraction as another layer

Your image is ready for you to add the extracted weeds to the Egret image.

1 With the Weeds.psd file active, use the Move tool (⊹) to drag the extracted selection to the Egret image. Position the weeds so that they fill the bottom third of the Egret image.

The selection is added to the Egret image as a new layer.

2 In the Layers palette, decrease the opacity of the new layer by entering a value of **70%**.

Weed image copy added to egret image

New layer opacity set to 70%

3 Choose File > Save.

4 Close the Weeds.psd file without saving your changes.

Applying a filter effect to a masked selection

To complete the composite of the marsh grasses and Egret image, you'll isolate the egret as you apply a filter effect to the image background.

1 In the Layers palette, select the Background.

2 In the Channels palette, drag the Egret channel to the Load Channel As Selection button (○) at the bottom of the palette. Before continuing to the next step, make sure that the RGB channel is selected, not the Egret channel.

3 Choose Select > Inverse.

The previous selection (the egret) is protected, and the background is selected. You can now apply changes to the background without worrying about affecting the egret.

4 Click the Layers palette tab and make sure that the background layer is selected. Then choose Filter > Artistic > Colored Pencil. Experiment with the sliders to evaluate the changes before you apply the filter.

Note: *If the Filter menu is not available (dimmed), you may have accidentally selected the Egret channel when you dragged it to the Load Channel As Selection button. To try again, choose Select > Deselect now and make sure that the RGB channel remains selected when you load the Egret channel.*

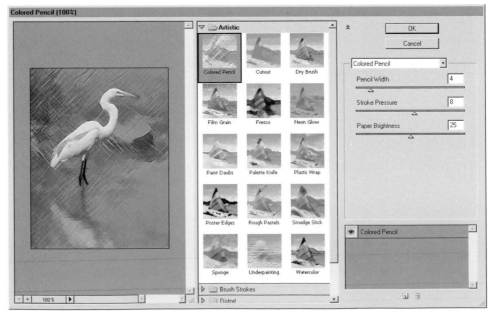

Colored Pencil filter dialog box

5 Click OK when you're satisfied with the Colored Pencil settings. The filter is applied to the background selection.

You can experiment with other filter effects for the background. Choose Edit > Undo to undo your last performed operation.

6 Choose Select > Deselect to deselect everything.

Before you save your file, you'll flatten your image to reduce the file size. Make sure that you are satisfied with the image before you go on to the next step, because you won't be able to make corrections to the separate layers after the image is flattened.

7 Choose Layer > Flatten Image, and then choose File > Save.

Creating a gradient mask

In addition to using black to indicate what's hidden and white to indicate what's selected, you can paint with shades of gray to indicate partial transparency. For example, if you paint in a channel with a shade of gray that is at least halfway between white and black, the underlying image becomes partially (50% or more) visible.

You'll experiment by adding a gradient (which makes a transition from black to gray to white) to a channel and then filling the selection with a color to see how the transparency levels of the black, gray, and white in the gradient affect the image.

1 In the Channels palette, create a new channel by clicking the New Channel button (▣) at the bottom of the palette.

The new channel, labeled Alpha 1, appears at the bottom of the Channels palette, and the other channels are hidden in the image window.

2 Double-click the Alpha 1 channel and type **Gradient** to rename it.

3 Select the Gradient tool (▭).

4 In the tool options bar, click the arrow to display the Gradients picker and select the Black, White gradient, if it is not already selected. (Use tooltips or another view option in the Gradients picker palette menu if you are unsure which thumbnail represents this option.)

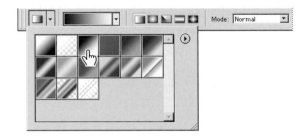

5 Hold down Shift to keep the gradient vertical, and drag the Gradient tool from the top of the image window to the bottom of the window.

The gradient is applied to the channel.

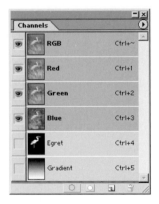

Applying effects using a gradient mask

When you load a gradient as a selection and then fill the selection with a color, the opacity of the fill color varies over the length of the gradient. Where the gradient is black, no fill color is present; where the gradient is gray, the fill color is partially visible; and where the gradient is white, the fill color is completely visible.

1 In the Channels palette, click the RGB channel to display the full-color preview, and then click the Gradient channel eye icon ( ) to hide that channel.

Next, you'll load the Gradient channel as a selection.

2 Without deselecting the RGB channel, drag the Gradient channel to the Load Channel As Selection button ( ) at the bottom of the palette to load the gradient as a selection.

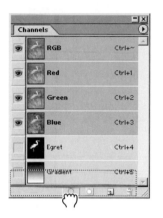

A selection border appears in the window. Although the selection border appears over only about half the image, it is correct.

3 Make sure that the foreground and background colors are set to their default (which are now white and black instead of black and white because of the active channel selection). If necessary, click the Default Foreground And Background Colors icon ( ) at the lower left corner of the color-selection boxes.

4 Press Delete to fill the gradient selection with the current background color (white).

5 Choose Select > Deselect to deselect everything.

6 Choose File > Save.

You have completed this lesson. Although it takes some practice to become comfortable using channels, you've learned all the fundamental concepts and skills you need to get started using masks and channels.

Review questions

1 What is the benefit of using a quick mask?

2 What happens to a quick mask when you deselect it?

3 When you save a selection as a mask, where is the mask stored?

4 How can you edit a mask in a channel once you've saved it?

5 How do channels differ from layers?

6 How do you use the Extract command to isolate an object with intricate borders from an image?

Review answers

1 Quick masks are helpful for creating quick, one-time selections. In addition, using a quick mask is an easy way to edit a selection using the painting tools.

2 The quick mask disappears when you deselect it.

3 Masks are saved in channels, which can be thought of as storage areas in an image.

4 You can paint directly on a mask in a channel using black, white, and shades of gray.

5 Channels are used as storage areas for saved selections. Unless you explicitly display a channel, it does not appear in the image or print. Layers can be used to isolate various parts of an image so that they can be edited as discrete objects with the painting or editing tools or other effects.

6 You use the Extract command to extract an object, and the Extract dialog box to highlight the edges of the object. Then, you define the object's interior and preview the extraction. Applying the extraction erases the background to transparency, leaving just the extracted object. You can also use the Force Foreground option to extract a monochromatic or uniform-colored object based on its predominant color.

7 | Retouching and Repairing

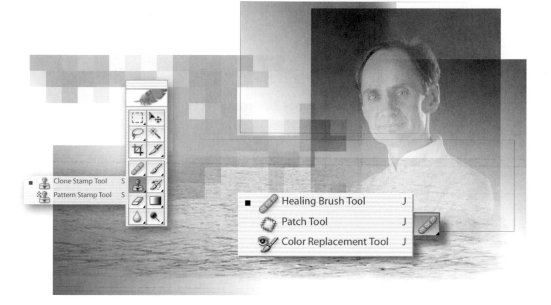

Photoshop includes a powerful set of cloning tools that makes retouching photographs easy and intuitive. Thanks to the underlying technology supporting these features, even touchups of the human face appear so lifelike and natural that it is difficult to detect that a photograph has been altered.

In this lesson, you'll learn how to do the following:

• Use the Clone Stamp tool to eliminate an unwanted part of an image.

• Use the Pattern Stamp tool and pattern maker to replace part of an image.

• Use the Healing Brush and Patch tool to blend in corrections.

• Make corrections on a duplicate layer and adjust it for a natural look.

• Backtrack within your work session using the History palette.

• Use the history brush to partially restore an image to a previous state.

• Use snapshots to preserve earlier states of your work and to compare alternate treatments of the image.

This lesson will take about 45 minutes to complete and must be done in Adobe Photoshop. Most of the specific image-editing features used in this lesson are not available in ImageReady.

If needed, remove the previous lesson folder from your hard drive, and copy the Lesson07 folder onto it. As you work on this lesson, you'll overwrite the start files. If you need to restore the start files, copy them from the *Adobe Photoshop CS Classroom in a Book* CD.

Note: Windows 2000 users need to unlock the lesson files before using them. For more information, see "Copying the Classroom in a Book files" on page 3.

Getting started

In this lesson, you'll work on three separate projects, editing three different photographs. Each of these employs the different retouching tools in unique ways, so you'll witness the strengths and special uses of the various tools.

You'll start by using the File Browser to preview the three finished images that you'll retouch in this lesson and to open your first start file.

1 Start Adobe Photoshop, holding down Ctrl+Alt+Shift (Windows) or Command+Option+Shift (Mac OS) to restore the default preferences. (See "Restoring default preferences" on page 4.)

As messages appear, select Yes to confirm that you want to reset preferences, No to defer setting up your color monitor, and Close to close the Welcome Screen.

2 Click the File Browser button ( ) on the tool options bar to open the File Browser.

3 In the upper left pane of the File Browser, locate and select the Lessons/Lesson07 folder.

4 In the right pane, select the thumbnail for the 07A_End.psd file. If necessary, enlarge the Preview palette by dragging the bars between palettes, or by double-clicking one of the other palette tabs to close them and fill the space with the Preview palette.

The image shows a photograph of a women's crew team with translucent text superimposed on the foreground.

5 Select the other thumbnails in the Lesson07 folder to see the "before" and "after" states of all three images you'll work on in this lesson:

• In the first project, you'll repair a torn-off corner of the scanned image and then remove some distracting areas where a boat and its wake appear beyond the rowers.

• In the second project, you'll clean up the stone wall beside the climber to remove some graffiti and scars from old bolt holes on the surface of the rock.

• In the third project, you'll retouch the portrait to remove some of the fine lines from the man's forehead and around his eyes.

6 When you have finished previewing the files, double-click the thumbnail for the 07A_Start.psd to open the file. If necessary, zoom in to 100% and resize the image window so that you can see the entire image.

7 Click the File Browser or the File Browser button ( ) to bring it forward, and then click the File Browser button again to close the File Browser.

Repairing areas with the Clone Stamp tool

The Clone Stamp tool uses pixels from one area of an image to replace the pixels in another part of the image. Using this tool, you can not only remove unwanted objects from your images, but you can also fill in missing areas in photographs you scan from damaged originals.

You'll start by filling in the torn corner of the photograph with cloned water from another area of the picture.

1 Select the Clone Stamp tool ( ).

2 In the tool options bar, open the Brush pop-up palette and select a medium-sized brush with a soft edge, such as Soft Round 21. Then, make sure that the Aligned option is selected in the tool options bar.

3 Move the Clone Stamp tool pointer to the center of the image so that it is at the same horizontal level as the top edge of the torn corner. Then, hold down Alt (Windows) or Option (Mac OS) so that the pointer appears as target crosshairs, and click to start the sampling at that part of the image. Release the Alt or Option key.

4 Starting at the top edge of the torn corner of the photograph, drag the Clone Stamp tool over a small area at the top of the torn area of the image.

Notice the crosshairs that appear to the right of the Clone Stamp tool. The crosshairs indicate the source area of the image that the Clone Stamp tool is reproducing as you drag.

5 Release the mouse button and move the pointer to another area of the missing corner, and then start dragging again.

Notice that the crosshairs reappear not at the original source spot that you selected in Step 3, but at the same spatial relationship to the Clone Stamp tool pointer that they had when you made the first stroke. This happens because you selected the Aligned option, which resets the crosshairs at that position regardless of the position of the brush.

Note: When the Aligned option is not selected and you make multiple brush strokes, the crosshairs and the brush maintain the same spatial relationship (distance and direction) that they had when you started your first brush stroke, regardless of the location of the original sample site.

6 Continue cloning the water until the entire missing corner of the image is filled in with water.

If necessary to help make the surface of the water appear to blend in naturally with the rest of the image, you can adjust your cloning by resetting the sample area (as you did in Step 3) and recloning. Or, you can try deselecting the Aligned option and cloning again.

7 When you are satisfied with the appearance of the water, choose File > Save.

Using the Pattern Stamp tool

The next task to be done is to remove the boat and its wake from the upper area of the image. You could do this with the Clone Stamp tool, but instead you'll use another technique. Since the entire area has a similar pattern, you can use the Pattern Maker feature to create a realistic pattern that you can use to paint out the wake and boat.

Creating a pattern

You'll begin by defining a new pattern for your project.

1 In the toolbox, select the Rectangular Marquee tool ([□]). Then, drag to select an area of the water between the right end of the rowing shell and the wake. Make sure that your selection includes only water and that it does not include any of the wake behind the passing motor boat.

2 Choose Filter > Pattern Maker.

3 Under Tile Generation in the Pattern Maker dialog box, click the Use Image Size button.

4 Click Generate. The Pattern Maker image area fills with your water pattern.

You can click Generate again to create variations on the pattern. Then, you can use the arrow buttons at the bottom of the right side of the dialog box to review the different patterns and select the one you want to use. However, for the water image, these will probably be quite similar.

5 Under Tile History in the lower right area of the dialog box, click the Saves Preset Pattern button (⊞).

6 In the Pattern Name dialog box, type **Water,** and click OK to return to the Pattern Maker dialog box.

7 In the Pattern Maker dialog box, click Cancel to close the dialog box without replacing the image with the Water pattern.

If you clicked OK instead of Cancel, the Pattern Maker dialog box would replace the entire image with the new pattern you've just created and saved. Replacing the image is not what you want to do, so Cancel is the correct button to click.

Note: *If you accidentally filled the image with water, choose Edit > Undo. Because you already saved your Water pattern, it is not lost and there is no need to redo this procedure. Furthermore, this pattern is now a permanent part of your Pattern set until you actively delete it, so you can apply it to other Photoshop images, even in later work sessions.*

Applying a pattern

Now you're ready to use your pattern to take out the boat and wake.

1 Choose Select > Deselect.

2 In the toolbox, select the Pattern Stamp tool (), hidden under the Clone Stamp tool ().

3 In the tool options bar, change the Brush selection to a brush about 13 pixels in diameter. Leave the Mode set to Normal, Opacity at 100%, Flow at 100%, and the Aligned checked box selected.

4 Click the arrow for the Pattern option to open the pattern picker. Then, select the Water pattern you created earlier, and double-click it or click outside the palette to close it. The Water thumbnail now appears in the Pattern option on the tool options bar.

To identify a pattern, let the pointer hover over the thumbnail in the pattern picker for a few seconds until a tooltip appears, showing the pattern name and information about its dimensions and mode. Or, click the arrow button in the upper right area of the pattern picker to open the palette menu, and select another display option, such as Text Only, Small List, or Large List.

5 In the image window, drag the Pattern Stamp tool brush over the wake and boat to replace them with the Water pattern. Continue painting with the Pattern Stamp tool until you are satisfied with the results.

You'll add just one final tweak to this retouching project, and then you'll be finished working on this image.

6 In the Layers palette, click to place an eye icon (👁) in the CREW layer, so that the text is visible in the image window.

7 Choose File > Save, and then close the 07A_Start.psd file.

Using the Healing Brush and Patch tools

The Healing Brush and Patch tools go one step beyond the capabilities of the Clone Stamp and Pattern Stamp tools. Using their ability to simultaneously apply and blend pixels from area to area, they open the door to natural-looking touchups in areas that are not uniform in color or texture.

In this project, you'll touch up the stone wall, removing some graffiti and bolt holes left over from obsolete climbing techniques. Because the rock has variations in its colors, textures, and lighting, it would be challenging to successfully use the Clone Stamp tool to touch up the damaged areas. Fortunately, the Healing Brush and Patch tools make this process easy.

If you want to review the "before" and "after" versions of this image, use the File Browser, as described in "Getting started" on page 222.

Using the Healing Brush to remove flaws

Your first goal for this image is to remove the initials marring the natural beauty of the rock wall.

1 Click the File Browser button in the tool options bar to open the File Browser, and then find and open the 07B_Start.psd file. Close the File Browser.

2 Select the Zoom tool (🔍) and click the initials "DJ" that have been scratched into the lower left area of the rock, so that you see that area of the image at about 200%.

3 In the toolbox, select the Healing Brush tool (🩹).

4 In the tool options bar, click the Brush option arrow to open the pop-up palette of controls, and drag the slider or type to enter a Diameter value of **10 px**. Then, close the pop-up palette and make sure that the other settings in the tool options bar are set to the default values: Normal in the Mode option, Sampled in the Source option, and the Aligned check box deselected.

| | Brush: • 10 | Mode: Normal | Source: ⦿ Sampled ○ Pattern: | ☐ Aligned |

5 Hold down Alt (Windows) or Option (Mac OS) and click a short distance above the scratched-in graffiti in the image to sample that part of the rock. Release the Alt/Option key.

6 Starting above the graffiti "D," paint straight down over the top part of the letter, using a short stroke.

Notice that as you paint, the area the brush covers temporarily looks as if it isn't making a good color match with the underlying image. However, when you release the mouse button, the brush stroke blends in nicely with the rest of the rock surface.

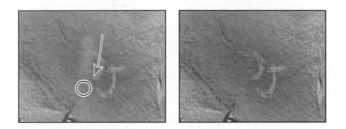

7 Continue using short strokes to paint over the graffiti, starting at the top and moving down until you can no longer detect the graffiti letters.

When you finish removing the graffiti, look closely at the surface of the rock, and notice that even the subtle striations in the stone appear to be fully restored and natural in the image.

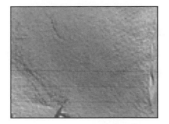

8 Zoom out to 100%, and choose File > Save.

About snapshots and History palette states

When you do retouching work, it can be easy to over-edit images until they no longer look realistic. One of the safeguards you can take to save intermediate stages of your work is to take Photoshop snapshots of the image at various points in your progress.

The History palette automatically records the actions you perform in a Photoshop file. You can use the History palette states like a multiple Undo command to restore the image to previous stages in your work. For example, to undo the most recent six actions, simply click the sixth item above the current state in the History palette. To return to the latest state, scroll back down the History palette and select the state in the lowest position on the list.

The number of items saved in the History palette is determined by a Preferences setting. The default specifies that only the 20 most recent actions are recorded. As you make more changes to the image file, the earliest states are lost as the latest ones are added to the History palette.

When you select an earlier stage in the History palette, the image window reverts to the condition it had at that phase. All the subsequent actions are still listed below it in the palette. However, if you select an earlier state in your work and then make a new change, all the states that appeared after the selected state are lost, replaced by the new state.

Note: *The following technique is not recommended when you work with large or complex images, such as ones with many layers, because this can slow down performance. Saving many previous states and snapshots is RAM-intensive. If you work frequently with complicated images that require maximum RAM, you should consider reducing the number of history states saved by changing that setting in your Photoshop preferences.*

Snapshots give you an opportunity to try out different techniques and then choose among them. Typically, you might take a snapshot at a stage of the work that you are confident you want to keep, at least as a base point. Then, you could try out various techniques until you reached a possible completed phase. If you take another snapshot at that phase, it will be saved for the duration of the current work session on that file. Then, you can revert to the first snapshot and try out different techniques and ideas for finishing the image. When that is finalized, you could take a third snapshot, revert to the first snapshot, and try again.

When you finish experimenting, you can scroll to the top of the History palette to where the snapshots are listed. Then, you can select each of the final snapshots in turn and compare the results.

Once you identify the one you like best, you can select it, save your file, and close it. At that time, your snapshots and History palette listings would be permanently lost.

Note: *You can keep an Edit History Log on a Photoshop file. The Edit History Log is a textual history of what has been done to the image file. For more information, see the Looking at the Work Area section of Photoshop Help.*

Taking a snapshot

Because you are satisfied with the results of your healing the graffiti marks, now is a good time to take a snapshot. This will serve as a baseline for any future experimentation during this work session. (Remember that snapshots and history listings are discarded when you close a file.)

1 Close the Navigator, Color, and Layer palette groups for this session—you won't use them in this lesson—and use the space to expand the History palette so that you can see as many items as possible. If necessary, scroll to the bottom of the History palette so that you can see the last change you made to the image.

2 With the most recent state in the History palette selected, click the New Snapshot button () at the bottom of the History palette to create a snapshot of the current state.

3 Scroll to the top of the History palette. A new snapshot, Snapshot 1, appears at the top of the palette.

4 Double-click the words *Snapshot 1* and type **Post-graffiti** to rename the snapshot.

Note: *You can also take snapshots of earlier phases of your current work session. To do this, scroll to that item in the History palette, select it, and click the New Snapshot button at the bottom of the palette. After you rename the snapshot, reselect the state at which you want to continue working.*

5 Make sure that either the Post-graffiti snapshot or the last state in the History list is selected in the History palette. Then, choose File > Save.

Using the Patch tool

The Patch tool combines the selection behavior of the Lasso tool with the color-blending properties of the Healing Brush tool. With the Patch tool, you can select an area that you want to use as the source (area to be fixed) or destination (area used to do the fixing). Then, you drag the Patch tool marquee to another part of the image. When you release the mouse button, the Patch tool does its job. The marquee remains active over the mended area, ready to be dragged again, either to another area that needs patching (if the Destination option is selected) or to another sampling site (if the Source option is selected).

It may be helpful to zoom in before you begin so that you can easily see the details of the image.

1 In the toolbox, select the Patch tool ( ), hidden under the Healing Brush tool ( ).

2 In the tool options bar, make sure that Source is selected.

3 Drag the Patch tool cursor around a few of the bolt holes to the right of the climber, as if you were using the Lasso tool, and then release the mouse.

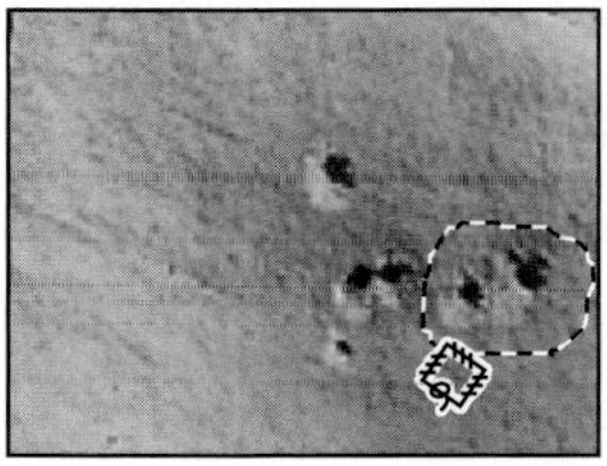

4 Drag the selection to an unblemished area of the rock, preferably—but not necessarily—one that is similar in color to the rock around the bolt holes.

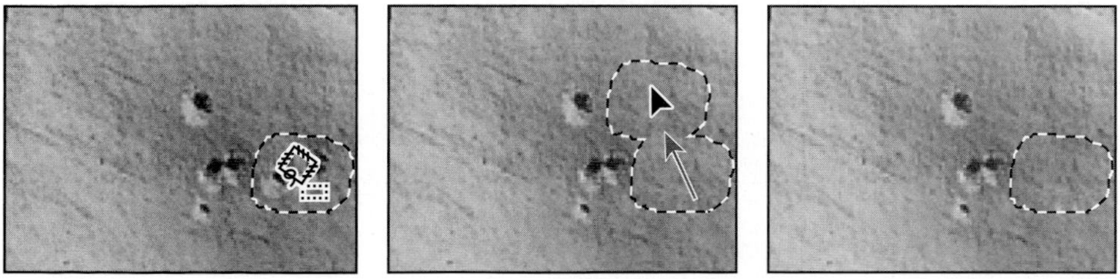

As you drag, the original selected area shows the same pixels as the lassoed selection you are dragging. When you release the mouse, the color—but not the texture—readjust back to the original color scheme of the selection.

5 Drag a new selection around some of the other bolt holes and then drag to an unblemished area of the image. Continue to patch the image until all the scars are repaired to your satisfaction. (Don't overlook the holes on the left side of the image.)

6 Choose Select > Deselect.

7 Choose File > Save.

Using the History Brush tool to selectively reedit

Even with the best tools, retouching photographs so that they look completely natural is an art and requires some practice. Examine your rock-climber image critically to see if any areas of your work with the Healing Brush or Patch tools are now too uniform or smooth, so that the area no longer looks realistic. If so, you can correct that now with another tool.

The History Brush tool is similar to the Clone Stamp tool. The difference between them is that instead of using a defined area of the image as the source (as the Clone Stamp tool does), the History Brush tool uses a previous History palette state as the source.

The advantage of the History Brush tool is that you can restore limited areas of the image. Because of this, you can keep the successful retouching effects you've made to some areas of the image and restore other, less successfully retouched areas to their previous state so that you can make a second attempt.

1 In the toolbox, select the History Brush tool ( ).

2 Scroll to the top of the History palette and click the empty box next to the Post-graffiti snapshot to set the source state that the History Brush tool will use to paint.

3 Drag the History Brush tool over the area where the bolt holes appeared before you edited them, to start restoring that part of the image to its previous condition. The bolt holes reappear as you paint.

4 Using the tool options bar, experiment with the different settings for the History Brush tool, such as Opacity and Mode. Notice how these affect the appearance of the rock as you paint.

If you don't like the results of an experiment, choose Edit > Undo, or click an earlier action at the bottom of the History palette to revert to that state.

5 Continue working with the History Brush and Patch tools until you are satisfied with the final appearance of your image.

6 Choose File > Save, and then choose File > Close.

You've finished your work on this image.

Retouching on a separate layer

In the previous project, you safeguarded your retouching work by using snapshots and the History Brush tool. Another method of protecting your original image is to do your retouching work on a duplicate layer of the original image. Then, you can retouch the duplicate layer. When you finish retouching, you can blend the two layers. This technique usually enhances the results, making your touchup work look more natural and realistic.

Using the Healing Brush on a duplicate layer

For this project, you'll work on a portrait photograph.

1 Choose Window > Workspace > Reset Palette Locations to move, reopen, and resize any palette groups that you rearranged in the previous project.

2 Use the File Browser button ( ) on the tool options bar to open the File Browser, and double-click the 07C_Start.psd thumbnail to open the file.

You can close the File Browser now, or leave it open if you prefer.

3 In the Layers palette, drag the Background layer onto the New Layer button (🔲) at the bottom of the palette to create a duplicate layer. Double-click the new layer and type **Retouch** to rename the layer; leave the Retouch layer selected.

4 In the toolbox, select the Healing Brush tool (✎), which may be hidden under the Patch tool (◔).

5 In the tool options bar, open the pop-up Brush palette and set the brush diameter at **12** pixels. Close the palette and select the Aligned check box. Leave the other settings at the defaults (Normal selected as the Mode option and Sampled selected for Source).

Notice the two wrinkles running horizontally across the man's forehead.

6 Hold down Alt (Windows) or Option (Mac OS) and click a smooth area of the forehead, on the left side of the image, to set the sample point. Then, drag the Healing Brush tool over the lower of the two forehead wrinkles.

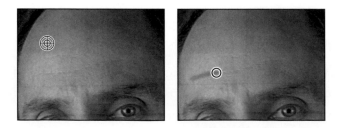

As you drag, the image looks as if you must be doing something terribly wrong, because the painted pixels appear much, much darker than the man's natural skin tones. However, when you release the mouse button the colors self-correct, so that the wrinkle is covered and the skin looks quite natural.

7 Continue painting with the Healing Brush tool to remove the upper forehead wrinkle and the furrow line between the eyebrows.

Patching and softening using the separate layer

You'll continue to do cosmetic work on the face image, using the Patch tool and the duplicate layer (Retouch) you created in the previous topic. Make sure that the Retouch layer is selected in the Layers palette before you begin.

1 In the toolbox, select the Patch tool ( ), hidden under the Healing Brush tool ( ). Then, drag a marquee around the wrinkles under one of the man's eyes.

2 Move the Patch tool inside the selected area and drag it to a smooth area on the man's forehead. Then use the same technique to erase the wrinkles under the other eye.

3 Continue to touch up the man's face with the Patch tool until most of the wrinkles are hidden, or at least softened.

It is especially important that cosmetic touchups on the human face look as natural as possible. There's an easy way to make sure that your corrections aren't too smooth or plastic looking. You'll do that now.

4 In the Layers palette, change the Opacity value of the Retouch layer to **65%**. Now hints of the heaviest skin creases appear in the image, giving the enhanced image a convincing realism.

5 Click the eye icon (👁) for the Retouch layer off and on to see the difference between the original image and the corrected one.

Look at the two numbers on the Info Bar, just to the right of the zoom percentage. The first number (ours is about 1.26 MB) represents the size the file would be if the two layers were flattened into one layer. The second number (ours is about 2.52 MB) shows the current size of the file with its two layers. However, after you flatten the image, you cannot separate the two layers again. When you are sure that you are satisfied with the results of your retouching efforts, it's smart to take advantage of the space-saving of flattening.

6 Choose Layers > Flatten Image, or choose Flatten Image on the Layers palette menu.

7 Choose File > Save.

Now the image has just one layer, combining the unaltered original background and the partly transparent retouched layer.

Congratulations; you've finished your work on this lesson. Close any open files.

Review questions

1 Describe the similarities and differences of the Clone Stamp tool, the Pattern Stamp tool, the Healing Brush tool, the Patch tool, and the History Brush tool.

2 What is a snapshot and how is it useful?

3 What difference does it make if you select or don't select the Aligned option for a retouching tool?

4 Can you use patterns and snapshots in later work sessions or other image files?

Review answers

1 The retouching tools have the following similarities and differences:

• Clone Stamp tool: As you paint, the tool duplicates the pixels from another area of the image. You set the sample area by holding down Alt (Windows) or Option (Mac OS) and clicking the Clone Stamp tool.

• Pattern Stamp tool (Photoshop only): As you paint, the tool lays down pixels based on a pattern that you designate. You can create this pattern from an area of the current image, from another image file, or from the default set provided with Adobe Photoshop CS.

• Healing Brush tool (Photoshop only): This tool works like the Clone Stamp tool except that Photoshop calculates a blending of the sample pixels and the painting area, so that the restoration is especially subtle, yet effective.

• Patch tool (Photoshop only): This tool works like the Healing Brush tool except that instead of using brush strokes to paint from a designated area, you drag a marquee around the area to be fixed and then drag the marquee over another area to mend the flawed area.

• History Brush tool: This tool works like the Clone Stamp tool except that it paints pixels from a designated previous state or snapshot that you select in the History palette.

2 A snapshot is a temporary record of a specific stage in your work session. The History palette saves only a limited number of actions. After that, each new action you perform removes the earliest item from the History palette list. However, if you select any action listed in the History palette and take a snapshot of that state, you can continue working from that action or another one. Later in your work session, you can revert to the state recorded by the snapshot by selecting it in the History palette, regardless of how many changes you've made in the meantime. You can save as many snapshots as you please.

3 The Aligned option governs the relationship between the sample site and the brush. The difference between selecting or not selecting the Aligned option is significant only if you use multiple strokes as you retouch—that is, if you change the position of the pointer between brush strokes.

• If Aligned is selected, then the sampling crosshairs maintain the same relative position to the brush as when you started the first brush stroke, so that an imaginary line between the brush and the crosshairs would maintain the same length and direction.

• If Aligned is not selected, then the sampling crosshairs go back to the original sample site each time you start a new brush stroke, regardless of the distance or the angle between the brush and the source.

4 The patterns that you create and save in the Photoshop Pattern Maker dialog box are saved with the application. Even if you close the current file, switch to another project, quit Photoshop, or reset your Photoshop preferences, that pattern will still be available in the pattern picker. (However, you can actively remove patterns, which deletes the pattern permanently.) Snapshots are deleted when you close the image file and cannot be recovered in later work sessions on that file. Snapshots are available only in the image file in which you created them.

Lesson 8

8 Painting and Editing

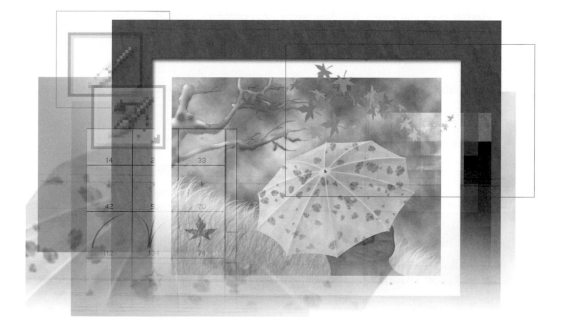

The Adobe Photoshop CS painting engine is so sophisticated and powerful that the possibilities for using it are virtually unlimited. This lesson gives you just a taste of the many techniques and approaches you can use in your work.

In this lesson, you'll learn how to do the following:

• Define a custom workspace that's tailored for painting tasks.

• Use layers to paint, adjust, add effects, and make color changes to specific portions of an image.

• Set the blending mode and opacity of a layer to adjust how overlapping colors and elements of the image combine with each other.

• Set the blending mode and opacity of a painting tool to adjust how a paint stroke combines with other pixels in the image.

• Use the History palette and history tools to make corrections and add effects.

• Use preset brushes.

• Create and use custom brushes.

• Create and apply a pattern from a different image to create a picture frame.

This lesson will take about an hour and a half to complete. The lesson is designed to be done in Adobe Photoshop.

If needed, remove the previous lesson folder from your hard drive, and copy the Lessons/Lesson08 folder onto it. As you work on this lesson, you'll overwrite the start files. If you need to restore the start files, copy them from the *Adobe Photoshop CS Classroom in a Book* CD.

Note: Windows 2000 users need to unlock the lesson files before using them. For more information, see "Copying the Classroom in a Book files" on page 3.

Getting started

You'll start the lesson by viewing the final Lesson file to see what you'll accomplish.

1 Start Adobe Photoshop and immediately hold down Ctrl+Alt+Shift (Windows) or Command+Option+Shift (Mac OS) to restore the default preferences. See "Restoring default preferences" on page 4.

As messages appear, select Yes to confirm that you want to reset preferences, No to defer setting up your color monitor, and Close to close the Welcome Screen.

2 On the tool options bar, select the File Browser button (![icon]) to open the File Browser.

3 In the File Browser Folders palette, go to the Lessons/Lesson08 folder and select the 08End.psd file in the thumbnails pane so that it appears in the Preview palette.

You can resize the other palettes to enlarge the image in the Preview palette, if needed.

4 When you have finished viewing the end file, close the File Browser without opening the start file yet.

Defining a custom workspace

When you use Adobe Photoshop CS to do a specific project, you'll typically make frequent use of some palettes and rarely need others. When you do a different type of Photoshop project, the palettes you use most frequently may change because the nature of the job has different requirements.

You already know that you can close unneeded palettes and open hidden ones that you do need, but with Photoshop CS you can save different combinations of open and closed palettes as workspaces. Painting is a good example of a situation that relies on specific palettes that are not opened by the default workspace definition.

1 Close the Navigator palette group, so that both the Navigator and Info palettes are hidden.

2 Drag the Brushes palette from the palette well in the tool options bar to the center of the work area. Position it so that you can see at least part of the History palette group.

Note: *If your work area size is 800 pixels by 600 pixels or less, the palette well does not appear. Instead, choose Window > Brushes.*

3 Drag the History palette tab into the Brushes palette. Then, click the Brushes tab to bring that palette forward in the palette group.

4 Close the Actions and Tool Presets palette group.

5 Drag the various palette groups to arrange them along the right edge of your work area, with the Color palette group at the top, the Layers palette group next, and the Brushes palette group at the bottom. (Depending on your monitor display area, the Layers palette group and Brushes palette group may overlap somewhat.)

6 Choose Window > Workspace > Save Workspace.

7 In the Save Workspace dialog box, type **Painting_8** (to remind you of the tasks you'll do in this workspace and the number of the associated lesson), and click Save.

You can experiment with different workspaces to see how your custom setting can save you the trouble of closing and arranging palettes the next time you restart Photoshop:

• Choose Window > Workspace > Reset Palette Locations. The palettes now appear as they did before you first opened Photoshop; that is, in the default arrangement.

• Choose Window > Workspace > Painting_8. Now the palettes are selectively closed, opened, and regrouped to match the positions they had at the end of Step 5.

After you close Photoshop or switch to a different Photoshop project, the Painting workspace remains available in Photoshop for use in future sessions.

Blending an image with the background

The blending mode controls how pixels in an image are affected by painting and editing tools. It's helpful to think in terms of the following types of colors when visualizing a blending mode's effect:

• The *base color* is the original color in the image.

• The *blend color* is the color being applied with the painting or editing tool.

• The *result color* is the color resulting from the blend.

Throughout this lesson, you will learn how to specify a blending mode for a layer in the Layers palette and for a tool in the tool options bar.

For color illustrations of the different blending modes available in Photoshop and ImageReady, see figure 8-1 of the color section. For descriptions of each blending mode, see "Selecting a blending mode" in Photoshop Help.

You'll use the Multiply blending mode to blend the white background of a tree outline on one layer with the opaque layer behind it.

1 Select the File Browser button on the tool options bar, or choose File > Open and open the 08Start.psd file in your Lessons/Lesson08 folder.

The file opens, showing you one of the layers that has been prepared for you: a mottled blue-and-white texture. This coloration covers the entire image window, simulating a thin layer of wispy clouds against a deep blue sky.

2 In the Layers palette, click the empty box to the left of the Tree layer set to place an eye icon (👁), which reveals that entire layer set in the image window.

3 Again in the Layers palette, click the arrow next to the Tree folder icon to expand the layer set. Two layers are nested in the set: an Outline layer and a Bark layer.

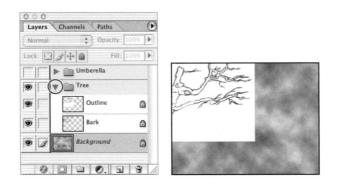

An outline drawing of tree branches against a white background now blocks part of the sky.

4 Select the Outline layer in the Tree layer set. Then, at the top of the palette, use the pop-up menu to change the blending mode from Normal to Multiply.

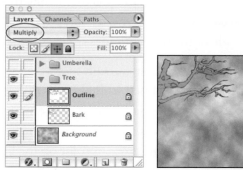 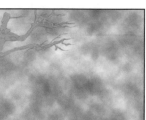

The white background disappears, and the brown paint on the Bark layer shows up. The Multiply blending mode calculates the color for each pixel by multiplying the color information in each channel (such as R, G, and B) by the color channels in the paint pixels. As a result, painting in Multiply blending mode creates colors that are darker than the original colors.

5 With the Outline layer still active, change the Opacity value in the Layers palette to **30%**, to soften the outline so that it looks more artistic and less cartoon-like. You'll make more adjustments to the appearance of the tree limb in the next procedures.

6 Choose File > Save.

Painting shadows and highlights in nontransparent areas

In this part of the lesson, you'll lock the transparency on the Bark layer. This restricts your painting on the layer so that you can add shadows and highlights to only the tree itself. Because all the transparent areas are protected, you don't have to worry about any paint strokes spilling onto the background outside of the tree outline.

There are two techniques for protecting the transparent areas. One is to select the layer you'll paint on and use the Lock Transparent Pixels option (✛) in the Layers palette. The other technique, which you'll use here, is to create a new layer and then group it with the previous one. When you apply brush strokes or effects to a layer that is grouped with a second layer, those brush strokes or effects apply only to pixels of color on the first layer. (Any transparent areas will be unaffected.)

1 In the Layers palette, select the Bark layer (in the Tree layer set), and then select New Layer from the Layers palette menu. (Don't use the New Layer button this time.)

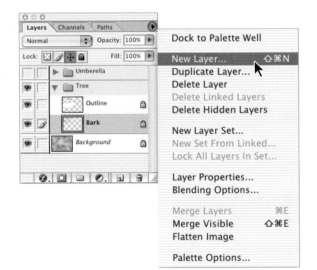

2 In the New Layer dialog box, type **Highlights** and select the Use Previous Layer to Create Clipping Mask check box. Then click OK.

The Highlights layer appears with a small arrow pointing to the Bark layer, indicating that these two layers are grouped. (This arrow may be difficult to see while the Highlights layer is selected.)

3 On the Swatches palette, select a warm brown color from the bottom row of the swatches, using a color that is somewhat darker than the tree-bark color.

4 In the toolbox, select the Brush tool. Then, use the Brushes palette to select a brush, such as the Soft Round 21-pixel brush.

5 Make sure that the Highlights layer is active in the Layers palette, and then paint shadows on the right sides and lower edges of the branches of the tree, as if a light source is outside the image to the upper left. Also paint shadows into the gnarly areas of the main branch.

As you paint, you don't need to worry about painting outside the tree area (because those areas are protected) or that the effect isn't subtle (because you'll adjust that later).

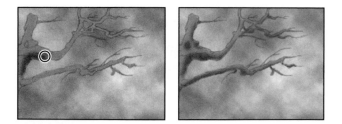

💡 *You can adjust the brush size and opacity of the paint as you work, using the settings on the tool options bar. To change the brush size on the fly, press left-bracket ([) to move to the next smaller brush size; press right-bracket (]) to switch to the next larger brush size.*

6 In the Swatches palette, select a brown color that is lighter than the original bark color, and use it to paint highlights on the upper and left sides of the branches. Then select white, and add touches of bright highlights to some of these areas.

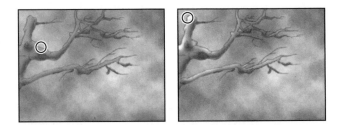

7 When you are satisfied with the highlights and shadows (although the results are still not subtle), choose File > Save.

Smoothing the edges of a stroke

Now you'll use the Blur tool to soften the edges of your paint strokes, smoothing out the color transitions among the brown shadows, the underlying bark, and the bright highlights.

1 In the toolbox, select the Blur tool (💧). Then, in the Brushes palette, select a small brush, such as the Soft Round 21 Pixel brush you used earlier. Make sure that tool options bar is set with Mode at Normal and Strength at 50%.

💧 ▾	Brush: ● 21 ▾	Mode: Normal ▴▾	Strength: 50% ▸	☐ Use All Layers

2 Make sure that the Highlight layer is active (selected) in the Layers palette.

3 Drag the Blur tool brush over the shadows and highlights of the tree branch to soften the color transitions. (It may be helpful to zoom in to see the results as you blur the image.)

4 As you blur the image, try adjusting the Strength option value in the tool options bar. If you don't like the results one percentage produces, choose Edit > Undo, and try a different one.

5 When you are satisfied with the blend of highlights and shadows, choose File > Save.

Changing images with the history tools

As you work on an image, you may want to undo an operation or correct a mistake. There are many ways to correct mistakes in Adobe Photoshop. In the following sections, you'll use the History palette and History Brush tools to restore your image to an earlier state.

About the history painting tools

Two brush tools include the word *history* in their names, but their functions are quite distinct. Each has its unique advantages. One similarity between them, however, is that both can apply what are ordinarily layer- or image-level changes to a limited area of an image.

The *History Brush tool* can selectively restore areas of an image to a previous state without changing the subsequent work you've done in other areas of the image. It works in a way similar to the way the Clone Stamp and Healing Brush tools work. Brush strokes made with the History Brush tool change pixels in the image back to pixels as they were in the state or snapshot that you've designated in the History palette.

The name of the *Art History Brush tool* refers to classic brush strokes you might see in painting masterpieces from over the centuries, but it is also related to the History palette. The brush strokes apply pixels based on the selected state or snapshot in the History palette, but the paint strokes are also filtered so that the results are altered in a particular way. The type of filtering is determined by the Style option for the Art History Brush tool. You can apply the Art History Brush tool selectively, painting in some areas of the active layer and leaving other areas of the active layer unchanged. With ordinary filters, the change applies to the entire selected layer.

Using the history painting tools

In this section, you'll work with both the History Brush tool and the Art History Brush tool. By using them in the same task, you'll get a better idea of the differences between them.

Your goal here is to make the flow of color among the highlights, body, and shadows of the tree branches more subtle, as if they were part of a watercolor painting.

1 In the History palette, click the New Snapshot button (▣). A snapshot state, Snapshot 1, appears at the top of the History palette.

2 At the top of the History palette, click in the empty box at the left of the Snapshot 1 thumbnail without actually selecting the snapshot.

An icon ( ) appears in the box, indicating that Snapshot 1 determines the source pixel state you'll paint into the current state of the image.

3 In the Layers palette, select the Outline layer.

4 In the toolbox, select the Art History Brush tool ( ), hidden under the History Brush tool ( ).

5 In the Brushes palette, choose a small brush size (such as Hard Round 3 Pixel). Then, for Style in the tool options bar, choose a style from the pop-up menu (or leave this at the default setting, Tight Short, as we used in the example).

Important: *Be sure that the most recent state is still selected (highlighted) at the bottom of the History palette list, or select it now.*

6 Using the Art History Brush tool, paint over the entire tree to smear and blur the outline. You can also experiment with just clicking on an area rather than dragging.

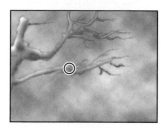

When you finish applying the Art History Brush tool, your image is probably a little more smeared than is ideal. You'll use the History Brush tool to remove some of the strokes you made with the Art History Brush tool, which won't affect other areas that you want to leave looking smeary.

7 Select the History Brush tool ( ), hidden under the Art History Brush tool ( ), and drag the pointer over the areas of the tree where you want to restore the focus to the dark details, such as the smaller twigs and branches and some areas on the shadowed side of the tree.

Notice that the strokes you make with the History Brush tool remove the strokes that you made with the Art History Brush tool and uncover the original dark lines of the image.

8 When you are satisfied with the look of the tree, click the arrow beside the Tree layer set in the Layers palette to collapse the list, and then choose File > Save.

Getting the most from the Brush tool

The Brushes palette includes a variety of preset brush tips with different sizes, shapes, and densities. The Brushes palette and tool options bar for the Brush tool also include a complex variety of settings that you can use with your selected brush. This flexibility gives you a powerful set of combinations that challenges you to use brushes in imaginative new ways.

One of the useful properties of brushes is that you can select different blending modes and opacity settings as you paint on a single layer. These settings are independent of each other and of any blending modes or opacity settings that you apply to the entire layer.

For color illustrations of brush blending modes, see figure 8-2 of the color section.

Another enhancement in Photoshop CS is that you can do more with the custom brush shapes that you create and save. You can now assign different sizes and other properties to your custom brushes and even change them on the fly like any other brush.

Painting with a specialty brush

Among the preset brushes are several that paint in preshaped units, so that a single stroke paints a series of stars, leaves, or blades of grass. You'll use one of the grass-shaped brushes to create a hillside for your image landscape.

1 In the Layers palette, select the Tree layer set and click the New Layer button (■). Double-click Layer 1, and type **Grass** to rename the layer.

2 In the toolbox, select the Brush tool (✎), and then scroll down the Brushes palette and select the Dune Grass brush shape.

♀ *To reduce the amount of scrolling needed in the Brushes palette, open the Brushes palette menu and choose Small Thumbnail (the display shown in the illustration below Step 3). You can confirm your brush choice by letting the pointer hover over the thumbnail until a pop-up appears, identifying the brush by name. If you prefer to see the brush descriptions as you scroll, you can still reduce your scrolling by choosing Small List on the Brushes palette menu.*

3 Above the sample displayed at the bottom of the Brushes palette, drag the Master Diameter slider or type to change the value to **60 px**.

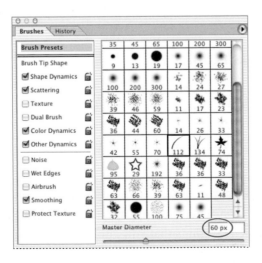

4 In the Color palette, select a pale yellow color, such as R=**230**, G=**235**, B=**171**.

5 If necessary, adjust the size and magnification of the image window so that you can see the entire image. Then, drag the Brush tool in a gently waving line from the center of the left side of the image to the lower right corner. (Refer to the 08End.psd file as a guide.)

6 Continue dragging the Brush tool across the lower left area of the image to fill in the hillside of grass. Do not try to fill the area with solid color, but leave a little bit of the sky showing through so that you can still see most of the individual blades of grass.

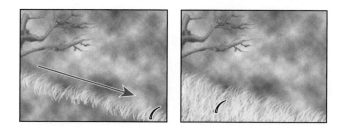

7 In the Color palette, select a light olive-green color, such as R=**186**, G=**196**, B=**93**.

8 In the tool options bar, select Multiply in the Mode pop-up menu, and change the Opacity value to **50%**.

9 Resume painting over the same area of your image, building up color until you are satisfied with the results. If you make a mistake or want to start over, select a previous state in the History palette, and start again from that state.

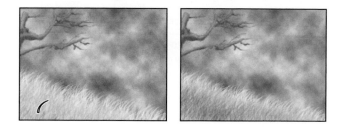

Notice that when you first start painting the olive color, the results are relatively faint. As you continue to drag the brush over the same areas, the color you add multiplies itself by the underlying pixel colors, producing increasingly darker shades of green. This process effectively demonstrates the way the Multiply blending mode works.

10 Choose File > Save.

Creating new color swatches for the umbrella image

Now, you'll use traditional painting techniques and brushes to complete more painting layers that have been started for you, and which together become an umbrella.

1 In the Layers palette, click the eye-icon box for the Umbrella layer set to make those layers visible in the image window. Then click the arrow to expand the layer set, so that five layers appear within that set, only some of which are visible.

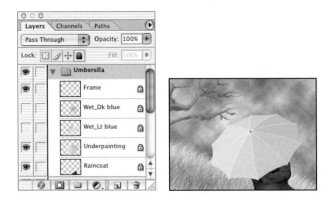

2 Click to set an eye icon (👁) for the Wet_Lt blue layer. A series of brush strokes have been laid down for you, so that the color and shape are gaining some definition.

3 Click to set an eye icon for the Wet_Dk blue layer.

Seven of the ten segments of the umbrella have been painted with additional color, but the three segments on the left side of the umbrella have not. Before you begin painting, you'll define two new color swatches that you'll use for this task.

4 Drag the Swatches palette tab out of the Color palette group so that it becomes a stand-alone palette. Move the Swatches palette so that it is near the Color palette and you can see both palettes completely.

5 In the Color palette, select a medium blue color, such as R=**150**, G=**193**, B=**219**.

6 Move the pointer into the blank (gray) area to the right or below the last swatch in the bottom row of the Swatches palette. When the pointer appears as a paint bucket icon ( ), click to add the medium blue color to the collection of swatches.

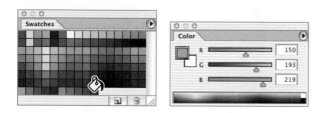

7 In the Color Swatch Name dialog box, click OK to accept the default name.

8 Define a darker blue color in the Colors palette, such as R=**132**, G=**143**, B=**199**, and add that color to the Swatches palette, using the technique you just learned.

Adding brush libraries to the Brushes palette

The brushes available to you go beyond the default set. You'll add a new brush library to the brush presets in the Brushes palette, and select settings for one of those brushes.

1 On the Brushes palette menu, choose Large List. Now, both the thumbnail of the tip and the name appear for each brush shape.

2 Again on the Brushes palette menu, choose Wet Media Brushes.

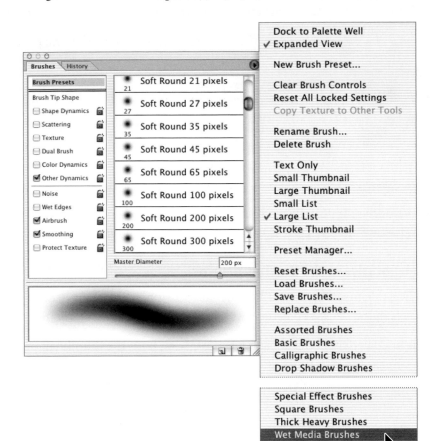

3 A small dialog box appears; select Append to add the Wet Media Brushes library to the set currently listed in the Brushes palette.

Note: If you accidentally click OK instead of Append, Photoshop replaces the existing brush set with the Wet Media Brushes set. To restore the original brush set, choose Reset Brushes on the Brushes palette menu, and then repeat Step 2 and 3 to append the Wet Media Brushes to the default brush library.

4 Scroll to the bottom of the list in the Brushes palette, and select the Watercolor Light Opacity brush. Then, just below the list, use the Master Diameter slider or type to set the value at **25** pixels.

5 In the tool options bar, select Normal on the Mode pop-up menu and change the Opacity value to **15%**.

6 In the Swatches palette, select the medium blue swatch you created in the previous topic.

Creating form and dimension with wet media brushes

Before you begin painting, you'll load one of the alpha channels that has been prepared for you. You'll use three different prepared alpha channels to restrict your painting to each of the three segments you're going to paint, so you don't have to worry about getting paint in other areas of the image or painting out the ribs of the umbrella.

1 In the Layers palette, select the Wet_Dk blue layer.

2 Choose Select > Load Selection.

3 In the Load Selection dialog box, select Alpha 1 from the Channel pop-up menu, and then click OK.

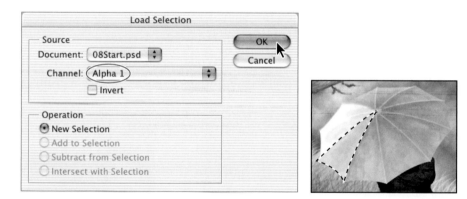

In the image window, a selection border appears around the lower of the three umbrella panels that you'll paint.

♀ *If you find the selection border distracting, you can hide it by pressing Ctrl+H (Windows) or Command+H (Mac OS). Even though the marquee is not visible, your painting is still restricted to the area within it. To make the selection border visible again, use the same keyboard shortcut.*

4 Starting near the center of the umbrella, paint with short, downward strokes to build up a subtle shading, concentrating on the areas next to the umbrella spokes.

As you work, you can experiment with different brush sizes and opacity settings to create varied texture and shadows.

5 In the Swatches palette, select the darker blue swatch that you created earlier, and continue to paint until that section of the umbrella coordinates nicely with the panels of the umbrella that are already painted.

6 Choose Select > Deselect. Then, choose Select >Load Selection and select the Alpha 2 Channel in the pop-up menu. Repeat Steps 4 and 5 to shade in the second of the three umbrella sections.

7 Repeat Step 6, but this time select the Alpha 3 Channel and paint the third umbrella section.

8 When you finish painting, click the arrow to collapse the Umbrella layer set in the Layers palette, drag the Swatches palette back into the Color palette layer group, and then choose File > Save.

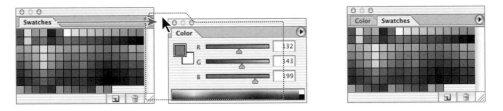

Saving a customized preset brush

Now you'll create and save a brush based on an existing preset, and use it in your painting.

1 In the Layers palette, select the Umbrella layer set, if necessary, and then click the New Layer button (⬛) at the bottom of the palette. Double-click the new layer and type **Leaves** to name the layer.

2 With the Brush tool selected in the toolbox, scroll through the Brushes palette and select the Scattered Maple Leaves brush.

3 On the left side of the Brushes palette, click the words *Shape Dynamics* to display the Shape Dynamics options on the right side of the palette. Enter the following settings, noticing how the stroke sample at the bottom of the palette changes each time you change a setting:

• In the Control pop-up menu near the top of the palette, select Fade, and then type **50** as the Fade value.

• In Roundness Jitter, drag the slider or type to set the value at **40%**.

4 Again on the left side of the Brushes palette, click the word *Scattering* and drag the sliders or type on the right side of the palette to change the following settings:

• For Scatter, set the value at **265%**.

• For Count, set the value at **1**.

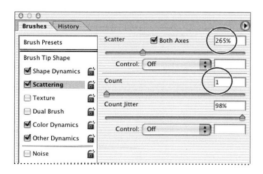

5 In the upper left corner of the Brushes palette, click the Brush Presets to display the list of brushes again. Then drag the Master Diameter slider or type **65 px**.

6 At the bottom of the Brushes palette, click the New Brush button (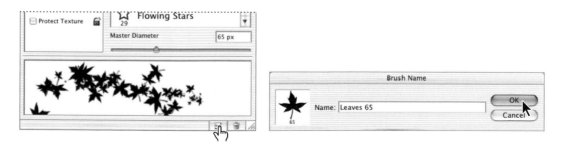), and then type **Leaves 65** as the brush name and click OK.

The new brush appears at the bottom of the list of brushes in the palette.

Painting from the image onto a created border

In the final artwork, a white border surrounds the painting, and leaves appear to fly outside the edges of the picture and onto the border area. To create that effect, your first step is to create the border.

1 In the toolbox, make sure that the background color is white. Then choose Image > Canvas Size.

2 In the Canvas Size dialog box, type **580** as the Width and select pixels from the units pop-up menu. Then type **440** as the Height and set those units to pixels also, and click OK.

3 On the Color palette, select a dark, warm yellow, such as R=**185**, G=**141**, B=**59**. This will be the base color for the autumn leaves you'll add.

You're now ready to start painting your leaves. Make sure that your Leaves 65 brush is still selected in the Brushes palette and that the tool options bar shows Normal as the Mode option and Opacity at 100%.

4 Drag the Leaves 65 brush in a gentle arc from the tips of the tree branches to the right, letting the stroke wander into the top border and onto the border on the right side. Refer to the 08End.psd file as a guide.

5 If you are not satisfied with the result, choose Edit > Undo, and try again.

Because brush Scatter settings are designed to create random patterns, each brush stroke produces slightly different results. It may take several tries before you get a pattern that you like. Remember that you can use either the Undo command or the History palette to backtrack through these attempts.

To save some results of the painting as potential candidates, use the History palette to take a snapshot of the image and then revert to an earlier state. Try painting again from that state to see if you can improve on your results. By taking snapshots of a series of attempts, you can compare them and select the one you like best as the basis for the remaining work in this lesson.

6 When you get the results you want, choose File > Save.

Creating a custom brush

Now that you've tried out the maple-leaf and dune-grass brush shapes, you may be wondering about other similar brushes you could use in your work. With Photoshop CS, you can create and save brushes in any shape you choose, even using other photographs as the basis of your custom brush shapes. You can then set options for the brush.

1 Choose File > Open, and open the Flower.jpg file in the Lessons/Lesson 08 folder.

2 Choose Edit > Define Brush. In the Brush Name dialog box, type **Flower**, and click OK. The Flower brush appears in the Brushes palette and is selected.

3 Close the Flowers.jpg image file.

4 In the Brushes palette, click Brush Tip Shape near the top of the left side of the palette. Then, on the right side, drag the sliders or type to set the Diameter value at **25** and the Spacing at **80%**.

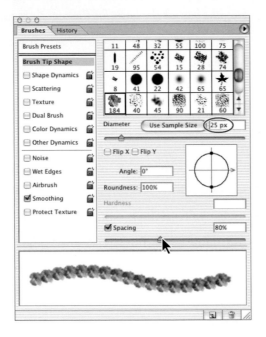

5 On the left side of the palette, click Shape Dynamics. Then, on the right side, set the following options:

- In the Control pop-up menu, select Off.
- For Roundness Jitter, drag the slider or type **44%**.

• For Minimum Roundness, drag the slider or type **39%**.

6 Once more on the left side of the palette, click Scattering, and use the slider or type to set the Scatter value at **500%** and the Count at **1**.

7 Finally, click Color Dynamics on the left side of the palette and change the Hue Jitter to **15%**.

Your brush is now ready for show business.

Painting with a custom brush

You're going to use your custom flower brush to paint a design on the fabric of the umbrella. To prevent yourself from accidentally painting the other parts of the image, you'll use another alpha channel, in the same way that you used alpha channels when you painted the shadings into the umbrella earlier in this lesson.

1 In the Layers palette, click the Umbrella layer set to make it active, and then click the arrow to expand it so that you can see the five layers nested in that set.

2 Click the New Layer button (⬛) at the bottom of the Layers palette. Double-click the new layer, which appears at the top of the layers in the Umbrella layer set, and type **Flowers** to name the layer.

3 Drag the Flowers layer down in the Layers palette so that it is between the Frame layer and the Wet_Dk blue layer.

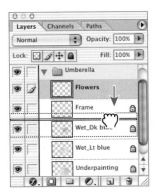

4 Choose Select > Load Selection, and then select the Alpha 4 option from the pop-up menu in the Load Selection dialog box, and click OK.

This alpha channel selects the entire umbrella shape. Remember that you can hide the selection marquee using Ctrl+H (Windows) or Command+H (Mac OS) if you prefer not to be distracted by the movement in the marquee.

5 Make sure that the Brush tool is still selected in the toolbox and that the Flower brush is still selected in the Brushes palette.

6 In the Color palette or Swatches palette, select a bright red color.

7 Using a series of short brush strokes, paint flowers onto the surface of the umbrella, creating a random pattern of fairly uniform density. Continue painting until you are satisfied with the result.

8 In the Layers palette, keep the Flowers layer selected and select Multiply from the blending-mode pop-up menu. Then set the Opacity value for the layer to **70%**.

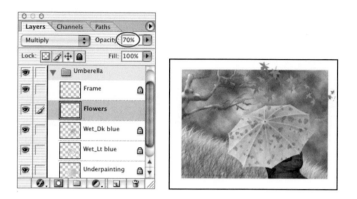

9 Choose File > Save.

Using the Pattern Maker to create a picture frame

In previous versions of Photoshop you could generate tiled patterns, but the new Pattern Maker in Photoshop CS marks a significant improvement in this functionality. Using this new feature, you can generate multiple, seamless patterns that you can use anywhere in your images.

Defining a new pattern

You'll use a prepared texture file as the basis of your custom pattern.

1 Choose File > Open, and open the Texture.jpg file in your Lessons/Lesson08 folder.

2 In the toolbox, make sure that the background color is white, and then choose Image > Canvas Size.

3 In the Canvas Size dialog box, change the units to pixels, and set Width at **780** and Height at **580**. Then click OK.

4 Choose Filter > Pattern Maker.

5 In the Pattern Maker dialog box, use the rectangular marquee tool (⬚) in the upper left corner of the dialog box to select a large area of the textured image. Be careful not to include any of the white background in your selection.

💡 *If you want to change your selection, hold down Alt (Windows) or Option (Mac) and click the Reset button in the upper right corner of the Pattern Maker dialog box (which appears as the Cancel button when you release Alt/Option); then make a new selection.*

6 Click the Generate button.

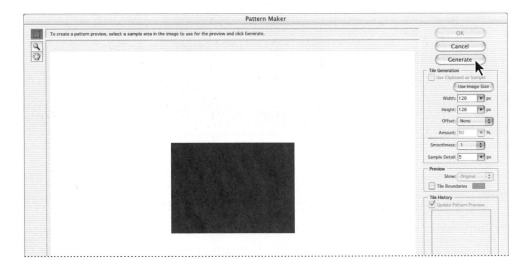

Notice the dimension information listed in the dialog box. The default tile size is 128x128 pixels, so that is the size of the pattern generated.

7 Under Preview (on the right side of the dialog box), select the Tile Boundaries check box.

A grid appears over your pattern, displaying the boundaries of the individual pattern tiles, each 128x128 pixels. Click the Tile Boundaries check box again to deselect it and hide the grid.

8 Under Tile Generation (on the right side of the dialog box), click the Use Image Size button so that the tile size matches the image size. Notice that the dimensions in the Width and Height displays are now the same as the dimensions of the image.

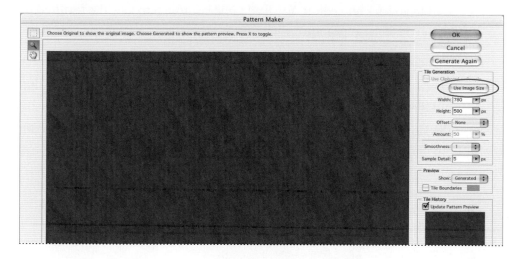

9 Click the Generate Again button a few times to generate variations of your pattern. Then, use the Previous and Next buttons at the bottom of the Tile History area of the dialog box to cycle through the patterns you've created. Select one of the patterns to use, and click OK.

In the image window, a new, seamless pattern fills the entire canvas.

10 Choose File > Save As, and name the file **Matte.psd**, saving it in your Lessons/Lesson08 folder.

Patterns can be saved and used repeatedly in any number of projects. Because you'll use this pattern just once, you won't bother to save it as a permanent pattern.

Composing the patterned image with your painting

This is it—the final phase of your work. Because you're going to flatten the painting image as part of the process, you'll create a duplicate of the original as a safeguard, in case you ever need to go back and edit it. You'll add one last touch to give the textured picture frame a dimensional appearance.

1 Click the image window for your umbrella painting to make it active.

2 Choose Image > Duplicate to create a duplicate image file, and name the duplicate **Autumn_flat.psd**. Click OK.

3 In the Layers palette menu, choose Flatten Image to combine all the layers in the Autumn_flat file.

4 In the toolbox, select the Move tool (⊕).

5 Hold down Shift and drag the painting from the Autumn_flat.psd image window into the Matte.jpg image window. The flattened painting appears as Layer 1 in the Matte.jpg Layers palette.

Holding down the Shift key as you drag in the painting image automatically centers it in the Matte.jpg image, so that the textured picture frame is equally sized around the painting.

6 With Layer 1 selected in the Layers palette, click the Add A Layer Style button (⊘) at the bottom of the palette to open the pop-up menu, and choose Inner Shadow.

7 In the Layer Style dialog box, set the Inner Shadow options, with the Opacity value at **85%**, the Distance at **6**, and the Size at **7**. Leave the other settings unchanged, and click OK.

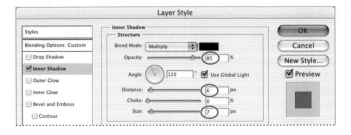

Congratulations; you've finished your painting. You can save your file or print it on a color printer as a souvenir.

This lesson represents just the tip of the metaphorical iceberg in terms of the potential of the painting tools. For more information, see the painting topics in Photoshop Help.

Review questions

1 What is a blending mode, and what are the three types of color that are helpful for visualizing a blending mode's effect?

2 What do the History palette, Eraser tool, and History Brush tools have in common?

3 What is the difference between the Art History Brush tool and the History Brush tool?

4 Describe two techniques for protecting transparent areas.

5 How can you add to your brush collection?

Review answers

1 A blending mode controls how pixels in an image are affected by the tools or other layers. It's helpful to think in terms of the following colors when visualizing a blending mode's effect:

• The *base color* is the original color in the image.

• The *blend color* is the color being applied with the painting or editing tool.

• The *result color* is the color resulting from the blend.

2 The History palette, Eraser tool, and History Brush tools can all restore your image to an earlier state, so that you can undo an operation or correct a mistake.

3 The Art History Brush tool paints with a stylized stroke based on a selected state or snapshot. The stylized stroke of the Art History Brush tool simulates the look of different paint styles. The History Brush tool paints a copy of the selected state or snapshot into the current image window. You can use the History Brush tool to remove the strokes made with the Art History Brush tool.

4 One method of preserving areas of transparency on a layer that you are painting is to use the Lock Transparent Pixels option—one of four Lock options on the Layers palette. A second method is to create a new layer above the layer with the transparent pixels that you want to protect and then to group the new layer with the layer below it. With the layers grouped, you can paint freely on the new layer because the paint applies only to areas with colored pixels in the underlying layer.

5 Two ways of adding to the default set of available brushes are to load additional brush libraries and to create new custom brush shapes. Adobe Photoshop CS includes a number of brush libraries that are available but not loaded by default, keeping the number of brushes on the Brushes palette down to a manageable number. You can switch from one library of brushes to another, or you can open more libraries and append them to the current set. You can define custom libraries that include the brushes you use most often, just as you can define custom brush shapes to suit your work needs. For more information, see "Managing libraries with the Preset Manager" in Photoshop Help.

1-1: Toolbox overview

The marquee tools *make rectangular, elliptical, single row, and single column selections.*

The Move tool *moves selections, layers, and guides.*

The lasso tools *make freehand, polygonal (straightedged), and magnetic* (snap-to) selections.*

The Magic Wand tool *selects similarly colored areas.*

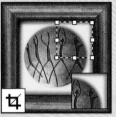

The Crop tool *trims images.*

The Slice tool *creates slices.*

The Slice Select tool *selects slices.*

The Healing Brush tool* *paints with a sample or pattern to repair imperfections in an image.*

The Patch tool* *repairs imperfections in a selected area of an image using a sample or pattern.*

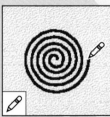

The Color Replacement tool* *substitutes one color for another.*

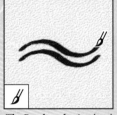

The Brush tool *paints brush strokes.*

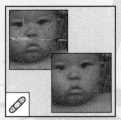

The Pencil tool *paints hard-edged strokes.*

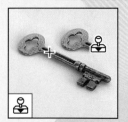

The Clone Stamp tool *paints with a sample of an image.*

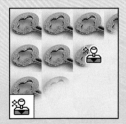

The Pattern Stamp tool* *paints with a part of an image as a pattern.*

The History Brush tool* *paints a copy of the selected state or snapshot into the current image window.*

The Art History Brush tool* *paints stylized strokes that simulate the look of different paint styles, using a selected state or snapshot.*

* Photoshop only
$ ImageReady only

The Eraser tool *erases pixels and restores parts of an image to a previously saved state.*

The Magic Eraser tool *erases solid-colored areas to transparency with a single click.*

The Background Eraser tool * *erases areas to transparency by dragging.*

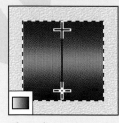

The gradient tools *create straight-line, radial*, angle*, reflected*, and diamond* blends between colors.*

The Paint Bucket tool *fills similarly colored areas with the foreground color.*

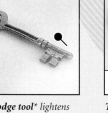

The Blur tool * *blurs hard edges in an image.*

The Sharpen tool * *sharpens soft edges in an image.*

The Smudge tool * *smudges data in an image.*

The Dodge tool * *lightens areas in an image.*

The Burn tool * *darkens areas in an image.*

The Sponge tool * *changes the color saturation of an area.*

The path selection tools * *make shape or segment selections showing anchor points, direction lines, and direction points.*

The Type tool *creates type on an image.*

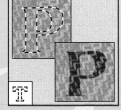

The type mask tools * *create a selection in the shape of type.*

The pen tools * *draw smooth-edged paths.*

The Custom Shape tool * *makes customized shapes selected from a custom shape list.*

* *Photoshop only*
$ *ImageReady only*

The annotations tools * make notes and audio annotations that can be attached to an image.

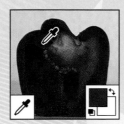

The Eyedropper tool samples colors in an image

The Measure tool * measures distances, locations, and angles.

The Color Sampler tool * samples up to four areas of the image.

The Hand tool moves an image within its window.

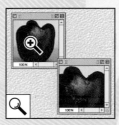

The Zoom tool magnifies and reduces the view of an image.

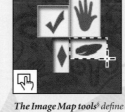

The Image Map tools § define image map areas in an image.

The Image Map select tool § selects image maps.

The Toggle Image Map Visibility tool § toggles between showing and hiding image maps.

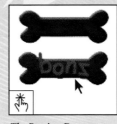

The Toggle Slices Visibility tool § toggles between showing and hiding slices in an image.

The Preview Document tool § previews rollover effects directly in ImageReady.

The Preview In Default Browser tool § previews animations in a Web browser.

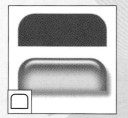

The Tab Rectangle tool § draws a rectangle with rounded upper corners.

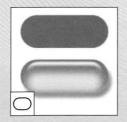

The Pill Rectangle tool § draws a rectangle with all corners rounded.

* *Photoshop only*
§ *ImageReady only*

3-1: **Removing a color cast**

Before Auto Color command

After Auto Color command

3-2: **Adjusting saturation with the sponge tool**

Before Sponge tool

After Sponge tool

6-1: **Selecting in Standard mode and Quick Mask mode**

Lesson 5 start file

Standard mode

Quick Mask mode
A. Selected areas
B. Hidden areas

6-2: **Painting in Quick Mask mode**

Quick Mask mode

Painting with white

Resulting selection

Painting with black

Resulting selection

6-3: **Extracting an object from its background**

Highlighting edges of foxtail tip

Filling highlighted tip area

6-4: **Extracting an intricate image**

Highlighting weed edges

Selecting top third of weeds

8-1: **Layer blending mode samples**

Layer 1

Background

Normal

Dissolve, 70% opacity

Darken

Multiply

Color Burn

Linear Burn

Lighten

Screen

Color Dodge

Linear Dodge

Overlay

Soft Light

Hard Light

Vivid Light

Linear Light

8-1: **Layer blending mode samples (cont.)**

Pin Light

Difference

Exclusion

Hue

Saturation

Color

Luminosity

8-2: **Application of brush strokes to background using blending modes**

Original

Normal

Dissolve, 70% opacity

Darken

Multiply

Color Burn

Linear Burn

Lighten

Screen

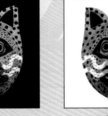

Color Dodge

Linear Dodge

Overlay

Soft Light

Hard Light

Vivid Light

Linear Light

Pin Light

Difference

Exclusion

Hue

Saturation

Color

Luminosity

Original

Behind

Clear

12-1: **Hand-coloring selections on a layer**

Original

After desaturating a selection

After hand-painting the selection

After adding a gradient fill to a selection

16-1: **Optimized continuous-tone images**

GIF, 128 colors,
88% dither

GIF, 128 colors,
No dither

GIF, 32 colors,
88% dither

GIF, 32 colors,
No dither

GIF, 64 colors,
88% dither

GIF, 64 colors,
No dither

GIF, Web palette,
auto colors

JPEG, Quality 60

JPEG, Quality 10

16-2: **Optimized solid graphics**

GIF, 128 colors,
88% dither

GIF, 128 colors,
No dither

GIF, 32 colors,
88% dither

GIF, 32 colors,
No dither

GIF, 64 colors,
88% dither

GIF, 64 colors,
No dither

GIF, Web palette,
auto colors

JPEG, Quality 60

JPEG, Quality 10

19-1: **Setting the monitor's white point**

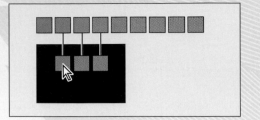

A shade cooler

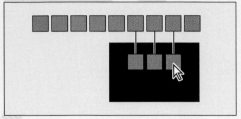

A shade warmer

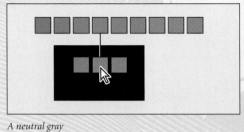

A neutral gray

20-1: **: RGB image with red, green, and blue channels**

20-2: CMYK image with cyan, magenta, yellow, and black channels

20-3: Color gamuts

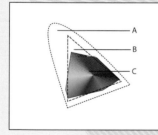

A. *Natural color gamut*
B. *RGB color gamut*
C. *CMYK color gamut*

20-4: RGB color model

20-5: CMYK color model

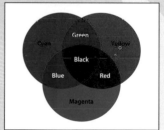

9 | Basic Pen Tool Techniques

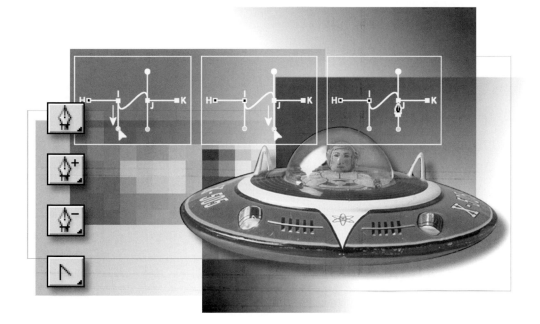

The Pen tool draws precise straight or curved lines called paths. You can use the Pen tool as a drawing tool or as a selection tool. When used as a selection tool, the Pen tool always draws smooth, anti-aliased outlines. These paths are an excellent alternative to using the standard selection tools for creating intricate selections.

In this lesson, you'll learn how to do the following:

• Practice drawing straight and curved paths using the Pen tool.

• Save paths.

• Fill and stroke paths.

• Edit paths using the path-editing tools.

• Convert a path to a selection.

• Convert a selection to a path.

This lesson will take about 50 minutes to complete. The lesson is designed to be done in Adobe Photoshop. Adobe ImageReady does not have a Pen tool and does not support paths.

If needed, remove the previous lesson folder from your hard drive, and copy the Lesson09 folder onto it. As you work on this lesson, you'll overwrite the start files. If you need to restore the start files, copy them from the *Adobe Photoshop CS Classroom in a Book* CD.

Note: Windows 2000 users need to unlock the lesson files before using them. For more information, see "Copying the Classroom in a Book files" on page 3.

Getting started

You'll start the lesson by viewing a copy of the finished image that you'll create. Then, you'll open a series of template files that guide you through the process of creating straight paths, curved paths, and paths that are a combination of both. In addition, you'll learn how to add points to a path, how to subtract points from a path, and how to convert a straight line to a curve and vice versa. After you've practiced drawing and editing paths using the templates, you'll open an image of a toy space ship and get more practice in making selections using the Pen tool.

1 Start Adobe Photoshop, holding down Ctrl+Alt+Shift (Windows) or Command+Option+Shift (Mac OS) to restore the default preferences. (See "Restoring default preferences" on page 4.)

As messages appear, select Yes to confirm that you want to reset preferences, No to defer setting up your color monitor, and Close to close the Welcome Screen.

2 On the tool options bar, select the File Browser button ( ) to open the File Browser.

3 In the File Browser Folders palette, go to the Lessons/Lesson09 folder and then select the 09End.psd file in the thumbnails pane so that it appears in the Preview palette.

The 09End file represents the finished state of the flying-saucer image, which you'll begin working on when you reach "Using paths with artwork" on page 322, after you finish practicing on the drawing templates. (If you are already skilled at drawing vector graphics in other programs, such as Adobe Illustrator, you can skim through the first part of this lesson to note the locations of the Photoshop tools and settings, and then start working on the flying-saucer exercise.)

4 Double-click the Straight.psd thumbnail to open it in Photoshop.

5 If desired, select the Zoom tool ( ), and click or drag over the image to magnify the view.

About paths and the Pen tool

The Pen tool draws straight and curved lines called *paths*. A path is any contour or shape you draw using the Pen tool, Magnetic Pen tool, or Freeform Pen tool. Of these tools, the Pen tool draws paths with the greatest precision; the Magnetic Pen tool and Freeform Pen tool draw paths as if you were drawing with a pencil on paper.

Press P on the keyboard to select the Pen tool. Pressing Shift+P repeatedly toggles between the Pen and Freeform Pen tools. (In this lesson, you'll stay with the regular Pen tool.)

Paths can be open or closed. Open paths have two distinct endpoints. Closed paths are continuous; for example, a circle is a closed path. The type of path you draw affects how it can be selected and adjusted.

Paths that have not been filled or stroked do not print when you print your artwork. (This is because paths are vector objects that contain no pixels, unlike the bitmap shapes drawn by the Pencil tool and other painting tools.)

Before you start drawing, you'll configure the Pen tool options and your work area in preparation for the procedures in this lesson.

1 In the toolbox, select the Pen tool (✒).

2 In the tool options bar, select or verify the following option settings:

• Select the Paths (▨) option.

• Click the arrow for Geometry Options and make sure that the Rubber Band check box is *not* selected in the Path Options pop-up palette.

• Make sure that the Auto Add/Delete option is selected.

• Select the Add To Path Area option (▣).

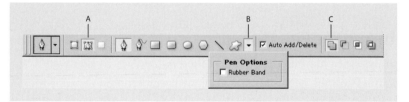

*A. Paths option **B.** Geometry Options menu **C.** Add To Path Area option*

3 Click the Paths palette tab to bring the palette to the front of the Layers palette group.

The Paths palette displays thumbnail previews of the paths you draw. Currently, the palette is empty because you haven't started drawing.

Drawing straight paths

Straight paths are created by clicking the mouse button. The first time you click, you set a starting point for a path. Each time that you click (thereafter), a straight line is drawn between the previous point and the current point.

1 Using the Pen tool, position the pointer on point A in the template and click the Pen tool. Then click point B to create a straight-line path.

As you draw paths, a temporary storage area named Work Path appears in the Paths palette to keep track of the paths you draw.

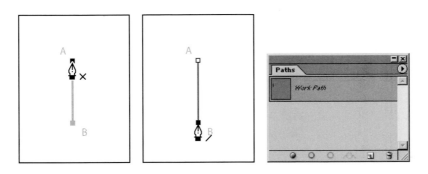

2 End the path in the image by clicking the Pen tool (✒) in the toolbox.

The points that connect paths are called *anchor points*. You can drag individual anchor points to edit segments of a path, or you can select all the anchor points to select the entire path.

3 In the Paths palette, double-click the Work Path to open the Save Path dialog box. For Name, type **Straight Lines**, and click OK to rename and save the path.

The path remains selected in the Paths palette.

Saving a work path is a good habit to acquire and a necessity if you use multiple discrete paths in the same image file. If you deselected an existing Work Path in the Paths palette and then started drawing again, a new work path would replace the original one, which would be lost.

However, if you deselect a Work Path in the Paths palette, the Work Path and your drawing on it remain there while you perform other non-drawing tasks. You can also reselect the Work Path and continue to add to your drawing.

About anchor points, direction lines, direction points, and components

A path consists of one or more straight or curved segments. Anchor points mark the endpoints of the path segments. On curved segments, each selected anchor point displays one or two direction lines, ending in direction points. The positions of direction lines and points determine the size and shape of a curved segment. Moving these elements reshapes the curves in a path.

A path can be closed, with no beginning or end (for example, a circle), or open, with distinct endpoints (for example, a wavy line).

Smooth curves are connected by anchor points called smooth points. Sharply curved paths are connected by corner points.

When you move a direction line on a smooth point, the curved segments on both sides of the point adjust simultaneously. In comparison, when you move a direction line on a corner point, only the curve on the same side of the point as the direction line is adjusted.

A path does not have to be one connected series of segments. It can contain more than one distinct and separate path component. Each shape in a shape layer is a path component, as described by the layer's clipping path.

Moving and adjusting paths

You use the Direct Selection tool to select and adjust an anchor point, a path segment, or an entire path.

1 Select the Direct Selection tool (▸), hidden under the Path Selection tool (▸) in the toolbox.

💡 *To select the Direct Selection tool by using a keyboard shortcut, press A. Also, when the Pen tool is active you can temporarily switch to the Direct Selection tool by holding down Ctrl (Windows) or Command (Mac OS).*

2 Click the A-B path in the window to select it, and then move the path by dragging anywhere on the path using the Direct Selection tool.

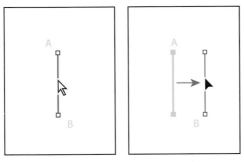

Selecting a path   *Moving a path*

3 To adjust the slope or length of the path, drag one of the anchor points with the Direct Selection tool.

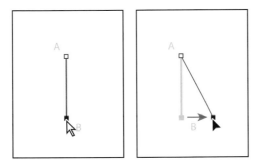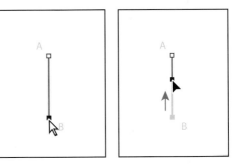

Adjusting the path angle   *Adjusting the path length*

4 Select the Pen tool (✒).

5 To begin the next path, hold the pointer over point C so that an *x* appears in the Pen tool pointer, indicating that clicking will start a new path; then click point C.

6 Click point D to draw a path between the two points.

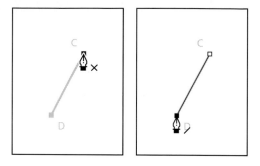

7 End the path using either of the following methods:

• Click the Pen tool in the toolbox.

• Hold down Ctrl (Windows) or Command (Mac OS) to temporarily switch to the Direct Selection tool, and then click away from the path.

Drawing straight paths with multiple segments

So far, you've worked only with two-point paths. You can draw complex straight-segment paths with the Pen tool simply by continuing to add points. These segments and anchor points can be moved later, either individually or as a group.

1 Using the Pen tool (✒), click point E to begin the next path. Then, hold down Shift and click points F, G, H, and I. Holding down Shift as you click restricts the positions along 45° angles.

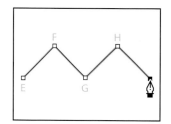

Note: *If you make a mistake while you're drawing, choose Edit > Undo to undo the last-placed anchor point. Then try again.*

2 End the path using one of the methods you've learned.

When a path contains more than one segment, you can drag individual anchor points to adjust individual segments of the path. You can also select all of the anchor points in a path to edit the entire path.

3 Select the Direct Selection tool (▶).

4 Click a segment of the zigzag path and drag to move the whole segment. As you drag, both anchor points for that segment move and the connecting segments adjust accordingly. The length and slope of the selected segment and the positions of the other anchor points do not change.

5 Select one of the individual anchor points on the path and drag it to a new position. Notice how this changes the adjacent segment or segments of the path.

6 Alt-click (Windows) or Option-click (Mac OS) to select the entire path. When an entire path is selected, all the anchor points are solid.

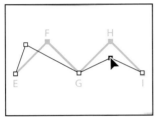
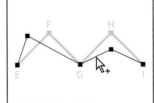

Dragging individual points   *Alt/Option-clicking to select entire path*

7 Drag the path to move the entire path without changing its shape.

Creating closed paths

Next, you'll draw a closed path. Creating a closed path differs from creating an open path in the way that you end the path.

1 Select the Pen tool (◊).

2 Click point J to begin the path; then click point K and point L.

3 To close the path, position the pointer over the starting point (point J), and click.

When you position the pointer over the starting point of a path (J), a small circle appears with the Pen tool, indicating that the path will be closed when you click.

Closing a path automatically ends the path. After the path closes, the Pen tool pointer again appears with a small x, indicating that your next click would start a new path.

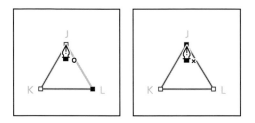

4 For more practice, draw another closed path, using the star-shape template.

5 Examine the thumbnail in the Paths palette.

At this point, all of the paths you've drawn appear in the Straight Lines work path in the Paths palette. Each individual path on the Straight Lines path is called a *subpath*.

Painting paths

Paths and anchor points are non-printing elements of the image. Because the black lines you see on-screen as you draw with the Pen tool are paths—not strokes—they do not represent any pixels in the image. When you deselect a path, the anchor points and path are hidden.

You can make a path visible in your printed image by painting the stroke, which adds pixels to the image. *Stroking* paints color along the path. *Filling* paints the interior of a closed path by filling it with color, an image, or a pattern. To stroke or fill a path, you must first select it.

1 Click the Swatches palette tab to bring the palette forward. Click any swatch (except white) to select a foreground color to use to paint the path.

2 Select the Direct Selection tool (⬚), and click to select the zigzag line in the image window.

3 On the Paths palette menu, choose Stroke Subpath to open the Stroke Subpath dialog box.

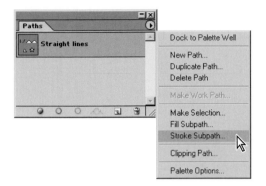

4 For Tool, select Brush from the pop-up menu, and click OK.

The path is stroked with the current brush settings.

Note: You can select a painting tool and set attributes before you select the tool in the Stroke Subpath dialog box.

Now you'll fill one of the paths.

5 Click the triangular closed path with the Direct Selection tool. Then, choose Fill Subpath from the Paths palette menu. The Fill Subpath dialog box appears.

6 In the Fill Subpath dialog box, click OK to accept the defaults.

The triangular path is filled with the foreground color.

7 To hide the paths, click the empty area below the path names in the Paths palette.

8 Choose File > Close, and don't save changes.

Drawing curved paths

Curved paths are created by clicking and dragging. The first time you click and drag, you set a starting point for the curved path and also determine the direction of the curve. As you continue to drag, a curved path is drawn between the previous point and the current point.

When you drag the Pen tool, Photoshop draws *direction lines* and *direction points* from the anchor point. You can use these direction lines and points to adjust the shape and direction of the curve. You'll edit paths using the direction lines and direction points after you practice drawing curved paths.

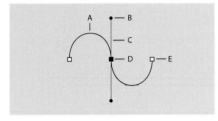

A. *Curved line segment* **B.** *Direction point*
C. *Direction line* **D.** *Selected anchor point*
E. *Unselected anchor point*

Like unpainted paths, direction lines and points do not print when you print your artwork, because they are vector objects that contain no pixels.

1 Use the File Browser or choose File > Open to open the Curves.psd file in the Lessons/Lesson09 folder.

2 Select the Pen tool (ϕ).

3 Drag the Pen tool pointer, starting at point A and stopping at the red dot above it at the tip of the directional line. When you release the mouse button, an anchor point appears at point A and two direction lines extend above and below the anchor point.

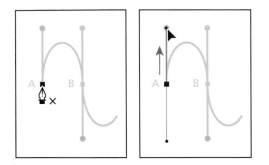

4 Drag from point B to the red dot below it.

Note: If you make a mistake while you're drawing, choose Edit > Undo New Anchor Point to undo the last point you drew, and try again.

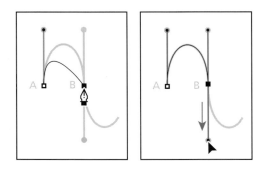

If you hold down Shift as you click and drag, you constrain the slope of the directional line to 45° increments.

5 Complete the curved path by dragging from point C to its red dot and from point D to its red dot. End the path using one of the methods you learned.

Now you'll save the temporary work path so that you don't lose its contents.

6 Double-click the Work Path in the Paths palette to open the Save Path dialog box. In Name, type **Curve 1**, and then click OK.

The named path is selected in the Paths palette.

Creating separate work paths

When you drew straight segments earlier in this lesson, you drew a vertical line, an angled line, a zigzag line, and a closed line (the triangle). All of these lines were *subpaths* of the Straight Lines work path in the Paths palette.

Sometimes you'll want to separate the different lines you draw as entirely distinct named paths, so that you can assign additional properties on the path level. In such a case, you start a new Work Path by first deselecting the current path in the Paths palette and then starting to draw.

1 In the Paths palette, click in the blank area below the Curve 1 path to deselect the path.

Note: When you deselect a path in the Paths palette, any paths or subpaths on it are deselected. This hides them, because paths contain no pixel-altering properties in themselves.

2 Drag up from point E to the red dot. When you release the mouse button, a new Work Path appears in the Paths palette.

3 Drag from point F to its red dot.

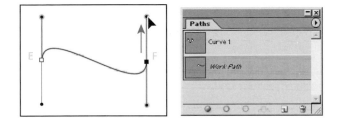

4 End the path using one of the methods you've learned.

5 Double-click the Work Path in the Paths palette to open the Save Path dialog box, type **Curve 2** to name the path, and then click OK.

6 In the Paths palette, click the empty area below Curve 2 to deselect it.

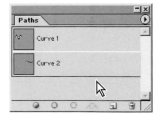

Drawing a closed curve path

In this task, you'll create a circle path, using the techniques you've already learned for drawing curves.

1 Drag up from point G to the red dot; then drag down from point H to the red dot.

2 Close the path by positioning the pointer over point G and clicking (without dragging).

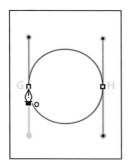

3 In the Paths palette, double-click the Work Path, type **Closed Path** to rename it, and then click away from the path to deselect it.

Modifying curved paths

Now, you'll edit the curved paths you've drawn.

1 Select the Direct Selection tool (⬈).

💡 *Press A to switch to the Direct Selection tool, or hold down Ctrl (Windows) or Command (Mac OS) when the Pen tool is selected to temporarily activate the Direct Selection tool.*

2 In the Paths palette, click Curve 2 to select it; then click the path in the image window to select it.

3 Click point E and then drag one of its two direction points in any direction to change the length, the slope, or both for that direction line.

Notice that the slope of the other direction line for that point also changes so that it is always 180° from the one you're dragging.

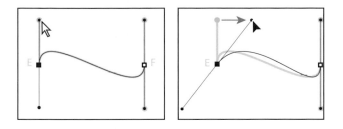

4 Now drag the point E anchor point to change the location of the curve.

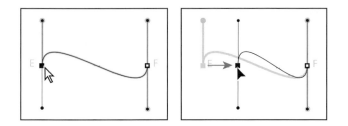

5 Try dragging the segment itself and notice what happens to the direction lines and anchor points.

Stroking and filling paths

Earlier in this lesson, you used the Stroke command on the Paths palette menu to create colored pixels on straight paths. You can stroke or fill paths by dragging a named path onto one of the special buttons at the bottom of the Paths palette. To designate the painting options you want to apply to a path, you'll select a painting tool and paint options before you drag the path onto the appropriate button in the Paths palette.

Note: These buttons on the Path palette apply painting to the entire set of subpaths associated with that path. To apply painting to only some of the subpaths, use the Stroke command instead. See "Painting paths" on page 306.

1 Select the Brush tool ( ).

2 Drag the Curve 1 path onto the Stroke Path With Brush button (○) at the bottom of the Paths palette to stroke the path with the current brush settings.

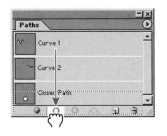

Notice that performing this action does not select the Curve 1 path; the Curve 2 path is still selected in the Paths palette.

If you want to add a fill or stroke to the path that is already selected in the Paths palette, you do not have to drag it to one of the buttons in the Paths palette—you can just click the button you want to apply.

3 In the Paths palette, drag Closed Path onto the Fill Path With Foreground Color button (●) at the bottom of the palette to fill it with the current foreground color.

When you fill an open path, Photoshop automatically draws an invisible line between the starting point and the ending point, and fills the segments between them.

4 In the Swatches palette, select a different color swatch.

5 In the Paths palette, drag the Curve 1 path to the Fill Path With Foreground Color button.

6 Choose File > Close, and don't save changes.

Combining curved and straight path segments

Now that you've learned how to draw straight and curved paths individually, you'll put them together to create paths that combine corner points and smooth ones. Smooth anchor points have directional lines that are opposite each other, 180° apart. Corner points either have no directional lines, only one directional line, or two directional lines that are at an angle that is not 180°.

Combining two curved segments at a sharp angle

One of the more challenging combinations is two curved paths that come together in a corner angle. You'll do that now and discover that it's not so difficult after all.

1 Use the File Browser or choose File > Open to open the Combo.psd file in the Lessons/Lesson09 folder.

2 Select the Pen tool ( ).

3 Drag up from point A to the red dot; then drag from point B downward to the red dot below it.

At point B, you must create a corner point to change the direction of the next curve.

4 Alt-click (Windows) or Option-click (Mac OS) point B to set a corner point.

Notice that the pointer icon includes a small caret arrow when you hold down the Alt or Option key.

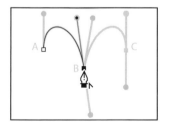

5 Again holding down Alt or Option, drag up from point B to its red dot, to add a direction line. The new line will affect the direction of the curve you'll draw next, when you add another anchor point.

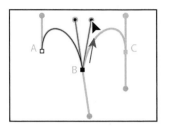

6 Drag down from point C to the red dot to complete the path. End the path using one of the methods you've learned.

Combining curved path segments with straight ones

When you create a path that combines straight and curved lines, you create corner points to indicate the transition from a straight line to a curved line (or vice versa).

In this procedure, you'll draw two separate line segments, creating two differently shaped curves: a half-circle curve and an s-curve. The position of the direction lines for the corner points determines which type of curve you create.

1 To start the second path (which begins with a straight line), click point D with the Pen tool; then, hold down Shift and click point E (don't drag).

Holding down Shift constrains the position so that the segment is perfectly horizontal.

2 Move the pointer over point E and drag to the red dot to set the directional line for the next segment (which will be an upward half-circle curve).

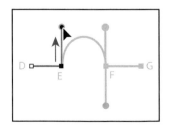

3 Drag from point F to the red dot; then Alt-click (Windows) or Option-click (Mac OS) point F to set a corner point.

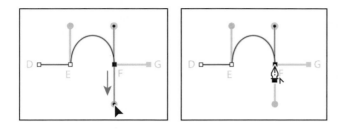

4 Hold down Shift, and click point G to create a straight line. End the path using one of the methods you learned.

5 Click with the Pen tool on point H to start a path for the s-curve; then, hold down Shift and click point I.

6 At point I, Alt-drag (Windows) or Option-drag (Mac OS) down from point I to the red dot to make point I a corner point.

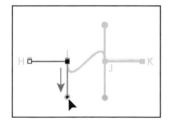

7 Drag down from point J to the red dot.

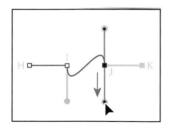

8 Alt-click (Windows) or Option-click (Mac OS) point J to make it a corner point.

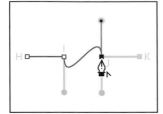

9 Shift-click point K, and then end the path using one of the methods you've learned.

10 Choose File > Close, and don't save changes.

Editing anchor points

One of the advantages of drawing with the Pen tool is that it's easy to go back and alter the paths you've drawn. You've already learned how to move anchor points, segments, and direction lines. In this section, you'll see how easy it is to add new anchor points to an existing path, delete anchor points, and convert different anchor points from one type to another.

Adding and subtracting anchor points

You can add points to a path to increase the number of segments in the path, and you can subtract unneeded or unwanted points from a path.

1 Use the File Browser or choose File > Open to open the Edit.psd file in the Lessons/Lesson09 folder.

Two paths have been named and saved in the Paths palette. You'll edit the paths using the Pen tool and the Convert Point tool.

2 In the Paths palette, click the upper path (named the "Add and delete points" path) to make it the active path. Two subpaths appear in the image window.

3 Select the Add Anchor Point tool (✒️⁺), hidden under the Pen tool (✒️). Then, position the pointer over the red dot at the center of the straight path and click.

An anchor point with direction lines is added to the segment, and the pointer appears as a hollow arrow (▹), so that you can select and manipulate the path.

4 Now select and drag the path upward.

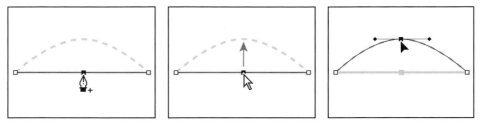

Clicking with the   *Dragging the anchor point*   *Result*
Add Anchor Point tool

Next, you'll subtract an anchor point from a path.

5 Select the Direct Selection tool (⊠) and select the second path.

Note: *You must select a path before you can delete points from it. However, you can select the path and the anchor points without first selecting a tool. If a path is selected, just move the Pen tool over a segment to change it to the Add Anchor Point tool. Move the Pen tool over an end point to change the tool to the Delete Anchor Point tool.*

6 Select the Delete Anchor Point tool (⊠), hidden under the Add Anchor Point tool (⊠), position the pointer on the red dot over the center anchor point, and then click to remove the anchor point.

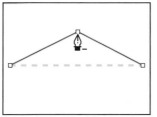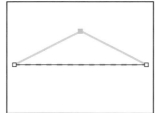

Clicking with the   *Result*
Delete Anchor Point tool

Converting points

Occasionally, you may want to change a curve to a corner point or vice versa. Using the Convert Point tool, you can easily make the adjustment.

Using the Convert Point tool is very much like drawing with the Pen tool. To convert a curve to a corner point, you click the anchor point, and to convert a corner to a curve, you drag from the anchor point.

1 In the Paths palette, select the Convert Directions path.

The shaped path has both corner points and curves. You'll start by converting the corner points to curves, and then you'll convert the curves to corner points.

2 Using the Direct Selection tool (✦), select the outer subpath.

3 Select the Convert Point tool (Ν), hidden under the Delete Anchor Point tool (✎⁻).

4 Position the pointer on a point of the outer path; then click and drag clockwise to convert the point from a corner point to a curve.

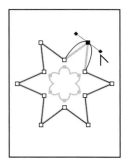

5 Convert the rest of the corner points to smooth points to complete the outer path.

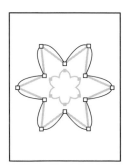

6 Using the Convert Point tool (⌐), click the inner subpath to select it and then click the anchor point at the tips of each curve to convert the curves to corner points.

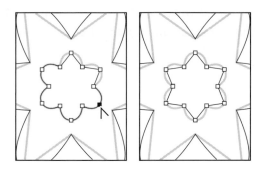

You can also use the Convert Point tool to adjust only one side of a curved segment. You'll try this on the outer path.

7 Click the outer path with the Direct Selection tool (⬆); then, click a curved segment so that direction lines and direction points emanate from the anchor point.

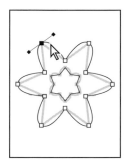

8 Select the Convert Point tool (⌐) again, and drag one of the direction points to change the shape of only one side of the curve.

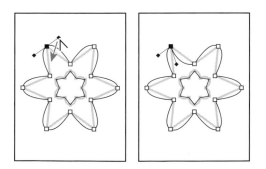

9 Choose File > Close, and don't save changes.

Using paths with artwork

Now that you've had some practice using the templates, you'll use the Pen tool to make selections in the fanciful image of a flying saucer traveling through outer space. The saucer has long, smooth, curved edges that would be difficult to select using other methods.

You'll draw a path around the image and create two paths inside the image. After you've drawn the paths, you'll convert them to selections. Then you'll subtract one selection from the other so that only the saucer and none of the starry sky are selected. Finally, you'll make a new layer from the saucer image and change the image that appears behind it.

Note: *If you want to review the final results of this project, choose File > Open and select the 09End.psd file in your Lessons/Lesson09 folder.*

When drawing a freehand path using the Pen tool, use as few points as possible to create the shape you want. The fewer points you use, the smoother the curves are and the more efficient your file is.

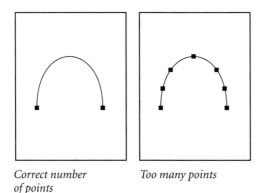

Correct number of points   *Too many points*

Essentially, in this procedure you're going to use the Pen tool to connect the dots from point A to point N and then back to point A, practicing what you learned earlier in this lesson about how to set different kinds of points.

• You'll set some straight segments (by simply clicking the points) at points C, F, J, and M.

• You'll set smooth curve points (by dragging to the red dots) for points A, D, E, G, H, I, K, and L.

• You'll set a corner point for a transition from a curved to a straight segment at point B by first creating a smooth curve point—again, by dragging to the red dots—and then removing one of the directional lines by Alt+clicking (Windows) or Option+clicking (Mac OS) the point itself.

• You'll set a corner point for a transition from a straight to a curved segment at point N by first clicking without dragging to create a corner point, and then holding down Alt or Option and clicking the point.

If you're ready to challenge yourself, you can try to do this task using just the instructions above. Or, follow the steps below first, to be sure that you make all the right moves.

Drawing the outline of a shape

Use the following steps to create a path, outlining the shape of the space ship.

1 Use the File Browser or choose File > Open to open the Saucer.psd file in the Lessons/Lesson09 folder.

2 Select the Pen tool (✒), hidden under the Convert Point tool (⌁).

If necessary, zoom in so that you can easily see the lettered points and red dots on the shape template that has been created for you.

3 Position the pointer on point A, and drag to the red dot to set the first anchor point and the direction of the first curve. Do the same thing at point B.

At the corner of the cockpit (point B), you'll need to make the point a corner point, to create a sharp transition between the curved segment and the straight one.

4 Alt-click (Windows) or Option-click (Mac OS) point B to convert the smooth point into a corner point by removing one of the direction lines.

Setting a smooth point at B   *Converting the smooth point to a corner point*

5 Click point C to set a straight segment (don't drag).

If you make a mistake while you're drawing, choose Edit > Undo to undo the step. Then resume drawing.

6 Drag up from point D to the red dot. Then, drag down from point E to its red dot.

7 Click point F.

8 Set curve points at G, H, and I by dragging from the points to their respective red dots.

9 Click point J.

10 Set curve points at K and L by dragging from each one to its respective red dot.

11 Click point M and then point N.

12 Hold down Alt (Windows) or Option (Mac OS) and drag from point N to the red dot, to add one direction line to the anchor point at N.

13 Move the pointer over point A so that a small circle appears in the pointer icon, and click to close the path. (The small circle may be difficult to see because the image is dark and the circle is faint.)

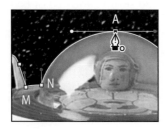

14 In the Paths palette, double-click the Work Path, type **Saucer** in the Name text box, and click OK to save it.

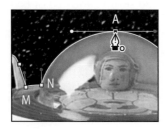

15 Choose File > Save to save your work.

Converting selections to paths

You'll create a second path using a different method. First, you'll use a selection tool to select a similarly colored area, and then you'll convert the selection to a path. (You can convert any selection made with a selection tool into a path.)

1 Click the Layers palette tab to display the palette, and then drag the Template layer to the Trash button at the bottom of the palette. You no longer need this layer.

2 Select the Magic Wand tool (✷).

3 In the Magic Wand tool options bar, make sure that the Tolerance value is **32**.

4 Carefully click the black area inside one of the saucer's vertical fins.

5 Shift+click inside the other fin to add that black area to the selection.

6 Click the Paths palette tab to bring the Paths palette to the front. Then, click the Make Work Path From Selection button () at the bottom of the palette.

The selections are converted to paths, and a new Work Path is created.

Note: If desired, adjust the points on the path, using the tools and techniques you've learned.

7 Double-click the Work Path, and name it **Fins**; then click OK to save the path.

8 Choose File > Save to save your work.

Converting paths to selections

Just as you can convert selection borders to paths, you can convert paths to selections. With their smooth outlines, paths let you make precise selections. Now that you've drawn paths for the space ship and its fins, you'll convert those paths to a selection and apply a filter to the selection.

1 In the Paths palette, click the Saucer path to make it active.

2 Convert the Saucer path to a selection using either of the following methods:

• On the Paths palette menu, choose Make Selection, and then click OK to close the dialog box that appears.

• Drag the Saucer path to the Load Path As Selection button (○) at the bottom of the Paths palette.

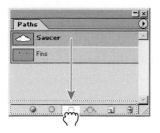

Next, you'll subtract the Fins selection from the Saucer selection, so that you can see the background change through the vacant areas in the fins.

3 In the Paths palette, click the Fins path; then, on the Paths palette menu, choose Make Selection.

4 In the Operation area of the Make Selection dialog box, select Subtract from Selection, and click OK.

The Fins path is simultaneously converted to a selection and subtracted from the Saucer selection.

Leave the paths selected, because you're going to use the selection in the next procedure.

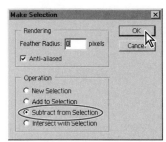

Subtracting the Fins selection   *Result*
from the Saucer selection

Adding layers to complete the effect

Now, just for fun, you'll see how creating the selection with the Pen tool can help you achieve interesting effects in an image. Because you've now isolated the space ship, you can create an exact duplicate of the selection on a new layer. Then, when you add a new object to a layer between the original layer and the duplicate saucer layer, that new object appears to be between the saucer and the starry sky background.

1 In the Layers palette, make sure that the background layer is selected, so that you see the selection outline in the image window. If you deselected it, you need to repeat the previous procedure ("Converting paths to selections" on page 327).

2 Choose Layer > New > Layer Via Copy.

A new layer appears in the Layers palette, named Layer 1. The Layer 1 thumbnail shows that the layer contains only the image of the flying saucer, not the sky areas of the original layer.

3 In the Layers palette, double-click Layer 1 and type **Saucer** to rename the layer.

4 Use the File Browser or choose File > Open to open the Planet.psd file in your Lessons/Lesson09 folder.

This is a Photoshop image of a planet, with a transparent area already defined around it.

5 If necessary, move the image windows so that you can see at least part of both the Saucer.psd window and the Planet.psd window.

6 In the toolbox, select the Move tool (▶⊕), and drag from the Planet.psd image window into the Saucer.psd image window.

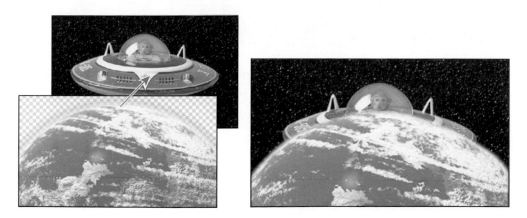

7 Close the Planet.psd image, leaving the Saucer.psd file open and active.

The planet appears to be in front of the space ship. You'll correct that now so that the saucer is flying away from the planet.

8 In the Layers palette, drag the Planet layer between the Saucer layer and the Background layer.

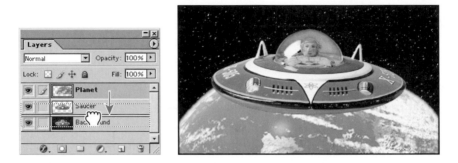

9 Still using the Move tool, drag the Planet layer to change its position in the Saucer.psd window until you are satisfied with the appearance of your composition.

10 Choose File > Save.

You've completed the Basic Pen Tool lesson. Try drawing paths around different objects in your artwork to practice using the Pen tool. With practice, you'll find that the Pen tool can be invaluable for creating intricate outlines and selections.

Review questions

1 How do you modify individual segments of a path?

2 How do you select an entire path?

3 How do you add points to a path?

4 How do you delete points from a path?

5 When you drag with the Pen tool to create a curved path, how does the direction in which you drag affect the curve?

6 How can the Pen tool be useful as a selection tool?

Review answers

1 To modify individual segments of paths, you drag the anchor points on the path using the Direct Selection tool. You can also edit the shape of curved segments by dragging the direction points at the ends of the direction lines that extend from the anchor point of the curve.

2 To select an entire path, hold down Alt (Windows) or Option (Mac OS), and click the path using the Direct Selection tool. When an entire path is selected, all the anchor points are solid.

3 To add points to a path, you select the Add Anchor Point tool, hidden under the Pen tool, and then click the path where you want to add an anchor point.

4 To delete points from a path, you select the Delete Anchor Point tool, hidden under the Pen tool, and then click the anchor point you want to remove from the path.

5 The direction in which you drag with the Pen tool defines the direction of the curve that follows.

6 If you need to create an intricate selection, it can be easier to draw the path with the Pen tool and then convert the path to a selection.

10 | Vector Masks, Paths, and Shapes

Unlike bitmap images, vector images retain their crisp edges at any enlargement. You can draw vector shapes and paths in your Photoshop images and add vector masks to control what is shown in an image. This lesson will introduce you to advanced uses of vector shapes and vector masks.

In this lesson, you'll learn how to do the following:

- Differentiate between bitmap and vector graphics.

- Draw and edit layer shapes and layer paths.

- Describe and use the thumbnails and link icon for a shape layer.

- Create complex layer shapes by combining or subtracting different shapes.

- Combine vector paths to create a shape.

- Use edit mode to add and edit a text layer.

- Use a text layer to create a work path.

- Use a work path to create a vector mask.

- Load and apply custom layer shapes.

This lesson will take at least an hour or an hour and a half to complete. The lesson is designed to be done in Adobe Photoshop, but information on using similar functionality in Adobe ImageReady is included where appropriate.

If needed, remove the previous lesson folder from your hard drive, and copy the Lesson10 folder onto it from the *Adobe Photoshop CS Classroom in a Book* CD.

Note: *Windows 2000 users need to unlock the lesson files before using them. For more information, see "Copying the Classroom in a Book files" on page 3.*

About bitmap images and vector graphics

Before working with vector shapes and vector paths, it's important that you understand the basic differences between the two main categories of computer graphics: *bitmap images* and *vector graphics*. You can use Photoshop or ImageReady to work with either type of graphics; moreover, in Photoshop you can combine both bitmap and vector data in an individual Photoshop image file.

Bitmap images, technically called *raster images*, are based on a grid of colors known as pixels. Each pixel is assigned a specific location and color value. In working with bitmap images, you edit groups of pixels rather than objects or shapes. Because bitmap graphics can represent subtle gradations of shade and color, they are appropriate for continuous-tone images such as photographs or artwork created in painting programs. A disadvantage of bitmap graphics is that they contain a fixed number of pixels. As a result, they can lose detail and appear jagged when scaled up on-screen or if they are printed at a lower resolution than that for which they were created.

Vector graphics are made up of lines and curves defined by mathematical objects called *vectors*. These graphics retain their crispness whether they are moved, resized, or have their color changed. Vector graphics are appropriate for illustrations, type, and graphics such as logos that may be scaled to different sizes.

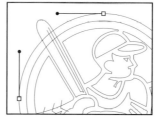

Logo drawn as vector art

Logo rasterized as bitmap art

Getting started

In the previous lesson, you learned how to use the Pen tool to create simple shapes and paths. In this lesson, you'll learn advanced uses of paths and vector masks to create a poster for a fictitious golf tournament. You'll learn how to add text to an image by incorporating the tournament information.

You'll start the lesson by viewing the final image, which is an example of a poster for an early autumn golf tournament.

1 Start Adobe Photoshop, holding down Ctrl+Alt+Shift (Windows) or Command+Option+Shift (Mac OS) to restore the default preferences. (See "Restoring default preferences" on page 4.)

As messages appear, select Yes to confirm that you want to reset preferences, No to defer setting up your color monitor, and Close to close the Welcome Screen.

2 On the tool options bar, select the File Browser button (⬚) to open the File Browser.

3 In the File Browser Folders palette, go to the Lessons/Lesson10 folder and select that folder.

4 Click the 10Start.psd thumbnail and then Shift-click to select the 10End.psd thumbnail.

5 On the File Browser menu bar, choose File > Open to open both files in Photoshop.

If a notice appears asking whether you want to update the text layers for vector-based output, click Update.

Note: The "update text layers" notice might occur when transferring files between computers, especially between Windows and Mac OS.

6 Select each file in turn and examine the display in the image window and the Layers palette listings. If you wish to do so, you can minimize the 10End.psd file by clicking the appropriate button on the file title bar.

7 Close the File Browser.

Now you'll start the lesson by creating a new document for the poster.

Creating the poster background

Many posters are designed to be scalable, either up or down, while retaining a crispness to their appearance. You'll create shapes with paths and use masks to control what appears in the poster.

Adding a colored shape to the background

You'll begin by creating the backdrop for a poster image.

1 If the 10Start.psd file is not still open and selected, do that now.

Some work on the file has been done for you; the image already contains a background layer with a green gradient fill and a series of horizontal and vertical guides. The guides are locked in position. (If you do not see the guides, choose View > Show to open the submenu and make sure that the Guides command is checked, or choose it now.)

2 Choose View > Rulers to display a horizontal and a vertical ruler.

3 In the Layers palette group, drag the tab for the Paths palette out of the palette group. Since you'll be using the Layers and Paths palettes frequently in this lesson, it's convenient to have them separated.

4 In the Color palette, set the foreground RGB color to a deep blue color by typing **0** as the R value, **80** as the G value, and **126** as the B value.

5 On the toolbox, select the Rectangle tool (▢). Then, in the tool options bar, make sure that the Shape Layers option is selected.

6 Drag a rectangle from the intersection of the top and leftmost guides to the intersection of the third horizontal guide (about three-fourths of the way down the image, slightly below the 5-inch mark) and the vertical guide near the right margin of the page.

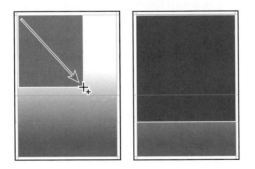

You've created a rectangle with a deep blue fill, set within enough of the edge to form a white border. (If you don't get that result, make sure that you've selected the Rectangle tool—which is below the Type tool on the toolbox—and not the Rectangular Marquee tool. Also, make sure that the Shape Layers option is selected in the tool options bar.)

7 In the toolbox, select the Direct Selection tool (↖), hidden under the Path Selection tool (↖), and click anywhere on the path (edge) of the blue rectangle to select the path, so that selection handles appear in the four corners.

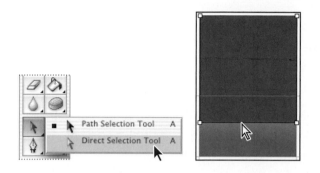

8 Select the lower left handle of the blue shape, being careful to select just the handle and not a path segment.

9 Shift+drag the handle upward to the next horizontal guide (at about the four-inch mark on the ruler) and release the mouse button when the handle snaps into place against the guide.

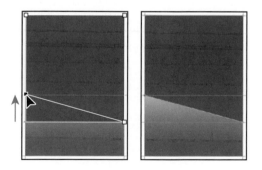

Now the lower edge of the blue shape slopes down from left to right.

10 Choose View > Show > Guides to hide the guides, because you are finished using them for this lesson. You'll be using the rulers again, so do not hide them yet.

11 Click anywhere inside or outside the blue rectangle in the image window to deselect the path and hide its handles.

Notice that the border between the blue shape and the green background has a grainy quality. What you see is actually the path itself, which is a non-printing item. This is a visual clue that the Shape 1 layer is still selected.

About shape layers

A shape layer has two components: a fill and a shape. The fill properties determine the color (or colors), pattern, and transparency of the layer. The shape is a layer mask that defines the areas in which the fill can be seen and those areas in which the fill is hidden.

In the blue layer you've just created, the fill is your dark blue color. The color is visible in the upper part of the image, within the shape you drew, and is blocked in the lower part of the image so that the green gradient can be seen behind it.

In the Layers palette for your poster file, you'll see a new layer, named Shape 1, above the Background layer. There are three items represented along with the layer name: two thumbnail images and an icon between them.

The left thumbnail shows that the entire layer is filled with the deep blue foreground color. The small slider underneath the thumbnail is not functional, but symbolizes that the layer is editable.

The thumbnail on the right shows the vector mask for the layer. In this thumbnail, white indicates the area where the image is exposed, and black indicates the areas where the image is blocked.

The icon between the two thumbnails indicates that the layer and the vector mask are linked.

A. *Fill thumbnail* **B.** *Layer-mask link icon* **C.** *Mask thumbnail*

Subtracting more shapes from a shape layer

After you create a shape layer (vector graphic), you can set options to subtract new shapes from the vector graphic. You can also use the Path Selection tool and the Direct Selection tool to move, resize, and edit shapes. You'll add some stars to your "sky" (the blue rectangle you just created) by subtracting star shapes from the blue shape. To help you position the stars, you'll refer to the Star Guides layer, which has been created for you. Currently, that layer is hidden.

1 In the Layers palette, click the box to the far left of the Star Guides layer to display the eye icon (👁) for that layer (but leave the Shape 1 layer selected). The Star Guides layer is now visible in the image window.

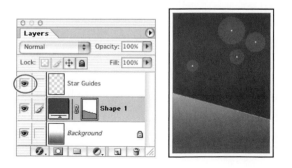

2 In the Paths palette, make sure that the Shape 1 Vector Mask is selected.

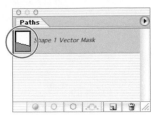

3 In the toolbox, select the Polygon tool (⬭), hidden under the Rectangle tool (▢).

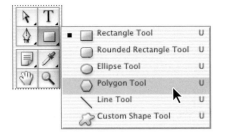

4 In the tool options bar, select the following:

• In Sides, type **9** and press Enter.

• Click the Geometry Options arrow (immediately to the left of the Sides option) to open the Polygon Options. Select the Star check box, and type **70%** in the Indent Sides By option. Then click anywhere outside the Polygon Options to close it.

• Select the Subtract From Shape Area option (⬓) or press either hyphen or minus to select it with a keyboard shortcut. The pointer now appears as crosshairs with a small minus sign (+.).

5 Move the crosshairs pointer over the center of one of the white dots and drag outward until the tips of the star rays reach the edge of the faint circle around the dot.

Note: As you drag, you can rotate the star by dragging the pointer to the side.

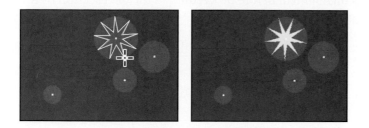

When you release the mouse, the star shape appears to fill with white. However, this is not a fill; the star is a cutout from the blue shape, and the white you see is the background layer underneath it. If the background layer were another image, pattern, or color, that's what you would see inside the star shape.

6 Repeat Step 5 for the other three white dots to create a total of four stars.

Notice that all the stars have grainy outlines, reminding you that the shapes are selected. Another indication that the shapes are selected is that the Shape 1 vector mask thumbnail is highlighted (outlined in white) in the Layers palette.

7 In the Layers palette, click the eye icon for the Star Guides layer to hide it.

Notice how the thumbnails have changed in the palettes. In the Layers palette, the left thumbnail is as it was, but the mask thumbnails in both the Layers palette and Path palette show the slant of the blue shape with the star-shaped cutouts.

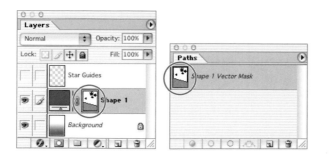

Deselecting paths

Deselecting paths is sometimes necessary to see the appropriate tool options bar when you select a vector tool. Deselecting paths can also help you view certain effects that might be obscured if a path is highlighted. Before proceeding to the next section of this lesson, you'll make sure that all paths are deselected.

1 Select the Path Selection tool (➤), which is currently hidden under the Direct Selection tool (➤).

2 In the tool options bar, click the Dismiss Target Path button (✔).

Note: An alternate way to deselect paths is to click in the blank area below the paths in the Paths palette.

Your paths are now deselected and the grainy path lines have disappeared, leaving a sharp edge between the blue and green areas. Also, the Shape 1 Vector Mask is no longer highlighted in the Paths palette.

Drawing paths

Next, you'll add more elements to your poster, but you'll work with these elements on different layers. Throughout this lesson, you'll create new layers so you can draw, edit, paste, and reposition elements on one layer without disturbing other layers.

Before you begin, make sure that the Shape 1 layer is still selected in the Layers palette.

1 In the Layers palette, click the New Layer button (⬒) at the bottom of the palette to create a new layer.

A new layer, named Layer 1, appears above the Shape 1 layer in the Layers palette and is automatically selected.

2 Select the Ellipse tool (◯), which is currently hidden under the Polygon tool (◯).

3 In the tool options bar, select the Paths option (▨).

4 Start dragging the Ellipse tool in the upper left area of the poster and then hold down Shift as you continue dragging. Release the mouse button when the circle is close to the bottom edge of the blue shape.

5 Hold down Shift and draw a second circle within the first.

6 Compare the sizes and positions of your circles to the 10End.psd image and make any necessary changes:

• To move a circle, select the Path Selection tool (▶) and use it to drag the circle to another location. (If necessary, choose View > Snap To > Guides to deselect this command so that you can move the circles exactly where you want them.)

• To resize a circle, select it with the Path Selection tool and choose Edit > Free Transform Path; then hold down Shift and drag a corner handle to resize the circle without distorting its shape. When you finish, press Enter to apply the transformation.

Note: In the Paths palette, only the new Work Path appears at this time. The Shape 1 Vector Mask that you created earlier (the blue shape with star cutouts) is associated with the Shape 1 layer. Since you are not working on the Shape 1 layer now, that vector mask does not appear in the Paths palette.

Understanding work paths

When you draw a shape in Photoshop, the shape is actually a vector mask that defines the areas in which the foreground color appears. That's why you see two thumbnails in the Layers palette for each shape layer: one for the layer color and a second one for the shape itself (as defined by the layer mask).

A work path is sort of a shape-for-hire: It stands at the ready, independent of any specific layer but available to serve as the basis of a vector mask on a layer. You can use the work path repeatedly to apply it to several different layers.

This concept differs from the approach used by many popular vector-graphics applications, such as Adobe Illustrator, so if you are used to working in that kind of program, this may take some getting used to. It may help you to understand this if you bear in mind that the underlying metaphor behind Photoshop is traditional photography, where the admission of light into a camera lens determines the shapes, colors, and transparencies of the negative, and then darkroom exposure determines what areas of the photographic paper develop into areas of color or darkness and light.

The Paths palette displays only two types of paths. The first type includes any vector paths associated with the currently selected Layer. The other type is the Work Path—if one exists—because it is available to be applied to any layer.

Because a vector path is automatically linked to a layer when you create it, transforming either the layer or the vector path (such as by resizing or distortion) causes both the layer and the vector path to change. Unlike a vector path, a work path is not tied to any specific layer, so it appears in the Paths palette regardless of which layer is currently selected.

7 Using the Path Selection tool ( ), select the second (inner) circle. Then select the Exclude Overlapping Path Areas option ( ) in the tool options bar.

In the Paths palette, the thumbnail now shows a white area only between the two subpaths.

Note: *This may be difficult to see if the palette icons are small. To enlarge them, choose Palette Options on the Paths palette menu and select a larger Thumbnail Size option.)*

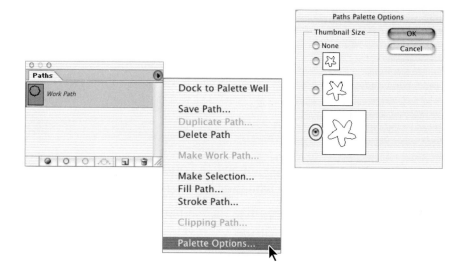

Combining paths into a filled shape

Your next task is to define the two circles as a single element, so that you can add a colored fill.

1 Using the Path Selection tool (⬆), click and Shift-click as necessary to select both of the circle paths.

2 In the tool options bar, click the Combine button.

The Combine button is now dimmed because the two paths are now treated as one shape.

3 In the toolbox, click the Default Foreground And Background Colors button (■), which is to the lower left of the two larger color swatches and changes them back to black and white.

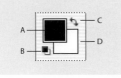

A. *Foreground Color button*
B. *Default Foreground And Background Colors button*
C. *Switch Foreground And Background Colors button*
D. *Background Color button*

4 In the same area of the toolbox, click the Switch Foreground And Background Colors button (↰), so that the foreground is white and the background black.

5 In the Paths palette, drag the work path to the Fill Path With Foreground Color button (●) at the bottom left of the palette.

6 In the Layers palette, change the Opacity to **40**%, either by scrubbing the Opacity label, typing in the text box, or dragging the pop-up slider.

You can try different Opacity values and compare the results they produce.

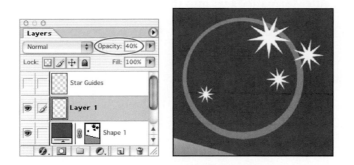

7 If the circle shape is still selected, click the Dismiss Target Path button (✔) in the tool options bar, and then choose File > Save.

Unlike the star-shaped cutouts on the Shape 1 layer, the area between the two circles on Layer 1 now has a white fill. Otherwise, you could not change the opacity of the white area. For example, if you experimented with reducing the layer opacity for the Shape 1 layer, the blue shape would become more transparent, but the stars would remain solid white because that is the color on the layer behind that area of Layer 1.

Working with type

In Adobe Photoshop, you create and edit type directly on-screen (rather than in a dialog box), and quickly change the font, style, size, and color of the type. You can apply changes to individual characters and set formatting options for entire paragraphs. In this part of the lesson, you'll learn about working with type by adding text to your logo.

When you click in an image with the Type tool (T) to set an insertion point, you put the Type tool in *edit mode*. You can then enter and edit characters on the currently targeted layer. Before you can perform other actions or use other tools, you must commit your editing in the layer or cancel it.

For example, if you select another tool in the toolbox, this automatically commits your text changes. Or, on the tool options bar, you can click the Commit Any Current Edits button (✔) to accept the text edits, or click the Cancel Any Current Edits button (⊘) to reject them. Any of these actions takes the Type tool out of edit mode.

Adding type to the image in edit mode

Your first editing task is to enter formatted text into the image.

1 Select the Type tool (**T**), and then choose Window > Character to open the Character palette group.

2 In the Character palette, select the following options:

• For the font family, select a sans serif font (such as Myriad, one of the fonts included on the *Adobe Photoshop CS Classroom in a Book* CD).

• For the font style, select Roman (sometimes called Plain or Regular, depending on the font family you use).

• For the font size (**T**), type **38** pt.

• For the leading (**A**), type **28** pt.

3 In the Character palette group, click the Paragraph palette tab, and then select the Center Text alignment option.

Notice that most of these character and paragraph options are also available in the tool options bar. Of the selections you've made so far, only the Leading option is not there.

4 In the toolbox, make sure that the foreground color is white.

Try the following keyboard shortcuts for setting black and white colors: First, press D. This is the same as clicking the Default Foreground And Background Colors button in the toolbox, which sets the foreground to black and the background to white. Then, press X. This is the same as clicking the Switch Foreground And Background Colors button in the toolbox, which reverses the colors, making the foreground white and the background black.

5 Click the Type tool just below the "horizon" (where the blue rectangle meets the green gradient background) and slightly to the left of center. Then type the following three lines, pressing the Return key so that the lines break as shown:

the full

moon

pro-am

6 Double-click the word *moon* to select it, and then using either the tool options bar or the Character palette, change the font size to **48**.

Note: *If you need to adjust the placement of the text, select the Move tool (▶⊕) and drag the text. Then reselect the Type tool.*

7 Choose File > Save.

Stylizing and warping text

In keeping with the spirit of the tournament, you'll distort the text so that it suggests a full moon. After you warp the text, you can continue to edit it with the Type tool, as needed. Before you begin, make sure that the "the full moon pro-am" text layer is still targeted.

1 With the Type tool (T) selected in the toolbox, click the Create Warped Text button (⊥) on the tool options bar to open the Warp Text dialog box.

2 In the Style pop-up menu, select Inflate and then click OK to close the dialog box, leaving the other settings at the default values.

3 Drag the Type tool to select the words *full* and *moon*.

4 In the Character palette or the tool options bar, select Bold as the font style.

5 Double-click the word *full* to select it (but not the word *moon*).

6 In the Color palette, select a bright yellow color by entering the following values: R=**239**, G=**233**, B=**7**.

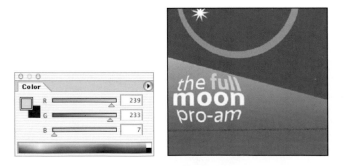

7 In the tool options bar, click the Commit Any Current Edits button (✔) to deselect the text so that you can see the results.

8 Choose File > Save.

When you select the Commit Any Current Edits button, you deselect the text. However, that doesn't mean that the text has to be absolutely final. You can still reselect it later with the Type tool and make additional edits.

Adding a new text layer

You'll get a little more practice using text by adding another word to your poster.

1 In the Layers palette, select Layer 1.

2 With the Type tool (T) selected, click the Default Foreground And Background Colors button to set them to black and white, respectively. (Or, press T and then D to do these.)

3 In the Character palette, select the same sans serif font that you used to type *the full moon pro-am*, select Roman as the font style, **36** as the font size, and **28** as the leading.

4 Click anywhere in the upper area of the poster (so that it is clearly separated from the area of the warped "full moon" text) and type **invitational**.

The word appears in black text in the image window. In the Layers palette, a new, active layer, named Layer 2, is above Layer 1.

5 Select the Move tool (▸⊕) and drag the word *invitational* to center it in the lower part of the image window, just below the "the full moon pro-am" text block.

Notice that the layer name changes from "Layer 2" to "invitational" in the Layers palette.

6 Close the Character palette group.

7 Choose File > Save.

Creating work paths from text

Currently, the word *invitational* appears on a type layer, not as a work path. That's about to change. After you use the type layer to create a work path, you can save the work path and manipulate it like any other path. Because it is a vector path instead of rasterized, the characters maintain their sharp edges.

Before you begin, compare the position of the word *invitational* in the 10End.psd sample file to your file and make sure that it is sized, spelled, and positioned exactly the way you want it to be. After you create the work paths, you won't be able to change the position easily and may have to start the process over if you aren't satisfied with the results.

1 In the Layers palette, make sure that the "invitational" type layer is selected, and then choose Layer > Type > Create Work Path.

On the Paths palette, notice that a new Work Path listing appears, including a thumbnail of the "invitational" text.

2 In the Layers palette, select the "invitational" text layer and drag it to the Delete Layer button (🗑) at the bottom of the palette, and then choose File > Save.

Now, only the grainy outlines of the work path remain to represent the word *invitational*.

Creating work paths from a type layer leaves the original type layer intact and fully editable as text—that is, you can still use the Type tool to select and alter it. However, you are going to use just the work paths to manipulate the shape of the text. You don't want to keep the "invitational" text layer because it would appear in the poster and visually compete with what you're going to create from the work path.

Altering the appearance of the work paths

You can now start working with the new work paths as vector shapes. You'll use the Direct Selection tool, which can be used to edit any path.

1 Zoom in to 200% so that you can easily see the details in the letter L of the word *invitational* and at least an inch of the blue shape directly above it.

2 In the toolbox, select the Direct Selection tool (▶), hidden under the Path Selection tool (▶).

3 In the image window, click the "L" part of the work path.

4 Select the two path points at the top of the L subpath by clicking one of the points and then Shift-clicking the other. (The points appear solid when selected and hollow when not selected.)

5 Start dragging the two points upward and then hold down Shift to constrain the movement, stopping when the L extends to about the level of the lower edge of the shape you created from two circles. The L is now about five or six times as tall as it was originally.

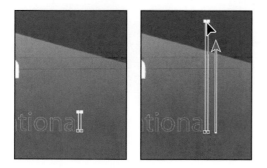

6 Click outside the work path to deselect it, and then zoom out again so that you can see the entire poster.

Double-click the Zoom tool (🔍) to switch quickly to 100% view. To switch to Fit on Screen view, double-click the Hand tool icon (✋).

7 Choose File > Save.

Adding a gradient layer

Right now, your "invitational" element is merely a work path, not something that would show up in print. To start the process of making it appear in the poster, you'll create a gradient layer that you can combine with the work path in the procedure following this one.

1 In the Layers palette, click the New Layer button (⬚) to create a new Layer 2.

2 In the toolbox, select the Gradient tool (▭).

3 Set the foreground to white and the background to black, by pressing D to set the default colors (black and white) and then pressing X to reverse them (white and black).

4 In the tool options bar, click the pop-up arrow to open the gradient picker.

5 Select the second gradient option in the top row (Foreground to Transparent), and then press Enter.

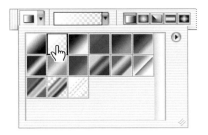

6 Shift-drag the Gradient tool from left to right across the image.

The gradient covers the entire image, with the underlying layers showing through the transparent areas.

Applying a work path to a layer as a vector mask

Your "invitational" work path is not yet applied to any layer. Now, you'll use it to create a vector mask for the gradient layer, limiting the visible area of the gradient fill to the insides of the letter shapes.

1 In the Paths palette, make sure that the Work Path is selected.

2 Choose Layer > Add Vector Mask > Current Path.

The work path becomes the basis of a new layer mask, shown in the thumbnails on Layer 2 in the Layers palette and in the Paths palette, where the mask is identified as "Layer 2 Vector Mask." This mask now hides the gradient in all areas of the image except the area inside the letter shapes of the word *invitational*.

3 Select the Path Selection tool ( ), hidden under the Direct Selection tool ( ), and then click the Dismiss Target Path button (✔) in the tool options bar to deselect all paths.

Note: You can also click the blank area below the paths in the Paths palette to deselect all paths.

4 In the Layers palette, click the link icon ( ) in Layer 2 to unlink the path from the gradient layer.

5 Select the Move tool ( ), and drag left or right in the image to adjust the placement of the gradient behind the vector mask. When you are satisfied with the appearance of the gradient, choose File > Save.

Creating a flag image and more text

In this section, you'll create a light red triangular shape for a flag in one layer and add new text in a separate layer. Before you begin, make sure that Layer 1 is selected in the Layers palette.

1 In the Layers palette, select Layer 2, and then click the New Layer button ( ) to create another layer, Layer 3.

2 Select the Polygon tool ( ), hidden under the Ellipse tool ( ).

3 In the tool options bar, do the following:

• Select Fill Pixels (▫), which is the third of three buttons near the left end of the bar.

• Click the Geometry Options arrow (to the left of the Sides option) to open the Polygon Options pop-up palette. Deselect the Star check box, and then close the pop-up.

• In the Sides option, type **3**.

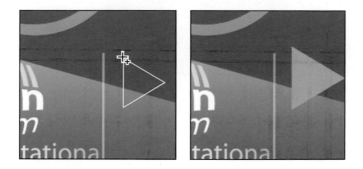

Note: *The Fill Pixels option converts vector graphics into rasterized images. This helps reduce the file size and speeds up processing. The flag image is a good opportunity for using this option.*

4 In the Color palette, set the foreground to a salmon color, using R=**244**, G=**128**, and B=**118**.

5 Hold down Shift and drag the Polygon tool to draw a triangle. Make the triangle large enough to just fit between the word *invitational* and the right edge of the image, and so that the left side of the triangle is parallel to the elongated L.

💡 *You can rotate polygon shapes by changing the angle at which you drag as you create them. Holding down Shift constrains the rotation to specific angles.*

6 Select the Type tool (T), and select the following options in the tool options bar:

• For font family, select the same sans serif font that you used for the word *invitational*.

• For font style, select Bold.

• For font size, select **30** pt.

• Click the text color swatch and select white. Or, you can use the Color palette or the Foreground Color box in the toolbox to select white.

7 Type **oct 2nd** anywhere in the image. This automatically creates a new type layer (Layer 4), which appears immediately above the flag layer (Layer 3).

8 Select the Move tool (⯈₊) and drag the "oct 2nd" text over the triangular flag shape.

When you select the Move tool, Layer 4 is renamed "oct 2nd" in the Layers palette. The text does not fit within the flag area, but you'll fix that next.

9 With the "oct 2nd" layer selected in the Layers palette, choose Edit > Free Transform. Handles now appear around the text element.

10 Drag the center-left and center-right handles as needed to compress the text bounding box so that all the text fits within the triangle. Then press Enter or Return.

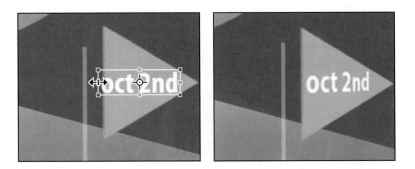

Leave the "oct 2nd" layer selected in the Layers palette for the next task.

Merging and distorting layer combinations

By merging layers, layer paths, vector masks, linked layers, or adjustment layers, you can combine several layers into one and keep your file size manageable. Typically, you want to be sure that you've finalized the characteristics and position of each layer's contents before you merge the layers, so make sure that you're satisfied with the appearance of the flag and the date text before starting this procedure.

1 With the "oct 2nd" layer selected, open the Layers palette menu and choose Merge Down.

The "oct 2nd" layer and polygon-shape layer are now merged into a single layer, Layer 3. From now on, you can no longer use the Type tool to edit the "oct 2nd" graphic.

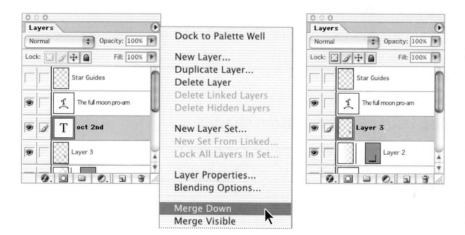

2 With Layer 3 selected, choose Edit > Transform > Distort. To create the illusion of foreshortening, drag the center right handle to the left until the flag is about 1 inch wide.

3 Drag the upper right handle slightly down and the lower right handle slightly up to further enhance the effect of a perspective view.

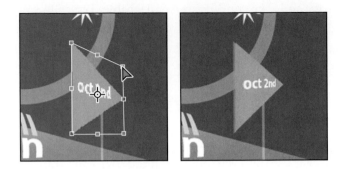

4 Press Enter (Windows) or Return (Mac OS) to apply the transformation.

5 Select the Move tool (▶⊕), and drag the flag shape into position near the top of the stretched letter L in "invitational."

6 Choose File > Save.

Working with defined custom shapes

Whenever you create a shape, you can save it as a custom shape. You can load the saved shape into the Custom Shape picker and use it in other areas of an image or even in different Photoshop projects without having to redraw the shape. This is especially useful when you have logos or other symbolic elements that you use repeatedly and that require multiple steps to create.

Placing a custom shape

A custom shape, representing a golf ball balanced on a tee, has been created for you. In this scenario, the tournament organizers intend to print this image on various types of collateral items—mailing letterheads, registration forms, advertisements, name tags, T-shirts, Web pages, and so forth—that may be printed in different sizes and colors.

You'll now load that shape into your Custom Shape picker and then use it in your poster for the golf tournament.

1 In the toolbox, select the Custom Shape tool ( ), hidden under the Polygon tool ( ).

2 In the tool options bar, click the pop-up arrow for the Shape option to open the custom-shape picker. Then, click the arrow button on the right side of the picker to open the palette menu, and choose Load Shapes.

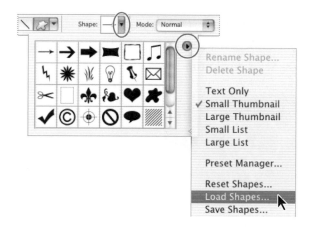

3 In the Load dialog box, go to the Lessons/Lesson10 folder on your hard disk and select Golfball.csh. Click Load.

4 Select the golf-ball shape at the bottom of the custom-shape picker (you may need to scroll or drag the corner of the picker to see the shape), and double-click it to select it and simultaneously close the custom-shape picker.

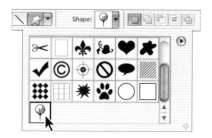

5 In the tool options bar, select the Shape Layers option ( ), which is the first of the three buttons on the left side of the tool options bar.

6 Make sure that the foreground color is white (or select white now), and then hold down Shift and drag diagonally in the image window to draw and size the shape. (Holding down Shift constrains the shape to its original proportions.)

A new layer, Shape 2, is automatically created.

7 Adjust the golf-ball shape as needed:

• To move the shape, select the Path Selection tool ( ) and drag it into position so that the bottom of the golf tee is just to the right of the word *moon*.

• To resize the shape, choose Edit > Free Transform, and Shift-drag one of the corner handles. The golf ball should be about half the height of the poster.

8 When you are satisfied with the golf-ball image, press Enter or click the Dismiss Target Path button (✔) on the tool options bar (if it is available).

Adding layer styles to a custom shape

You're almost finished with your poster project. Right now, your golf-ball shape is simply a composite, solid-white shape, unlike the golf ball you saw in the sample End file. You'll create the same results with very little effort by applying layer styles to the custom shape.

1 In the Layers palette, make sure that the Shape 2 layer is selected.

2 Click the Layer Style button (⊘) at the bottom of the Layers palette, and choose Bevel And Emboss on the pop-up menu that appears.

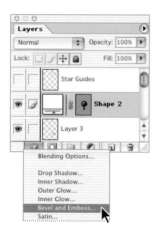

3 Make sure that the Preview check box is selected and then move the Layer Style dialog box so that you can watch the changes to the golf-ball shape as you make style selections.

4 In the Structure area of the Layer Style dialog box, use the following settings:

• For Style, select Inner Bevel.

• For Technique, select Smooth.

• For Depth, type or drag the slider to set the value at about **150**%.

• For Direction, select Up.

• For Size, select **5** px.

• For Soften, type or drag the slider to set the value at **6** px.

Do not close the dialog box yet.

5 In the Shading area of the Layer Style dialog box, select the following settings:

• For Angle, select **–41°** (being careful to make the number negative).

• For Altitude, select **28°**.

Leave the dialog box open for the next step.

6 In the Styles list on the left pane of the Layer Style dialog box, select the Gradient Overlay check box. Do not click OK yet.

7 Also in the Styles list, click the Outer Glow listing so that it is highlighted and its check box is automatically selected. Then select the following settings on the right side of the dialog box:

• In the Structure section, click the color swatch to open the color picker, and select a pale yellow color by setting the following values: R=**255**, G=**255**, B=**190**, and then click OK to close the color picker.

• In the Elements section, leave Technique set as Softer, enter **8%** for Spread, and enter **24** for Size.

8 Review the settings and then click OK to close the dialog box.

Although you opened the Layer Styles dialog box just once, you applied a total of three different layer styles: Bevel and Emboss, Gradient Overlay, and Outer Glow.

9 If necessary, click a blank area in the Paths palette to deselect the Shape 2 Vector Mask, and then save your work.

Congratulations! You've finished your work on the poster.

Review questions

1 What is the difference between a bitmap image and a vector graphic?

2 What does a layer shape do?

3 What tools are used to move and resize paths and shapes?

4 Does the Type tool create vector shapes?

5 What is the purpose of merging layers?

Review answers

1 Bitmap or raster images are based on a grid of pixels and are appropriate for continuous-tone images such as photographs or artwork created in painting programs. Vector graphics are made up of shapes based on mathematical expressions and are appropriate for illustrations, type, and drawings that require clear, smooth lines.

2 A layer shape stores the outline of a shape in the Paths palette. You can change the outline of a shape by editing its path.

3 You use the Path Selection tool (▶) and the Direct Selection tool (▶) to move, resize, and edit shapes. You can also modify and scale a shape or path by choosing Edit > Free Transform Path.

4 No, the Type tool adds text, not vector shapes, to an image. If you want to work with the characters as vector shapes, you must create a work path from the type. A work path is a temporary path that appears in the Paths palette. Once you create a work path from a type layer, you can save and manipulate it like any other path. You cannot edit characters in the path as text. However, the original type layer remains intact and editable.

5 Merging combines several layers into one to keep your file size manageable. When you've finalized the characteristics and positioning of a layer's contents, you can merge that layer with one or more other layers to create partial versions of your composite image.

Lesson 11

11 | Advanced Layer Techniques

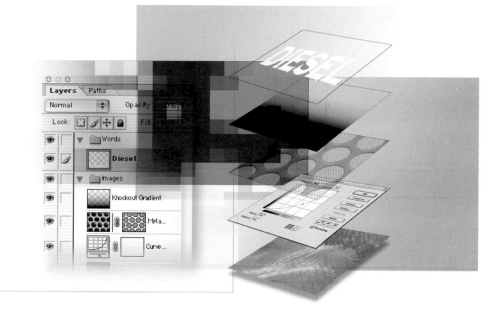

After you've learned basic layer techniques, you can create more complex effects in your artwork using layer masks, path groups, filters, adjustment layers, and more style layers.

In this lesson, you'll learn how to do the following:

• Create clipping groups, with which you can use an image on one layer as a mask for artwork on other layers.

• Create layer sets to organize and manage layers.

• Add adjustment layers to an image, and use them to apply color and tonal adjustments without permanently changing pixel data.

• Create knockout layers to use one layer selectively to reveal others.

• Import layers from other Photoshop files.

• Work with type layers.

• Duplicate and clip layers.

• Add layer styles to a layer, and apply the effects to multiple layers.

• Rasterize layers.

• Convert clipping paths to masks.

• Liquify a layer, giving it a melted appearance.

• Flatten and save layered files, greatly reducing their file size.

This lesson will take less than an hour to complete. The lesson is designed to be done in Adobe Photoshop, but information on using similar functionality in Adobe ImageReady is included where appropriate.

If needed, remove the previous lesson folder from your hard drive, and copy the Lessons/Lesson11 folder onto it. As you work on this lesson, you'll overwrite the start files. If you need to restore the start files, copy them from the *Adobe Photoshop CS Classroom in a Book* CD.

Note: *Windows 2000 users need to unlock the lesson files before using them. For more information, see "Copying the Classroom in a Book files" on page 3.*

Getting started

In this lesson, you'll work with an image that has two layers plus a background layer. You'll get more experience with adjustment layers, layer effects, layer masks, and layer filters. Beyond this lesson, there is no substitute for experimentation and creativity for teaching you what you can do by combining the many filters, effects, layer properties, layer masks, and layer properties in new ways.

1 Start Adobe Photoshop, and immediately hold down Ctrl+Alt+Shift (Windows) or Command+Option+Shift (Mac OS) to restore the default preferences.

As messages appear, select Yes to confirm that you want to reset preferences, No to defer setting up your color monitor, and Close to close the Welcome Screen.

2 Click the File Browser button ( ) and use the Folder palette to go to the Lessons/Lesson11 folder. Select the 11End.psd thumbnail and examine it in the Preview palette. If necessary, enlarge the Preview palette so that you can get a good look.

3 Double-click the 11Start.psd thumbnail to open the file in Photoshop.

4 Close the File Browser, either by clicking the close button or by clicking the File Browser button.

5 Close (or minimize) the Navigator, Color, and History palette groups, and move the Layers palette group to the top of the work area. Drag the corner of the Layers palette group to elongate it so that you'll be able to see about ten layers without scrolling.

Right now, there are only three layers in the palette. Only the Metal Grille layer is visible in the image window. The Rust layer and the Background are stacked underneath it, so the metal grille image blocks your view of these underlying layers.

6 Using the eye icons (👁) in the Layers palette, examine the layers one by one, hiding each of the other layers so that you can see exactly what each layer image looks like.

7 Reset eye icons for all the layers so that all are as they were when you opened the file.

Creating paths to clip a layer

You can use a vector path to clip a layer, creating a sharp-edged mask on that layer. In this part of the lesson, you'll draw a circle and use it to knock out the holes in the metal grille image. This will let you see through the holes to the layers below.

Drawing the vector work path

You'll begin by drawing the basic path on the Metal Grille layer.

1 Click the Metal Grille layer in the Layers palette to select it.

2 Select the Ellipse tool ( ), hidden behind the Rectangle tool ( ). (Be careful not to select the Elliptical Marquee tool.) On the tool options bar, click the Paths option ( ).

3 Move the pointer to the center of one of the holes in the metal grille and start dragging. Then, hold down Shift+Alt (Windows) or Shift+Option (Mac OS) and continue to drag until the circle is the size of the hole. Carefully release the mouse button first, and then release the keyboard keys.

Note: If the circle is not exactly centered when you're done, hold down Ctrl (Windows) or Command (Mac OS) and drag the circle path into position. If the circle fills with black, choose Edit > Undo, and go back to Step 2, making sure that you select the Paths option in the tool options bar.

Next, you'll make copies for the rest of the metal grille.

4 In the toolbox, select the Path Selection tool ( ),which is beside the Type tool, and click to select the circle you just drew.

5 Hold down Alt (Windows) or Option (Mac OS) so that a small plus sign appears below the pointer icon (▶⊕), and then drag the circle to place a copy of the path over another hole in the metal grille.

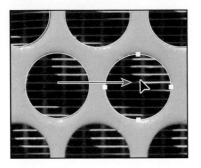

6 Repeat this step to place copies over the remaining holes, including the holes that extend outside the edges of the image.

💡 *When you have position copies of the circle path over several holes, you can Shift-click to select them all, and then Alt-drag or Option-drag to duplicate and move them.*

Note: *You can adjust the position of a selected circle using the arrow keys on the keyboard. You may also find it helpful to choose View > Snap To > and click any of the commands that are checked on the Snap To submenu to deselect them, so that none of these are active.*

Creating a layer mask from the work path

You're ready to use these circles as a layer vector mask.

1 Shift-click to select all 16 circle paths.

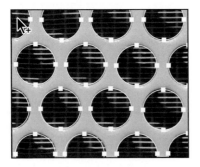

2 In the tool options bar, click the Subtract From Shape Area option ( ), or press hyphen (-) to select it with the keyboard shortcut.

The subtraction option sets up Photoshop to use the circle shapes to define where it will remove pixels from the layer, so that those areas of the Metal Grille layer become transparent when you apply the path as a vector mask.

3 Choose Layer > Add Vector Mask> Current Path.

The Rust layer appears through the holes you cut in the Metal Grille layer. In the Layers palette, a thumbnail of the vector mask appears in the Metal Grille layer.

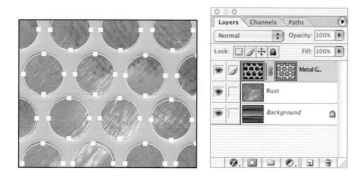

4 Click the Dismiss Target Path button ( ) in the options bar to deselect the multicircle path you created.

5 Choose File > Save to save your work.

Creating layer sets

You have already had some practice with layer sets in earlier lessons in this book. Layer sets help you organize and manage individual layers by grouping them. You can then expand the layer set to view the layers contained in it or collapse the set to simplify your view. You can change the stacking order of layers within a layer set.

Layer sets can function like layers in a number of ways, so that you can not only select, duplicate, and move entire sets of layers, but you can also apply attributes and masks to the entire layer set. Any changes you make at the layer-set level apply to all the layers within the layer set.

In this section, you'll create two layer sets, one for type and another for the metal grille.

1 In the Layers palette, click the Create a New Set button (⬛) twice to create two layer sets.

2 Double-click the name *Set 2* and type **Words**.

3 Double-click the name *Set 1* and type **Images**, and press Enter (Windows) or Return (Mac OS).

4 In the Layers palette, drag the Metal Grille layer onto the folder icon (⬛) for the Images layer set (the name of the Images layer set should be highlighted when you release the dragged layer), and release the mouse button. The Metal Grille layer now appears indented under the Images layer set.

5 Drag the Rust layer to add it to the Images layer set, too. Notice that the Rust layer is also indented and below the Metal Grille layer in the layer set.

6 Choose File > Save.

Using adjustment layers (Photoshop)

You can use an adjustment layer to experiment with color or tonal adjustments to an image without permanently modifying the pixels in the image. The color or tonal changes reside within the adjustment layer, which acts as a veil through which the underlying image layers appear.

Keep in mind that an adjustment layer affects all the layers below it. You can correct multiple layers by making changing the adjustment layer, rather than making the corrections to each layer separately.

Note: *Adjustment layers can be applied and edited only in Photoshop; however, they can be viewed in ImageReady. When you apply an adjustment layer to a layer set, Photoshop adds the new adjustment layer in the layer set above the existing layers.*

Creating an adjustment layer

Adjustment layers can be added to an image to apply color and tonal adjustments without permanently changing the pixel values in the image. For example, if you add a Color Balance adjustment layer to an image, you can experiment with different colors repeatedly, because the change occurs only on the adjustment layer. If you decide to return to the original pixel values, you can hide or delete the adjustment layer.

Here, you'll add a Curves adjustment layer to create a greater contrast between the grille and the rust layer behind it. You'll do this by darkening the entire rust image. An adjustment layer affects all layers below it in the image's stacking order. Because you'll place the Curves adjustment layer below the Metal Grille layer, the adjustment will affect the Rust layer and the Background but not the metal grille.

1 Select the Rust layer in the Layers palette.

2 Click the Create New Fill Or Adjustment Layer button (⬤) at the bottom of the Layers palette and choose Curves from the pop-up menu.

3 Click the middle of the diagonal line in the grid (the color curve) to add a control point on the curve that will adjust the midtones.

4 Drag the control point down and to the right or enter values in the Input and Output text boxes. (We moved the control point so that the value in the Input text box was **150%** and the value in the Output text box was **105%**.)

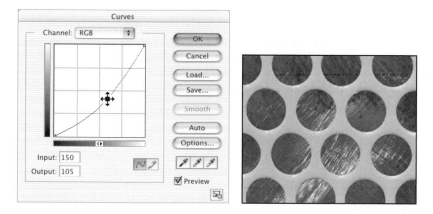

5 Click OK to close the dialog box.

An adjustment layer named Curves 1 appears in the Layers palette. The thumbnails for the new layer include one of the Curves 1 graph and one of the layer mask.

6 Choose File > Save.

You can experiment by clicking the eye icons for the Curves 1 and Rust layers off and on, to see the effect of the adjustment layer on the other layers. When you finish, be sure to return all layers to their visible state.

Creating a knockout gradient layer

Knockout layer options specify how one layer reveals other layers. In this section, you'll create a knockout gradient layer so that the lower third of the image reveals the Background layer.

You'll begin by creating a new layer in the Images layer set.

1 Select the Images layer set in the Layers palette and click the Create a New Layer button (⬛) at the bottom of the palette.

This creates a new layer (Layer 1) in the Images layer set, above the Metal Grille, Curves 1, and Rust layers.

2 Double-click the new Layer 1, and type **Knockout Gradient** to rename it. Press Enter (Windows) or Return (Mac OS), and keep the Knockout Gradient layer selected.

3 Select the Gradient tool (⬛) in the toolbox.

4 If necessary, click the Default Foreground And Background Colors icon (⬛) in the toolbox to set the foreground color to black and the background color to white.

5 If necessary, click the Linear Gradient button (⬛) in the tool options bar to create a linear gradient.

6 Click the arrow (▾) to the right of the gradient display in the tool options bar to open the gradient picker.

7 Click the arrow button (⦿) to open the gradient-picker palette menu, and choose Small List. Select Foreground To Transparent in the gradient picker, and close the gradient picker by clicking outside it or double-clicking the Foreground To Transparent option.

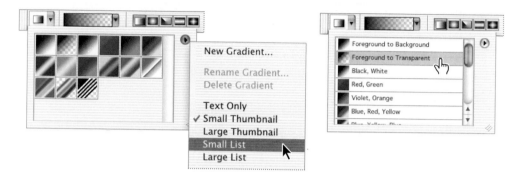

8 Shift-drag from the bottom of the image to slightly above the midpoint to create a gradient that goes from black at the bottom to transparent at the top.

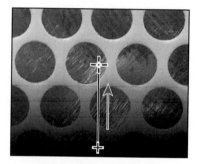

9 In the Layers palette, click the Layers Style button (⦿) at the bottom of the palette and choose Blending Options from the pop-up menu.

10 In the Layer Style dialog box, do the following:

• Under Advanced Blending, drag the Fill Opacity slider or type to enter **0** as the value. (Be careful to adjust the Fill Opacity, not the Opacity option under General Blendings.)

• In the Knockout pop-up menu, select Deep.

- Click OK to close the dialog box.

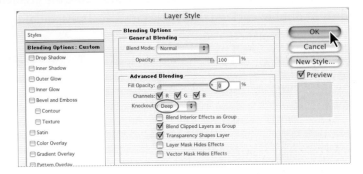

Now the horizontal stripes of gradient colors on the Background layer start to show through the layers in the Images layer set.

11 Choose File > Save.

Importing a layer from another file

In this part of the lesson, you'll import an existing layer from another file into your artwork. Although the imported layer contains the word *diesel* and was originally created with the Type tool, the text has now been converted to a graphic. You can no longer edit it with the Type tool, but the advantage here is that you also don't have to worry about whether or not your users or other people working on the file have the same font installed on their machines in order to see the image correctly.

1 Select the Words layer set in the Layers palette.

2 Use the File Browser or choose File > Open to find and open the Diesel.psd file in your Lessons/Lesson 11 folder.

3 With the Diesel.psd file active, drag the Diesel layer from the Layers palette into the 11Start.psd image.

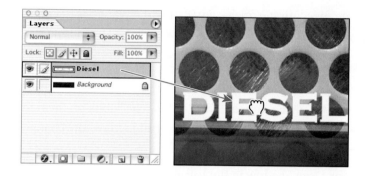

Because the Words layer set was selected in the 11Start.psd image, the Diesel layer is added to that set.

4 Select the Move tool (⊹) and drag the Diesel layer image into position so that it is in the center of the 11Start.psd image and near the bottom.

5 Choose File > Save to save your 11Start.psd file.

6 Choose Window > Diesel.psd, and then close that file without saving it.

Applying layer styles

Layer styles are automated special effects that you can apply to a layer.

Once you have the text arranged on the image, you can add layer styles to enhance the look of the type. Here, you'll add two different layer styles to the Diesel type layer.

1 With the Diesel layer selected in the Layers palette, click the Layer Styles icon ( ) at the bottom of the palette and select Drop Shadow from the pop-up menu.

2 In the Layer Style dialog box, make sure that the Preview check box on the right side of the dialog box is selected, or select it now so that you'll be able to see the changes as you work.

3 Examine the options for Drop Shadow in the Layer Style dialog box. You can either leave them at the default settings or experiment with various changes until you like the results these create in the image window.

4 On the left side of the dialog box, click the words *Bevel and Emboss* so that they are highlighted and a checkmark appears in the Bevel and Emboss check box.

5 In the Structure area on the right side of the dialog box, adjust the sliders for Depth and Size until you achieve a fairly subtle beveled look in the Diesel image. (We used **2%** for Depth and **2** pixels for Size, but you may think this is too subtle. Instead, you can leave them set at the default values: 100% and 5.)

💡 *Also watch the example located directly below the Preview check box. This thumbnail image shows you the results the layer-style options you've selected would have on a plain, medium-gray square.*

6 Click OK to close the dialog box.

7 Choose File > Save.

Duplicating and clipping a layer

In this section, you'll learn how to copy the Rust layer and then use the compound shape of the Diesel layer to clip away some of the Rust layer.

First, you'll copy the Rust layer and move it above the Diesel layer.

1 Select the Rust layer in the Layers palette and drag it onto the Create a New Layer button (⬛) at the bottom of the palette.

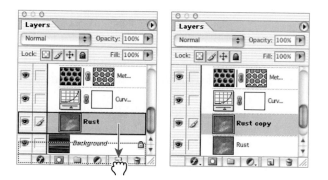

A new layer called "Rust copy" is created directly above the Rust layer in the palette.

2 In the Layers palette, drag Rust copy just above the Diesel layer inside the Words layer set.

Because Rust copy is the top layer, the rust image is all you can see in the image window.

3 Hold down Alt (Windows) or Option (Mac OS) and move the mouse pointer over the line dividing the Rust copy and Diesel layers in the Layers palette. When the pointer changes to two overlapping circles (•⊛), click the mouse button.

The Rust copy layer is clipped away so that it appears inside the Diesel shape and you can see the other layers in the other areas of the image.

4 Choose File > Save.

Note: The rust layer that appears inside the Diesel lettering is separate from the rust that appears within the circular holes in the yellow metal. You can prove this to yourself by clicking off the eye icon in the Rust Copy layer. The rust disappears from the Diesel letters but remains visible behind the yellow metal.

Liquifying a layer

The Liquify command adds a melted look to the image that you control. In this part of the lesson, you'll make the metal grille look as if it has melted from one side to the other.

Note: The Liquify filter in Photoshop CS includes enhancements over previous versions. If you think you'll want to experiment with other Liquify effects after you finish the next procedure, save a copy of your 11Start.psd file now (choose File > Save As and give the copy a different name, such as 11Testing.psd), and then close it and reopen your 11Start.psd file to continue working.

Rasterizing the mask

Before you can apply the Liquify feature to the metal grille, you must rasterize its vector mask and merge the mask and image to create just one image.

1 In the Layers palette, select the Metal Grille layer in the Images layer set.

2 Choose Layer > Rasterize > Vector Mask. This converts the circles path, which is a vector graphic and resolution-independent, into a mask that is a raster image and resolution-dependent.

To view a mask by itself, Alt-click (Windows) or Option-click (Mac OS) the mask thumbnail in the Layers palette.

3 Choose Layer > Remove Layer Mask > Apply to merge the layer with its mask, creating a single rasterized image on that layer Notice that there is now only one thumbnail in the Layers palette for the Metal Grille layer, whereas before there were two: one for the image and one for the mask.

Using the Liquify command

Using the Liquify command, you can interactively push, pull, rotate, reflect, pucker, and bloat any area of an image. The distortions you create can be subtle or drastic, which makes the Liquify command a powerful tool for retouching images as well as creating artistic effects.

Note: *The Liquify command is available only for 8-bit images in RGB Color, CMYK Color, Lab Color, and Grayscale image modes.*

You can use tools or alpha channels to freeze areas of the preview image to protect them from further changes, or thaw the frozen areas.

Certain reconstruction modes change unfrozen areas in relation to the distortions in frozen areas. You can hide or show the mask for frozen areas, change the mask color, and use a Brush Pressure option to create partial freezes and thaws.

Applying the Liquify filter

The Liquify filter works by applying a hidden grid that you can warp. This distorts the image by dragging handles at the intersection of the hidden grid or *mesh.* Turning on the mesh visibility can help you understand more clearly how you're manipulating this grid and the different effects created by the various liquify tools.

1 With the Metal Grille layer selected in the Layers palette, choose Filter > Liquify.

2 In the Liquify dialog box, select the following options:

• In the upper left corner of the dialog box, make sure that the Forward Warp tool (🖉) is selected.

• On the upper right side of the dialog box under Tool Options, select a brush size that's the same size as the holes in the grille (we used 133). Then for Brush Pressure, select a moderate value (we used 20).

Note: *Under View Options , you could select the Show Backdrop check box (as shown in the illustration above. Then you can set options for which layers to show as the backdrop (the Use option), whether to show the backdrop in front of the selected layer or behind it (the Mode option) and the level of Opacity for the backdrop. However, these options can be visually confusing at first, so leaving the Show Backdrop option unselected is recommended for this lesson.*

• Under View Options, select the Show Backdrop check box. Then select All Layers for the Use option, Behind for the Mode option, and 50% for Opacity.

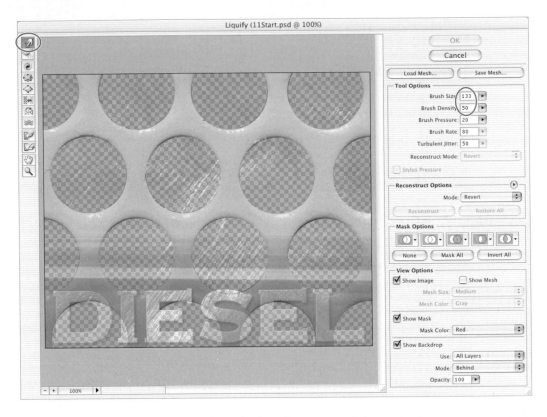

3 Still in the Liquify dialog box, drag the brush across and down the image once to start applying the Liquify filtering effect.

The view showing the backdrop, including the original, undistorted version of the Metal Grille layer in addition to the distorted version you're working on, can be visually confusing, especially when you're just learning the process.

4 Under View Options in the Liquify dialog box, select the Show Mesh check box, and deselect the Backdrop check box.

Notice how the mesh has been distorted by the Forward Warp tool. You can drag the Forward Warp Tool brush in the image some more to create different results.

Removing distortions in the Liquify dialog box

If you want to undo some or all of your distorting work, you don't have to cancel your efforts and start over completely. While the Liquify dialog box is open, you have several other choices for removing or reducing distortions from an area or from the entire image. The method you select depends on how much of your work you want to undo.

- *You can press Ctrl+Z (Windows) or Command+Z (Mac OS) to undo your most recent action, but only by one step.*

- *You can select the Reconstruct tool in the Liquify dialog box and drag it freehandedly across an area of the image that you want to restore to its original condition.*

- *You can click the Reconstruct button on the right side of the dialog box to reduce the entire distortion by degrees.*

- *You can use the Freeze tool to protect an area of the image that you want to remain distorted and then use either the Reconstruct tool or the Reconstruct button to remove or reduce the distortion of the areas that are not frozen.*

- *You can click the Restore All button to revert to the original (undistorted) condition of the image. The Restore All button restores even any frozen areas, so it is the equivalent of clicking Cancel and then choosing Filter > Liquify again in the Photoshop CS menu bar.*

You can also select different reconstruction modes (under Reconstruct Options) and modes for the Reconstruction tool (under Tool Options). For more information, see Photoshop Help.

5 On the left side of the dialog box, select the Turbulence tool (≋), and drag the brush across another area of the metal grille image.

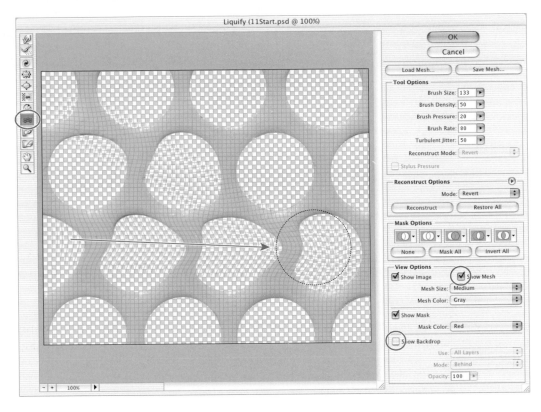

6 Move the Turbulence tool to an undistorted area of the image and hold down the mouse button for several seconds without moving the pointer.

As you hold down the mouse button, you can watch the grille appearing to melt under the influence of the Turbulence tool. Look closely for other the differences between the results created with the Forward Warp and Turbulence tools.

7 Continue to apply different effects to the metal grille. When you are satisfied with the results, click OK to close the Liquify dialog box, and then choose File > Save.

Note: If you make mistakes or don't like one of the brush strokes you apply, press Ctrl+Z (Windows) or Command+Z (Mac OS) to undo that step. You can also use the Reconstruct tool in the Liquify dialog box, which selectively and gradually removes the distortion from the areas that you paint with that tool, as specified by the selection in the Reconstruct Mode option on the right side of the dialog box, which is Revert by default.

This lesson merely scratches the surface of the Liquify filter. Beyond giving an image a "melted" look, you can achieve many other special effects. See Photoshop Help to learn more about:

• How to limit the distortion area by selecting an area before choosing the Liquify filter.

• How to freeze an area of the image within the Liquify dialog box, thereby protecting it with a temporary mask.

• How to distort a channel or mask instead of a layer.

• How to use the reconstruction modes to restore areas you've distorted.

• How to use and customize the other tools in the Liquify dialog box.

Creating a border layer

To give the image a finished look, you'll add a border to it.

1 Click the Create a New Layer button (▣) in the Layers palette. (It doesn't matter which layer is currently selected, because you're going to move the new layer a little later.)

2 Double-click the new Layer 1, and type **Image Border** to rename it.

3 Drag the Image Border layer to the top of the Layers palette stack, until a black line appears immediately above the Words layer set, and then release the mouse button.

The Image Border layer is now the top layer in the image.

4 Choose Select > All to select the entire image in the image window.

5 Choose Edit > Stroke. In the Stroke area, enter **5 px** for Width and click OK. (Or, for a more dramatic black border, enter a larger number, such as **10** or **15** pixels.)

A 5-pixel-wide black stroke now appears around the entire image.

6 Choose Select > Deselect to deselect the entire image.

7 Choose File > Save.

Flattening a layered image

If you plan to send a file out for proofs, it's also a good idea to save two versions of the file—one containing all the layers so that you can edit the file if necessary, and one flattened version to send to the print shop. When you flatten a file, all layers are merged into a single background, greatly reducing the size of the file.

1 First, note the values in the lower left corner of the application window (Windows) or the 11Start.psd image window (Mac OS). If the display does not show the file size (such as "Doc: 909K/6.4M"), click the arrow on the bottom of the window to open a pop-up menu, and choose Document Sizes.

The first number is the printing size of the image, which is about the size that the saved, flattened file would have in Adobe Photoshop format. The number on the right indicates the approximate document size of the file as it is now, including layers and channels.

2 Choose Image > Duplicate, name the duplicate file **11Final.psd**, and click OK.

3 On the Layers palette menu, choose Flatten Image. The layers for the 11Final.psd file are combined onto a single background layer.

Now the file sizes shown in the lower left area of the work area or image window are the same, smaller number that you saw earlier.

4 Choose File > Save. If n the Save As dialog box, click Save to save the file in Photoshop format.

You've completed the Advanced Layer Techniques lesson.

Review questions

1 Why would you use layer sets?

2 What are clipping path layers?

3 How do adjustment layers work, and what is the benefit of using an adjustment layer?

4 What are layer styles? Why would you use them?

Review answers

1 Layer sets help you organize and manage layers. For example, you can move all the layers in a layer set as a group and apply attributes or a mask to them as a group.

2 A clipping path is when you configure the artwork on the base layer as a mask for the layer above it. In this lesson, you used the Metal Grille layer (which had holes in it created by the vector mask you created) as a clipping path for the rust layer, so that the rust appeared only in the holes in the grille. You also used the Diesel layer as a clipping path for the copy of the rust layer, so that it appeared only inside the shapes of the word.

3 Adjustment layers are a special type of Photoshop layer that works specifically with color and tonal adjustments. When you apply an adjustment layer, you can edit an image repeatedly without making a permanent change to the colors or tonal range in the image. You can view adjustment layers in ImageReady, but you can create or edit them only in Photoshop.

4 Layer styles are customizable effects that you can apply to layers. You can use them to apply changes to a layer that you can modify or remove at any time.

12 | Creating Special Effects

With the huge assortment of filters available for Adobe Photoshop, you can transform ordinary images into extraordinary digital artwork. You can select filters that simulate a traditional artistic medium—a watercolor, pastel, or sketched effect—or you can choose from filters that blur, bend, wrap, sharpen, or fragment images. In addition to using filters to alter images, you can use adjustment layers and painting modes to vary the look of your artwork.

In this lesson, you'll learn how to do the following:

- Record and play back an action to automate a series of steps.

- Add guides to help you place and align images precisely.

- Save selections and load them as masks.

- Apply color effects only to unmasked areas of an image.

- Add an adjustment layer to make a color correction to a selection.

- Apply filters to selections to create various effects.

- Add layer styles to create editable special effects.

This lesson will take about an hour to complete. The lesson is designed to be done in Adobe Photoshop, but information on using similar functionality in Adobe ImageReady is included where appropriate.

If needed, remove the previous lesson folder from your hard drive, and copy the Lessons/Lesson12 folder onto it. As you work on this lesson, you'll overwrite the start files. If you need to restore the start files, copy them from the *Adobe Photoshop CS Classroom in a Book* CD.

Note: *Windows 2000 users need to unlock the lesson files before using them. For more information, see "Copying the Classroom in a Book files" on page 3.*

Getting started

You'll start the lesson by viewing the final Lesson file, to see what you'll accomplish.

1 Start Photoshop and then immediately hold down Ctrl+Alt+Shift (Windows) or Command+Option+Shift (Mac OS) to restore the default preferences. (See "Restoring default preferences" on page 4.)

As messages appear, select Yes to confirm that you want to reset preferences, No to defer setting up your color monitor, and Close to close the Welcome Screen.

2 On the tool options bar, select the File Browser button (🗁) , and use the Folders palette to navigate to and select the Lessons/Lesson12 folder on your hard disk.

3 In the thumbnails palette, select the 12End.psd file, so that it appears in the Preview palette in the File Browser.

This end file is a montage that is comprised of four pictures. Each quadrant has had a specific filter or effect applied to it.

4 In the File Browser, select the 12End_copy.psd thumbnail.

This copy of the end file is a version of the same montage that has been partially flattened and adjusted in color so that the four quadrants have similar color schemes.

Leave the File Browser open.

Automating a multi-step task

An *action* is a set of one or more commands that you record and can then play back to apply to a single file or a batch of files. In this section of the lesson, you'll see how the Actions palette can help you save time by applying a multi-step process to the four images you'll use in this project.

Using actions is one of several ways that you can automate tasks in Adobe Photoshop and Adobe ImageReady. To learn more about recording actions, see Photoshop Help.

Opening and cropping the files

You'll start by opening and resizing four files. Since this part of the task involves aesthetic choices about where and how much of the image to crop, you'll do these steps manually rather than recording them with the Actions palette.

1 In the File Browser, double-click the 12Start.jpg thumbnail to open it in Photoshop.

2 Click the Info tab in the Navigator palette group so that the Info palette is visible.

3 In the toolbox, select the Crop tool (⌗). Hold down Shift to constrain the shape to a square and drag around the pears. When you finish dragging, be careful to release the mouse key first and then the Shift key.

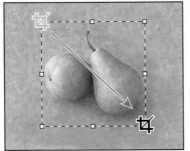

Dragging and pressing Shift   *Cropped image*

4 Examine the width (W) and height (H) values in the Info palette. If you've drawn a perfect square, the pixel counts will be identical.

5 If necessary, make any adjustments to the selection so that the pears are centered in the cropping marquee and fit fairly snugly inside it:

• To correct the dimensions if the width and height are not equal, drag a corner until the W and H values in the Info palette are identical. (Do not hold down Shift.)

• To move the marquee, click inside it and drag until it is positioned properly.

• To resize the marquee, hold down Shift and drag one of the corners to make the marquee larger or smaller.

6 When you are satsified with the crop selection, double-click inside the crop area, or press Enter (Windows) or Return (Mac OS) to apply the cropping.

Because you're working with a number of files, you'll rename the 12Start.jpg file with a descriptive name so that it will be easy to identify.

7 Choose File > Save As, and save the cropped image as **Pears.jpg** in your Lesson12 folder. If a dialog box appears with options for image quality, click OK to accept the default settings.

8 Repeat Steps 1 through 6 for three of the other images in the Lesson12 folder: Leaves.jpg, Dandelion.jpg, and Sand.jpg, and then choose File > Save instead of Save As to save each of the files. (You don't need to rename them.)

Note: It is not necessary to make all the cropped images the same size. You will adjust their sizes again later in this lesson.

Cropped versions of the Leaves, Dandelion, and Sand JPEG files

Leave all the newly cropped files open for the next procedures.

Preparing to record an action

You use the Actions palette to record, play, edit, and delete individual actions. You also use the Actions palette to save and load action files. You'll start this task by opening a new document and preparing to record a new action in the Actions palette.

1 Click the Actions tab in the History palette group to bring the Actions palette forward, or choose Window > Actions to accomplish the same thing.

2 In the Actions palette, click the New Set button (🗀) at the bottom of the palette. Or, you can create a new set by choosing New Set on the Actions palette menu (opened by clicking the arrow button (⊙) in the upper right corner of the palette).

3 In the New Set dialog box, type **My Actions**, and click OK.

4 Choose Window > Dandelion.jpg to make that file active.

Recording a new action set

For this project, you'll want the images to be identical sizes and for each to be surrounded by a narrow white border. You're now ready to perform those tasks on the dandelion image. You'll do this by setting the image dimensions to a specific number of pixels and by setting a stroke and stroke properties that will surround the image. As you work, you'll setup the Actions palette to record each step of the process.

Note: *It is important that you finish all the steps in this procedure without interruption. If you become distracted and need to start over, skip ahead to Step 9 to stop the recording. Then, you can delete the action by dragging it onto the Delete button (🗑) in the Actions palette, and start again at Step 1.*

1 In the Actions palette, click the New Action button (▣) or choose New Action on the Actions palette menu.

2 In the New Action dialog box, type **Size & Stroke** in the Name option and make sure that My Actions is selected in the Set pop-up menu. Then click Record.

Note: *Take all the time you need to do this procedure accurately. The speed at which you work has no influence on the amount of time required to play a recorded action.*

3 Choose Image > Image Size.

4 Make sure that both the Constrain Proportions and the Resample Image check boxes are selected at the bottom of the Image Size dialog box. Then, for the Width, type **275** and make sure that **pixels** is selected as the unit of measurement. Then click OK.

5 Choose Select > All.

6 Choose Edit > Stroke.

7 In the Stroke dialog box, make sure that the following options are selected, or select then now:

• In the Width option, leave the value at **1** pixel.

• In the Color swatch, use white, or select it by clicking the swatch to open the color picker, selecting white (C, M, Y, and K=0), and clicking OK to close the color picker.

• Under Location, leave Center selected.

• Under Blending, leave Mode set to Normal and Opacity set at 100%.

• Then click OK to close the Stroke dialog box.

8 Choose Select > Deselect.

Stroke dialog box settings and close-up of resulting border on image

9 In the Actions palette, click the green Stop button (■) at the bottom of the palette to stop recording steps. Save your work.

Your action is now saved in the Actions palette. You can click the arrows to the left of the My Actions set, the Size & Stroke action, and beside each step of that action to expand and collapse them at your convenience. With these expanded, you can examine each recorded step and the specific selections you made. When you finish reviewing the action, click the arrows to collapse the steps.

Playing an action on an individual file

Now that you've recorded the process of setting the image size and stroke characteristics for the dandelion image, you can use the action as an automated task. You'll apply the Stroke & Size action to one of the other three image files you cropped earlier in this section.

1 If the Leaves.jpg, Pears.jpg, and Sand.jpg files are not still open, choose File > Open and open them now.

2 Choose Window > Document > Sand.jpg to make that image active.

3 In the Actions palette, select the Size & Stroke action in the My Actions set, and then click the Play button (▶), or choose Play on the Actions palette menu.

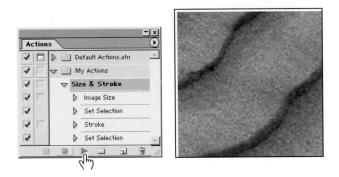

The Sand.jpg image is automatically resized and given a stroke so that it now matches the Dandelion.jpg image for these properties.

4 Choose File > Save.

Batch-playing an action

Applying actions is a time-saving process for performing routine tasks on files, but you can streamline your work even further by applying actions to all open files. You have two more files in this project that need to be resized and given strokes, so you'll apply your automated action to them simultaneously.

1 Close the Dandelion.jpg and Sand.jpg files. Make sure that only the Pears.jpg and Leaves.jpg files are open.

2 Choose File > Automate > Batch.

3 Under the Play section of the Batch dialog box, make sure that My Actions is selected for Set and that Size & Stroke is selected for Action.

4 In the Source pop-up menu, select Opened Files.

5 Leave Destination set as None, and click OK.

The action is applied to both the pears and leaves images, so that the files have identical dimensions and strokes surrounding them.

6 Choose File > Save and then File > Close for each of the two files.

In this exercise, you batch-processed only two files instead of making all the same changes in each of them; this was a mild convenience. But creating and applying actions can save significant amounts of time and tedium when you have dozens or even hundreds of files that require any routine, repetitive work.

Setting up a four-image montage

Now that you've finished preparing the four images, you'll place them together in a new composite image. Using guides, you'll be able to align the images precisely without a lot of effort.

Adding guides

Guides are non-printing lines that help you line up elements in your document, either horizontally or vertically. You can choose a Snap To command so that the guides behave like magnets: Objects you drag to positions that are close to a guide will snap into place along the guide when you release the mouse button.

1 Use the File Browser or choose File > Open, and open the Montage.psd file in the Lesson12 folder.

2 Choose View > Rulers. A vertical ruler appears along the left side of the window and a horizontal ruler appears along the top of the window.

Note: If the ruler units are not inches, choose Edit > Preferences > Units & Rulers (Windows) or Photoshop > Preferences > Units & Rulers (Mac OS), and select Inches from the Rulers pop-up menu; then click OK.

3 If the Info palette is not visible, click the Info palette tab or choose Window > Info to bring it forward in its palette group.

4 Drag down from the horizontal ruler to the middle of the image window, watching the Info palette to see the Y coordinates as you drag. Release the mouse when Y = 3.000 inches. A blue guide line appears across the middle of the window.

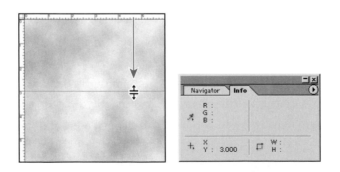

5 Drag another guide from the vertical ruler to the middle of the image and release the mouse when X = 3.000 inches.

6 Choose View > Snap To > and make sure that the Guides command is checked, or select it now.

7 Choose View > Rulers to hide the rulers again.

Snapping images into position

Your guides are in place, so now you're ready to arrange your four cropped images in the montage.

1 Choose File > Open Recent > Pears.jpg. The pears image opens in a separate image window.

2 In the toolbox, select the Move tool (⊕), if it is not already selected.

3 Click the Move tool anywhere in the pear image and drag from that image window to the larger Montage.jpg window, and release the mouse button.

4 Still using the Move tool, drag the pears image into the upper left quadrant of the image so that its lower right corner snaps into place against the intersection of the two guides at the center of the window.

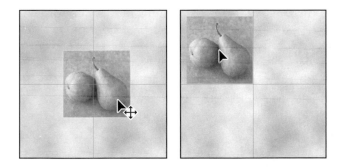

In the Layers palette, you'll notice that the pears image is on a new layer, Layer 1.

5 Choose Window > Pears.jpg to make it active again, and then close it, either by clicking the close button or by choosing File > Close.

6 Repeat Steps 1–5 for the three other cropped files, placing the leaves image in the upper right quadrant, the dandelion in the lower left quadrant, and the sand in the lower right quadrant. All the images should fit snugly against the intersection of the guides in the center of the window.

7 Choose View > Show > Guides to hide the guides.

Saving selections

Next, you'll select the two pears and save the selection itself. Later, you can reload the selection and use it as needed. Later in this lesson, you'll use your saved selection to colorize the pears and to add a special effect.

1 In the toolbox, select the Zoom tool (🔍), and drag a marquee around the pears to magnify your view. Make sure that you can see all of both pears in the image window.

2 Hold down the mouse on the Lasso tool (🔍) to open the hidden tools list, and select the Magnetic Lasso tool (🔍).

For best results when tracing the pear stem with the Magnetic Lasso tool, decrease the tool's lasso width and frequency values on the tool options bar. For example, try tracing the pear using a Lasso Width of **1** or **2** pixels and a Frequency of **40**.

Note: ImageReady does not include the Magnetic Lasso tool.

3 Click once to set a point on the edge of the pear on the right, and then move the pointer (you do not need to hold down the mouse button) around the pear to trace its outline.

As you move the pointer, the active segment snaps to the strongest edge in the image. Periodically, the Magnetic Lasso tool adds fastening points to the selection border to anchor previous sections. Try to make your selection a reasonably accurate outline of the pear, but don't worry if it's not perfect.

You can also click the Magnetic Lasso tool as you trace the outline to add your own fastening points. This might be especially helpful around the stem or where the highlights or shadows make the edge between the pear and the background less distinct.

4 When you get back to your starting point and a small circle appears in the lower right area of the Magnetic Lasso pointer (⌕), click to close the segment.

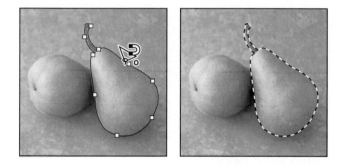

If you want to fix any flaws in the selection, try switching to Quick Mask mode and using the techniques you learned in Lesson 6, "Masks and Channels."

5 Choose Select > Save Selection, and then type **Right Pear** for Name, and click OK to save the selection in a new channel.

6 Choose Select > Deselect to deselect the right pear.

7 Repeat the process (Steps 1–6), this time selecting the left pear and saving the selection as **Left Pear**. Then choose Select > Deselect, or press Ctrl+D (Windows) or Command+D (Mac OS).

You now have two selections saved. To see them, click the Channel palette tab to open it, and scroll down, if necessary. Click each pear channel name in turn to make the channel masks appear in the image window.

When you are ready to continue working, scroll to the top of the Channels palette and click the RGB channel to select it and click to remove the eye icons from the Right Pear and Left Pear channels, if necessary. Click the tab for the Layers palette to bring it forward in the palette group so it will be ready for the next procedure.

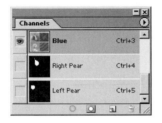

Hand-coloring selections on a layer

You'll start to add special effects to your montage by hand-coloring the pears, beginning with the pear on the right. To select it, you'll simply load the first selection you created in the previous procedure. Then, you'll remove the color from the selection so that you can color it by hand. Finally, after adding a layer above the pears, you'll be ready to apply new color by adding it to the new layer. In this way, you can simply erase the layer and start over if you don't like the results.

You could do most of the following tasks in ImageReady rather than Photoshop, but this is not recommended. ImageReady has the same Load Selection command and filters, and many of the same color-collection options, blending modes, and tools for applying and tracking color that you find in Photoshop. However, ImageReady uses a slightly different technique for creating gradients (see "Adding a gradient" on page 416), and cannot create or edit an adjustment layer (see "Changing the color balance" on page 418). Because of this, it's better to do these procedures in Photoshop.

Desaturating a selection

You'll use the Desaturate command to *desaturate*—that is, to remove the color from—the selected pear area. Saturation is the presence or absence of color in a selection. When you desaturate a selection within an image, you create a grayscale-like effect without affecting the colors in other parts of the image.

1 In the Layers palette, select Layer 1, the layer with the pears image.

2 Choose Select > Load Selection.

3 In the Load Selection dialog box, select Right Pear from the Channel pop-up menu, and click OK. A selection border appears around the right pear in your image.

4 Choose Image > Adjustments > Desaturate. The color is removed from the selection.

5 Choose Select > Deselect.

6 Choose File > Save to save your work.

Creating a layer and choosing a blending mode

Now, you'll add a layer and specify a layer blending mode for painting the desaturated pear image. By painting on a separate layer, you won't permanently alter the image. This makes it easy to start over if you aren't satisfied with the results.

You use layer blending modes to determine how the pixels in a layer blend with underlying pixels on other layers. By applying modes to individual layers, you can create myriad special effects.

1 In the Layers palette, click the New Layer button (▣) to add Layer 5 to the image, just above Layer 1 in the palette.

2 Double-click Layer 5 and type **Paint** to rename the layer.

3 In the Layers palette, choose Color from the pop-up mode menu to the left of the Opacity text box.

The Color mode option is a *blending mode.* These modes determine how the pixels in this layer blend with underlying pixels on the Background layer.

Note: *Next to the New Layer button, you'll see the Trash button. If you ever you want to delete a Paint layer, you can drag that layer to the Layers palette Trash button. Or, simply select the layer you want to delete and then click that Trash button, which will bring up a message asking you to confirm that you want to delete the layer.*

You can use the Color mode to change the hue of a selection without affecting the highlights and shadows. This means that you can apply a variety of color tints without changing the original highlights and shadows of the pears.

Applying painting effects

To begin painting, you must again load the selection that you created earlier. By loading the Right Pear channel, you protect the unselected areas of the image as you apply colors, making it easy to paint within the lines.

For an illustration of hand-painting the pears, see figure 12-1 in the color section.

1 Choose Select > Load Selection. Then select Right Pear for the Channel option in the Load Selection dialog box, and click OK.

Notice in the Load Selection dialog box that the color-mode change you just made also was saved as a selection, called *Paint Transparency.*

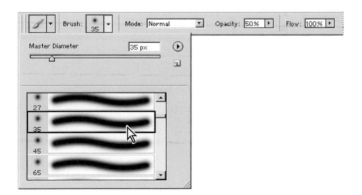

2 Select the Brush tool ( ). Then, in the tool options bar, type, scrub, or drag the slider to set the Opacity to about **50%**.

Change the brush opacity by pressing a number on the keypad from 0 to 9 (where 1 is 10%, 9 is 90%, and 0 is 100%).

3 In the Brush pop-up palette, select a large, soft-edged brush, such as the Soft Round 35-pixel brush.

4 Choose Window > Swatches to bring the Swatches palette forward (or click its tab in the Color palette group), and then select any yellow-green color that appeals to you as your foreground color.

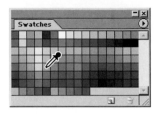

5 Drag the brush over the entire pear to apply the color.

Next, you'll use a darker and a lighter shade to add highlights and shadows.

6 Select a darker green from the Swatches palette. In the tool options bar, set the brush opacity to about **30%**. Paint around the edges in the pear selection, avoiding the highlight area.

7 Select a rose color from the Swatches palette. In the tool options bar, select a smaller brush size and decrease the paint opacity to about **20%**. Then, paint highlights on the pear.

8 When you are satisfied with your results, choose Select > Deselect, and then choose File > Save.

Adding a gradient

Now you'll use the Gradient tool to add a gradient to the other pear for a highlight effect. (ImageReady does not have a Gradient tool. Instead, gradients are created as ImageReady layer effects.)

First, you'll need to load the selection of the left pear that you made earlier.

1 Choose Select > Load Selection. Select Left Pear in the Load Selection dialog box, and click OK. A selection border appears around the left pear in your image.

2 Click the Color palette tab to bring it forward, and then select red as the foreground color by typing or dragging the R slider to **255** and the G and B sliders to **0**.

3 Click the Set Background Color icon in the upper left area of the Color palette and then select yellow as the background color by setting R and G at **255** and B at **0**.

Foreground color *Background color*

4 Select the Gradient tool (▭). On the tool options bar, select the following options:

• Select the Radial Gradient icon.

• Open the gradient picker and make sure that Foreground To Background is selected, so that the color blends from the foreground color (red) to the background color (yellow).

• Set the Opacity to **40%**.

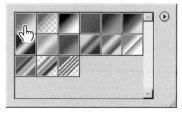

A. *Linear gradient*   *Selecting Foreground To Background*
B. *Radial gradient*
C. *Angle gradient*
D. *Reflected gradient*
E. *Diamond gradient*

5 Position the Gradient tool near the pear's highlight, and drag toward the stem end.

6 When you're satisfied with the results, choose Select > Deselect.

Merging layers

The next step, merging layers, helps you to keep the file size relatively small. However, after you merge, you cannot easily go back and restore the image or start the process over, so be sure that you are happy with your results before you choose a merge command.

1 In the Layers palette, make sure that the Paint layer is selected.

2 Choose Layer > Merge Down to merge the Paint layer with the pear-image layer (Layer 1) below it.

Now the two layers are fused as Layer 1.

3 Double-click the Hand tool (🖐) so that the entire image fits in the image window, or double-click the Zoom tool (🔍) to reduce the view to 100%.

4 Choose File > Save.

Changing the color balance

Now, you'll use an adjustment layer to adjust the color balance on the leaves image. ImageReady has many of the same color-correction features as Photoshop, but they cannot be applied to adjustment layers or channels because you cannot create or edit adjustment layers or channels in ImageReady.

Altering the color for a channel or a regular layer permanently changes the pixels on that layer. However, with an adjustment layer, your color and tonal changes reside only within the adjustment layer and do not alter any pixels in the layers beneath it. The effect is as if you were viewing the visible layers through the adjustment layer above them. By using adjustment layers, you can try out color and tonal adjustments without permanently changing pixels in the image. You can also use adjustment layers to affect multiple layers at once.

1 In the Layers palette, select the layer containing the leaves (in the upper right quadrant of the montage).

In our example this is Layer 2, but it may be on another layer in your file if you originally placed the images in a different sequence.

2 Choose Layer > New Adjustment Layer > Color Balance.

3 In the New Layer dialog box, select the Use Previous Layer To Create Clipping Mask check box, which ensures that your adjustment layer will affect only the leaves image, not the other three sections of the montage. Then click OK to create the adjustment layer with the default name, Color Balance 1.

The Color Balance dialog box opens, where you can change the mixture of colors in a color image and make general color corrections. When you adjust the color balance, you can keep the same tonal balance, as you'll do here. You can also focus changes on the shadows, midtones, or highlights.

4 Move the dialog box so that you can see the leaves in the image window and make sure that the Preview check box is selected.

5 In the Color Balance dialog box, experiment with different Color Levels for the image. (The example uses +10, −20, and −20.)

6 When you are happy with the result, click OK, and then save your work.

Adjustment layers act as layer masks, which can be edited repeatedly without permanently affecting the underlying image. You can double-click an adjustment layer to display the last settings used and adjust them as many times as you want. You can delete an adjustment layer by dragging it to the Trash button at the bottom of the Layers palette.

Applying filters

In this phase of the project, you'll apply two different styles of filters to the leaves and dandelion images. Because there are so many different filters for creating special effects, the best way to learn about them is to try out different filters and filter options. ImageReady supports the same filters that are included with Photoshop.

To save time when trying various filters, experiment on a small, representative part of your image or on a low-resolution copy.

Improving performance with filters

Some filter effects can be memory-intensive, especially when applied to a high-resolution image. You can use these techniques to improve performance:

• Try out filters and settings on a small portion of an image.

• Apply the effect to individual channels—for example, to each RGB channel—if the image is large and you're having problems with insufficient memory. (With some filters, effects vary if applied to the individual channel rather than the composite channel, especially if the filter randomly modifies pixels.)

• Free up memory before running the filter by using the Purge commands. (See "Correcting mistakes" in Photoshop Help.)

• Allocate more RAM to Photoshop or ImageReady (Mac OS). You can also exit any other applications to make more memory available to Photoshop or ImageReady.

• Try changing settings to improve the speed of memory-intensive filters such as Lighting Effects, Cutout, Stained Glass, Chrome, Ripple, Spatter, Sprayed Strokes, and Glass filters. (For example, with the Stained Glass filter, increase cell size. With the Cutout filter, increase Edge Simplicity, decrease Edge Fidelity, or both.)

If you plan to print to a grayscale printer, convert a copy of the image to grayscale before applying filters. However, applying a filter to a color image and then converting to grayscale may not have the same effect as applying the filter to a grayscale version of the image.

Applying and fading the Accented Edges filter

The Accented Edges filter exaggerates the margins between areas with different colors. You can adjust the extent of the exaggeration by changing the edge-brightness control, but in this procedure, you'll use a Fade command to mute the results.

1 In the Layers palette, select the layer with the leaves image. Make sure that you select the layer itself and not the adjustment layer.

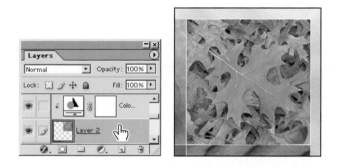

2 Choose Filter > Brush Strokes > Accented Edges. Click OK to accept the default settings in the Accented Edges dialog box.

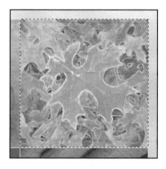

This image is somewhat too bright, so you'll tone it down slightly.

3 Choose Edit > Fade Accented Edges.

4 In the Fade dialog box, drag the Opacity slider to **60%**; then click OK.

5 Save your work.

Note: The Fade command settings determine how the modified pixels in the selection appear in relation to the original pixels. The blending modes in the Fade dialog box are a subset of those available in the painting and editing tools Options palette.

Using filters

To use a filter, choose the appropriate submenu command from the Filter menu. These guidelines can help you in choosing filters:

- *The last filter chosen appears at the top of the menu.*

- *Filters are applied to the active, visible layer.*

- *Filters cannot be applied to Bitmap-mode or indexed-color images.*

- *Some filters work only on RGB images.*

- *Some filters are processed entirely in RAM.*

- *Gaussian Blur, Add Noise, Median, Unsharp Mask, High Pass, and Dust & Scratches filters can be used with 16-bit-per-channel images, as well as 8-bit-per-channel images.*

Applying the ZigZag filter

Next, you'll use the ZigZag filter to create the impression that you're viewing the reflection of a dandelion on the surface of a rippled pool of water.

1 In the Layers palette, select the layer with the dandelion image.

2 In the toolbox, select the Elliptical Marquee tool (◯), which is hidden behind the Rectangular Marquee tool (⬚).

3 Drag across the dandelion image to select most of the seed head and stem, but do not extend the selection so that it reaches the borders of the image.

The selection restricts the area that the filter will affect within the dandelion-image layer. If the selection is too large, the border will also be wavy and start to overlap the other quadrants of the montage image.

4 Choose Filter > Distort > ZigZag.

5 At the bottom of the ZigZag dialog box, make sure that Pond Ripples is selected in the Style pop-up menu. Then, experiment with different settings for Amount and Ridges by dragging the sliders. (The example uses 10% for Amount and 11 for Ridges.)

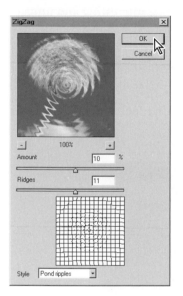

6 When you are satisfied with the result, click OK.

7 Choose Edit > Deselect, and then File >Save to save your work.

Using filter shortcuts

Try any of these techniques to help save time when working with filters:

* *To cancel a filter as it is being applied, press Esc or Command-(.) (period) (Mac OS).*

* *To undo a filter, press Ctrl+Z (Windows) or Command+Z (Mac OS).*

* *To reapply the most recently used filter with its last values, press Ctrl+F (Windows) or Command+F (Mac OS).*

* *To display the dialog box for the last filter you applied, press Ctrl+Alt+F (Windows) or Command+Option+F (Mac OS).*

Combining selections

Before you apply a filter to the remaining image quadrant, the sand, you'll load and combine the two selections you made earlier of the individual pears. By applying these selections to a different part of the image, you can create interesting and unusual results.

1 Choose Select > Load Selection.

2 In the Channel pop-up menu in the Load Selection dialog box, select Right Pear and click OK.

3 Repeat Step 2, but this time select Left Pear as the Channel and select the Add To Selection option. Click OK.

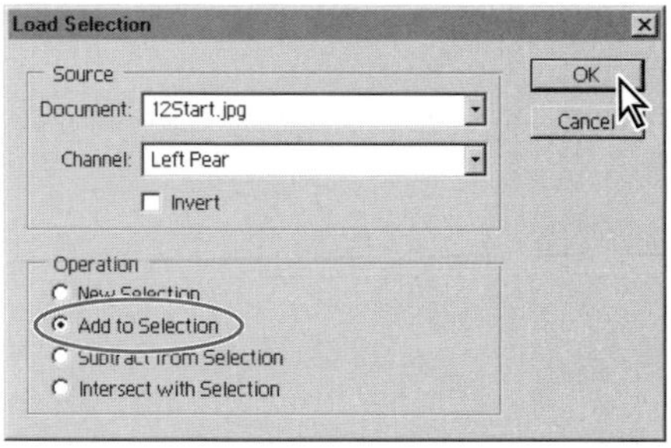

Now both pears are selected.

Editing a selection in Quick Mask mode

When you combine selections as you've just done, small unselected gaps can remain between the two loaded selections. In this task, you'll review the selection and repair any holes that may be there.

1 Using the Zoom tool ( ), zoom in to the image so that the area where the two pears overlap fills the image window.

2 In the toolbox, click the Quick Mask Mode button ( ), or press Q to select it with the keyboard shortcut.

All the areas in the image that are not included in the selection appear with a 50% red tint.

You can double-click the Edit in Quick Mask Mode button to open the Quick Mask Options dialog box, where you can change the opacity and color of the tint that indicates the unselected areas.

3 Look closely at the area where the two pears overlap to see if there are any red pixels there.

4 In the toolbox, make sure that the foreground and background colors are black and white, respectively, or click the small Default Foreground And Background Colors button to reset them.

5 Select the Eraser tool ( ) and drag it over the area between the two pears to erase any red tint that appears there. If necessary, you can adjust the diameter of the Eraser tool in the tool options bar. Continue erasing until there are no more red pixels in that area.

Leave the selection active for the next procedure.

Moving a selection

The next phase of your job is a simple task: moving the selection to another area of the image. This sets the stage for the final work, creating a different effect in the shape of the pears.

1 In the toolbox, click the Standard Mode button ( ), or press Q.

2 Double-click the Zoom tool ( ) so that the entire image fits in the image window.

3 In the toolbox, select the Rectangular Marquee tool ( ).

4 Move the pointer inside the pear selection and then drag the selection marquee (not the pear images) into the lower right quadrant, centering it over the sand image.

If you want to move the selection at exactly a 45° angle, start dragging and then hold down Shift.

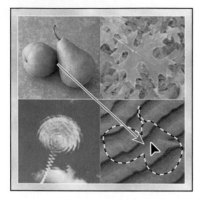

Be careful not to deselect yet because you'll need this selection for the next procedure.

Creating a cutout effect

In this task, you'll use your selection and some layer styles to create the illusion of a cutout in the sand image. Make sure that your combined pears-shaped selection is still active. If you have accidentally deselected, you'll have to start this process over, beginning with "Combining selections" on page 424.

1 In the Layers palette, click the layer with the sand image to make it the target layer.

2 Choose Layer > New > Layer Via Copy to create a new layer above the original Sand layer, based on your combined selection. The new layer automatically becomes the active layer in the Layers palette, and the pears-shaped marquee disappears.

You can quickly create a selection marquee around a layer by Ctrl+clicking (Windows) or Command+clicking (Mac OS) the layer name in the Layers palette. You can try this with the new Layer 5 to make the pear marquee reappear. Before you continue with this lesson, choose Select > Deselect.

3 At the bottom of the Layers palette, click the Add A Layer Style button (⊘) and then select Pattern Overlay from the pop-up menu.

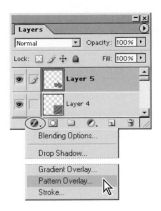

4 Drag the Layer Style dialog box aside, as needed, so that you can see both the dialog box and the image window.

5 Click the Pattern arrow (in the long, narrow button to the right of the thumbnail) to open the pattern picker, which displays smaller thumbnails of an assortment of patterns.

6 Click the arrow button (⊙) to open the palette menu for the pattern picker, and select Load Patterns.

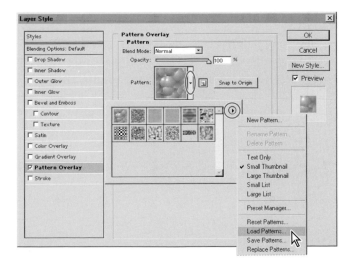

7 In the Load dialog box, go to the Lessons/Lesson12 folder and select the Effects.pat file. Click Load. When the dialog box closes, notice the new pattern that appears as the last thumbnail in the pattern picker.

8 Select the pattern thumbnail you added in Step 7. The pattern replaces the default pattern inside your pears selection. At this point, you can drag the pattern in the image window to adjust the area of the pattern that appears in the selection—even without closing the Layer Style dialog box.

9 On the left side of the Layer Style dialog box, under Styles, select Inner Shadow to add that effect to the selection, and adjust the Inner Shadow options on the right side of the dialog box. (The example uses the default settings for Blend Mode, Opacity, and Angle, but uses 13 for Distance and 10 for Size.)

10 You can continue to experiment with other Styles and settings until you create results that you think are interesting. When you are satisfied with the results, click OK.

For detailed information on individual filters and a gallery of examples, see "Using filters" in Photoshop Help.

Matching color schemes across images

Another innovation in Photoshop CS is the ability to coordinate different images by matching color palettes. In this final task, you'll create a different version of the file that harmonizes the color schemes in the four images by matching the target image to the dominant colors in a source.

1 With your working file (Montage.psd) still open, choose File Save, and then choose Image > Duplicate.

2 Click OK in the Duplicate Image dialog box, without changing the default name (12Montage_copy).

3 With the 12Montage_copy image window active, scroll down the Layers palette to the Background layer and click the eye icon (👁) to hide that layer. If the Background layer is selected, select any other layer.

4 On the Layers palette menu, choose Merge Visible.

Notice that the Layers palette has been reduced to two layers: Background and a merged layer with the same name as the layer that was selected at the end of Step 3.

5 Choose Image > Adjustments > Match Color to open the Match Color dialog box, and do the following:

• Select the Preview option, if it is not already selected.

• For Source, select 12Montage.psd (the original working file with all layers still unmerged) on the pop-up menu.

- On the Layer pop-up menu, select the layer containing the pears image, as shown in the thumbnail to the right of the Source option. Observe the effect this has on the 12Montage_copy.psd image in the image window.

- One by one, select the other layers and study the results shown in the image window. After you have seen how the various layers affect the image. You can also try out the Image Options by adjusting the sliders for Luminence, Color Intensity, and Fade, with or without the Neutralize option selected.

6 When you arrive at the selections you think do the best job of unifying the image and giving it the look you want, click OK to close the dialog box. (We used the pears-image layer and the default Image Options settings.)

7 In the Layers palette, make the Background layer visible again by clicking to set the eye icon (👁).

8 Choose File > Save.

You can use Match Color with any source file to create interesting and unusual effects. The Match Color feature is also useful for certain color corrections in some photographs. See Photoshop Help for more information.

You have completed Lesson 12, so you can now close the 12Start.psd and 12Start_copy.psd files.

Review questions

1 What is the purpose of saving selections?

2 Describe one way to isolate color adjustments to an image.

3 Describe one way to remove color from a selection or image for a grayscale effect.

Review answers

1 By saving a selection, you can create and reuse time-consuming selections and uniformly select artwork in an image. You can also combine selections or create new selections by adding to or subtracting from existing selections.

2 You can use adjustment layers to try out color changes before applying them permanently to a layer.

3 You can use the Desaturate command to desaturate, or remove the color, from a selection. Or, you can use the Hue/Saturation command and adjust only the Saturation component. Photoshop also includes the Sponge tool for removing color.

Lesson 13

13 | Preparing Images for Two-Color Printing

Not every commercially printed publication requires four-color reproduction. Printing in two colors using a grayscale image and spot color can be an effective and inexpensive alternative. In this lesson, you'll learn how to use Adobe Photoshop to prepare full-color images for two-color printing.

In this lesson, you'll learn how to do the following:

- Convert a color image to monochrome, and improve its overall quality.

- Adjust the tonal range of the image by assigning black and white points.

- Sharpen the image.

- Convert a color image to grayscale.

- Add spot color to selected areas of the image.

This lesson will take about 45 minutes to complete. The lesson is designed to be done in Adobe Photoshop. ImageReady does not support channels or spot color.

If needed, remove the previous lesson folder from your hard drive, and copy the Lessons/Lesson13 folder onto it. As you work on this lesson, you'll overwrite the start files. If you need to restore the start files, copy them from the *Adobe Photoshop CS Classroom in a Book* CD.

Note: Windows 2000 users need to unlock the lesson files before using them. For more information, see "Copying the Classroom in a Book files" on page 3.

Printing in color

Color publications are expensive to print commercially because they require four passes through the press—one for each of the four process colors used to create the full-color effect. The colors in the publication must be separated into cyan, magenta, yellow, and black plates for the press, which also adds to the expense.

Printing images in two colors can be a much less costly yet effective approach for many projects, even if they begin with an image in full color. With Photoshop, you can convert color to grayscale without sacrificing image quality. You can also add a second spot color for accent, and Photoshop will create the two-color separations needed for the printing process.

Note: Spot color is intended for images that will be printed to film during the printing process. The spot-color techniques covered in this lesson are not appropriate for color images printed to desktop printers or for images designed for electronic distribution.

Using channels and the Channels palette

Channels in Adobe Photoshop are used for storing information, and they play an important role in this lesson. *Color channels* store the color information for an image, and *alpha channels* store selections or masks you can use when you want to edit specific parts of an image. A third channel type, the *spot-color channel*, is used to specify color separations for printing an image with spot-color inks. For more information about channels, see Lesson 6, "Masks and Channels."

In this lesson, you'll use all three types of channels. You'll learn to mix color channels to improve the quality of an image. You'll select areas of the image by loading a selection from an alpha channel. And you'll use a spot-color channel to add a second color to the image.

Getting started

You'll start the lesson by viewing the final Lesson file to see the duotone image that you will create.

1 Start Adobe Photoshop, holding down Ctrl+Alt+Shift (Windows) or Command+Option+Shift (Mac OS) to restore the default preferences. (See "Restoring default preferences" on page 4.)

As messages appear, select Yes to confirm that you want to reset preferences, No to defer setting up your color monitor, and Close to close the Welcome Screen.

2 On the tool options bar, select the File Browser button, and use the Folders palette to navigate to and select the Lessons/Lesson13 folder on your hard disk.

3 In the thumbnails palette, select the 13End.psd file, so that it appears in the Preview palette in the File Browser.

4 When you have finished viewing the file, double-click the thumbnail for the 13Start.psd file to open it in Photoshop.

5 Close the File Browser.

6 If guides are showing, choose View > Show > Guides to remove the checkmark and hide the guides.

Using channels to change color to grayscale

Sometimes it's possible to improve the quality of an image by blending two or more color channels. For instance, one channel in an image may look particularly strong, but would look even better if you could add some detail from another channel. In Photoshop, you can blend color channels with the Channel Mixer command in either RGB mode (for on-screen display) or CMYK mode (for printing). For more information on color modes, see Lesson 19, "Setting Up Your Monitor for Color Management."

In this lesson, you'll use the Channel Mixer command to improve the quality of an RGB image that you'll then convert to grayscale mode. But first, you'll use the Channels palette to view the different channels in the image.

1 Choose Window > Channels (or click the Channels tab) and drag the palette from group that also contains the Layers and Paths palettes. Place the Channels palette on your screen where you can easily access it.

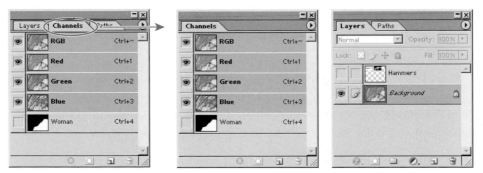

Drag the Channels palette from the Layers palette to make both palettes visible at the same time.

Because the image is in RGB mode, the Channels palette displays the image's red, green, and blue channels. Notice that all the color channels are currently visible, including the RGB channel, which is a composite of the separate red, green, and blue channels. To see the individual channels, you can use the palette's eye icons.

2 Click the eye icons (👁) to turn off all color channels in the Channels palette except the Red channel. The colors in the Start image change to shades of gray.

All channels off except red   *Red channel*

3 Drag the eye icon from the Red channel to the Green channel and then to the Blue channel. Notice how the monochrome image in the image window changes with each channel. The Green channel shows the best overall contrast and the best detail in the woman's face, while the Blue channel shows good contrast in the framework behind the woman.

Green channel   *Blue channel*

4 In the Channels palette, click the box to set an eye icon for the composite RGB channel to display all the color channels in the image.

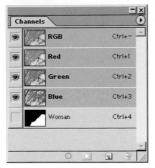

All channels displayed

RGB image

Now you'll use the Channel Mixer command to improve the image in this lesson. Specifically, you'll divide the image into two areas, the woman and the framework, and mix different amounts of source channels in each selection.

Mixing the woman's image

First, you'll select the woman's image by loading a premade selection.

1 In the Layers palette, make sure that the Background layer is selected.

2 Choose Select > Load Selection. In the dialog box, select Woman from the Channel menu to load a selection that outlines the image of the woman. Click OK.

Now you'll mix the Green and Blue channels to improve the selection's contrast. You'll use Green as the base channel because it has the best overall contrast for the image.

3 Choose Image > Adjustments > Channel Mixer.

4 In the Channel Mixer dialog box, choose Green for the Output Channel. The Source Channel for Green changes to 100%.

5 Select the Monochrome check box to change the image to shades of gray. This option gives you an idea of how the selection will look in grayscale mode, so that you can more accurately adjust the selection's tonal range.

Note: *The Output Channel option now shows Gray selected instead of Green.*

The resulting image is a little flat. You can bring out the contrast and improve the highlights by blending in some of the Blue channel.

6 Drag the slider for the Blue Source Channel or type **10%**. Click OK.

Selection loaded   *Channel Mixer dialog box with 10% blue*

Mixing the framework's image

Next, you'll select the framework, convert this part of the image to monochrome, and again mix channels to improve the contrast and detail.

1 Choose Select > Inverse to select the framework behind the woman.

2 Choose Image > Adjustments > Channel Mixer.

3 In the Channel Mixer dialog box, choose Green for the Output Channel, and select Monochrome. Again, the image appears in grayscale and the Output Channel option automatically switches from Green to Gray.

This time the resulting image is dark and lacks contrast. You can improve the image again by blending in some of the Blue channel to increase the contrast.

4 Drag the slider for the Blue Source Channel or type **26%**. Click OK.

Inverse of selection   Channel Mixer dialog box with 26% blue

5 Choose Select > Deselect.

Both the woman and the framework now show better contrast and detail. But the image is still an RGB color image (one that contains only gray values). To convert the image to grayscale mode, you will use the Grayscale command.

6 Choose Image > Mode > Grayscale. When prompted, select Don't Flatten to keep the image's two layers separate. (You'll use the second layer later in this lesson.) The image converts to grayscale mode, and the color channels in the Channels palette are replaced by a single Gray channel.

7 Choose File > Save to save your work.

Assigning values to the black and white points

You can further improve the quality of the image by adjusting the black and white limits of its tonal range. In Lesson 3, "Basic Photo Corrections," you learned to use the sliders on the Levels command histogram to adjust the range. In this lesson, you'll control the range more accurately by using the Levels command eyedropper to assign specific values to the darkest and lightest points.

1 Choose Image > Adjustments > Levels.

2 In the Levels dialog box, double-click the White Eyedropper tool (✐), which is on the right, to open the color picker for the white point.

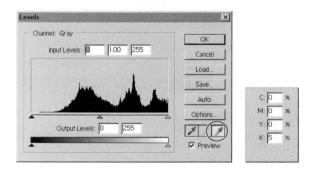

3 Enter **0, 0, 0,** and **5** in the CMYK text boxes, and click OK. These values generally produce the best results when printing the white points (highlights) of a grayscale image onto white paper.

4 Next, double-click the Black Eyedropper tool (✐) in the Levels dialog box to open the color picker for the black point.

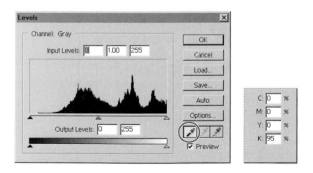

5 Enter **0, 0, 0**, and **95** in the CMYK text boxes, and click OK. These values generally produce the best results when printing the black points (shadows) of a grayscale image onto white paper.

Now that you've defined the values for the black and white points, you'll use the Levels command eyedropper to assign the values to the darkest and lightest areas in the image.

6 Make sure that the Black Eyedropper tool is selected, and position it in the darkest area of the framework behind the woman's elbow. Click to assign this area the values you set in Step 5.

7 Next, select the White Eyedropper tool in the Levels dialog box, position the tool in the lightest area of the woman's collar, and click to assign this area the values you set in Step 3.

Black Eyedropper tool selecting   *White Eyedropper tool selecting*
darkest area behind elbow   *lightest area in collar*

8 Click OK to close the dialog box and apply the changes. If an alert message appears, click No so that the new target colors do not become the defaults.

Assigning the black and white points shifts the image's histogram to produce a more evenly distributed tonal range.

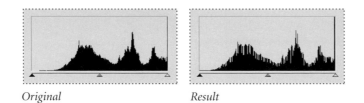

Original   *Result*

9 Choose File > Save.

Sharpening the image

By applying the Unsharp Mask filter to the image, you can create the illusion of a more focused image.

1 Choose Filter > Sharpen > Unsharp Mask. Make sure that the Preview option is selected so that you can view the effect before you apply it. To get a better view, you can place the pointer within the preview window and drag to see different parts of the image (we focused on the woman's face). You can also change the magnification of the preview image with the plus and minus buttons located below the window.

2 Drag the Amount slider until the image is as sharp as you want (we used 57%), and make sure that the Radius is set to 1 pixel.

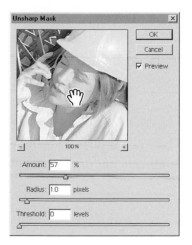

3 Click OK to apply the Unsharp Mask filter to the image.

Setting up for spot color

Spot colors, also called *custom colors*, are premixed inks that are used instead of, or in addition to, the cyan, magenta, yellow, and black process-color inks. Each spot color requires its own color separation or printing plate. Graphic designers use spot colors to specify colors that would be difficult or impossible to achieve by combining the four process inks.

You'll now add spot color to the image in this lesson by creating a spot-color channel.

1 In the Channels palette menu, choose New Spot Channel.

2 In the New Spot Channel dialog box, click the color box, and select Custom in the color picker.

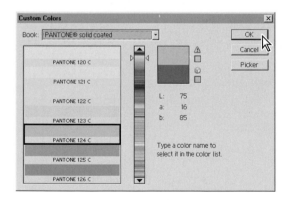

3 When the Custom Colors dialog box opens, type **124** to scroll automatically to the PANTONE® custom color 124 C. (There is no text box; you just type. Avoid long pauses between keystrokes. If you make a mistake, pause, and then try again.) Click OK.

4 In the New Spot Channel dialog box, type **100**% for Solidity.

The solidity setting can simulate on-screen the ink solidity of the printed spot color. Inks range from transparent (0% solidity) to opaque (100% solidity). The Solidity option affects the on-screen preview only and has no effect on the printed output.

5 Click OK to create the spot-color channel. A new spot-color channel named PANTONE 124 C is added to the Channels palette.

6 Choose File > Save.

About spot colors

Note the following when working with spot colors:

• *For spot-color graphics that have crisp edges and knock out the underlying image, consider creating the additional artwork in a page-layout or illustration application.*

• *To apply spot color as a tint throughout an image, convert the image to Duotone mode and apply the spot color to one of the duotone plates. You can use up to four spot colors, one per plate.*

• *The names of the spot colors print on the separations.*

• *Spot colors are overprinted on top of the fully composited image. Each spot color is overprinted in the order in which it appears in the Channels palette.*

• *You cannot move spot colors above a default channel in the Channels palette, except in Multichannel mode.*

• *Spot colors can't be applied to individual layers.*

• *Printing an image with a spot-color channel to a composite color printer will print the spot colors at an opacity indicated by the solidity setting.*

• *You can merge spot-color channels with color channels, splitting the spot color into its color-channel components.*

Adding spot color

You can add spot color to selected areas of an image in different ways with varying effects. For instance, you can apply spot color to part of a grayscale image so that the selection prints in the spot color rather than in the base ink. Because spot colors in Photoshop print over the top of a fully composited image, you may also need to remove the base color in an image when adding spot color to it. If you do not remove the base color, it may show through the semitransparent spot-color ink used in the printing process.

You can also use spot color to add solid and screened blocks of color to an image. By screening the spot color, you can create the illusion of adding an extra, lighter color to the printed piece.

Removing a grayscale area and adding spot color

You'll begin your work in spot color by changing the framework behind the woman to the spot color. You must first select the framework, remove it from the grayscale image, and then add the selection to the spot-color channel.

1 In the Channels palette, select the Gray channel.

2 Choose Select > Load Selection. In the dialog box, choose Woman from the Channel menu and select the Invert option. Click OK to load a selection of the framework behind the woman.

3 Choose Edit > Cut to cut the selection from the image. Make sure that black is set as the foreground color.

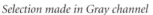
Selection made in Gray channel   *Selection cut from Gray channel*

4 In the Channels palette, select the PANTONE 124 C channel.

5 Choose Edit > Paste to paste the framework selection into the spot-color channel. In the 13Start window, the framework reappears in the Pantone color.

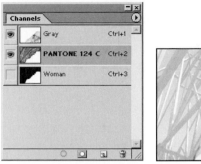 

Selection pasted into spot-color channel

6 Choose Select > Deselect.

7 Choose File > Save.

Removing spot color from a grayscale area

Now, you'll remove some spot color where it overlaps the grayscale area of a second layer of the image.

1 In the Layers palette, click the box to set an eye icon (👁) next to the Hammers layer to make it visible. (Click just the box to set the eye icon. Do not select the layer.)

Notice that the spot color of the framework overlaps part of the Hammers layer. You'll remove this overlap by making a new selection and cutting it from the spot-color channel.

2 Choose View > Show > Guides.

3 Select the Rectangular Marquee tool (▢), and make sure that Normal is selected in the tool options bar.

4 Drag a selection across the image, from one edge to the other and from the top edge to the uppermost horizontal guide.

5 Make sure that the spot-color channel in the Channels palette is still active, and press Delete to remove the rectangular selection from the channel. In the image window, the spot color disappears from the hammers image.

Making selection   *Selection cut from spot-color channel*

6 Choose Select > Deselect.

7 Choose File > Save.

Adding solid and screened areas of spot color

Next, you'll vary the effect of adding spot color by adding a solid block of the color and then a block of the color screened to 50%. The two areas will appear to be different colors even though you have used the same Pantone custom color on the same color separation.

First, you'll make a selection for the solid block of color and fill the selection using a keyboard shortcut.

1 Using the Rectangular Marquee tool ([⬚]), drag a selection marquee around the white square area in the upper right corner of the image (bounded by the two guides).

2 Hold down Alt (Windows) or Option (Mac OS), and press Delete to fill the selection with the foreground color. Because the PANTONE 124 C channel is selected, the foreground color is actually PANTONE 124 (not black) and appears in the selected area.

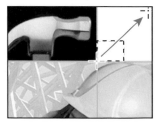

Making selection for spot color   *Selection filled with solid color*

Now you can add a lighter block of spot color to the image.

3 Make a rectangular selection directly below the left hammer and bounded by the guides.

4 In the Color palette, drag the color slider to 20% (do not type this time) to set the value for the new block of color.

5 Hold down Alt/Option and press Delete to fill the selection with a 20% screen of PANTONE 124.

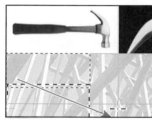 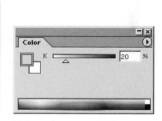 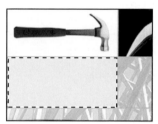

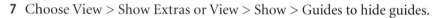

Making selection   *Color value set to 20%*   *Selection filled with 20% color*

6 Choose Select > Deselect.

7 Choose View > Show Extras or View > Show > Guides to hide guides.

8 Choose File > Save.

Adding spot color to text

Text in an image can also appear in spot color. There are different methods for creating this effect, but the most straightforward is to add the text directly to the spot-color channel. Note that text in a spot-color channel behaves differently from text created on a type layer. Spot-color–channel text is uneditable. Once you create the type, you cannot change its specifications, and once you deselect the type, you cannot reposition it.

Now, you'll add text to the spot-color channel and place the text in the light block of spot color.

1 In the Color palette, return the color slider to 100%.

2 Select the Type tool (T), and click the image in the light block of color. A red mask appears over the artwork, and an insertion point for the text flashes.

3 In the Type tool options bar, select a sans serif typeface from the Font menu (such as Myriad, which is included on the *Adobe Photoshop CS Classroom in a Book* CD, or Arial). Also choose Bold, and scrub or type **66** to set the font size.

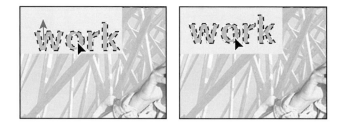

4 Type **work** in the image window.

5 Select the Move tool (⯈⊕), and drag the text so that it is centered in the light block of color.

6 Choose Select > Deselect.

7 Choose File > Save.

You have finished preparing the image for two-color printing. To see how the color separations for the printed piece will look, try alternately hiding and displaying the two color channels in the Channels palette.

8 Click the eye icon (👁) for the Gray channel in the Channels palette. The Gray channel is hidden, and the image window changes to just the areas of the image that will print in the spot color.

9 Redisplay the Gray channel by clicking to set an eye icon (👁). Then hide the PANTONE 124 C channel by clicking its eye icon. Just the grayscale areas of the image appear in the image window.

10 Click to set an eye icon for the PANTONE 124 C channel to make it visible again.

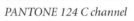

| Final image | Black channel | PANTONE 124 C channel |

If you have a printer available, you can also try printing the image. You'll find that it prints on two sheets of paper—one representing the color separation for the spot color and one representing the grayscale areas of the image.

For the Web: Creating two-color Web graphics

Two-color images are used in print to keep costs down and expand the tonal range of grayscale images. Even when printing costs aren't an issue, you can use two-color images for effect. Try this technique in ImageReady for creating effective two-color graphics for the Web that deliver maximum impact without increasing the file size. You can start with an image in Photoshop, or you can work exclusively in ImageReady.

1 For a duotone effect, start by creating a grayscale image in Photoshop or by desaturating an ImageReady image. To convert your color Photoshop image to grayscale, choose Image > Mode > Grayscale.

In ImageReady, it's not possible to create a grayscale image, but you can use the Image > Adjustments > Desaturate command. ImageReady supports only RGB files. Even an image that may appear to be grayscale in ImageReady is actually an RGB file.

2 In Photoshop, choose Image > Mode > RGB Color to convert your grayscale image to RGB mode.

3 In the Layers palette, click the New Layer button (⊡) at the bottom of the palette to create a new layer. Then drag the new layer into position below the grayscale image layer.

In Photoshop, if the grayscale image is the Background, you must convert the Background to a layer by double-clicking the Background in the Layers palette and naming it in the New Layer dialog box.

4 In the image, fill the new layer with a second color, using a two-step process:

• In the Color palette, enter values for the color to set the foreground color. (Or, you can select a color swatch in the Swatches palette.)

• Press Alt+Delete (Windows) or Option+Delete (Mac OS).

The new foreground color fills the new layer.

Note: *There are several other ways to fill a new layer with the selected color, such as choosing Layer > New Fill Layer > Solid Color, or selecting the New Fill Or Adjustment Layer button at the bottom of the Layers palette and then selecting Solid Color on the pop-up menu.*

5 Select the top layer of the image and choose Multiply from the Layers palette mode menu.

Multiply mode looks at the color information in each layer and multiplies the base color by the blend color. The resulting color is always darker. Multiplying any color with another color produces progressively darker colors.

6 Duplicate the top layer by dragging it to the New Layer button at the bottom of the Layers palette.

Grayscale image with color layer beneath

Duplicating the top layer

7 With the new layer selected, choose Hard Light from the Layers palette mode menu. This mode brings out the color underneath.

Hard Light filter applied

This technique works most effectively on the top layer of an image with the Hard Light mode applied. Hard Light mode multiplies or screens the colors, depending on the blend color. The effect is similar to shining a harsh spotlight on the image. If the blend color (light source) is lighter than 50% gray, the image is lightened as if it were screened. This is useful for adding highlights to an image. If the blend color is darker than 50% gray, the image is darkened as if it were multiplied. This is useful for adding shadows to an image.

8 Select the middle layer. Choose Image > Adjustments > Levels, and adjust the histogram using the sliders to let more or less color from the bottom layer show through.

9 If desired, decrease the opacity of the different layers and note the effect.

10 Save the file in the GIF file format for the Web, optimizing the file as needed.

As a variation, select the Dodge tool or Burn tool and adjust one detail or object in your image at a time.

Review questions

1 What are the three types of channels in Photoshop, and how are they used?

2 How can you improve the quality of a color image that has been converted to grayscale?

3 How do you assign specific values to the black and white points in an image?

4 How do you set up a spot-color channel?

5 How do you add spot color to a specific area in a grayscale image?

6 How can you apply spot color to text?

Review answers

1 Channels in Photoshop are used for storing information. Color channels store the color information for an image; alpha channels store selections or masks for editing specific parts of an image; and spot-color channels create color separations for printing an image with spot-color inks.

2 You can use the Color Mixer command to blend color channels to bring out the contrast and detail in an image. You can extend the tonal range of the image by adjusting its black and white points. You can also sharpen the image by applying the Unsharp Mask filter.

3 You assign specific values with the Levels command Black Eyedropper and White Eyedropper tools.

4 You set up a spot-color channel by choosing New Spot Channel from the pop-up menu on the Channels palette, and by specifying a color from the Custom color picker in the New Spot Channel dialog box.

5 With the Gray channel active, you select the area, cut it from the Gray channel, and paste it into the spot-color channel.

6 You can add the text to the spot-color channel. However, text created in this way is not editable and cannot be repositioned once it is deselected.

14 | Arranging Layer Objects in ImageReady

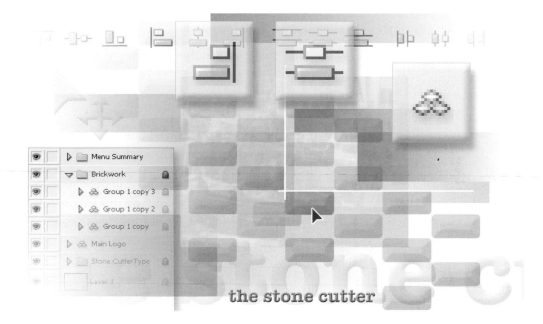

Adobe ImageReady CS makes it even easier to position layer elements in an image. The new Smart Guides show you alignment relationships as you drag objects from one spot to another. Perhaps best of all, you can now use a keyboard shortcut that creates a duplicate of an object as you drag, a feature that can save you bundles of time.

In this lesson, you'll learn how to do the following:

- Align an individual object to other objects as you move it in the image.

- Duplicate and move an object in one action.

- Create layer groups and layer sets, and to distinguish between the two.

- Apply changes to layer sets.

- Lock a layer set to prevent further changes.

- Move an object that is part of a layer group without moving the rest of the group.

- Align objects using tool options bar buttons.

- Change the attributes of multiple text objects.

This lesson will take less than an hour to complete. Smart Guides for layer objects are not available in Photoshop, so you must do this lesson in ImageReady.

If needed, remove the previous lesson folder from your hard drive, and then copy the Lessons/Lesson14 folder onto your computer. As you work on this lesson, you'll overwrite the start files. If you need to restore the start files later, recopy them from the *Adobe Photoshop CS Classroom in a Book* CD.

Getting Started

In this lesson, you'll have the pleasure of working with a new efficiency in ImageReady CS: Smart Guides. As usual, you'll start by restoring the default preferences and reviewing the End file before opening the Start file and getting to work.

Note: Do not look for the File Browser in ImageReady, because that feature is found only in Photoshop.

1 Start Adobe ImageReady while holding down Ctrl+Alt+Shift (Windows) or Command+Option+Shift (Mac OS) to restore the default preferences. (See "Restoring default preferences" on page 4.)

As messages appear, select Yes to confirm that you want to reset preferences, No to defer setting up your color monitor, and Close to close the Welcome Screen.

2 Choose File > Open and select the 14End.psd file in the Lessons/Lesson14 folder that you copied from the *Adobe Photoshop CS Classroom in a Book* CD. Click Open.

3 Examine the End file in the image window and notice the listings in various palettes, especially the Layers palette. When you finish, either close the file without saving any changes or minimize it by clicking the appropriate button on the image window title bar.

4 Choose File > Open, select the 14Start.psd file in the Lessons/Lesson14 folder, and click Open.

The 14Start.psd file already contains several layers that have been prepared for you, to save time. One layer is an image of a single building block, which you'll duplicate and arrange easily into a precise grid pattern.

Note: The type layers in this lesson file are set in Myriad. If this font is not installed on your computer, the appearance of the text in the image may not match the illustrations in this book. You can install the Myriad font, which is provided on the Adobe Photoshop CS Classroom in a Book CD. See "Installing the Classroom in a Book fonts" on page 3.

Duplicating and aligning layers

The new Smart Guides is a Snap-To feature found only in ImageReady. Smart Guides help you align layer objects to other elements in the file. Unlike regular guides that you drag from the Rulers to place, Smart Guide lines are temporary, appearing only during the dragging process. They appear when the edges or center (vertical or horizontal) of the object you're moving crosses the center line or an edge of another layer object.

1 Choose View > Snap if the Snap command is not already selected (checked), and then choose View > Snap To and verify that Guides and Layers are also selected (checked). If not, choose these commands now.

2 In the Layers palette, select the Stone layer and drag it to the Create A New Layer button (🔲) at the bottom of the palette. Leave the Stone Copy layer selected.

3 In the toolbox, select the Move tool (▸⊕), and then look in the tool options bar to verify that the Layer Select tool (▸) is selected, or select it now.

4 In the image window, drag the Stone Copy layer up and to the left, so that its lower right corner snaps into alignment with the upper left corner of the original Stone layer.

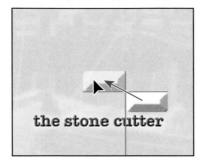

As you drag, the blue Smart Guide lines appear whenever the dragged object aligns with another object in the image. The Smart Guides extend from the object you're moving to the alignment points in the other object.

Note: If you do not see the Smart Guides as you drag, make sure that the appropriate commands are selected in the Snap To submenu. See "Getting Started" on page 460.

5 Hold down Alt (Windows) or Option (Mac OS) and drag up and to the right from the Stone Copy layer.

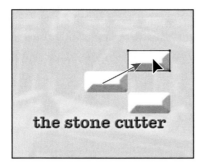

Holding down the designated key as you drag duplicates the selected layer, so that when you release the mouse, you'll have three stones in place.

Note: As you drag, the Smart Guides show you any alignment to the edge or center of any other layer objects in the image. Be sure to watch the Smart Guides carefully as you work so that you line up the object you're moving with the correct other object. This will be more pronounced as you continue because the number of objects in the image is growing.

6 Using the same technique as in Step 5, drag three more new stones into position so that they form the pattern shown in the illustration below.

Creating a layer group

You'll use the simple arrangement of stone objects from the previous task as a pattern that you'll repeat across the image. This will make it easier to fill in the rest of the pattern.

1 In the image window, drag the Move tool (▸⊕) across the six stone objects to select them.

Note: Be sure to use the Move tool, not one of the selection marquee tools.

Bounding boxes and corner anchor points appear around each of the objects, and the six layers are highlighted in the Layers palette, indicating that they are selected.

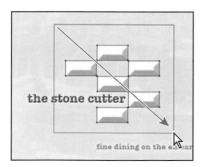

2 Choose Layer > Group Layers so that a large bounding box encloses the selected objects, replacing the six individual bounding boxes.

Notice that the six Stone layers are now nested in the Layers palette under a layer group named Group 1.

3 In the Layers palette, click the arrow to collapse the Group 1 layer group.

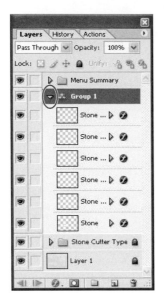

4 Choose File > Save.

Duplicating and aligning layer groups

You can treat layer groups like individual layer objects. You can duplicate, move, and transform them as a unit. In ImageReady—unlike Photoshop—you can also select multiple layers, layer sets, or layer groups in the Layers palette. Once you've selected these, you can drag them to the buttons at the bottom of the Layers palette to duplicate, delete, or group the entire collection of selected layers, layer sets, and layer groups.

Before you begin, make sure that the Move tool (⬆) is still selected in the toolbox and that the Layer Select tool is selected in the tool options bar, or select them now.

1 In the Layers palette, select the Group 1 layer group and drag it to the Create A New Layer button (⬛).

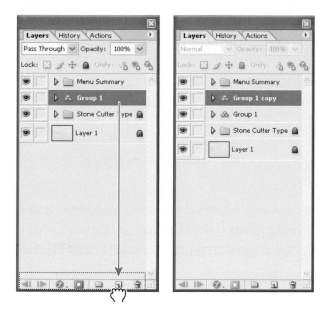

2 Using the Move tool in the image window, drag the Group 1 Copy layer group up and to the right, so that it aligns as shown below, with the individual stones lined up in three diagonal rows of four stones each.

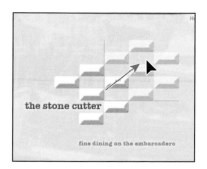

3 In the Layers palette, click the Group 1 Copy layer so that the group bounding box replaces the individual bounding boxes in the image window, and then set the Opacity at 35%, either by dragging the slider or typing.

4 In the image window, select the Group 1 Copy and hold down Alt (Windows) or Option (Mac OS) and drag down and to the right, aligning the group to the original layer group.

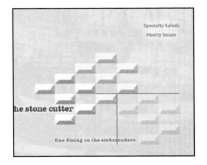

As you drag, the Smart Guides will appear whenever the layer group aligns with any other object in the image. Watch where the Smart Guides connect so that you are sure you're aligning the layer group copy to the original layer group, not to the text blocks in the image.

5 Repeat Step 4, but this time drag the new layer group up and to the left, as shown below, even though this position doesn't exactly balance yet with the rest of the pattern.

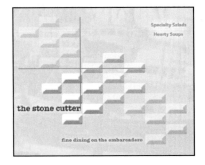

Transforming a layer group

In the previous task, you changed the opacity of an entire group of objects by changing the Opacity value for the group. Now, you'll transform a group by turning it upside down.

1 In the Layers palette, select the Group 1 Copy 3 layer set so that the group bounding box replaces the individual bounding boxes.

2 Choose Edit > Free Transform.

3 Move the pointer outside one of the corners of the layer group so that it appears as a curved, double-headed arrow. Then, hold down Shift as you drag to rotate the layer group 180°, turning it upside down.

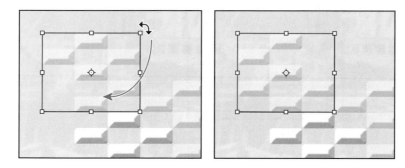

4 Release the mouse button first and then the Shift key.

5 Press Enter (Windows) or Return (Mac OS) to commit the transformation.

6 If necessary, use the Move tool to nudge the rotated layer group into alignment. Then save your work.

Creating a layer set and applying changes

A layer set is similar to a layer group, but there are a few functional differences between the two. (See sidebar, "About layer groups and layer sets," after this topic.) Both help you organize the Layers palette. You can nest both layer groups and layer sets within other layer groups or sets.

1 In the Layers palette, Shift-click to select the three copies of the Group 1 layer group. Be careful to select only the copies, not the Group 1 layer group itself.

2 Drag the selected layers to the Create A New Set button (▭) at the bottom of the Layers palette.

The three copies of the stone-image layer groups now appear nested under a layer set with the default name, Set 1.

3 Double-click the name Set 1 so that it can be edited and type **Brickwork** to rename it. Press Enter (Windows) or Return (Mac OS) to set the name.

About layer groups and layer sets

Layer groups and layer sets have much in common: You can select them and move them as a unit. You can transform an entire layer group or layer set, such as rotating, skewing, or scaling it. You can also apply opacity changes to a whole group or set. Either one organizes specified layers in the Layers palette into a hierarchy that can be collapsed to a single level or expanded to show its contents. Both can contain multiple levels of mixed layer sets and layer groups nested inside them.

The most important differences between them are:

• You select a layer set by clicking it in the Layers palette, not in the image window. You can select a layer group either by clicking it in the Layers palette or by clicking in the image window. To do the latter, you must select the Move tool (with the default Layer Select option selected on the tool options bar) and click any object that is a part of that layer group.

• Layer sets are available in both Photoshop and ImageReady. Layer groups are found exclusively in ImageReady. If you open an ImageReady file that includes layer groups in Photoshop, the layer groups will appear in the Layers palette as layer sets while you work on the file in Photoshop. When you reopen the same file in ImageReady, the layer groups are restored, so that the layer groups you defined as such in ImageReady appear again as groups (and those defined as layer sets remain layer sets).

In ImageReady, you can convert an existing layer set into a layer group and vice versa. This process is controlled by the Treat Layer Set As A Group check box, which appears in the Layer Set Options or Layer Group Options dialog box that opens from the Layers palette menu. When the Treat Layer Set As A Group option is selected, the item is a layer group. When the option is not selected, the item is a layer set. To change from a set to a group or vice versa, just click to add or remove the checkmark.

If you want to see this for yourself, try temporarily unlocking the Brickwork layer set that you just finished creating in the previous procedure. Then, click a blank area of the Layers palette to deselect that layer set, or choose Select > Deselect Layers. When you click any of the low-opacity stones in the image window with the Move tool (with the Layer Select tool option selected in the tool options bar), it selects one of the groups nested within the Brickwork layer set, not the entire set. If you want to select all three of these groups, you can either Shift-click to select them in the image window or you could select the Brickwork layer set in the Layers palette.

• Be sure to relock the Brickwork layer set before you continue.

4 Click the arrow for the Brickwork layer set to collapse it, but leave the layer set selected for the next two steps.

5 On the Layers palette, change the Opacity to 75%, either by dragging the slider or typing **75** in the percentage box.

6 Click the Lock button (🔒) near the top of the Layers palette to prevent further changes to the Brickwork layer set. A lock icon appears to the left of the layer set name, indicating that it is indeed locked.

Why would you change the Opacity of the layer set now? You might do it for aesthetic reasons, or at the request of your client. Instead of expanding the layer set and the layer groups to adjust the opacity of the individual layers, you can make the change at the layer-set level. This means that you enter the change once instead of 17 times (once for each individual Stone layer).

Modifying objects within a layer group

You can change the attributes of individual layer objects within layer groups and layer sets. You can even add new layer objects to an existing group simply by creating them while the group is selected or dragging them to different positions in the Layers palette.

For convenience, you'll start by doing something now that could have been done earlier but wasn't: renaming the layer groups that are nested inside the Brickwork layer set.

1 In the Layers palette, double-click the name Group 1 to make the name editable, and type **Main Logo** to rename it. Then press Enter (Windows) or Return (Mac OS).

Keep the Main Logo group selected.

2 Make sure that the Move tool (⤢) is selected, and then select the Direct Select tool (⤢) in the tool options bar.

3 In the image window, click to select any one of the stone objects in the Main Logo.

In the Layers palette, the Main Logo layer group expands automatically. The bounding box in the image window shrinks to surround only the selected stone.

4 Press Alt (Windows) or Option (Mac OS) and drag to move a copy of the selected stone into alignment with the stonework pattern, as shown in the illustration below.

A seventh layer now appears within the layer group in the Layers palette.

5 Collapse the Main Logo layer group in the Layers palette and choose File > Save.

Duplicating and editing text objects

In ImageReady, text can be selected and manipulated like any other layer object. This includes the power to align text objects precisely and easily with Smart Guides.

1 In the tool options bar for the Move tool, select the Layer Select tool ( ).

2 Select the Hearty Soups layer object in the image window.

3 Press Alt (Windows) or Option (Mac OS) and drag down to create and move a copy of the Hearty Soups layer. (At this stage, exact position isn't important.)

4 Use the same technique from Steps 2 and 3 to create two more copies of the Hearty Soups layer.

5 Select the Type tool (**T**) in the toolbox, and drag or double-click and drag to select the words *Hearty Soups* in the first copy you made of this layer.

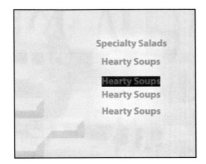

6 Type **International Entrees**.

7 Using the same process, rename the remaining two copies of the Hearty Soups layer, but type **Fresh Seafood** in one copy and **Chocolate** in the other.

Aligning and grouping text objects

Another quick method of lining up layers is to use the alignment buttons that appear in the tool options bar when you select the Move tool. This array of over a dozen different types of alignments and distributions provides a one-click, intuitive way to tidy up your Web illustrations so that they're easy to understand and use.

1 Select the Move tool (▸₊) in the toolbox. Make sure that the Layer Select tool (▸) is selected in the tool options bar.

2 In the image window, select the Chocolate layer and drag it so that it aligns as follows:

• The baseline of the text aligns with the lower edge of the topmost stone in the Main Logo layer group (the group with 100% Opacity).

- The right edge of the text aligns with the right edge of the Brickwork layer set.

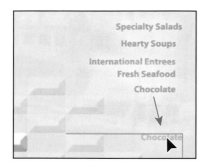

3 In the tool options bar, select the Direct Select tool (![]).

4 Starting above and to the right of the top line of text, drag a selection marquee that covers at least part of each of the five lines of text.

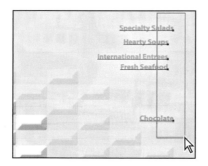

If you accidentally select one of the stone objects, either Shift-click the selected stone object to deselect it or try dragging over the text layers again.

5 In the tool options bar, select the Align Layer Right Edges button (![]).

6 Also in the tool options bar, select the Distribute Layer Vertical Centers button (![]).

The five lines of text are now right-aligned and evenly spaced.

Changing multiple lines of type

Unlike most word-processing programs, you can change the type characteristics of multiple lines of text in ImageReady without double-clicking or dragging a cursor to select all the words. You'll see for yourself how easy this is when you select font attributes for the list of menu specialties in the image file.

1 If the five text layers are not still selected, expand the Menu Summary layer set and Shift-click to select them, or drag a marquee as you did in the previous procedure.

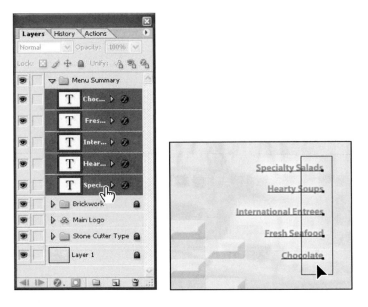

2 Choose Window > Character to open the Character palette.

3 In the Character palette, specify the following font options:

• For Font Family, select a serif font from the pop-up menu. (We used Adobe Garamond.)

• For Font Style, select Regular, if it is not already selected.

• For Font Size, type **19 px.**

4 Click the color swatch in the Character palette to open the color picker.

5 In the color picker, select a dark rose color. (We used R=**133**, G=**109**, B=**109**.) Then click OK to close the color picker.

6 Choose File > Save, and then admire your finished work because you've now completed this lesson.

Review questions

1 What are Smart Guides?

2 Describe three methods of duplicating a layer in ImageReady.

3 What is the easiest method of duplicating multiple layers in ImageReady?

4 Why did you have to press Enter or Return after you rotated a layer group? Would you have to do so if you rotated only one layer object?

5 What are the three versions of the ImageReady Move tool on the tool options bar? How do their functions vary?

6 What are layer groups and layer sets? How do you create them?

Review answers

1 Smart Guides are temporary guide lines that appear when an object that you are moving aligns with another layer object in the image. The Smart Guides are only long enough to connect the edge or center of the object you're moving with the edge or center of the object it's aligned with in the image.

2 One method of duplicating a layer is to use the Layers palette to drag the layer you want to duplicate to the Create New Layer button at the bottom of the palette. A second method is to choose Layer > Duplicate Layer. The third method is to hold down Alt (Windows) or Option (Mac OS) and drag the layer with the Move tool. Because this third method accomplishes two tasks in one action, many users prefer it.

3 To duplicate multiple layers, first select them by holding down the Shift key and clicking the layers either in the Layers palette or in the image window, using the Move tool. Then duplicate them all at once using one of the three methods for duplicating an individual layer, as described in the previous Review answer. If the layers you want to duplicate are already organized into a layer set or layer group, you can select the layer set or group and then duplicate all of them at once.

4 When you select the Free Transform, another Transform command, or work with the Type tool, you switch into transform or text-edit mode, respectively. Until you press Enter or Return, Photoshop or ImageReady remains in that mode so that you can continue to edit or transform objects. When you commit those changes, you leave transform or text-edit mode and can then perform other kinds of actions in your file.

5 The three tool options for the Move tool in Image Ready are the Layer Move tool (⬆⊕), the Layer Select tool (▸), and the Direct Select tool (▸). Use the Layer Move tool to move an entire layer that is already selected. Use the Layer Select tool to select and move an ungrouped layer or a grouped layer as a single object. Use the Direct Select tool to select and move only a specific layer within a layer group. You can also hold down Shift and use the Direct Select tool to select and move multiple individual layers that are grouped within one or more layer groups.

6 Both layer groups and layer sets are ways of organizing layers on the Layers palette. You can select a layer group or layer set and apply changes to the layers nested within as a unit.

You can create layer sets in Photoshop or ImageReady by either clicking the New Layer Set button in the Layers palette (and then adding layers to it) or dragging an existing layer to the same button to nest that layer within it as you create it. In ImageReady, you can also select multiple layers and drag them to the New Layer Set button to nest them all in the new layer set.

Layer grouping is available only in ImageReady. You create a new layer group by selecting one or more layers and choosing Layer > Group Layers or using the keyboard shortcut Ctrl+G (Windows) or Command+G (Mac OS).

After you create the layer group or a layer set, you can add layers to it by dragging them in the Layers palette into the group or set.

Lesson 15

Lesson 15

15 Creating Links within an Image

This lesson deals with basic slices and image maps—features that you can use to create multiple hypertext links within a single graphic. Users can click one part of your sliced or image-mapped graphic on a Web page to open one site and click another area to open a different site.

There are two techniques you can use to create linked subdivisions of an image that users click to open different sites in a Web browser. One method is to define *slices*, which are rectangular subdivisions of the image in Adobe Photoshop or Adobe ImageReady. The other is to create *image maps*, which are not necessarily rectangular.

In this lesson, you'll learn how to do the following:

• Create image slices, using several methods.

• Distinguish between user slices and auto slices.

• Link user slices to other HTML pages or locations.

• Create "no image" slices to contain text that is editable in HTML.

• Define image-map areas using three different methods.

• Link image-map areas to other HTML pages and locations.

• Generate an HTML page that contains the sliced image in a table.

This lesson will take about 90 minutes to complete. You can do the slices work in either Adobe Photoshop or Adobe ImageReady, but only ImageReady has the tools for creating image maps.

If needed, remove the previous lesson folder from your hard drive, and copy the Lessons/Lesson 15 folder onto it. As you work on this lesson, you'll overwrite the start files. If you need to restore the start files, copy them again from the *Adobe Photoshop CS Classroom in a Book* CD.

Note: *Windows 2000 users need to unlock the lesson files before using them. For more information, see "Copying the Classroom in a Book files" on page 3. (This is not required for Windows XP or Mac OS.)*

Getting started

In this lesson you'll work on graphics that are destined for a Web home page. Your goal is to embed multiple hypertext links within a complex image that is a single .psd file. Different areas, or *hotspots*, of the image map link to different files, so that the user can click one area of the home page to open a linked page or click a different area of the home page to open a different linked page. There will also be unlinked areas of the home page that produce no change if the user clicks randomly or by accident.

Later lessons in this book cover the processes for optimizing individual slices with settings that are different from the rest of the image and how to animate slices by defining rollover effects.

About slices and image maps

The first method is to create *slices*. Slices are areas in an image that you define based on layers, guides, or precise selections in the image, or by using the Slice tool. When you define slices in an image, Photoshop or ImageReady creates an HTML table or cascading style sheet to contain and align the slices. If you want, you can generate and preview an HTML file that contains the sliced image along with the table or cascading style sheet.

An *image map* is also an image area that serves to support a hypertext link. The controls for making image maps appear only in Adobe ImageReady; so you must jump over to ImageReady to do this work if the file is open in Photoshop. ImageReady creates both client-side image maps and server-side image maps. Unlike slices, which are always rectangular, image maps can be any shape.

Previewing the results

You'll start the lesson by viewing an example of the finished HTML home page that you'll create. For this procedure, you'll use your favorite Web browser application (such as Netscape, Internet Explorer, or Safari) instead of Photoshop or ImageReady. You do not need connect to the Internet.

1 Start a Web browser, and open the end file 15End.html in the Lessons/Lesson15/15End folder.

The file contains an HTML table that links to several Web images, all created from Photoshop and ImageReady slices.

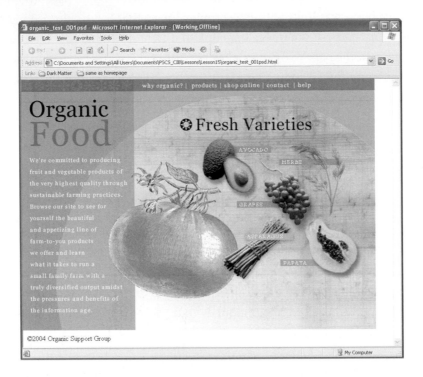

2 Click the "why organic?" button at the top of the Organic Foods Web page.

A new Web browser window opens to a new page. (It's not a fully developed page; it's more of a placeholder page to show that the things you click really do represent links.)

3 Close the Why page instance of the Web browser.

4 In the Web browser open to the Organic Foods page, click the "products" button at the top of the Web page. Then, close the new instance of the Web browser that is showing the Products page.

5 Again in the Web browser open to the Organic Foods page, move the pointer over the picture of asparagus on the right side of the page. Notice that the pointer changes to a pointing-finger icon (🖑), indicating that this area is linked. Move the pointer on and off the different areas of the page and notice when the pointer appears as an arrow and when as a hand.

6 Click the bunch of asparagus to open yet another linked Web page. Then close that Web browser to see the main page. Click some of the other links you find on the page.

7 When you finish viewing the end files, close all the Web browser windows and quit that application.

In this procedure, you witnessed two different types of links: slices (in the menu buttons at the top of the Web page) and image maps (the asparagus, papaya, and herbs image areas, in which the linked area matches the shape of the item pictured).

You'll start by working with slices, which are always rectangular.

Slicing an image in Photoshop

You can define slices in Photoshop by dragging the Slice tool or by converting layers or selections into slices. You'll begin the lesson by slicing menu buttons for the Web page, using the Slice tool in Photoshop.

About designing Web pages with Photoshop and ImageReady

When designing Web pages using Adobe Photoshop and Adobe ImageReady, keep in mind the tools and features that are available in each application.

• *Photoshop provides tools for creating and manipulating static images for use on the Web. You can divide an image into slices, add links and HTML text, optimize the slices, and save the image as a Web page.*

• *ImageReady provides many—but not all—of the same image-editing tools as Photoshop. In addition, it includes tools and palettes for advanced Web processing and creating dynamic Web images such as animations and rollovers.*

Preparing to create slices

Before you start doing any work in your file, you'll customize the work options so that everything is ready to go.

1 Start Adobe Photoshop, holding down Ctrl+Alt+Shift (Windows) or Command+Option+Shift (Mac OS) to restore the default preferences. (See "Restoring default preferences" on page 4.)

2 Click the File Browser button ( ) and use the File Browser Folders palette to locate and select the Lessons/Lesson15 folder in the File Browser Folders palette.

3 Double-click the 15Start.psd thumbnail, or select that file and choose File > Open on the File Browser menu bar.

If a notice appears asking whether you want to update the text layers for vector-based output, click Update.

The lesson file includes blue horizontal and vertical guide lines. You'll use the guides and the snap-to commands when you draw marquees, so that they are tightly aligned.

4 Click the close button on the File Browser title bar or click the File Browser button on the tool options bar twice to close the File Browser to reduce clutter in the work area.

5 Make sure that the following commands are selected (checked), or select them now if they are not.

- View > Show > Guides
- View > Show > Slices
- View > Snap
- View > Snap To > Guides
- View > Snap To > Slices

The blue guide lines have been created to help you draw slices accurately. As you create slices close to the guides, the edges of the slice will snap to the guides so that your slices are uniform and efficient.

Using the Slice tool to create slices

You might wonder why the heading for this topic uses the word "slices" instead of "a slice." The answer is that unless you create a slice that includes the whole image—which would be a fairly useless thing to do, especially since that slice is created automatically—you can't create just one slice. Any new slice within an image (a *user slice*) also causes the creation of other slices (*auto slices*) that cover all the area of the image outside the user slice you create.

Notice the very small gray rectangle in the upper left corner of the image. In that area, you'll see the number 01 and an even smaller icon or *badge*, resembling a miniature mountain. This rectangle identifies slice 01, which includes the entire image. The gray color tells you that it is an auto slice, not a user slice. The symbol indicates that the slice contains image content.

1 In the toolbox, select the Slice tool ().

2 Drag the Slice tool diagonally across the *why organic?* text area, starting and ending close to the guides surrounding the text.

A blue rectangle, similar to the one for slice 01, appears in the upper left corner of the slice you just created, slice 02. The blue color reminds you that this is a user slice, not an auto slice.

The original gray rectangle for auto slice 01 remains unchanged, but the area included in slice 01 is smaller, covering only the left side of the page.

Slice 03—another auto slice, as indicated by its gray color—covers the remaining area of the menu bar that is to the right of slice 02. A third auto slice, slice 04, covers the area below the menu bar and to the right of slice 01.

Creating more user slices

Now that you've seen how easy it is to create slices, you'll slice up the rest of the text for the menu bar into four more buttons.

1 With the Slice tool still selected in the toolbox, drag across the *products* text to create another user slice.

The new slice becomes slice 03. The number of each slice after slice 03 automatically increases by one.

⚲ *You can change the way the pointer appears on-screen for the Slice tool by changing your Photoshop preferences. To change the Slice tool's standard pointer (⬚) to the precise pointer (⊹), choose Edit > Preferences > Display & Cursors (Windows) or Photoshop > Preferences > Display & Cursors (Mac OS 10), select Precise for the Other Cursors option, and click OK.*

2 One at a time, draw slice marquees around each of the other text items in the same row: around the words *shop online, contacts,* and *help* to create three more slices for menu buttons.

Your image should have a total of eight slices: five user slices and three auto slices. If your numbers are different, don't worry because you'll fix that now.

3 In the toolbox, select the Zoom tool (🔍) and click the area of your button slices to enlarge the view to 300% or 400%.

4 Carefully examine the user slices you created to see if there are any gaps between the slices. (If there are, these gaps would be auto slices.) If there are no gaps between your user slices, you can skip Steps 5 and 6.

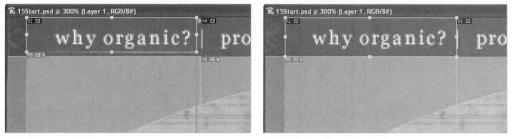

Gaps between slices   No gaps between slices

5 In the toolbox, select the Slice Select tool ( ), hidden behind the Slice tool, and select one of the user slices that did not snap to the guides—that is, a slice with a gap between it and the adjacent user slice.

6 Drag a selection handle for the selected slice until the slice boundaries snap into position against the guides and the other slices.

Note: *You can also use the Slice Select tool to drag the slice from one position to another.*

7 Double-click the Zoom tool to return to 100%, and choose File > Save.

 If you find the indicators for the auto slices distracting, select the Slice Select tool and then click the Hide Auto Slices button on the tool options bar. You can also hide the guides by choosing View > Show > Guides, because you won't need them again.

Setting slice options in Photoshop

Slices aren't particularly useful until you set options for them. Slice options include the slice name and the URL opened when the user clicks the slice. The process for setting slice options in Photoshop differs slightly from the method you'll use in ImageReady. In Photoshop, you set options in a dialog box. In Image Ready, you set them on a palette. Either way, it's a fairly simple process, but it's important that you're able to do the job in either application if you're going to do a lot of Web work.

Note: *You can set options for an auto slice, but doing so automatically promotes the auto slice to a user slice.*

1 Select the Slice Select tool (🔪), and use it to select slice 02, with the *why organic?* text.

2 In the tool options bar, click the Slice Options button.

By default, Photoshop names each slice based on the filename and the slice number, so the current filename appears as "15Start_02," representing slice number two in the 15Start.psd file.

3 In the Slice Options dialog box, enter the following information: In Name, type **Why_button**; in URL, type **pages/why.html**; and in Target, type **_blank**. (Be careful to include the underscore before the letter "b.") Then click OK.

Note: The Target option controls how a linked file opens when you click the link. The _blank option opens the linked page in a new instance of the Web browser. If you wanted the link to open in the original instance of the Web browser, you could type another code instead of _blank. For more information, see Adobe Photoshop Help or an HTML reference (such as a printed book or a Web site that explains HTML code).

4 Using the Slice Select tool, select slice 03, which encloses the *products* text, and then click Slice Options in the tool options bar.

5 Enter the following information:

- For Name, type **Products_button**.

- For URL, type **pages/products.html**.

- For Target, type **_blank**.

6 Click OK to close the dialog box.

7 Choose File > Save.

Leave the file open for the next procedure.

You may have noticed that there are more options in the dialog box than the three you filled in for these slices. For example, you can type something in the Alt Tag option if you wish. Usually, the Alt Tag text is used to identify the slice contents that cannot be seen or that may be confusing. It may appear in tooltips in some Web browsers or as a placeholder during a long download. It may also be read aloud by some screen-reader applications. For more information on how to use these options, see Photoshop Help.

Working with slices in ImageReady

Although you could continue to set slice options in Photoshop, it's more efficient to do this specific job in ImageReady. You'll use the Jump To button to switch to ImageReady. The Jump To button will not only launch ImageReady but also "jumps" the file that is open in Photoshop, transferring control to ImageReady until you either close the file or jump back to Photoshop.

Once ImageReady is open, you'll define a custom workspace to serve the specific need of this lesson. You begin this procedure with the 15Start.psd file open in Photoshop.

Note: Workspaces define which palettes are open, how they are grouped, and their locations in the work area. Workspace definitions do not affect the size, location, or view setting of the image window.

1 Make sure that you have saved the file. Then, in the Photoshop toolbox, click the Jump to ImageReady button ( ).

The ImageReady application opens and the 15Start.psd file opens, too. Notice that ImageReady has a Slices menu and a Slices palette, neither of which appear in Photoshop.

2 Choose Window > Workspace > Interactivity Palette Locations to close some of the palettes you won't need for this lesson.

3 Close the Animation and the Web Content palette groups by clicking the close buttons on the palette title bars or by deselecting those palettes in the Window menu.

4 Drag the Slice palette group to the right until it snaps into place at the edge of the work area. Your work area now looks like the following illustration.

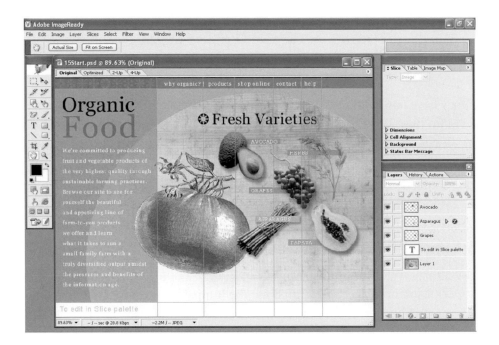

5 Choose Window > Workspace > Save Workspace.

6 In the Save Workspace dialog box, type **15_Links**, and click OK.

The 15_Links workspace now appears on the Workspace submenu of the Window menu. You can test it by choosing another workspace and then choosing 15_Links again.

Note: The custom workspaces you create and save for either ImageReady or Photoshop are not lost when you close the application or reset the default preferences. Your workspaces will always be available on the Workspace submenu until you actively delete them. Of course, ImageReady workspaces do not transfer over to Photoshop or vice versa, because the two applications have different palettes.

Setting slice options in ImageReady

The ImageReady work area has an advantage over the Photoshop workspace for the task of assigning slice options. The Slices palette in ImageReady makes it possible to enter the slice options you want without requiring the extra actions of opening a dialog box and then closing it again.

This next procedure continues the unfinished job of setting options for the last three user slices on the menu bar.

1 In the toolbox, select the Slice Select tool ( ), which is beside the Slice tool rather than hidden behind it.

2 Select slice 04, which encloses the *shop online* text.

3 In the Slice palette, enter the following information:

• For Name, type **Shop_button**.

• For URL, type **pages/shop.html**.

• For Target, select _blank from the pop-up menu.

4 Select slice 05 and type **Contact_button** for Name and **pages/contact.html** for URL. Select _blank for Target.

5 Select slice 06 and type **Help_button** for Name and **pages/help.html** for URL. Select _blank for Target.

6 Choose File > Save.

💡 *Once you've typed an URL in any slice, ImageReady places that listing on the URL pop-up menus in the Slices and Image Maps palettes. If you create another link to the same page, you can select that URL from the list instead of having to type.*

Creating a layer-based slice

Another method for defining slices in Photoshop and ImageReady is to convert layers into slices. A layer-based slice includes all the pixel data in the selected layer. When you edit the layer, move it, or apply a layer effect to it, the layer-based slice adjusts to encompass the new pixels. To unlink a layer-based slice from its layer, you can convert it to a user slice.

You'll create a slice based on the copyright text layer, and then apply a layer effect to it so you can see how the slice adjusts to the new effect.

1 In the Layers palette, select the "To edit in Slice palette" text layer.

2 Choose Layer > New Layer Based Slice.

ImageReady replaces areas of the auto slices with one layer-based slice for the entire layer. Notice the layer symbol (▣) in the upper left corner of the slice, indicating that the slice is layer-based. Also, a slice icon (✎) appears on the "To edit in Slice palette" text layer, reminding you that the layer is the basis of a slice.

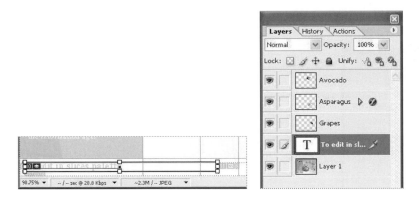

Note: *You can still apply layer styles to the layer that you used to create the layer-based slice. The dimensions of the slice automatically increase to accommodate any extra space required to show the effect if you do this in this order. If not, may need to go back later and resize the slices, as you'll see in Lesson 17, "Creating Rollover Web Visuals."*

3 Choose File > Save to save your work in ImageReady.

Creating No Image slices

In ImageReady and Photoshop, you can create *No Image* slices and then add text or HTML source code to them. No Image slices can have a background color and are saved as part of the HTML file.

The primary advantage of using No Image slices for text is that the text can be edited in any HTML editor, saving you the trouble of having to go back to Photoshop or ImageReady to edit it. The disadvantage is that if the text grows too large for the slice, it will break the HTML table and introduce unwanted gaps. The answer is to make the slice large enough to accommodate changes and to select font properties suitable for the slice dimensions.

1 Make sure that the layer-based slice that you created for the copyright information is selected in the image window. If it is not, use the Slice Select tool ( ) to select it now.

2 In the Slice palette, choose No Image from the Type pop-up menu.

3 Using the Text box in the Slice palette (*not* the image window), type some copyright information. (We used ©**2004 Organic Support Group**.) Make sure that the Text is HTML option is selected.

💡 *You can add a copyright symbol by pressing Alt+0169 on the numeric keypad (Windows) or Option+G (Mac OS).*

Because you chose No Image for the slice type, the layer of placeholder text ("To edit in Slice palette") that you see now in the image window will not appear in the Web page. The text that you typed in the Slice palette will appear in the Web page; however, it does not appear in your sliced image in ImageReady or Photoshop.

4 Click a blank area in the Layers palette to deselect the slice.

5 Choose File > Save.

Previewing a No Image slice in a Web browser

You should now make sure that the text you type will fit in the table cell, so you'll preview the image in a Web browser. You must have a Web browser installed on your computer to do this task.

Note: *(Mac OS only) Make sure that you have a Mac OS 10 browser alias in place so that the browser doesn't open in classic mode.*

1 In the toolbox, click the Preview In Default Browser button (such as 🅔 or 🅗) or choose a browser from the button's pop-up menu.

The image appears in the browser window, and the HTML source for the preview appears in a table below the image.

2 Read the copyright text in the lower right corner of the image and make sure that it matches the information you typed in the Slice palette, not the placeholder text in the ImageReady image window.

3 Quit the browser.

4 In ImageReady, select the Toggle Slices Visibility button (▨) in the toolbox (or press Q) to hide the slice markers and remove the ghosting from the image.

Note: Adding your choice of browsers to the Preview In Default Browser button is a simple task you do on the desktop. You create a shortcut (Windows) or alias (Mac OS) for your Web browser application and then drag it into the Preview In folder on your desktop. This folder is located inside the Helpers folder in the Photoshop CS folder.

More about creating slices

You've finished the slices work for this lesson. You've explored some of ways to slice an image and set slice options in Photoshop and ImageReady, but not all of them. There are other methods of creating slices that you can try on your own. For example:

• If you use custom guides in your design work, you can instantly divide up an entire image into user slices with an option on the tool options bar (Photoshop) or the Slices menu (ImageReady). However, this technique should be used with caution, because it discards any previously created slices and any options associated with those slices. Also, all the slices it creates are user slices, and you may not need that many of them.

• When you want to create identically sized, evenly spaced and aligned slices, try creating a single user slice that precisely encloses the entire area. Then, use the Divide Slice feature on the Slice Select tool options bar (Photoshop) or on the Slices menu (ImageReady) to divide the original slice into as many vertical and horizontal rows of slices as you need.

• If you have already selected an area with the ImageReady selection marquee tools that you want to designate as a slice area, you can use the Create Slice From Selection command on the Select menu. Be aware that even if the selection is an irregular shape, the slice you create will always be a rectangle.

Working with image maps (ImageReady)

Creating image maps is one of the functions that you must do in Adobe ImageReady. You can use Photoshop to create slices, which share certain functionality with image maps, but you cannot create image maps with Photoshop.

In this section, you'll create an image map within the same image that you've been working on in this lesson, the organic food home page. Your task is to create links to different Web pages that match the shapes of the pictured produce items—something that would be difficult to do with slices because slices are always rectangular.

If ImageReady is not already open, start it now, holding down the key combination for your operating system that restores the default preferences. (See "Restoring default preferences" on page 4.) Then, select the workspace you defined earlier from the Workspace submenu of the Window menu. (See "Working with slices in ImageReady" on page 491.)

Using layers to create image maps

You'll define image-map areas based on some of the layers that make up the home page design. By using layers to define the hotspots, you easily gain control over the shapes of those areas. If the 15Start.psd file is not still open in ImageReady, open it now.

1 In the Layers palette, select the Asparagus layer.

Notice that a layer style, the Drop Shadow effect, has already been applied to this layer.

2 Choose Layer > New Layer Based Image Map Area.

A ghosted rectangular area surrounded by a red line appears, enclosing the asparagus area of the image. The red line and ghosting define the hotspot area included in the image map.

3 In the Slice palette group, click the Image Map tab to bring the Image Map palette forward.

4 Click the arrow to expand the Layer Based Settings options (if necessary), and choose Polygon from the Shape pop-up menu.

Now the red outline approximates the shape of the asparagus bunch, including the Drop Shadow on the lower right side.

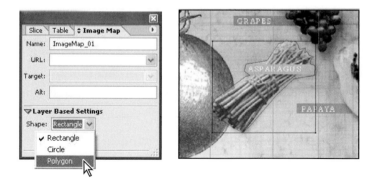

5 In the Quality option on the Image Map palette, drag the slider or type **90** to make the red line more closely conform to the asparagus area shape.

6 In the Image Map palette, type **Asparagus** in Name, type **pages/veggies.html** for URL, and select _blank from the Target pop-up menu.

In the Layers palette, a pointing-finger icon now appears on the Asparagus layer, indicating that it has a layer-based image map.

7 Click a blank area of the Layers palette to deselect the Asparagus layer, and then choose File > Save.

Using the image map tools

When the elements you want to use for image maps are conveniently located on separate layers, it's simple to define those image-map areas, as you saw in the previous procedure. This procedure and the next one show you a couple of techniques for defining image maps within a single layer.

The first method is similar to the Photoshop technique you used earlier in this book when you selected elements with the Pen tool. Before you begin working, you'll turn off the snap-to options, which will make it easier to position anchor points exactly where you want them.

1 Choose View > Snap so that the command is deselected (unchecked).

2 In the toolbox, select the Polygon Image Map tool ( ), which is hidden behind the Rectangle Image Map tool ( ).

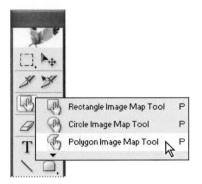

3 Click the edge of the papaya to set an anchor point.

4 Move along the outside edge of the papaya and the papaya label, clicking frequently to set more anchor points.

Don't worry if the points are not perfectly placed because you'll get a chance to adjust them later.

5 When the anchor points are almost completely around the papaya, click the original anchor point to close the image-map shape. (The pointer icon changes when you're at the right spot, showing a little circle that indicates a click will close the shape.)

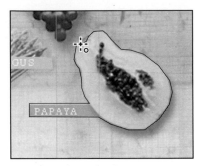

The red image-map boundary appears around the papaya, with anchor points where you set them.

Using selections to create image maps

You can also convert selections you make with the selection tools into image maps. You'll try that now with the fennel herb, selecting it with the Magic Wand tool.

1 Select the Zoom tool (🔍) and click the fennel ("HERBS") until the magnification is 300%.

2 In the Layers palette, select the Background layer.

3 Select the Magic Wand tool ( ), which is hidden behind the Marquee tool ( ).
Then, in the tool options bar, type **42** in the Tolerance option and make sure that the
Contiguous check box is selected, or select it now.

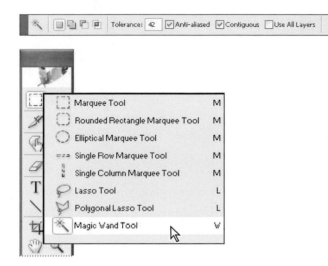

4 Click the fennel branch where the "Herbs" label crosses it.

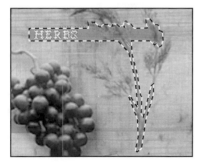

5 Hold down Shift, so that the Magic Wand tool pointer includes a plus sign, and carefully click an unselected area of the fennel branch. Repeat a couple of more times until most of the fennel is selected—the selection doesn't need to be perfect.

Note: If the selection marquee seems to disappear after a click, you may have accidentally clicked the wood grain, so that the marquee includes a very large area. In that case, choose Edit > Undo and try again.

6 Choose Select > Create Image Map From Selection to open the Create Image Map dialog box. Select the Polygon option with the Quality set at 80, and click OK.

In the image window, the fennel image appears ghosted. A red line indicating the shape of the image map surrounds the fennel.

7 Choose Select > Deselect to remove the selection marquee.

Refining image map shapes and assigning links

The previous two procedures did not attempt to create image-map shapes that were perfect matches for the items pictured. You'll improve the shapes now, and then assign URL and name information to your image maps. Since the fennel is already in view and enlarged to 300%, you'll start with that image map.

1 Select the Image Map Select tool ( ). If the fennel image map is not already selected (so that the image-map border appears as a red line with anchor points), select it now.

2 Select one of the anchor points that doesn't match the shape of the fennel and drag it to a better position.

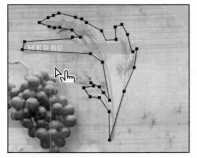 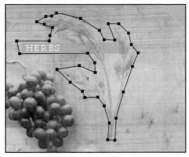

Dragging an anchor point   *Finished image map area*

3 One by one, select other anchor points and drag them into position until you are satisfied with the shape of the image map.

💡 *You can add individual anchor points by Shift-clicking: First, position the pointer where you want to add a point. Hold down Shift, so that a small plus (+) sign appears in the pointer icon, and click. To remove anchor points, Alt-click (Windows) or Option-click (Mac OS). In this case, a minus (-) sign appears in the pointer icon .*

4 In the Image Map palette, type **Herbs** for Name, **pages/herbs.html** for URL, and select _blank for Target.

5 Finish up your work on the papaya image map by doing the following:

• Hold down the spacebar to switch temporarily to the Hand tool and drag until you can see the papaya image-map area.

• Select and move anchor points until you are satisfied with the image-map shape.

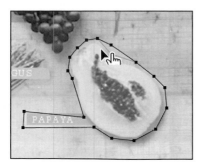

- Select options in the Image Map palette, and type **Papaya** for Name, **pages/fruits.html** for URL, and select _blank for Target.

6 Choose Select > Deselect Image Maps.

7 Double-click the Hand tool (✋) or Zoom tool (🔍) to reduce the view.

8 Choose File > Save.

Note: If you want to see your image without the light blue image-map lines and ghosting, select the Toggle Image Maps Visibility button [🔲] in the toolbox, or press A. Reselect the button or press A again to see the image-map indicators.

So far in this lesson you have created three image map links and five slice links within your Web page image. You could go ahead and create additional image maps for the avocado and grapes if you want to practice, or you can go on now to the next topic.

Examining all linked areas and creating an HTML file

When you save an image map in an HTML file, the basic HTML tags needed to display the image on a Web page are generated automatically. The easiest way to do this is simply to choose the HTML And Images option when you save the optimized image.

Once you have created the HTML file, it can easily be updated to reflect any changes, such as new or modified image-map areas or URLs.

1 In ImageReady, choose Window > Web Content to open that palette. If necessary, click the arrows to expand the Image Maps and Slices categories and drag the lower right corner of the palette down so you can see all the items listed.

2 Review the Web Content listings, which include thumbnails of the slices and image maps. Notice that the image-map thumbnails include the boundary lines of the image-map areas.

3 Close the Web Content palette or move it out of your way.

4 Choose File > Save Optimized As. (Be careful *not* to select Save As by mistake.)

5 In the Save Optimized As dialog box, accept the default name, **15Start.html**, and do the following:

- Select HTML And Images in the Save As Type pop-up menu (Windows) or Format pop-up menu (Mac OS).

- Locate and select the Lessons/Lesson15/15MyPage folder as the destination location.

• Click Save.

6 Switch to the desktop and double-click the 15Start.html file to open it in your default Web browser application.

7 Click several of the areas with slices or image maps that you created and examine them to see if any of them do not link properly (some of them don't). When you finish, switch to ImageReady, leaving the Web browser open to the 15Start.html page.

Note: In Photoshop, you create an HTML file in the Save Optimized As dialog box that appears after optimizing the image and clicking OK in the Save For Web dialog box.

Editing link information and updating the HTML file

Some of the image maps in the HTML file are not linked properly, because we changed the names of some of the destination pages to be more specific to the fruit or vegetable featured. This is easy to fix in the original ImageReady file and then to update to the HTML file.

1 In the ImageReady toolbox, select the Image Map Select tool ( ).

2 In the image window, click to select the papaya image-map area.

3 In the Image Map palette, change the URL to **pages/papaya.html**.

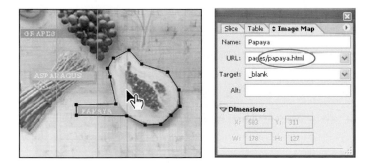

4 In the image window, select the asparagus image-map area, and then change the URL in the Image Map palette to **pages/asparagus.html**.

Note: You can change link information for slices in a similar way, using the Slice Select tool and Slice palette instead of the Image Map Select tool and Image Map palette.

5 Choose File > Update HTML.

6 In the Update HTML dialog box, select the 15Start.html file, and click Open. Click Replace when the Replace Files dialog box appears, and click OK in the update message.

7 Go back to your Web browser and choose the refresh or reload icon or View menu command. Click the links to make sure they're OK, and then go back to ImageReady.

8 Choose File > Close to close the image. If a message appears reminding you that the file is no longer open in Photoshop, click Yes to dismiss it.

You can use your Web browser to open and view the 15Start.html file. You can also open the file in a word-processing or Web-authoring application to make your own revisions to the HTML code.

For the Web: HTML File-Naming Conventions

Use the UNIX® file-naming convention, because many network programs truncate (shorten) long filenames. This convention requires a filename of up to eight characters, followed by an extension. Use the .html or .htm extension.

Do not use special characters such as question marks (?) or asterisks (*), or spaces between the letters in your filename—some browsers may not recognize the pathname. If you must use special characters or spaces in the filename, check with an HTML-editing guide for the correct code to use. For example, to create spaces between letters you will need to replace the space with **%20***.*

You have finished Lesson 15. To learn about using animations with your slices and rollovers, see Lesson 18, "Animating GIF Images for the Web" and ImageReady Help.

Review questions

1 What are slices?

2 Describe the five ways that image slices are created.

3 Describe the method for creating a slice with boundaries that exactly encompass a small or unusually shaped object.

4 How do you create a slice that contains no image? What purpose would such a slice serve?

5 What are the differences and similarities between slices and image maps?

Review answers

1 Slices are rectangular areas of an image that you can define in Photoshop or ImageReady for individual Web optimization. With slices, you can create animated GIFs, URL links, and rollovers.

2 You can actively create image slices by selecting areas in the image with the Slice tool. Other active methods of creating slices include converting layers, guides, or selections into slices using commands on the Layers, Slices, or Select menu. Indirectly, auto slices are created automatically for areas in the sliced image that you leave undefined as you use the other methods of creating user slices.

3 Using the Magic Wand tool (or another appropriate selection tool) in ImageReady, select the object, and choose Select > Create Slice From Selection. Or, if the object is a layer, select it and choose Layer > New Layer Based Slice.

4 Select the slice with the Slice Select tool. In the Slice Options dialog box (Photoshop) or Slice palette (ImageReady), choose No Image from the Type menu. No Image slices can contain a background color, text, and HTML source code, or they can serve as a place-holder for graphics to be added later.

5 Slices can be created in either Photoshop or ImageReady; they are always rectangular in shape; they can be defined as having Image, No Image, or Table content. Image maps can be created only in ImageReady; they can have any shape; and they always have image content. Both slices and image maps can be configured as hotspots with links to other pages. Both can be configured with rollover states, which you can learn more about in Lesson 17, "Creating Rollovers."

16 | Optimizing Web Images

For effective Web publishing, your images must strike a good balance between file size and display quality. Using Adobe Photoshop and Adobe ImageReady, you can optimize your images so that they have reasonable download times from a Web server without losing essential details, colors, transparencies, or navigational elements such as image maps.

In this lesson, you'll learn how to do the following:

• Optimize JPEG and GIF files, and adjust the optimization settings to achieve the desired balance between file size and image quality.

• Adjust the amount of dithering applied to an image.

• Define a transparent background for an image.

• Batch-process files to automate the optimization process.

This lesson will take about one and a half hours to complete. The lesson is designed to be done in Adobe Photoshop and Adobe ImageReady.

If needed, remove the previous lesson folder from your hard drive, and copy the Lessons/Lesson16 folder onto it. As you work on this lesson, you'll overwrite the start files. If you need to restore the start files, copy them from the *Adobe Photoshop CS Classroom in a Book* CD.

Note: *Windows 2000 users need to unlock the lesson files before using them. For more information, see "Copying the Classroom in a Book files" on page 3.*

Optimizing images using Photoshop or ImageReady

Optimizing is the process of selecting format, resolution, and quality settings so that an image has the efficiency, visual appeal, and utility for Web browser pages. Simply put, it's balancing file size against good looks. No single collection of settings can maximize the efficiency of every kind of image file; optimizing requires human judgment and a good eye.

Compression options vary according to the file format used to save the image. You should be familiar with the general format types.

• The JPEG format is designed to preserve the broad color range and subtle brightness variations of continuous-tone images (such as photographs or images with gradients). This format can represent images using millions of colors.

• The GIF format is effective at compressing solid-color images and images with areas of repetitive color (such as line art, logos, and illustrations with type). This format uses a palette of 256 colors to represent the image, and supports background transparency.

• The PNG format is effective at compressing solid-color images and preserving sharp detail. The PNG-8 format uses a 256-color palette to represent an image; the PNG-24 format supports 24-bit color (millions of colors). However, many older browser applications do not support PNG files.

• The WBNG format is the standard format for optimizing images for mobile devices, such as cell phones. WBMP supports 1-bit color, which means that WBMP images contain only black and white pixels.

Note: *For information about using PNG and WBNG formats, see Photoshop Help.*

Adobe Photoshop and Adobe ImageReady give you an effective range of controls for compressing the file size of an image while optimizing its on-screen display quality. You can apply a set of optimization settings to a collection of files, a single file, a layer, or a slice.

In this lesson, you'll optimize and save images in JPEG and GIF formats. In the exercises that follow, you'll work with a set of images designed to be used on a Web site for a fictitious travel organization.

Photoshop (through its Save For Web dialog box) and ImageReady (through its Optimize palette) share many of the same capabilities for optimizing images. For example, you can use either application to select from a wide array of file formats and settings, to suit the goals for your project. You can also use either one to compare side-by-side views of different optimized versions of a file. Using optimization features and color palettes in either Photoshop or ImageReady, you can maximize color integrity while minimizing file size.

Getting started

You'll do the first part of this lesson in Adobe Photoshop, but it could be done just as well in ImageReady. As you begin, you'll restore the default application settings for Adobe Photoshop so that the descriptions in the instruction match the settings in your Photoshop work area.

The lesson revolves around a primary home-page graphic for the fictitious travel organization.

1 Start Adobe Photoshop while holding down Ctrl+Alt+Shift (Windows) or Command+Option+Shift (Mac OS) to restore the default preferences. (See "Restoring default preferences" on page 4.)

As messages appear, select Yes to confirm that you want to reset preferences, No to defer setting up your color monitor, and Close to close the Welcome Screen.

2 Click the File Browser button on the tool options bar to open it.

3 In the File Browser Folders palette, locate and select the Lessons/Lesson16 folder.

Thumbnails of three different Start and End files appear in the thumbnails pane, many of which appear to be quite similar.

4 Select—but do not open—the 16Start1.psd thumbnail, so that the thumbnail is highlighted and metadata appears in the Metadata palette.

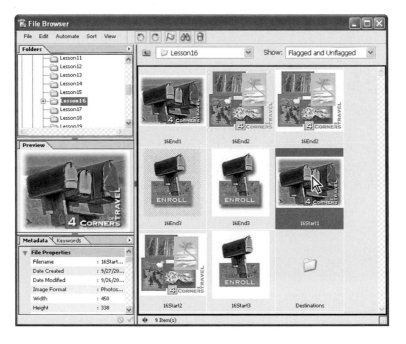

5 Select the 16End1.jpg thumbnail. Notice that the file size listed in the metadata is smaller but the image looks about the same as the 16Start1.psd.

6 One by one, select and preview the other Start and End files in the Lesson16 folder.

7 Double-click the 16Start1.psd file to open it in Photoshop. Close the File Browser by clicking either the File Browser button (⬛) on the tool options bar twice (once to bring it forward and once to close it) or the close button in the File Browser window.

Optimizing a JPEG image (Photoshop)

In this lesson, you will optimize files in both JPEG and GIF formats. You goal is to set optimization selections so that your files are small and efficient but still look great.

Currently, the 16Start1.psd file size is larger than ideal for use on a Web page. You'll compare different file-compression formats to see which one gives you the most compression without sacrificing too much image quality.

Using the Save For Web dialog box

The Photoshop Save For Web dialog box shows you different versions of an image side by side, using different optimization settings. You can compare versions as you work, adjusting optimization settings and examining the differences until you have the best possible combination of file size and image quality.

1 With the 16Start1.psd file open and active in Photoshop, choose File > Save for Web.

Note: If the 4-Up tab is not already selected in the image window, select it now.

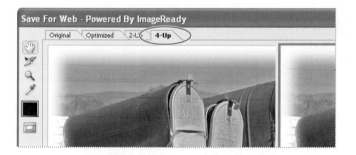

Photoshop automatically generates three different sets of optimization settings, besides the original image. Notice the information listed under each view of the image, including the file size and the number of seconds required to download the image. The first pane shows the original file. The second, third, and fourth panes show different combinations of optimization settings for the image, including the file format (such as GIF or JPEG) and color-reduction algorithm (such as Selective, Perceptual, or Web).

2 In the lower left corner of the Save For Web dialog box, select 300% or higher from the Zoom Level pop-up menu so that you can see the details of the image.

Compare the preset views of the different optimization settings.

3 Click one of the four images so that the pointer becomes a hand icon, and drag the image so that you can see the differences among the optimized views and the original.

4 Look carefully at the following areas: the text in the lower right corner of the image, the area where the top of the mail box sits in contrast against the blue sky, the shadow of the rusted door of the large mail box, the embossed area of the rusted mail box, and other image details.

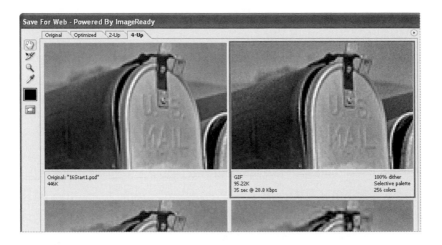

Comparing optimized GIF, JPEG, and PNG formats

You can customize any of the three optimized views in the Save For Web dialog box. To do this, you select one of the optimized image previews, and then select settings for it on the right side of the dialog box. By experimenting with different combinations of settings, you can get a good idea of which settings will best suit your purpose.

Note: As you perform tasks in this lesson, use the zoom controls frequently so that you can get an overall impression of the image and then see small details that show you flaws you might not notice at smaller enlargements. Don't wait for the instructions to tell you to zoom in and zoom out each time.

1 Select the optimized preview at the upper right of the Save For Web dialog box.

2 In the Preset pop-up menu on the right side of the dialog box, select GIF 128 Dithered (if it is not already selected).

The information that is listed immediately below the preview changes.

Notice the dark group of pixels around the rust-covered mailbox and in the green square background behind the number 4 in the logo.

You'll use the two bottom versions of the image to compare GIF 128 Dithered optimization with JPEG and PNG optimization.

3 Click the lower left version of the image to select it, and select the following JPEG options, one at a time, on the Preset pop-up menu:

• JPEG Low. Notice that the image details and text are unacceptably choppy.

• JPEG High. The image quality improves, but the file size more than triples.

JPEG Low   *JPEG High*

• JPEG Medium. At this setting, the image quality is acceptable and the file size is lower than either the JPEG High version or the GIF version.

Note: *You can select other intermediate levels of quality for JPEG files by typing or dragging the Quality slider option on the right side of the Save For Web dialog box.*

Now that you've tried different GIF and JPEG settings, you'll use the fourth image preview to try another format.

4 Select the lower right version of the image, and then use the Preset menu to select PNG-8 128 Dithered.

Although this results in a smaller file size than the original image, the image quality is not as good as the JPEG Medium version, which also has a smaller file size. Furthermore, many older browsers cannot read the PNG format. To make this image compatible with older browsers, you will save this file for the Web using the JPEG Medium optimization.

5 Select your JPEG Medium version of the optimized image (in the lower left corner of the dialog box), and then select the Progressive check box.

Note: *When Progressive is selected, any download of the image occurs in several passes, each of which increases the image quality.*

The Progressive JPEG download

6 Click Save. In the Save Optimized As dialog box, use the default name **16Start1.jpg**, and save the file in the same folder as the original Photoshop file.

7 Choose File > Close to close the 16Start1.psd file, and don't save your changes.

Optimizing a GIF image

Now, you'll optimize an image that has been stylized into stretches of flat color; that is, areas where the adjacent pixels have identical RGB color values. You'll optimize this image in GIF format and compare the results of different palette and dither settings. Although you could do this entire section in Photoshop, you'll use ImageReady.

Photoshop and ImageReady share many features, but there are certain tasks you can do in Photoshop that are not possible in ImageReady, and vice versa. Other tasks are merely more appropriately done in one application or the other.

If you have an open file when you jump from one application to the other, the file opens in the application to which you jump. If you have more than one file open, only the active file opens in the jumped-to application. If no files are open, you can still jump back and forth from one application to the other. In all these cases, it's just a one-click process.

Using a predefined ImageReady workspace

Before you begin working on a new file, you'll jump from Photoshop to ImageReady. Then, you'll rearrange the work area by selecting one of the predefined workspaces that are always available on the ImageReady Workspace submenu.

1 In Photoshop, click the Jump To ImageReady button ( ) at the bottom of the toolbox to switch from Photoshop to ImageReady.

Note: If you do not have enough memory to run both applications simultaneously, quit Photoshop and then start ImageReady.

2 In ImageReady, choose Window > Workspace > Optimization Palette Locations.

Only the bare-bones set of palettes needed for optimization tasks remains open in the work area: the Optimize palette group and the Color Table palette group, along with the toolbox and tool options bar. If you need another palette at some point, you can reopen it by selecting it on the Window menu.

Choosing basic optimization settings in ImageReady

Earlier in this lesson, you used Photoshop optimization settings that were integrated into the Save For Web dialog box. In ImageReady, the same options appear in the Optimize palette.

1 In ImageReady, choose File > Open, and open the 16Start2.psd file from the Lessons/Lesson16 folder.

This image was created in Adobe Illustrator, and then rasterized into Photoshop format. The image contains many areas of solid color.

2 Click the 2-Up tab in the image window.

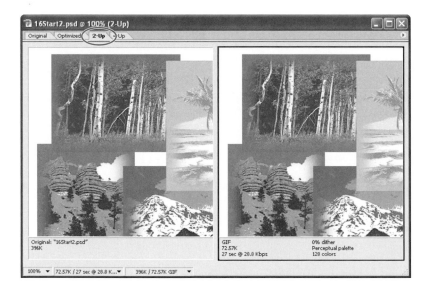

The optimized version of the image is selected on the right side of the window.

3 In the Preset pop-up menu on the Optimize palette, choose GIF 128 No Dither.

4 If necessary, click the arrow to expand the Color Table options on the Optimize palette, and then select Perceptual on the Reduction pop-up menu.

Selecting a color reduction algorithm

One of the ways to reduce image file size is to reduce the number of colors in the image. Photoshop can calculate the most needed colors for you, based on any of several available algorithms. You specify which algorithm is to be used by making a selection from the Color Reduction Algorithm menu, which includes the following options:

Perceptual *Creates a custom color table by giving priority to colors for which the human eye has greater sensitivity.*

Selective *Creates a color table similar to the Perceptual color table, but favors broad areas of color and the preservation of Web colors. This color table usually produces images with the greatest color integrity. Selective is the default option.*

Adaptive *Creates a custom color table by sampling colors from the spectrum appearing most commonly in the image. For example, an image with only the colors green and blue produces a color table made up primarily of greens and blues. Most images concentrate colors in particular areas of the spectrum.*

Web *Uses the standard 216-color color table common to the Windows and Mac OS 8-bit (256-color) palettes. This system ensures that no browser dither is applied to colors when the image is displayed using 8-bit color. (This palette is also called the Web-safe palette.) If your image has fewer colors than the total specified in the color palette, unused colors are removed.*

Custom *Preserves the current color table as a fixed palette that does not update with changes to the image.*

Windows or Mac OS *Uses the system's default 8-bit (256-color) color table, which is based on a uniform sampling of RGB colors. If your image has fewer colors than the total number specified in the color palette, unused colors are removed.*

The status bar at the bottom of the image window displays the view magnification and other useful information about the original and optimized versions of the image.

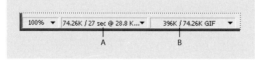

A. *File size and download time of optimized image*
B. *File sizes of original and optimized images*

You can customize the type of information that appears here.

5 In the status bar, choose Size/Download Time (56.6 Kbps Modem/ISDN) in the middle pop-up menu, and then choose Image Dimensions from the pop-up menu on the right.

The 56.6 Kbps is usually more common now than 28.8 Kbps. The dimension displays the size of the image in pixels, which is important to know when planning how to fit an image into a predesigned Web-page template.

About the Color Table

The Color Table palette displays the colors that the currently selected Reduction option uses for the currently active file. The count of the colors used in the image is listed at the bottom of the palette with the various buttons.

You can resize the palette or use the scroll bar to view all the colors. You can also change how the colors are arranged in the palette by clicking the small arrow to open the Color Table palette menu and then selecting a sorting method: by hue, luminance, or popularity.

Other symbols on the color swatches themselves indicate a current swatch (if one is selected), whether or not a color is locked, and whether or not a color is a Restricted (Web) color. You'll learn more about recognizing and using these features as you progress through this lesson.

***Note:** In Photoshop, the Color Table is in the Save For Web dialog box.*

Controlling dither and reducing colors

You may have noticed that certain areas of the image appear mottled or spotty. This spotty appearance results from *dithering*, the technique used to simulate the appearance of colors that are not included in the color palette. For example, a blue color and a yellow color may dither in a mosaic pattern to produce the illusion of a green color that is not included in the color palette.

When optimizing images, keep in mind the two kinds of dithering that can occur:

• *Application dither* occurs when ImageReady or Photoshop attempts to simulate colors that appear in the original image but not in the optimized color palette you specify. You can control the amount of application dither by dragging the Dither slider in the Optimize palette.

• *Browser dither* can occur in addition to application dither. A browser dither occurs when a Web browser using an 8-bit (256-color) display simulates colors that appear in the optimized image's color palette but not in the system palette used by the browser. You can control the amount of browser dither by shifting selected colors to Web-safe colors in the Color Table palette.

Before you do further optimizing, zoom in to 200% or more and compare the transition areas between the landscape images and the solid-color background in both the optimized version and the unoptimized original version. In the original, the stylized photographs fade smoothly into the background. In the optimized version, the shift is abrupt and has harsh borders. Also, notice the rainbow-like bands of color of the cloud in the upper right area of the canyon image.

Reducing the color palette

To compress the file size further, you can decrease the total number of colors included in the Color Table palette. A reduced range of colors will often preserve good image quality while dramatically reducing the file space required to store extra colors.

Currently, 128 colors compose the 16Start_2.psd file, as shown in the Colors option in the Optimize palette, under Color Table. Your ultimate goal in this entire section is to get that number down to 32 without ruining the appearance of the graphic.

1 Make sure that the optimized version of the image is selected and that Perceptual is selected in the Optimization palette. Notice the current file sizes.

2 On the zoom pop-up menu in the bottom of the image window, select 200% or higher, or use the Zoom tool (🔍) to enlarge your view. Make sure that you zoom in enough so that you start to see the pixelation of the image.

3 Using the Hand tool (✋), select the image on the right of the 2-up display, and drag so that you can see some of each of the following: the dark shadows in the aspen trees, some trees in the rock canyon, and the mountain top with some of the light blue sky to its right.

4 In the Colors option in the Optimize palette, type or select **32** from the pop-up menu.

Notice the significant reduction in the file size, but that there are problems. The shadows between the aspen trees are now dark brown instead of dark green, while the trees in the canyon image are dark green instead of brown. The clouds in the brown canyon sky look distinctly striped in multiple colors.

5 Reselect 128 as the Colors option.

Obviously, simply reducing the color palette without solving the problems that this creates is not a good idea. However, there are some techniques you'll try next that will produce better results.

Adding dither to simulate missing colors

Before you begin this procedure, make sure that the Optimize palette still shows Perceptual as the Reduction option and 128 for Colors. In the canyon image, notice the gradient brown bands in the cloud. You'll be focusing on this portion of the image and the aspen shadows as you make adjustments in this topic.

1 Under Dither in the Optimize palette, select Diffusion on the Method pop-up menu and drag the Amount slider to **100%**.

Now a speckling pattern softens the transition in color in the cloud area. Any change in the aspen area is either not noticeable or more subtle.

2 Reselect 32 as the Colors option.

The aspen image looks arguably even worse than before. The area that had been dark green now appears as a speckling of dark brown on a medium green. The clouds in the canyon area look smoother, but the skies over the canyon and mountain images—both of which used to be uniform colors—are now speckled.

3 Drag the Dither slider to **50%**, and then experiment with other dither percentages.

ImageReady minimizes the amount of dither in the image, but no percentage of dither will preserve the drop shadows without ruining the green background. Also, reducing the percentage of dither reintroduces the multicolored striping in the clouds above the canyon.

4 Set the dither back to **100%**.

5 Reset the Colors option to 128. (Leave the dither settings as they are.)

The aspen shadows turn dark green again and the speckling is not noticeable. But while the file size is smaller than the original (unoptimized) version, the optimized version is a little larger than it was without dithering. You have more work to do in optimizing this file, so go on to the next topic.

For an illustration of the effects of different dither percentages on an image, see figure 16-2 in the color section.

Locking colors to preserve image details

In the previous procedures, you saw how reducing the number of colors can compromise details in an illustration, even after you add dithering. You'll now learn how to lock specific colors to ensure that those colors do not drop out of the reduced palette.

As you begin this work, make sure that the Optimize palette shows Perceptual, 128 colors, and Diffusion dithering set at 100%.

1 In the toolbox, select the Eyedropper tool ( ), and click the darkest green you can find in the aspen shadows to sample that color.

Notice that the dark green now appears in the Foreground Color swatch in the toolbox and that the tiny swatch for the dark green in the Color Table is highlighted with a white border.

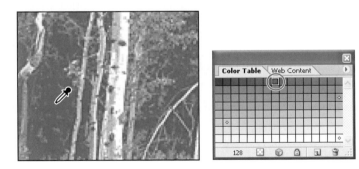

2 Click the Lock button ( ) at the bottom of the Color Table palette to lock the selected color of green.

Locking a color swatch gives that color priority over non-locked colors. If you reduce the number of colors from 128 to a lower number, locked colors can't be bumped from the list by non-locked colors.

3 In the Optimize palette, change the Colors value back to 32.

Now the green shadows look good, but notice the speckled dithering this introduces into the sky area in the brown canyon and the blue mountain portions of the graphic, which is starting to look something like a blizzard. Once again, the cayon trees, which should be brown, are dark green. Despite this, you shouldn't abandon the effort.

4 Hold down the spacebar so that the pointer changes from the eyedropper icon to the hand icon (🖐), and drag the image so that about half the viewing area is covered by the canyon image and half by the mountain image.

5 In the Optimize palette, select 128 in the Colors option.

Continue on to the next topic, where you'll lock more colors until the image achieves an acceptable appearance.

Note: You can unlock a locked color by selecting the color swatch in the Color Table and then clicking the Lock button again.

Locking more colors to prevent unwanted dithering

The challenge of working with 32 colors is finding the ideal 32 colors. As you saw in the previous procedure, correcting an unwanted dithering effect or color shift in one area tends to produce other problems in other areas.

Rather than giving up on the locking process, you'll continue to refine the image by locking more colors. You'll go back and forth between 32 and 128 colors, locking in the original colors when the reduction to 32 colors causes unwanted dithering or a change in color. Once you've locked a color, it's important to reexamine the entire image carefully, to see what kinds of problems that color lock has created.

1 Select the Eyedropper tool (✐), and click the dark brown that now appears in the center of the trees in the canyon image. Then, click the Lock button (🔒) at the bottom of the Color Table palette to lock the selected color.

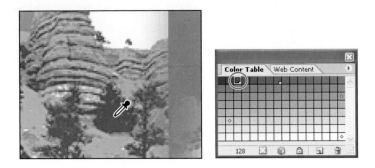

A small square appears in the lower right corner of the color swatch, indicating that the color is locked.

2 Repeat Step 1 three more times, sampling and locking the following:

• The medium brown sky in the canyon area.

• The dark blue sky to the upper left of the mountain top.

• The light blue sky to the right of the mountain top.

3 Reduce the Colors option to 32.

4 Hold down the spacebar so that the pointer changes to the hand icon (✋), and drag the image so that you can see the forested ridge in front of the mountain, the "4," and some of the text in the lower right area of the image.

Now the ridge in the blue image is unacceptably dithered.

5 Change the number of colors back to 128, and use the same technique you used in Steps 1 and 2 to lock the dark blue in the ridge. Then change the Colors options to 32.

The ridge looks good, but now the khaki-colored text is so dithered that it looks like multicolored confetti. Have courage; you're on the brink of reaching your goal.

6 Change the number of colors back to 128, and use the same technique you used in Steps 1 and 2 to lock the text color. Then change the Colors options to 32.

7 Examine every area of the image to make sure that there are no other color shifts, and then choose File > Save.

If you want to do so, you can continue to lock colors, such as the darker color at the center of the palm tree or some other color.

Note: There is some dithering that is unavoidable, such as in areas with gradients. Each of the four blocks of color images has a gradient separating the solid-colored background from the image it contains. Dithering is the best possible choice for balancing file efficiency and acceptable appearance for gradient color changes.

If you experiment with optimization of image files, you'll notice that significant image degradation can occur when the palette is reduced below 32 colors. In fact, for all but the simplest images, even 32 colors may be too drastic a reduction. For the best file compression of a GIF image, try to use the fewest number of colors that will still display the quality you need.

For an illustration of the image set to different palette values, see figure 16-1 in the color section.

Minimizing browser dither

In the Photoshop Save For Web dialog box and in ImageReady, you can view application dither directly in an optimized image. You can also preview the additional browser dither that will appear in the final image when viewed in a browser using an 8-bit display.

As you learned earlier, images that include non–Web-safe colors undergo a process of dithering when displayed in a Web browser using an 8-bit display, because the browser simulates colors that do not occur in the 8-bit system palette. From ImageReady, you can preview how an optimized image will look when dithered in a Web browser.

To protect a color from browser dither, you can Web-shift the color, converting the color to its nearest equivalent in the Web palette. Because the Web palette includes the subset of colors that appear in both the Windows and the Mac OS system palettes, Web palette colors will display without dithering in browsers on either platform.

1 With the optimized 16Start2.psd image open, choose View > Preview > Browser Dither (so that a checkmark appears next to the command).

Notice that browser dither occurs in the sky and the slope of the canyon image, even though you locked the medium brown color of the sky earlier in this lesson. You'll Web-shift that color to reduce the amount of browser dither in the image.

Note: If you don't see the dithering, increase the zoom or turn off the browser-dither preview and then turn it back on to observe the effects. You can toggle the browser-dither preview off and on by pressing Ctrl+Shift+Y (Windows) or Command+Shift+Y (Mac OS).

2 Switch out of Browser Preview mode, but this time do it by pressing Ctrl+Shift+Y (Windows) or Command+Shift+Y (Mac OS). Or, you can use the View > Preview >Browser Dither command again.

3 Select the Eyedropper tool (⟋) and click anywhere in the canyon sky area. The sampled color appears selected in the Color Table palette.

4 Click the Web-shift button (⬤) at the bottom of the Color Table palette.

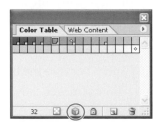

The swatch changes position in the palette and a small diamond appears in the center of the swatch, indicating that it has been shifted to its nearest Web-palette equivalent.

5 Using the same technique, select a sample of the lighter brown on the slope of the canyon and click the Web-shift button (⬡) again.

6 Choose View > Preview > Browser Dither, or press Ctrl+Shift+Y (Windows) or Command+Shift+Y (Mac OS) to preview the file in that mode.

The browser dither is gone from the selected areas and the rest of the image is acceptable.

7 Choose View > Preview > Browser Dither to deselect it, and then choose File > Save.

By Web-shifting the brown background, you changed its color to one that can be displayed without dithering by a Web browser on a 256-color system.

Note: *In Photoshop CS and ImageReady CS, you can also quickly map one color to another color or to a transparency. This remapping reassigns all the pixels that appeared in the selected color to the new color or transparency. For more information, see ImageReady Help.*

Optimizing slices

Professional designers often combine various types of graphic resources into a single Photoshop or ImageReady image. For example, you might create an image file composed of graphics with large areas of flat color and typography, combined with continuous-tone photographs or other images with complex shading and graduated fills. It would be difficult to get satisfactory results by optimizing such an image using just a single optimization scheme.

If you divide an image into slices, you can optimize any individual unlinked slices uniquely. For example, you could apply GIF optimization to some areas within an image while applying JPEG or PNG optimization to others. To do this, you simply select the individual slice (using the Slice Select tool) and set optimization options in the Save For Web dialog box (Photoshop) or Optimize palette (ImageReady).

Specifying background transparency

You can use background transparency to place a nonrectangular graphic object against the background of a Web page; the areas outside the borders of the object are defined as transparent, letting the Web-page background color show through. You can specify background transparency for GIF and PNG images.

Converting the Background into an ordinary layer

Before you can use the GIF file format's ability to preserve transparency, you must create some transparency in your image. You'll do that by removing the white backdrop surrounding the image. To start this process, you'll first convert the Background layer to a regular layer, because a Background layer is always locked and cannot have any transparency.

1 Make sure that the 16Start2.psd file is open in ImageReady.

2 Select the original (left) version of the image in the image window.

3 Choose Fit on Screen from the Zoom Level menu in the lower left corner of the image window.

4 Choose Window > Layers to open the Layers palette, and then open the Layers palette menu and choose Layer Options.

5 Click OK to close the Layer Options dialog box without changing the default settings (including the name, Layer 0). The layer now appears in the Layer palette as Layer 0.

A Background layer cannot contain any transparency information because, by definition, there is nothing behind it to be seen. If you tried to use one of the techniques that usually can replace colored pixels with transparent ones, the results would be that the original pixels would be changed to the currently selected background color instead of becoming transparent pixels.

Using the Magic Eraser tool to create transparency

In this part of the lesson, you'll use the Magic Eraser tool to quickly convert the white backdrop behind the images and lettering to transparent pixels.

However, you don't want to erase any white pixels that might appear inside the colored images themselves. You'll accomplish this in two phases.

1 Make sure that the original (left) version of the image is selected in the image window.

You can erase background pixels only in the unoptimized version, not in an optimized version.

2 Select the Magic Eraser tool (⌖), which may be hidden under the Eraser tool (⌖).

3 In the tool options bar, make sure that the Contiguous check box is selected.

4 Click the white background that surrounds the color images.

The checkerboard pattern replaces the white background, indicating that the area is transparent.

5 Click the rectangular white area that is trapped within the middle of the four colored blocks.

Now most of the white backdrop is erased, except for the small islands of white pixels in the closed areas of the lettering.

Converting isolated areas of white into transparency

The Magic Eraser tool did not remove the white areas that are isolated within enclosed areas of the lettering because the Contiguous option was selected in the tool options bar.

One way to correct this would be to zoom in further and click in each of the white areas within the letters, just like you clicked the white rectangle in the center of the image. Instead, you'll use a method that works much more efficiently in cases where there may be a large number of small, discontiguous areas that you want to erase, while preserving other areas of similarly colored pixels that you do not want to erase.

1 In the tool options bar for the Magic Eraser tool ( ), deselect the Contiguous option.

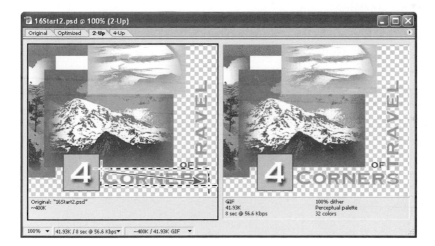

2 Select the Rectangular Marquee tool ( ), and carefully draw a rectangular selection marquee around the word "Corners" in the Original (left) version of the image.

3 Hold down Shift so that a small plus symbol appears in the pointer-icon crosshairs, and drag another selection rectangle around the word "Travel" and the word "of." The two selected areas merge into one selection shape. (You can do the word "of" separately, if you prefer by holding down Shift and dragging to add it to the selection. Or, you can either include a bit of the yellow block when you select both "Travel" and "of.")

4 Select the Zoom tool ($\mathcal{Q}$), and zoom in so that you can easily see the areas within the selection (about 300%).

5 Select the Magic Eraser tool ($\mathcal{D}$), and then carefully click the white background inside the letter "O."

The white pixels within the letter "O" are converted to transparent pixels, but so are the pixels inside the "A" and "R" characters in "Travel" and the "O" in "of."

6 Choose Select > Deselect, and then choose File > Save.

Finalizing the Color Table

Although it's not usual to think of transparency as a color, it does count as one of the 32 colors in the Color Table for the image. That means you need to inspect the image one more time to find any unacceptable dithering caused by the shift to transparency.

1 Scroll, or select the Hand tool ( ) and drag, to examine all the areas of the image.

Notice that there is now heavy dithering in the green around the aspen trees.

2 Select the optimized version on the right side of the image window.

3 In the Color option on the Optimize palette, select 128.

4 Select the Eyedropper tool and click the medium green in the upper right corner of the aspen image.

5 In the Color Table palette, click the lock icon to lock the color.

6 In the Optimize palette, select 32 as the number of colors.

7 Scroll or use the Hand tool ( ) to examine the image one more time, confirming that the image strikes an acceptable balance between dithering and file size. Then choose File > Save.

Previewing transparency

Now you will preview the transparency in your browser. Because the ImageReady preview feature displays the image on a Web page with a white background, you'll change the matte color of the image so that you can see the transparency.

1 In the image window, select the optimized (right) version of the image.

2 On the Optimize palette, make sure that the Transparency check box is selected.

Selecting Transparency converts areas in the original image with less than 50% opacity to background transparency in the optimized image.

3 Click the Matte swatch in the Optimize palette to open the color picker, and then select any color except white. Click OK to close the color picker.

4 Choose File > Preview In, and choose a Web browser from the submenu.

Note: *To use the Preview In command, you must have a Web browser installed on your system.*

If it is not already open, the browser first starts and then displays the optimized image in the upper left corner of the browser window. The browser also displays the pixel dimensions, file size, file format, and optimization settings for the image, along with the HTML code used to create the preview.

Transparency option selected   Transparency option deselected

5 Quit your browser when you're finished previewing the image.

Trimming extra background areas

Although the background of the image for the fictitious travel organization now contains transparent pixels that do not display, these pixels still take up file space, adding to the size of the image. You can trim away unneeded background areas to improve the layout of the image and optimize the file size.

1 In ImageReady, choose Image > Trim.

You use the Trim command to crop your image according to the transparency or pixel color of the extra border area.

2 In the Trim dialog box, select Transparent Pixels if it is not already selected, and click OK.

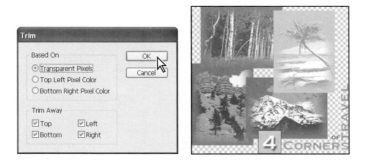

ImageReady trims the extra transparent areas from the image.

3 Choose File > Save Optimized As.

4 In the Save Optimized As dialog box, use the default name (**16Start2.gif**), and click Save.

5 In the Replace Files dialog box, click Replace (if it appears).

6 Choose File > Close.

You will be prompted to save the 16Start2.psd file before closing. Since you are finished with this file for this lesson, there is no need to save the last changes.

Creating a dithered transparency

In this section of Lesson 16, you'll create a dithered transparency for a graphic that will be used in another area of the Web site for the fictitious travel organization. By creating a dither from an opaque drop shadow to transparency, you'll make it possible to create a smooth transition from the image to any color backdrop on the page without having to redo any work.

You'll do this in two procedures. First, you'll apply a drop shadow to the image. Then, you'll add dithering to the drop shadow so that it blends into a background color for the Web page.

You can do this procedure in Photoshop or in ImageReady, using the same controls but in slightly different locations.

Adding a drop shadow

The file you'll be working on is intended to serve as a graphic that users click to open another page on the Web site. You'll add a drop shadow to the button to make the image appear to float above the background, emphasizing that it is an interactive element of the page.

1 Choose File > Open, and select the 16Start3.psd file in the Lessons/Lesson16 folder.

2 If necessary, choose Window > Layers to open the Layers palette, and then select Layer 1, if it is not already selected.

3 Select the Add A Layer Style button (⊘) at the bottom of the Layers palette, and then select Drop Shadow from the pop-up menu.

4 In the Layer Style dialog box, enter the following values:

- For Opacity, drag the slider or type **65%**.
- For Distance, drag the slider or type **15** px.
- For Spread, drag the slider or type **10%**.
- For Size, drag the slider or type **15** px.

5 Click OK to close the Drop Shadow dialog box.

6 Choose File > Save.

Adding transparency dithering to the drop shadow

As you've already learned, dithering is a method of creating gradations of color with a limited color palette. This makes it useful for Web pages, because you can simulate smoother gradations without sacrificing small file size and quick downloads.

1 (Photoshop only) With the 16Start3.psd active, choose File > Save For Web to open the Save For Web dialog box.

This step is not necessary in ImageReady.

2 Click the Optimized tab in the Save For Web dialog box (Photoshop) or image window (ImageReady), and then set the following options on the right side of the Save For Web dialog box (Photoshop) or the Optimize palette (ImageReady):

• In the Preset pop-up menu, select GIF 128 Dithered.

• Select the Transparency check box, if it is not already selected.

• In the Dither pop-up menu for Transparency, select Diffusion.

• In the Amount option, use the pop-up slider or type **64%**.

Save For Web dialog box
(Photoshop)

Optimize palette
(ImageReady)

3 Click the Matte swatch to open the color picker. Select any color other than white, and click OK. (We selected R=**250**, G=**234**, B=**212**, a neutral beige to set off the blues in the mailbox photograph.)

To see the effect of the matte setting, try zooming in so that you can see individual pixels in the dither—about 400% or even all the way to 1600%, which is the maximum. Notice that the pixels closest to the edge of the mailbox and blue frame area are dark, and that the others become increasing more blended with the matte color as they occur farther from the edge. Then zoom back to 100%.

4 Do one of the following:

• (In Photoshop) At the bottom of the Save For Web dialog box, click the button with the browser icon, or click the arrow to select your browser from the pop-up menu.

• (In ImageReady) Use the Preview In Default Browser button or the Preview In submenu on the File menu to open the file in a browser.

5 In the browser, notice how the drop shadow blends into the background matte color. When you finish viewing your document, close the browser or go back to Photoshop or ImageReady.

6 Click the Save button in the Save For Web dialog box (Photoshop) or choose File > Save Optimized (ImageReady).

7 In the Save Optimized dialog box, accept the default settings and filename (16Start3.gif) and save the file in your Lessons/Lesson16 folder.

8 Choose File > Save to save the 16Start3.psd file, or close the file without saving.

Batch-processing file optimization

ImageReady supports batch processing through the use of *droplets*—icons that contain actions for ImageReady to perform on one or more files. Droplets are easy to create and use. To create a droplet, you drag the droplet icon out of the Optimize palette and onto the desktop. To use it, you drag a file or folder over the droplet icon on the desktop.

1 In ImageReady, choose File > Open, and open any file in the Lessons/Lesson16/Destinations folder.

2 Experiment with different file formats and other settings in the Optimize palette as desired until you are satisfied with the result. (We used JPEG for Format, High (60) for Quality, and the Progressive option.)

3 Drag the droplet icon (🐾) out of the Optimize palette and drop it anywhere on your desktop. (If you are using Windows, you may have to resize the ImageReady window to make your desktop visible.)

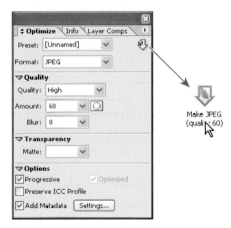

4 Close the file (without saving it).

5 From your desktop, drag the Destinations folder from the Lessons/Lesson16 folder and drop it onto the droplet to batch-process the photographic images within the folder.

ImageReady optimizes each file and adds the Web image to the Destinations folder.

6 In ImageReady, open any or all of the JPEG image files in the Destinations folder.

Notice that they have all been optimized according to the settings specified when the droplet was created.

7 Quit ImageReady. You have now finished this project and this lesson.

Review questions

1 For image optimization, what are the advantages of using ImageReady rather than Photoshop?

2 What is a color table?

3 When does browser dither occur, and how can you minimize the amount of browser dither in an image?

4 What is the purpose of assigning matte color to a GIF image?

Review answers

1 There aren't really any advantages to using one application over the other for optimization. Both Photoshop and ImageReady can perform a wide range of image-optimization tasks. ImageReady has many Web-specific features that you won't find in Photoshop, but image optimization is not one of them.

2 A color table is a table that contains the colors used in an 8-bit image. You can select a color table for GIF and PNG-8 images, and add, delete, and modify colors in the color table.

3 Browser dither occurs when a Web browser simulates colors that appear in the image's color palette but not in the browser's display system. To protect a color from browser dither, you can select the color in the Color Table palette, and then click the Web-shift button at the bottom of the palette to shift the color to its closest equivalent in the Web palette.

4 By specifying a matte color, you can blend partially transparent pixels in an image with the background color of your Web page. With matting, you can create GIF images with feathered or anti-aliased edges that blend smoothly into the background color of your Web page. You can also specify a dither to transparency.

Lesson 17

17 | Creating Rollover Web Visuals

Rollovers animate slices of an image on a Web page with visual changes that occur in response to mouse actions. Rollovers can go a long way toward making your Web pages more user-friendly. This in turn helps you achieve your goals for your Web sites by giving even casual users added clues about links and other items available to them.

In this lesson, you'll learn how to do the following:

• Divide one slice into several equally spaced slices.

• Group selected slices into a table.

• Apply a warped text style to a text layer.

• Define rollover states affecting layer visibility, layer styles, and warped text.

• Create Over, Down, and Selected rollover states.

• Specify different combinations of hidden and visible layers as the designated conditions of various rollover states.

• Generate an HTML page that contains the sliced image in a table.

This lesson will take about 60 minutes to complete. The lesson must be done in Adobe ImageReady.

If needed, remove the previous lesson folder from your hard drive, and copy the Lessons/Lesson17 folder onto it. As you work on this lesson, you'll overwrite the start files. If you need to restore the start files, copy them from the *Adobe Photoshop CS Classroom in a Book* CD.

Note: *Windows 2000 users need to unlock the lesson files before using them. For more information, see "Copying the Classroom in a Book files" on page 3.*

About rollovers

Rollovers are familiar Web effects that alter the usual appearance (Normal state) of the Web page without switching the user to a different Web page. The primary example is the namesake behavior: When a user rolls the mouse so that the pointer passes over a defined area of a Web page, that same area of the page changes appearance in some way. Usually, this is done as a visual cue, emphasizing that the area is a hotspot that the user can click to make something happen, such as open another Web page.

There are other kinds of rollovers. Some rollovers are tied to other types of user actions, such as clicking or holding down the mouse button. Some rollovers triggered by a user action in one area of the Web page can cause another part of the Web page to change.

Rollover effects or states represent different conditions in the Layers palette. These conditions may involve layer visibility, layer position, layer styles, and other options for formatting. This lesson is entirely devoted to exploring a representative sampling of what you can do with rollovers.

Note: This lesson assumes that you have a basic knowledge of slices either from your work in Lesson 15, "Creating Links within an Image," or from your own background.

Getting started

You'll start the lesson by viewing an example of an HTML page that you'll create based on a single .psd image file. Several areas of the artwork react to mouse actions. For example, some areas of the image change appearance when the pointer "rolls over" or when you click one of those spots.

For this procedure, you'll need to have a Web browser (such as Netscape Communicator or Microsoft Internet Explorer) installed on your computer.

1 On the desktop, locate the Lessons/Lesson17/17End folder and double-click the 17End.html file to open it in your default Web browser.

2 Move the mouse pointer over the Web page, especially over the left side. Look for:

• Changes in the appearance of the image.

• Changes in the appearance of the pointer (from an arrow to a pointing hand).

3 Click each of the menu buttons on the left side of the image, and notice the different reactions that occur on the page.

Note: The page is not necessarily finished because no links are set up yet, so clicking these buttons will not open additional Web pages. However, some actions in these buttons (which are slices) do cause changes on this same page. For more on configuring slices to link to URLs for other Web pages, see Lesson 15, "Creating Links within an Image."

4 When you finish viewing the Web page, quit the Web browser.

Creating rollover states

A *rollover state* is named by the event, such as a click or rolling the pointer over an area of the image, that triggers a change in the image or part of the image. All the ImageReady rollover states are described in the sidebar below, "Rollover states in ImageReady."

Remote rollovers tie a rollover state in one slice to changes in a different slice. For example, the user could click a button (the activating slice) that would make a previously hidden graphic or text block (the remote slice) visible in another area of the Web page.

Only user slices can have rollover states. However, you can choose Slices > Promote to convert an auto slice into a user slice, and then assign rollover states to that slice.

Rollover states in ImageReady

ImageReady automatically assigns one of the following states to new rollovers you create.

Over *Activates the image when the user rolls over the slice or image-map area with the mouse while the mouse button is not pressed.*

Down *Activates the image when the user presses the mouse button on the slice or image-map area. The state appears as long as the viewer keeps the mouse button pressed down on the area.*

Click *Activates the image when the user clicks the mouse on the slice or image-map area. The state appears until the user moves the mouse out of the rollover area.*

Note: *Different Web browsers, or different versions of a browser, may process clicks and double-clicks differently. See ImageReady Help for more information.*

Custom *Activates the image of the specified name when the user performs the action defined in the corresponding JavaScript code. (You must create JavaScript code and add it to the HTML file for the Web page in order for the Custom rollover option to function. See a JavaScript manual for more information.)*

None *Preserves the current state of the image for later use, but does not output an image when the file is saved as a Web page.*

Selected *Activates the rollover state when the user clicks the mouse on the slice or image-map area. The state appears until the viewer activates another selected rollover state, and other rollover effects can occur while the selected state is active.*

Out *Activates the image when the user rolls the mouse out of the slice or image-map area. (The Normal state usually serves this purpose.)*

Up *Activates the image when the user releases the mouse button over the slice or image-map area.*

Defining a workspace for this lesson

If you've already completed other lessons in this book, it's likely that you've had experience defining workspaces. ImageReady has several predefined workspaces that you can use for specific kinds of work, and you could certainly use one of those as a starting place for this lesson. But you can also create a specialized refinement of a predefined workspace and save it as a custom workspace, which is what you'll do now.

1 Start Adobe ImageReady. If the palettes are not in the default locations, choose Window > Workspace > Default Palette Locations.

2 Drag the Web Content palette group to the left of the Info palette, at the top of the work area.

3 Click the close buttons to close the Info palette group and the Color palette group. Or, you can close them by selecting Info and Color on the View menu.

4 Drag the Layers palette group to the upper right corner of the work area, next to the Web Content palette group (where the Info palette group was).

5 In the Slices palette group, select the Table tab to bring it forward, and then click the double arrows (‡) on that tab to fully expand the palette. Then drag it to the lower right corner of the work area.

6 Drag the lower right corners of the Web Content and Layers palettes so that they take full advantage of the available space below them.

7 Choose Window > Workspace > Save Workspace, and name it **17_Rollovers** in the Save Workspace dialog box.

Setting up work options for the lesson file

Another important preparation for work is to make sure that the work settings for ImageReady are set up in the right way. Some of these can't be configured unless a file is open, so you'll start with that step.

1 Choose File > Open.

2 In the Open dialog box, navigate to the Lessons/Lesson17 folder on your hard drive.

3 Select the 17Start.psd file and click Open.

4 If necessary, resize the image window and zoom in or out so that you can see the entire image.

5 Examine the View menu and submenus to make sure that the following commands are selected (checked), or select them now.

- Extras

- Snap

- Guides and Slices on the Snap To submenu

- Guides and Slices on the Show submenu

Creating a rollover with warped text

One of the fun things ImageReady can do with text is to warp the font shape. For example, you can make the words appear as they might look if they were painted on a three-dimensional object.

You'll combine that applied warping with a rollover state. As a result, the warped text will appear on the final HTML image only in response to specific user actions.

1 Select the Slice tool ( ), and drag a rectangle around the words "Museo Arte," using the guides as a reference so that the slice borders snap to them.

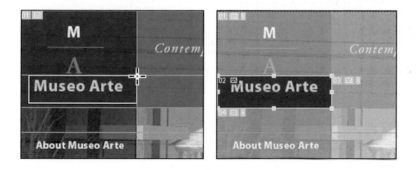

2 In the Web Content palette, double-click the automatically assigned name of the user slice (17Start_02) to activate it. Type **Museo Arte** to rename it, and press Enter (Windows) or Return (Mac OS).

3 Select the Create Rollover State button (▣). A new Over state rollover appears nested below the Museo Arte slice in the Web Content palette.

4 In the Layers palette, select the Museo Arte layer.

5 In the toolbox, select the Type tool (**T**) to display the text options in the tool options bar, and click the Create Warped Text button (ᴦ).

Note: You do not need to use the Type tool or select the text. The warping effect always applies to the entire text layer, not individual words or characters.

6 Select Fisheye in the Style pop-up menu, and drag the Bend slider to 30%. Leave the Vertical and Horizontal Distortion sliders at 0%, and click OK. Notice the distortion of the Museo Arte text.

7 In the Web Content palette, click Normal to deactivate the rollover-state display in the image window.

Note: Warping text is not the same as placing type on a path, which is a feature you can use in Photoshop. For information on how to arrange characters on geometric or freeform paths, see Photoshop Help. (This feature is not available in ImageReady.)

Previewing a rollover

Although the end result of this project is a Web page, you can test the interactive behaviors of your slices in ImageReady. You do this by stepping out of working mode into preview mode. While you are previewing, some palettes, such as the Layers palette, are dimmed because you cannot select layers or make adjustments in those palettes in preview mode.

1 In the Layers palette, click a blank area to deselect the Museo Arte layer.

2 In the toolbox, first select the Toggle Slices Visibility button (🔲) or press Q to hide the slice boundaries and remove the ghosting appearance over the image.

3 Select the Preview Document button ( ) or press Y to activate preview mode.

Note: *The guides are still visible in the image window. You can either ignore them as you preview or hide them by choosing View > Show > Guides, or with the keyboard shortcut using the semicolon key: Ctrl+; (Windows) or Command+; (Mac OS>. If you hide them now, be sure that you make them visible again after you finish previewing, because you'll need them for the next topic.*

4 Move the pointer over the Museo Arte text in the image window, and then move it away so that you can see the effect of the Over rollover state with the Warped Text applied.

Notice the effect the pointer position has on the highlighting in the Web Content palette. As you move the pointer over and then away from the Museo Arte slice in the image window, the slice selection in the Web Content palette shifts from Normal to the Museo Arte Over state.

5 Click the Preview Document and Toggle Slices Visibility buttons again to deactivate them, or press Q and Y to use the keyboard shortcuts.

The slice boundaries and the ghosted overlay reappear in the image window.

6 In the Web Content palette, select Normal, and click the arrow on the Museo Arte slice to hide the rollover listing.

Try to keep the Web Content and Layers palettes as organized and tidy as possible for your rollover work. By avoiding visual clutter, you'll make fewer mistakes, do less scrolling, and be able to find and focus on the next item in the palette that requires your attention. In this lesson, we'll frequently remind you to collapse grouped items when you finish working with them, even though this doesn't affect the end result of the lesson.

In this lesson, you won't go on to the next logical step for a Web page author: associating a link to another Web page with the Museo Arte slice. It's something you can do later on your own, if you want to do so. This process is covered in Lesson 15, "Creating Links within an Image."

Creating and dividing a slice and making a table

Slices are essentially the cells of an HTML table. You can use the improved tables features and new Table palette in ImageReady CS to create tables nested within the overall HTML table for your page. This produces a cleaner, more manageable HTML code and makes it easier for you to work with the table slices.

1 Select the Slice tool ( ) in the toolbox.

2 Drag to create a new slice, beginning at the intersection of the vertical and horizontal guides just above the "About Museo Arte" text and ending where the guide just below the "Contact" text meets the left edge of the document.

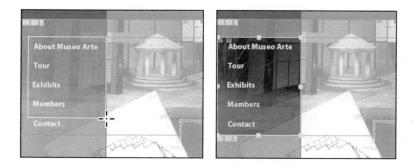

3 Choose View > Show > Guides to remove the check mark and hide the guides.

4 Choose Slices > Divide Slice to open the Divide Slice dialog box.

5 Under Divide Slice Horizontally Into, type **5** in the Slices Down, Evenly Spaced option. Then click OK.

6 With the five new slices still selected, click the Group Slices Into Table button (⊞) at the bottom of the Web Content palette.

Notice that the five slices are now nested under the new Table 02 in the Web Content palette and that the color of their bounding boxes has changed in the image window, indicating that they are a table. The Museo Arte slice remains outside the table.

Renaming and rearranging slices

As you've probably already guessed, you can change the order of the slices in the Web Content palette in the same way you change the arrangement of layers in the Layers palette. This includes rearranging slices within a defined table, like the one you just created for the menu panel in the image.

1 In the Web Content palette, double-click the Table_02 name to activate it and type **Menu Slices** to rename it, and then press Enter (Windows) or Return (Mac OS).

2 Select the first cell (slice) nested under the Menu Slices table, and notice that a differently colored selection border appears around the Contact button.

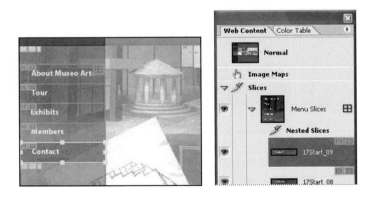

3 Double-click the selected slice name, type **Contact** to rename it, and press Enter (Windows) or Return (Mac OS).

4 Using the same technique, rename the remaining four slices in the table, typing **Members**, **Exhibits**, **Tour**, or **About** corresponding to the text enclosed in the selected slice.

5 Select the About slice in the table and drag it to the top of the table under Nested Slices, being careful to keep the slice indented. (Otherwise, you will remove the slice from the table.)

6 Select and drag the other slices so that their order in the table in the Web Content palette matches the order seen in the image window and in the second illustration below: About, Tour, Exhibits, Members, and Contact.

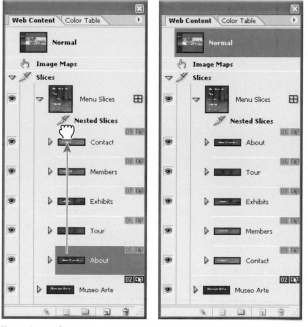

Dragging a slice   Final order of the table slices

7 Click Normal.

Creating rollovers affecting layer visibility

Perhaps one of the most common methods of animating a file is to change the visibility of different layers.

In this design, the original version of the central image was fully colored instead of the heavily blue-toned version that you see in Normal state. Sections of the original version have been copied onto layers in this file, above the blue-version Background layer. The original-color sections line up perfectly with the blue image, so making them visible appears to brighten just that area of the image by removing the blue color cast.

1 In the Web Content palette, select the About slice, and then click the Create Rollover State (⬛) button at the bottom of the palette to create a new Over state for that slice.

2 In the Layers palette, expand the Menu Color Bkgds layer set, and click the visibility box to set an eye icon (👁) by the Cell 1 layer.

The background behind the About Museo Arte text is now more brightly colored.

3 In the Web Content palette, click Normal, and click the arrow by the About slice to collapse its contents.

The eye icon disappears from the Cell 1 layer, and the About button in the image window returns to its monochromatic blue coloring.

4 Using the same process as Steps 1–2, create rollover states for each of the remaining four table slices:

• Select the Tour slice, create a new rollover, and make the Cell 2 layer visible.

• Select the Exhibits slice, create a new rollover, and make the Cell 3 layer visible.

• Select the Members slice, create a new rollover, and make the Cell 4 layer visible.

• Select the Contact slice, create a new rollover, and make the Cell 5 layer visible.

5 Hide all the rollover-state listings for the slices by clicking the arrow for each slice.

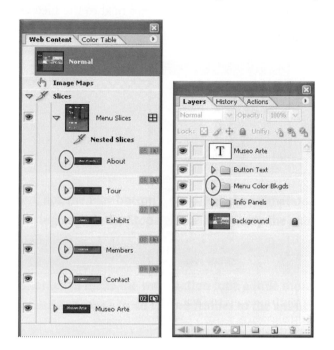

6 In the Layers palette, collapse the Menu Colored Bkgds layer set.

Previewing layer-visibility rollovers

Now it's time to test your rollover work by previewing the image.

1 Click a blank area of the Layers palette to ensure that no layers are selected. Then select the Preview Document button ( ) in the toolbox.

Note: *Do not select the Toggle Slices Visibility button this time, so that the slice boundaries and symbol boxes remain visible as you preview.*

2 Slowly move the pointer up and down over the different buttons in the table and notice the following:

• The changes in background coloring as the pointer moves over the different button areas.

• The Active Slice badge (✳) that appears in the symbol sets in the image window and slice listings in the Web Content palette, and also in the boxes next to the slice visibility symbols (👁).

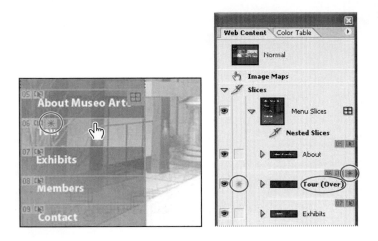

3 Click the Preview Document button again to deactivate it.

4 Choose File > Save to save your work.

About slice symbols

The slice symbols or badges that appear in the Web Content palette and in the image window can be useful reminders if you take the time to learn how to read them. One slice can contain as many badges as are appropriate. The following badges appear under the stated conditions:

(01) The number of the slice. (Numbers run sequentially from left to right and top to bottom of the image.)

(✳) The active rollover state is in this slice.

(⊠) The slice contains Image content.

(⊠) The slice contains No Image content.

(✦) The slice is layer-based (that is, it was created from a layer).

(⬛) The slice includes at least one rollover effect.

(⊞) The slice is a nested table.

(⬒) The slice is a remote trigger (causes a change in a remote slice).

(◉) The slice is a remote target (changes in response to a user action in an associated remote trigger slice).

(▨) The slice is linked to other slices (for optimization purposes).

Creating another rollover state using layer styles

All the rollovers you've created so far are Over states, which affect the appearance of the image when the pointer moves over the slice. Several other kinds of mouse actions can trigger rollover states. You can assign more than one rollover state to an individual slice, so that different things occur on-screen depending on what the user does, such as point to, click, or select a particular slice.

1 In the Layers palette, click the arrow to expand the Button Text layer set. If necessary, click the arrow to expand the "About Museo Arte" text layer within that set, so that you can see the effects nested below that layer.

2 In the Web Content palette, select the About slice in the Menu Slices table.

3 Select the Create Rollover State button at the bottom of the palette. The new rollover is labeled Down and is selected.

4 Double-click the new Down rollover to open the Rollover State Options dialog box.

5 Select the Click option, and then click OK to close the dialog box.

6 In the Layers palette, click the box to set an eye icon for Effects under the "About Museo Arte" text layer.

A slight yellow glow surrounds the words *About Museo Arte* in the image.

7 Click the Normal state at the top of the Web Content palette and then collapse the About slice to hide the rollover listing. Then, in the Layers palette, collapse the "About Museo Arte" layer to hide the Effects listing.

Finishing the remaining buttons and previewing the rollovers

Again, it's always a good idea to test your rollovers in preview mode before you go on.

1 Using the procedure you followed in the previous topic ("Creating another rollover state using layer styles" on page 569), create Click rollover states for the other four slices in the Menu Slices table. When you finish, the Tour text will glow when the user clicks the Tour button, the Exhibits text will glow when the user clicks the Exhibits button, and so forth.

2 In the Layers palette, click the arrow to collapse the Button Text layer set, and then click a blank area of the Layers palette to deselect all layers.

3 Select Normal in the Web Content palette.

4 In the toolbox, select the Toggle Slices Visibility button (🖼) and then the Preview Document button (👆).

5 Slowly move the pointer over the image window, concentrating on the changes to the colored background in the Over states.

6 Click individual buttons, and notice the glow that remains visible on the letters until you move the pointer off the button area.

Also notice that after you click, the more brightly colored background disappears, leaving the regular darker-toned background for the button.

7 Click the Toggle Slices Visibility button and Preview Document button again to return to normal work mode.

Preparing to do more rollover work

You can create sets for slices, just as you can for layers. Slice sets tidy up the list in the Web Content palette, helping you navigate quickly and accurately through the complexity of a sophisticated collection of slices and rollovers.

1 In the Web Content palette, make sure that Normal is the selected state or select it now, and then select the New Slice Set (🗀) button at the bottom of the palette.

2 Double-click the new slice set name (Slice Set 1) to activate it, and type **Info Slices** to rename it. Then press Enter (Windows) or Return (Mac OS).

Leave the Info Slices set selected in the Web Content palette.

3 In the Layers palette, do the following:

• Click the arrow for the Info Panels layer set to expand it.

• Select the Exhibit_info layer.

Adding new slices to a slice set

You can always drag slices in and out of a slice set in the Web Content palette, just as you can drag layers in and out of layer sets or layer groups in the Layers palette. But if you plan ahead, you can save yourself the trouble by automatically placing new slices inside a specific slice set as you create them. This topic shows you how.

1 In the Layers palette, click to set an eye icon ( ) for the Exhibit_info layer in the Info Panels layer set so that the "Spanish Master" graphic is visible in the image window.

The layer becomes visible in the image window.

2 Choose Select > Load Selection >Exhibit_info Transparency.

The animated selection border shows that the layer is now selected.

3 Choose Select > Create Slice From Selection.

A solid-colored border indicates that the layer is now also a slice, but the selection border is also visible.

4 Choose Select > Deselect, or press Ctrl+D (Windows) or Command+D (Mac OS).

5 In the Web Control palette, expand the Info Slices slice set by clicking the arrow by its name.

Because Info Slices was selected in the Web Content palette when you created the slice, the new slice appears nested inside that slice set.

6 Double-click the new slice name (17Start_11) and type **Exhibit Info** to rename it. Press Enter (Windows) or Return (Mac OS).

Troubleshooting rollover behaviors

Creating rollovers requires meticulous attention to detail in an environment that can be crowded with alternatives. One of the more common mistakes occurs when you unintentionally alter the Normal state.

1 In the Web Content palette, select Normal.

Notice that the previous procedure has created a problem: The Exhibit_info layer is now visible in Normal state. Fortunately, that's easy to correct.

2 With Normal state still selected, click the eye icon ( ) in the Layers palette for the Exhibits Info layer to hide the layer.

3 Test that this corrected the problem by selecting a rollover state in any of the slices (you will have to expand the slice to reveal the hidden rollovers), and then clicking Normal again.

Now the image appears correctly, as it did before you assigned any rollovers.

Creating a slice from a hidden layer

In this procedure, you'll create a slice from the Member_info layer just like the one you created for the Exhibits Info slice—but with a more efficient technique. You can create the slice from a layer that isn't even visible. Because this doesn't alter the view in Normal state, this makes it unnecessary to go back and fix the Normal state when you finish.

1 In the Layers palette, select the Members_info layer but do *not* click the eye icon to make it visible.

2 In the Web Content palette, select the Info Slices slice set.

3 Choose Select > Load Selection > Members_info Transparency.

In the center of the image window, the animated selection border around the unseen layer boundaries confirms that the layer is selected, even though you can't see any change in the art itself.

4 Choose Select > Create Slice From Selection.

5 Choose Select > Deselect, or press Ctrl+D (Windows) or Command+D (Mac OS) to deselect the layer but not the slice.

6 In the Web Content palette, double-click the new slice name (17Start_14) and type **Members Info** to rename the slice. Press Enter (Windows) or Return (Mac OS).

7 Click Normal.

Because you did not make the Member_info layer visible during this procedure, the Normal state is still as it was and there is no need to correct it as you had to do for the Exhibit Info slice.

Creating remote rollovers

A remote rollover is the association of one slice with another one so that an action in one slice affects the visibility or effects in the other slice.

For remote slices, it is not enough to change the visibility settings in the Layers palette for the remote slice. You must also create the relationship between the two slices. Fortunately, the pickwick (⦿) feature makes it easy and intuitive to accomplish this part.

1 In the Web Content palette, do the following:

• In the Menu Slices table, expand the Exhibits and Members slices so that you can see the Over and Click rollover states nested under each of those slices.

• Select the Click rollover state for the Exhibits slice.

2 In the Layers palette, select the Exhibit_info layer and click the visibility box to set an eye icon (👁) for that layer.

3 In the Web Content palette, drag the pickwick (🔘) from the Click rollover state of the Exhibits slice to the Exhibit_info layer in the image window, so that the slice boundary is highlighted by a dark border.

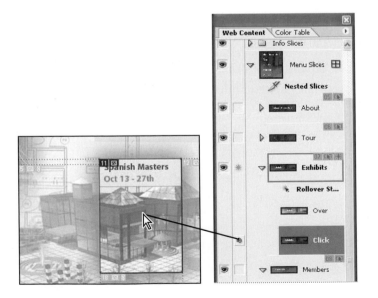

When you release the mouse button, notice the new badge (⊡) in the symbol sets for the Exhibits slice in the image window and Web Content palette. Also notice the badge (◈) next to the Exhibit Info slice.

Note: Instead of dragging the pickwick to the target slice in the image window, you can drag it to that slice in the Web Content palette. The result is the same with either method.

4 Select Normal in the Web Content palette, and click the arrow on the Exhibits slice to collapse the rollovers nested below it.

5 Select the Click rollover state for the Members slice.

6 Repeat Steps 2–4 but use the Members Info slice as the target for the remote rollover: Make that layer visible and then drag the pickwick from the Click state to the "Members Discount" image. Be careful to select Normal at the end of the process.

7 In the Layers palette, click the arrow to collapse the Info Panels layer set.

 If you accidentally release the pickwick at the wrong slice or decide later that you don't want to use the remote rollover at all, you can remove it. To do this, select the rollover state you want to edit, such as an Over or Down state nested under the triggering layer. Then find the Remote badge (◈) between the eye icon and the name of the target slice in the Web Content palette. Click that Remote badge to delete it, which removes the remote rollover relationship.

Previewing rollovers to detect problems

Catching errors isn't the only reason for testing rollovers. Sometimes unanticipated results occur that require additional adjustments, especially when you're just learning how to work with rollovers.

1 In the Web Content palette, expand the Exhibits and Members slices in the Menu Buttons slice set so that you can see the rollover states nested below them.

2 One at a time, select the two Click rollover states and notice the results in the image window. Pay particular attention to the partially transparent, dark halo effect that appears around the Info Panels layer art.

3 Click a blank area of the Layers palette to deselect all layers and select Normal in the Web Content palette.

4 In the toolbox, select the Toggle Slices Visibility button ( ) and then the Preview Document button ( ).

Shadowless slice (preview model)   *Shadowed layer (work mode)*

5 Move the pointer over the image window, and click the Exhibit button. Allow the pointer to remain inside that navigation button so that you can examine the information panel that appears. Notice that the shadowy halo around the panel does not appear.

6 Click the Members button and confirm that the same phenomenon occurs for that information panel.

7 Click the Toggle Slices Visibility button and Preview Document button again to return to normal work mode.

Resizing slices to correct visibility problems

In order to correct the view of the information panels so that the user can see the shadow layer style applied to them, you must make those layers visible as a reference. After you make the correction, you need to make them invisible again so that you don't change Normal state.

1 In the Web Content palette, select the Click state for the Exhibits slice.

2 In the toolbox, select the Slice Select tool (⟋) and click the Exhibit Info slice in the image window. (If you hid the Guides earlier, choose View > Show > Guides to make them visible.)

3 Select one of the corner anchor points on the upper slice boundary and drag it up and away from the center of the layer art until it completely surrounds the gradient dark shadow around the top and side of the art.

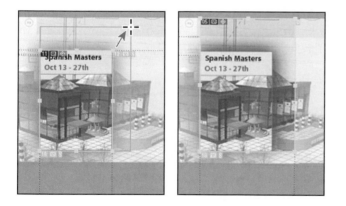

Note: You can drag the slice borders to the horizontal guides above and below the central third of the image because there are no other slices in that area. This is not necessary, but it reduces the number of auto slices required to completely divide up the image. If there were other user slices in the same area, overlapping their edges would block one slice or the other and create unwanted results.

4 Select the anchor point on the opposite corner of the slice and drag down and away from the center so that the slice encloses all the shadow on those sides.

5 In the Web Content palette, select the Click state of the Members slice. Then, repeat Steps 2–4 so that that slice encompasses the entire shadowy effect around the Members Info art.

6 In the Web Content palette, select Normal. In the Layers palette, click an empty area to ensure that no layers are selected.

7 Use the Toggle Slices Visibility and Preview Document buttons and preview the image to make sure that changing the slice dimensions corrected the problem. When you finish, select the buttons again to return to working mode.

Generating a Web page from the image

ImageReady does the hard work of converting your image-file information into a Web page consisting of an HTML file and supporting folders of files. There is one important step that you must do in order for the Web page to recognize the rollovers so that they work properly on the Web page. You'll do that step first.

1 Click the arrow to open the Web palette menu, and choose Find All Remote Slices.

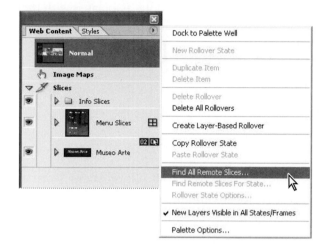

2 When a message appears, reporting the changes that ImageReady has made to the file, click OK.

3 Choose File > Save Optimized As.

4 In the Save Optimized As dialog box, navigate to the location in which you want to save the file, or save it in the Lessons/Lesson17 folder.

5 Leave the file name as it is and then make sure that the following options are selected:

• HTML And Images for Save As Type (Windows) or Format (Mac OS).

• Default Settings for the Settings option.

• All Slices for the Slices option.

6 Click Save.

7 On the desktop, locate the 17Start.html file you just generated and open it to view your final results. After you finish viewing it and testing the rollovers, quit the browser.

Nice job! You have finished your work on Lesson 17.

There is more to learn about rollovers, tables, and how to use them effectively for Web pages. Also, rollovers are not the exclusive feature of slices. You can also create rollovers from image maps, such as for the image maps you created in Lesson 15, "Adding Links to an Image."

Review Questions

1 Name two common rollover states and the mouse actions associated with them.

2 How many rollover states can a slice have?

3 Can you create a rollover state for an image map instead of a slice?

4 What is a remote rollover?

5 Can rollovers do more than cause changes in appearance?

Review Answers

1 Normal and Over are probably the two most common rollover states. Normal is the default appearance of the Web page, as it opens and before the user performs any mouse actions. Over is the state when the pointer tip is within the defined area but without the user pressing the mouse button in any way. There are a total of eight different rollover states you can create in ImageReady, if you count Custom and None. However, since you can create your own Custom states, there are innumerable other possibilities.

2 A slice can have multiple rollover states, but only one of each type. For example, a slice could not have two different Over states, but one Over state could trigger multiple changes in the slice and also in one or more remote slices. Because these different states are associated with different mouse actions, there is no conflict and no reason why they cannot coexist.

3 Yes, certainly! You can make the same kinds of changes in layer visibility, position, or effects that you can make with slices, just as you can link both slices and image maps to URLs.

4 A remote rollover is when a mouse action taking place in one slice affects the appearance of another slice in the image. These have sometimes been called *secondary* rollovers.

5 Yes. Properly set up, you can use remote rollovers to do other things, such as launch an application or run an animation. For more information, see ImageReady Help.

Lesson 18

18 Animating GIF Images for the Web

To add dynamic content to your Web page, use Adobe ImageReady to create animated GIF images from a single image. Compact in file size, animated GIFs display and play in most Web browsers. ImageReady provides an easy and convenient way to create imaginative animations.

In this lesson, you'll learn how to do the following:

• Use a multilayered GIF image as the basis for the animation.

• Use the Layers palette and Animation palette together to create animation sequences.

• Create animations based on changes in position, layer visibility, and layer effects.

• Make changes to single frames, multiple frames, and an entire animation.

• Use the Tween command to create smooth transitions between different settings for layer opacity and position.

• Preview animations in Adobe ImageReady and in a Web browser.

• Optimize the animation using the Optimize palette.

This lesson will take about 60 minutes to complete. The lesson must be done in Adobe ImageReady, not Adobe Photoshop.

If needed, remove the previous lesson folder from your hard drive, and copy the Lessons/Lesson18 folder onto it. As you work on this lesson, you'll overwrite the start files. If you need to restore the start files, copy them from the *Adobe Photoshop CS Classroom in a Book* CD.

Note: *Windows 2000 users need to unlock the lesson files before using them. For more information, see "Copying the Classroom in a Book files" on page 3.*

Creating animations in Adobe ImageReady

In Adobe ImageReady, you create animation from a single image using animated GIF files. An *animated GIF* is a sequence of images, or frames. Each frame varies slightly from the preceding frame, creating the illusion of movement when the frames are viewed in quick succession—just like movies. You can create animation in several ways:

• By using the Duplicate Current Frame button in the Animation palette to create animation frames, and then using the Layers palette to define the image state associated with each frame.

• By using the Tween feature to quickly create new frames that warp text or vary a layer's opacity, position, or effects to create the illusion of an element in a frame moving or fading in and out.

• By opening a multilayer Adobe Photoshop or Adobe Illustrator file for an animation, with each layer becoming a frame.

When creating an animation sequence, it's best to select the Original tab in the image window because this view doesn't require ImageReady to reoptimize the image as you edit the frame contents. Animation files are output as either GIF files or QuickTime movies. You cannot create a JPEG or PNG animation.

For the Web: About working with layers in animations

Working with layers is an essential part of creating animations in ImageReady. Placing each element of an animation on its own layer enables you to change the position and appearance of the element across a series of frames.

Frame-specific changes Some changes you make to layers affect only the active animation frame. By default, changes you make to layers using Layers palette commands and options—including layer opacity, blending mode, visibility, position, and style—are frame-specific. However, you can apply layer changes to all frames in an animation by using the unity buttons in the Layers palette.

Global changes Some changes affect every frame in which the layers are included. Changes you make to layer pixel values, using painting and editing tools, color- and tone-adjustment commands, filters, type, and other image-editing commands are global.

Each new frame starts out as a duplicate of the preceding frame—you edit the frame by adjusting its layers. You can apply layer changes to a single frame, a group of frames, or the entire animation.

Getting started

In this lesson, you'll work with a set of images designed to appear on the Web page of a fresh-juice company. If you have a browser application installed on your computer, you can preview the finished animations.

1 On the desktop, go to the Lessons/Lesson18 folder and double-click the 18End.html file to open it in your default Web browser application.

The page includes four animated areas: the "Making Waves" text, the whale tail rising and falling back into the ocean, the chemical formula for water moving into the image, and a dolphin swimming along and releasing bubbles that pop into the air. (The text and buttons are merely placeholders.)

2 When you have finished viewing the file, quit the browser.

3 Start Adobe ImageReady while holding down Ctrl+Alt+Shift (Windows) or Command+Option+Shift (Mac OS) to restore the default preferences. (See "Restoring default preferences" on page 4.)

4 As messages appear, select Yes to confirm that you want to reset preferences, No to defer setting up your color monitor, and Close to close the Welcome Screen.

Defining a workspace for animation tasks

Before you start working on the file, you'll define a new workspace especially for animation work. Having the right workspace available at any time reduces screen clutter and makes your task more efficient and more enjoyable.

ImageReady offers a predefined Interactivity Palette Locations workspace, which you're already familiar with if you've done the previous ImageReady lessons. Since the interactivity in this lesson is limited to animating, you can reduce the number of open palettes even further, starting from the default workspace configuration.

1 Choose File > Open, and select the Dolphin.psd file in the Lessons/Lesson18 folder. (The art work for the animation has been completed for you, so you won't need to enlarge the image window or zoom in for the tasks in this lesson.)

2 Close the Color, Web Content, and Slice palette groups.

3 In the Info palette group, select the Layer Comps tab to bring it forward.

4 Choose Window > Animation to open the Animation palette. Drag the lower right corner of the Animation palette to expand it so that you take advantage of available horizontal space in the work area.

(Optional) You can also move the Animation palette closer to the image window, to keep elements in the work area close together.

5 Choose Window > Workspace > Save Workspace.

6 Type **18_Animation** in the Save Workspace dialog box, and click OK.

Now you can quickly restore these palette sizes and positions by choosing Window > Workspace > 18_Animation at any time.

Animating by hiding and showing layers

Perhaps the simplest way to create a two-step animation is by toggling the visibility of two layers by changing the eye icons (👁) in the Layers palette. For example, you can make an animated character alternate between different expressions or make an object move back and forth in a simple pattern.

The Dolphin.psd image file includes five layers, as you can see by examining the Layers palette. You'll do this kind of animation with the two Dolphin layers.

Preparing layer comps

You worked with layer comps in Photoshop earlier in this book. ImageReady offers the same capabilities, which can make animating much easier to do.

1 In the Layers palette, make sure that eye icons (👁) appear in the visibility boxes for the Background and Dolphin 1 layers and that the visibility boxes for the other three layers are empty.

2 In the Layer Comps palette, click the Create New Layer Comp button (🖫).

3 In the New Layer Comp dialog box, type **Dolphin 1**, and then make sure that Visibility is selected (checked) before you click OK.

Now a new layer comp, Dolphin 1, appears in the Layer Comps palette.

4 In the Layers palette, click to hide the eye icon for the Dolphin 1 layer, and then click to set an eye icon for the Dolphin 2 layer.

5 Create a new layer comp, Dolphin 2, using the same techniques that you used in Steps 2 and 3, above.

6 Click the box on the left of the Dolphin 1 layer comp to apply those visibility conditions to the image. A badge (▣) appears in the box, indicating that this is the current layer comp.

You now have two layer comps that you can use as starting points for the frames you'll create in the animation.

Beginning the animation process

As you begin, only one frame, the default, appears in the Animation palette. This frame shows the current visibility settings in the Layers palette, with only two layers visible: Dolphin 1 and Background. The frame is selected (outlined with a border), indicating that you can change its content by editing the image.

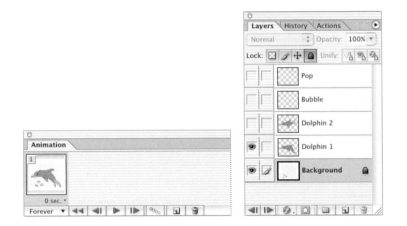

1 In the Animation palette, click the Duplicate Current Frame button (⬏) to create frame 2.

2 In the Layer Comps palette, click the box to set the Apply This Layer Comp badge (🖼) for the Dolphin 2 layer comp. Notice that in the Layers palette, the Dolphin 1 layer is now hidden and the Dolphin 2 layer is visible.

3 In the Animation palette, select frame 1. In the image window, the dolphin resumes its original appearance, with only Layer 1 visible.

4 Select frame 2 and then frame 1 repeatedly to manually animate the image.

Navigating animation frames and previewing the animation

You can use a number of techniques to preview and scroll through your animation frames. Understanding the controls available on the Animation and Layers palettes is essential to mastery of the animation process.

You've already tried out animating the image manually by selecting each of the frames in turn. In this procedure, you'll try out several of the other ways you can preview an animation in ImageReady. You'll also preview the animation in a Web browser.

Note: *To use the Preview In command, you must have a browser application installed on your system. For more information, find "Previewing an image in a browser" in ImageReady Help.*

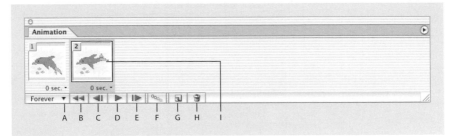

A. *Looping pop-up menu* **B.** *Select First Frame button* **C.** *Select Previous Frame button*
D. *Play/Stop Animation button* **E.** *Select Next Frame button* **F.** *Tween button* **G.** *Duplicate Current Frame button* **H.** *Trash* **I.** *Selected frame*

1 In the Animation palette, make sure that Forever is selected in the Looping pop-up menu in the lower left corner of the palette.

2 Click the Select Previous Frame button ( ) to move to the other frame. (Try clicking the button repeatedly in quick succession, and watch the manual playback of the animation in the image window.)

3 In the Layers palette, click the Backward or Forward button in the lower left corner of the palette, and notice results similar to the previous step.

A. *Layers palette Backward button*
B. *Layers palette Forward button*

4 Click the Play button ( ) in the Animation palette to preview the animation. The Play button becomes the Stop button ( ), which you can click to stop the playback.

5 Choose File > Preview In > and choose a browser application on the Preview In submenu. When you finish previewing the animation, quit the browser window and return to Adobe ImageReady.

[TIP] You can also do this step by pressing Ctrl+Alt+P (Windows) or Command+Option+P (Mac OS) to launch a browser preview quickly, or clicking the browser button in the toolbox.

6 Choose File > Save Optimized As.

7 In the Save As dialog box, open the Lessons/Lesson18 folder and click the icon for Create New Folder. Type **My_GIFs** to name the new folder, and then open it. Still in the Save As dialog box, type **Dolphin.gif** as the file name, and click Save.

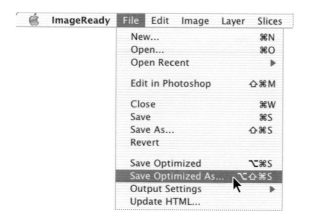

Preparing layer copies for an animation

Now you'll begin to animate a different element in the dolphin image, adding to the existing animation. In this procedure, you'll use the same basic technique—hiding and showing layers in different frames—to create your animation, but this time you'll also create the different layers by copying and transforming a single layer.

Before adding layers to an image that already contains an animation, it's a good idea to create a new frame. This step helps protect your existing frames from unwanted changes.

1 In the Animation palette, select frame 2 and click the Duplicate Current Frame button (▣) to create a new frame (frame 3) that is identical to frame 2. Leave frame 3 selected.

2 Open the Animation palette menu and choose the New Layers Visible in All States/Frames command to deselect it (remove the checkmark).

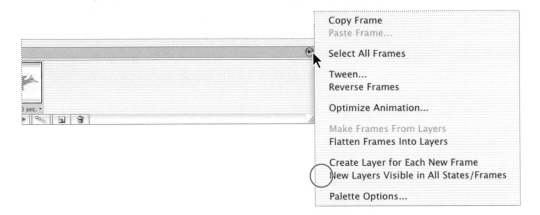

3 In the Layers palette, select the Bubble layer and click the box for the eye icon (👁) to make the layer visible. Leave the Bubble layer selected.

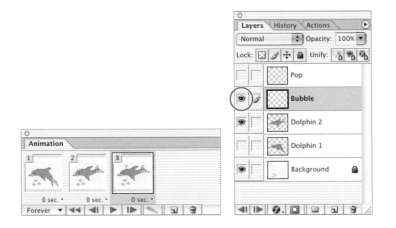

In the image window and in the frame 3 thumbnail, notice the bubble that appears above the dolphin's blow hole.

4 Choose View > Snap to deselect it so that no checkmark appears by this command.

5 Select the Move tool (►⊕) in the toolbox.

6 Hold down Alt (Windows) or Option (Mac OS) and drag the bubble up and to the right in the image window. When you release the mouse button, two bubbles now appear in the image, and a new layer, Bubble copy, appears in the Layers palette.

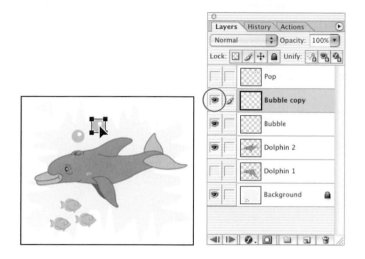

7 Again hold down Alt (Windows) or Option (Mac OS) and drag to create a third bubble, a little farther up and to the right of the second bubble.

You now have three bubble layers in the image window and the Layers palette: Bubble, Bubble copy, and Bubble copy 2.

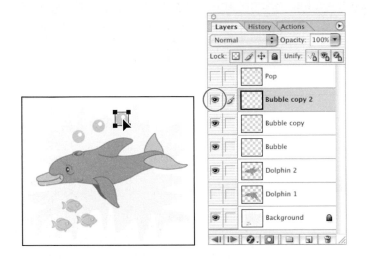

Note: *The duplicate layers would be visible in all three frames in the Animation palette if New Layers Visible in All States/Frames was not deselected in the Animation palette menu.*

Transforming layers for an animation

Now that you've prepared the duplicate bubble layers in the Dolphin.psd file, you'll apply a scale transformation to the two copies so that the bubble appears to grow as it trails behind the swimming dolphin.

1 If the Move tool (⤴⊕) is not still selected, select it now, and then make sure that the Layer Select tool (↖) is selected in the tool options bar.

2 In the image window, select the middle bubble, the Bubble copy layer object.

3 Choose Edit > Transform > Scale.

In the image window, the transformation bounding box appears around the Bubble copy layer.

4 In the tool options bar, select the Constrain Aspect Ration icon (⬚), and type **24** px for width (W:). Click anywhere outside the width text box and notice that the bubble assumes its new size but the transformation bounding box remains on the Bubble copy layer object.

5 Press Enter (Windows) or Return (Mac OS) to commit the transformation.

6 Select the third bubble and repeat Steps 3–5, but this time type **26** px as either the width or height dimension.

7 Still using the Move tool and the Layer Select tool option, refine the locations of the three bubble layers by dragging them in the image window, as needed.

Make sure that the third bubble does not extend beyond the tip of the dolphin's dorsal fin and that the three bubbles are nearly evenly spaced. Refer to the illustration below as a suggestion.

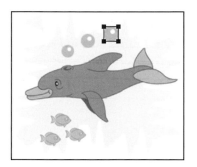

8 Choose File > Save.

Creating the simultaneous animations

Now you'll define the rising-bubble animation by successively hiding and showing the layers of the Dolphin.psd file. You'll combine this rising bubble with the swimming dolphin animation by duplicating frames and coordinating settings in the Layers and Animation palettes.

1 In the Animation palette, make sure that frame 3 is selected, or select it now.

2 In the Layers palette, click the visibility boxes to set or remove eye icons (👁) so that the Background, Dolphin 1, and the original Bubble layer are visible and the other layers are hidden.

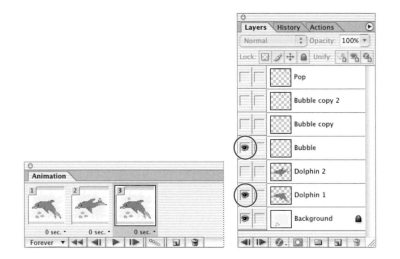

Note: *When you hide or show a layer in a frame, the visibility of the layer changes for that frame only.*

3 In the Animation palette, click the Duplicate Current Frame button (🖿) to create frame 4. Leave frame 4 selected in the Animation palette.

4 In the Layer Comps palette, select Dolphin 2. Then in the Layers palette, set an eye icon (👁) for the Bubble Copy layer.

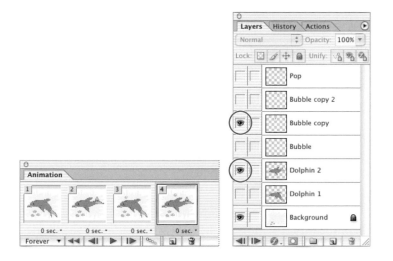

5 Click the Duplicate Current Frame two more times, and then use the Layer Comps and Layers palettes as follows:

• For frame 5, select the Dolphin 1 layer comp and make the Bubble Copy 2 layer visible.

• For frame 6, select the Dolphin 2 layer comp and make the Pop layer visible.

6 Select the Play button(▶) on the Animation palette to preview the results. When you are finished, click the Stop button (■) to stop the animation.

As the animation moves from frame to frame, the dolphin's tail moves up and down with each step. In each full cycle, the bubble emerges from the dolphin, rises, and pops in a four-step sequence.

If your results are different than described here, review the visibility settings on the Layers palette for each successive frame and make any necessary corrections.

Setting and previewing the timing sequence

Earlier, when you previewed your animation in the browser, you probably noticed that the rate at which the dolphin is swimming is nothing short of frenetic. You can calm down the motion by setting a delay between each frame in the animation. Then, you'll play the animation again to review the speed of the apparent action.

In your own projects, you can specify pauses for all frames or different pauses for various individual frames in your animation. For this file, you'll apply the same time delay between each pair of frames in the complete animation.

1 From the Animation palette menu, choose Select All Frames.

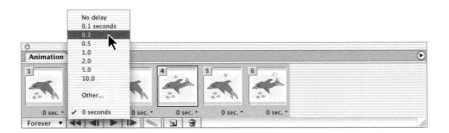

2 Click the time (0 seconds, which is the default) beneath any one of the frames to open the Frame Delay pop-up menu, and choose 0.2 seconds.

The new value appears below each frame thumbnail, indicating that the time delay applies to all the frames in the palette.

3 Click the Play button (▶) in the Animation palette to view your animation, and then click the Stop button (■) when you're ready to halt the animation.

4 Choose File > Preview In, and choose a browser application from the submenu to play the animation with accurate timing. When you finish previewing, return to ImageReady.

5 Choose File > Save Optimized As.

6 In the Save As dialog box, make sure that the image is named **Dolphin.gif** and that the location is inside your My_GIFs folder. Then click Save, and click Replace to replace the existing file.

The Save Optimized As command saves a file in the GIF, JPEG, or PNG format, for use in your Web pages. GIF is the only format that supports animations, so that's the format you need for this project.

7 Choose File > Close to close your original image without saving changes.

You've finished your work on the dolphin animation for the Web-page project. Next, you'll continue with work on other animated elements for the project.

Animating with layer opacity and position

You'll use a slightly different method for animation in the next facet of the project. This time, you'll animate a fly-in of a text logo, using a multilayered Photoshop image.

The good news is that you don't have to create more layers manually for each change in position, nor do you have to painstakingly create and adjust each individual frame. As soon as you create the beginning and end frames for the sequence, you can relax and let ImageReady do all the work for the frames in between them.

Opening the image file and starting the animation process

To get started, you'll open the new art file and review its current settings.

1 In ImageReady, choose File > Open, and open the H2O.psd file from the Lessons/Lesson18 folder on your hard disk.

The logo consists of four different components that reside on separate layers. You'll compose animation frames that show the characters of the logo appearing and moving into their final position from different areas. The initial state reflects how you want the image to appear at the end of the animation.

2 Make sure that the Animation and Layers palettes are visible, or choose Window > Workspace > 18_Animation to open them.

3 In the Animation palette, click the Duplicate Current Frame button ( ) to create a new animation frame.

Now that you have two frames, you've paved the way for a new animation. Your next tasks will be to change the status of various layers for the different frames.

Setting layer positions and opacity

In this part of the lesson, you'll adjust the position and opacity of layers in an image to create the starting and ending frames of an animation sequence. Changing the order in which frames appear in the animation is as simple as dragging the thumbnails in the Animation palette.

1 In the Animation palette, make sure that frame 2 is selected. Then, in the Layers palette, select the H layer.

2 Select the Move tool (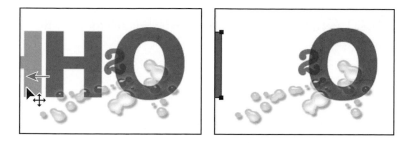), hold down Shift (to constrain the movement), and drag the "H" to the left side of the image window so that only a portion of the "H" is visible.

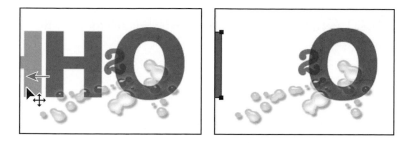

3 In the Layers palette, select the O layer, and then hold down Shift and drag to a similar position on the right side of image window.

4 Repeat Step 3, but this time select the 2 layer and drag it to the upper edge of the image window. The three layers should be arranged as shown in the illustration below.

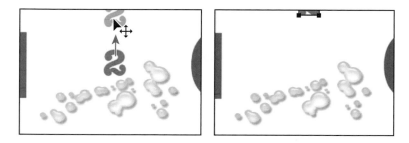

5 In the Layers palette, select the H layer and drag the Opacity slider to 20%. Repeat this process to reset the opacity of the 2 and O layers at 20% as well.

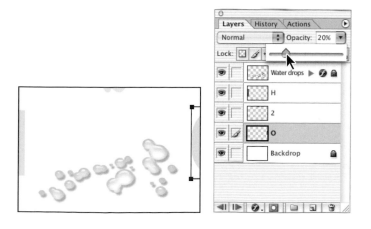

In the Animation palette, notice that frame 2 has updated to reflect the current image state. To make frame 2 the starting state of your animation, you'll switch the order of the two frames.

6 In the Animation palette, drag frame 2 to the left, releasing the mouse when the black bar appears to the left of frame 1.

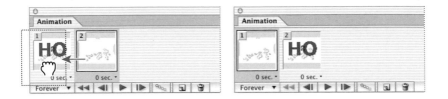

Tweening the position and opacity of layers

Next, you'll add frames that represent transitional image states between the two existing frames. When you change the position, opacity, or effects of any layer between two animation frames, you can instruct ImageReady to *tween*, which automatically creates as many intermediate frames as you specify.

1 In the Animation palette, make sure that frame 1 is selected; then choose Tween on the Animation palette menu.

2 In the Tween dialog box, set the following options (if they are not already selected):

• On the Tween With pop-up menu, select Next Frame.

• For Frames to Add, type **4**.

• Under Layers, select All Layers.

• Under Parameters, select Position and Opacity, as needed, so that checkmarks appear for those options. (You could select Effects if you were going to vary the settings of layer effects evenly between the beginning and ending frames. You won't choose this option now because you have not applied any layer effects.)

• Click OK to close the dialog box.

ImageReady creates four new transitional frames, based on the opacity and position settings of the layers in the original two frames.

3 On the Looping pop-up menu in the lower left of the Animation palette, choose Once.

Note: *In the sample End file for this lesson, the looping is configured slightly differently that you're asked to do here. In the End file, Forever is selected as the looping option but there is also a long delay after the final frame of the animation, which is not yet created at this phase.*

4 In the Animation palette, click the Play button (▶) to preview your animation in ImageReady.

For the Web: Tweening frames

You use the Tween command to automatically add or modify a series of frames between two existing frames—varying the layer attributes (position, opacity, or effect parameters) evenly between the new frames to create the appearance of movement. For example, if you want to fade out a layer, set the opacity of the layer in the starting frame to 100%; then set the opacity of the same layer in the ending frame to 0%. When you tween between the two frames, the opacity of the layer is reduced evenly across the new frames.

The term "tweening" is derived from "in betweening," the traditional animation term used to describe this process. Tweening significantly reduces the time required to create animation effects such as fading in or fading out, or moving an element across a frame. You can edit tweened frames individually after you create them.

If you select a single frame, you choose whether to tween the frame with the previous frame or the next frame. If you select two contiguous frames, new frames are added between the frames. If you select more than two frames, existing frames between the first and last selected frames are altered by the tweening operation. If you select the first and last frames in an animation, these frames are treated as contiguous, and tweened frames are added after the last frame. (This tweening method is useful when the animation is set to loop multiple times.)

Note: *You cannot select discontiguous frames for tweening.*

Animating a layer style

When you tweened to create the four new frames in the previous procedure, you noticed the Effects check box in the Tween dialog box. In this procedure, you will animate a layer effect or *layer style*.

The final result will be a little flash of light that appears and then disappears behind the 2 image.

1 In the Animation palette, select frame 6, and then click the Duplicate Current Frame button to create a new frame with all the same settings as frame 6. Leave frame 7 selected.

2 In the Layers palette, select the 2 layer, and then choose Outer Glow from the Layer Style pop-up menu at the bottom of the palette.

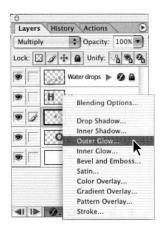

Notice the subtle light halo around the edges of the 2 image.

3 When the Layer Style dialog box opens, click OK to accept the default settings.

4 Duplicate frame 7 by clicking the Duplicate Current Frame button ( ).

5 In the Layers palette, double-click the Outer Glow effect for the 2 layer to open the Layer Style dialog box. Make sure that the Preview check box is selected, and then specify the following options:

• For Spread, drag the slider to **20%**.

• For Size, drag the slider to **49 pixels**.

6 Click OK, and then choose File > Save.

Tweening frames for the layer-style changes

As you've seen already in this lesson, the Tween feature can save you lots of time you might have spent doing tedious and exacting work. You'll use the Tween command again now to animate the change in layer style.

You'll also complete the glow effect by duplicating one more frame and moving it to the end of the animation. The resulting animation gives the impression of a little "pop" of light behind the 2 image as it comes into place.

1 In the Animation palette, select frame 7.

2 Choose Tween from the Animation palette menu.

3 In the Tween dialog box, specify the following options:

• For Tween With, select Next Frame.

• For Frames to Add, type **2**.

• Under Layers, select All Layers.

• Under Parameters, select Effects.

4 Click OK to close the dialog box.

5 In the Animation palette, select frame 6, and then select the Duplicate Current Frame button (⬓) to create a new frame 7, which will renumber the frames following 7.

6 Drag the new frame 7 to the end of the Animation palette so that it is to the right of (after) frame 11.

7 Choose File > Save.

Preserving transparency and preparing to optimize

Next, you'll optimize the H2O image in GIF format with background transparency and preview your animation in a Web browser. Remember that only the GIF format supports animated images.

We included the Backdrop layer in the H2O.psd file to make it easier to see the results as you work. That layer is not necessary for the final Web-page project because you're going to optimize the file with a transparent background. Your first step, then, is to hide the Backdrop layer.

1 On the Animation palette menu, choose Select All Frames.

2 On the Layers palette, click the eye icon (👁) for the Backdrop layer to hide it in all frames.

3 On the Optimize palette, set the following options:

• For the file format, choose GIF.

• Under Color Table, choose Perceptual for Reduction and **256** for Colors.

• Under Transparency, select the Transparency check box (to preserve the transparency of the original image).

• For Matte, select the white swatch from the pop-up palette, if it is not already selected.

4 With all frames still selected in the Animation palette, right-click (Windows) or Control-click (Mac OS) one of the frames in the Animation palette to open the Disposal Method context menu, and choose Restore to Background.

5 With all frames selected, use the pop-up menu at the bottom of any one of the frame thumbnails and select 0.1 sec.

6 On the Animation palette menu, choose Optimize Animation.

7 In the Optimize Animation dialog box, make sure that both the Bounding Box and Redundant Pixel Removal check boxes are selected, and then click OK.

The disposal options—Restore to Background (⌁) and Automatic—clear the selected frame before the next frame is played, eliminating the danger of displaying remnant pixels from the previous frame. The Do Not Dispose (⌁) option retains the frames. The Automatic option is suitable for most animations. This option selects a disposal method based on the presence or absence of transparency in the next frame and discards the selected frame if the next frame contains layer transparency.

For the Web: Setting the frame-disposal method

The frame-disposal method specifies whether to discard the current frame before displaying the next frame. You select a disposal method when working with animations that include background transparency in order to specify whether the current frame will appear through the transparent areas of the next frame.

The Disposal Method icon indicates whether the frame is set to Do Not Dispose or Restore to Background. (No icon appears when the disposal method is set to Automatic.)

• *Choose the Automatic option to determine a disposal method for the current frame automatically, discarding the current frame if the next frame contains layer transparency. For most animations, the Automatic option yields the desired results and is, therefore, the default option.*

Note: *Choose the Automatic disposal option when using the Redundant Pixel Removal optimization option, to enable ImageReady to preserve frames that include transparency.*

• *Choose the Do Not Dispose option to preserve the current frame as the next frame is added to the display. The current frame (and preceding frames) may show through transparent areas of the next frame. To accurately preview an animation using the Do Not Dispose option, preview the animation in a browser.*

• *Choose the Restore to Background option to discard the current frame from the display before the next frame is displayed. Only a single frame is displayed at any time (and the current frame will not appear through the transparent areas of the next frame).*

In addition to the optimization tasks applied to standard GIF files, several other tasks are performed for animated GIF files. If you optimize the animated GIF using an adaptive, perceptual, or selective palette, ImageReady generates a palette for the file based on all of the frames in the animation. A special dithering technique is applied to ensure that dither patterns are consistent across all frames, to prevent flickering during playback. Also, frames are optimized so that only areas that change from frame to frame are included, greatly reducing the file size of the animated GIF. As a result, ImageReady requires more time to optimize an animated GIF than to optimize a standard GIF.

The Bounding Box option directs ImageReady to crop each frame to preserve only the area that has changed from the preceding frame. Animation files created using this option are smaller but are incompatible with GIF editors, which do not support the option.

The Optimize by Redundant Pixel Removal option makes all pixels in a frame that are unchanged from the preceding frame transparent. When you choose the Redundant Pixel Removal option, the Disposal Method must be set to Automatic.

[?] For more information, see "Optimizing Images for the Web" in Photoshop Help.

Viewing the optimized GIF file

You've almost completed your work in the H2O.psd file that you'll use to save as an animated GIF image.

1 In the image window, click the Optimized tab.

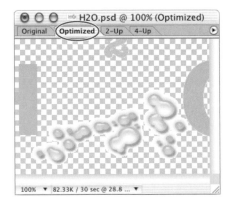

ImageReady rebuilds the image according to the options you entered.

2 In the image window, click the 2-Up tab and compare the information for the original and optimized versions of the animated image.

3 Choose File > Save Optimized As, name the image **H2O.gif**, select the My_GIFs folder, and click Save.

If you want to preview your animation in the browser, you can do that now by clicking the Preview In Default Browser button in the toolbox. Then close the browser.

4 In ImageReady, choose File > Close to close the original file.

You have finished your work on the fly-in logo.

Using vector masks to create animations

The rest of this lesson deals with masks, as they apply to animations. You'll work on two separate projects with different types of masks, first vector masks and then layer masks.

First, you'll create the effect of an ocean wave rising and falling inside the characters of the word *Waves*. You'll do this by creating a vector mask to partially block the Wave layer so that the ocean appears only inside the word, and then using position changes to define the different frames of the animation.

1 Choose File > Open, and open the Waves.psd file from the Lessons/Lesson18 folder.

2 In the Layers palette, make sure that all the layers are visible. If not, click the visibility boxes so that eye icons appear for each of the layers.

3 In the Layers palette, select the Wave layer.

4 Hold down Alt (Windows) or Option (Mac OS) and move the pointer (without clicking) over the solid line dividing the Wave and Text layers in the Layers palette until the pointer changes to two overlapping circles (⊗). Then click the dividing line between the layers to link the two layers together.

Or, you can do the same thing by choosing Layer > Group With Previous.

Notice that the waves now appear masked by the logo text. A downward-pointing arrow (⌐) appears in front of the Wave layer name and thumbnail in the Layers palette, indicating that the layer is grouped with the layer below.

Animating position changes within a vector-mask layer

Although the Wave and Text layers are linked, you can still make position changes to individual layers.

1 In the Animation palette, click the Duplicate Current Frame button to create a new frame.

2 If necessary, select frame 2 in the Animation palette. In the Layers palette, deselect the Text layer, leaving only the Wave layer selected.

3 Select the Move tool (▸⊕) in the toolbox.

4 Hold down Shift (to constrain the movement) and drag the Wave layer in the image window, moving it down until the top of the wave image rests just above the top of the text. (As you drag, the entire Wave layer is ghosted so that you can see the position of the wave as you move it.)

5 Click the Play button (▶) to play the animation. The wave moves up and down inside the logo. Click the Stop button (■) to stop the animation.

Smoothing the wave action

In order to make the wave action look a little more natural, you'll use the now-familiar tweening feature to add more frames to the animation.

Before you begin, make sure that frame 2 is selected in the Animation palette.

1 On the Animation palette menu, choose Tween to open the Tween dialog box, and then do the following:

- For Frames To Add, type **2**.

- For Tween With, select Previous Frame.

- Under Layers, select All Layers.

- Under Parameters, select Position.

• Click OK to close the dialog box.

2 In the Animation palette, select Forever on the pop-up menu.

3 Choose Select > Deselect Layers, and then click the Play button (▶) in the Animation palette to preview the animation. When you've seen enough, click Stop (■).

The animation is still bumpier than ideal, so you'll fix that next using the same or similar techniques as ones you used with the previous two animations in this lesson.

4 Select frame 2 and then Shift-click frame 3 to select both new frames. Then choose Copy Frames on the Animation palette menu.

5 Select frame 4, and then choose Paste Frames on the Animation palette menu to open the Paste Frames dialog box, and select Paste After Selection. Then click OK.

6 Click frame 5, so that it is the only frame selected, and drag it to the right, so that it becomes the last frame in the animation.

7 With frame 6 selected, hold down Shift and click frame 1 to select all the frames, and then select 0.2 from the time delay pop-up for any one of the frames. Then choose File > Save.

Previewing and saving the vector-mask animation

Now, you'll put your animation to the test by previewing it to see if the wave action meets your standards.

1 In the Animation palette, click the Play button (▶). When you are ready, click the Stop button (■) to halt the animation.

2 If necessary, make any adjustments to the delay or the order of the frames to correct errors or set the timing the way you want it to be.

3 Preview the animation again and continue to make adjustments until you are fully satisfied with the results.

4 (Optional) Select the Preview In Default Browser button in the toolbox, or choose File > Preview In > and select your preferred Web browser. When you finish, close the Web browser and return to ImageReady.

5 Choose File > Save Optimized As, specify the My_GIFs folder location, and type **Waves.gif** to name the file. Then click Save.

ImageReady saves the animation as a GIF file, using the current settings in the Optimize palette.

6 Choose File > Close to close the original file.

Animating with layer masks

As your final element of the Web-animation project, you'll hide just the lower portion of a layer object—in this case, a whale's tail—to create the illusion of the tail rising out of the water.

The file you'll work with in this section has just three layers: an ocean layer that serves as the background area, the whale's tail image, and a gradient fill that we created for you in Photoshop.

Creating and applying a layer mask

In this task, you'll create a layer mask based on the opacity differences of the gradient fill and then apply your mask to the whale tail. The gradient itself doesn't play a role in your final image, but you'll use the mask it can generate and apply it to a different layer.

Before you begin, take a close look at the appearance of the whale-tail image in the image window so that you'll be able to compare it to the results when you finish.

1 Choose File > Open and open the Whale.psd file in the Lessons/Lesson18/ folder.

2 In the Layers palette, click the visibility box for the Gradient layer to set an eye icon (👁) and make the layer visible.

3 Select the Gradient layer and choose Layer > Add Layer Mask > From Transparency.

Notice the new Layers palette thumbnail for the Gradient layer, showing the areas of transparency (white) and the areas of masking (black).

4 Click the eye icon to hide the Gradient layer.

5 Click the link icon (⊗) between the two Gradient layer thumbnails to unlink the gradient and the mask so that you can use the mask apart from the Gradient layer.

6 Select the mask thumbnail (on the right) and drag it to the Tail layer.

If you remember how the whale tail looked before you started making changes, you'll see the difference now in the image window: The lower area of the tail fades gradually as it sinks into the water.

Animating an image within a layer mask

The beauty of this technique is that although you change the layer object position, the mask stays in place. Here, you'll start the next phase of the animation process by moving the image of the tail itself. As you do this, the gradient mask won't change, so it will have the same effect on the visibility of the whale as it sinks and rises in and out of the water.

1 In the Animation palette, click the Duplicate Current Frame button (▣). Leave frame 2 selected.

2 Select the Move tool (►⊕), and make sure that Layer Selection (▶) is selected in the tool options bar.

3 In the image window, drag the tail image down until it almost disappears below the surface of the water.

4 In the Animation palette, drag frame 2 left, so that it becomes the new frame 1.

Refining the layer-mask animation

All that remains to be done is to smooth out the action with intermediate frames and delays between frame changes. By now, you are probably familiar enough with these processes that you could do this on your own. But we've added an extra twist to this task that should make it worth the effort of stepping through the procedure.

1 In the Animation palette, make sure that frame 1 is selected, and then choose Tween on the Animation palette menu. Or, choose the Tween button at the bottom of the palette.

2 In the Tween dialog box, select the Next Frame and type **3** for Frames To Add. Make sure that All Layers and Position are selected, and then click OK.

3 In the Animation palette, Shift-click to select frames 2, 3, and 4.

4 On the Animation palette menu, choose Copy Frames.

5 Select frame 5. Then choose Paste Frames on the Animation palette menu.

6 In the Paste Frames dialog box, select Paste After Selection, and click OK. Leave the three new frames selected.

7 On the Animation palette menu, choose Reverse Frames.

Now the frames show the whale tail rising and sinking in a smooth sequence.

8 Select all eight frames and select 0.2 on the delay pop-up menu for one of the frames to set the timing for all frames.

Previewing and saving the layer-mask animation

You've almost finished your final element for the Web-page project.

1 In the toolbox, select the Preview Document button (🖑) to preview the animation, and then click the button again to stop it.

Or, you can click the Play button and then the Stop button in the Animation palette.

2 Choose File > Preview In > *browser* to select an available Web browser.

3 When you finish previewing the animation, close the Web browser.

4 Choose File > Save Optimized As.

5 Select the My_GIFs folder and make sure that the name is Whale.gif. Then click OK.

6 Close the Whale.psd file.

Give yourself another pat on the back—you've finished all four elements in the Web page project.

If you want to test your images in the Web page you viewed at the beginning of this lesson, you can go to the desktop and drag contents of the My_GIFs folder into the Lessons/Lesson18/images folder to overwrite the GIF files inside. (Click Yes when messages appear asking you to confirm this action.) Then double-click the 18End.html. When the page opens in your default Web browser, it will utilize your GIF images rather than the samples provided for this lesson.

Review questions

1 Describe a simple way to create animation.

2 In what instances can you tween animation frames? When can't you tween frames?

3 How do you optimize an animation?

4 What does optimizing an animation accomplish?

5 What is frame disposal? Which frame-disposal method should you generally use?

6 How do you edit an existing animation frame?

7 What file formats can you use for animations?

Review answers

1 A simple way to create animation is to start with a layered Photoshop file. Use the Duplicate Current Frame button in the Animation palette to create a new frame, and then use the Layers palette to alter the position, opacity, or effects of one of the selected frames. Then, create intermediate frames between the selection and the new frame either manually, by using the Duplicate Current Frame button, or automatically, by using the Tween command.

2 You can instruct Adobe ImageReady to tween intermediate frames between any two adjacent frames. Tweening can change layer opacity or position between two frames, or to add new layers to a sequence of frames. You cannot tween discontiguous frames.

3 Click the Show Options button in the Optimize palette, and then choose File > Save Optimized to optimize animations. Choose Optimize Animation from the Animation palette menu to perform optimization tasks specific to animation files, including removing redundant pixels and cropping frames according to the bounding box.

4 When you optimize GIF files, ImageReady also generates an adaptive, perceptual, or selective palette for the file, based on all frames in the animation. ImageReady applies a special dithering technique to ensure that dither patterns are consistent across all frames, to prevent flickering during playback. The application also optimizes frames so that only areas that change from frame to frame are included, greatly reducing the file size of the animated GIF.

5 A frame-disposal method specifies whether to discard the selected frame before displaying the next frame when an animation includes background transparency. This option determines whether the selected frame will appear through the transparent areas of the next frame. Generally, the Automatic option is suitable for most animations. This option selects a disposal method based on the presence or absence of transparency in the next frame, and discards the selected frame if the next frame contains layer transparency.

6 To edit an existing animation frame, you first select the frame, either by clicking the frame thumbnail in the Animation palette or by navigating to the desired frame using the First Frame, Select Previous Frame, or Select Next Frame buttons in the Animation palette or Layers palette. Then, edit the layers in the image to update the contents of the selected frame.

7 Files for animations must be saved in GIF format or as a QuickTime movie. You cannot create animations as JPEG or PNG files.

Lesson 19

19 | Setting Up Your Monitor for Color Management

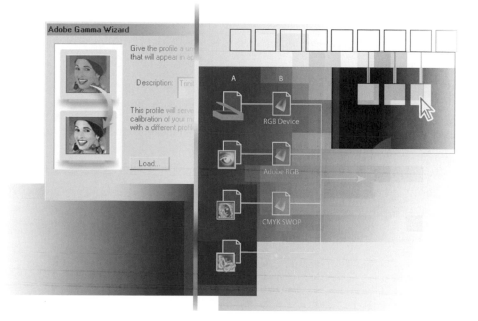

The most basic requirement for color management is to calibrate your monitor and create an ICC profile for it. Applications that support color management will use your monitor's ICC profile to display color graphics consistently. If you don't have a hardware-based calibration and profiling utility, you can get reasonably accurate results using Adobe Gamma.

In this lesson, you'll learn how to do the following:

- Examine the principles associated with color management.

- Calibrate your monitor using Adobe Gamma.

- Create an ICC profile for your monitor using Adobe Gamma.

This lesson will take about 45 minutes to complete.

Note: You can skip this lesson if you have already calibrated your monitor using a hardware-based tool or an ICC-compliant calibration tool, and if you haven't changed your video card or monitor settings.

Getting started

In this lesson, you'll learn some basic color-management concepts and terminology. In addition, you'll calibrate your monitor to a known color condition, and then create an ICC profile that describes your monitor's specific color characteristics. For information about setting up RGB and CMYK color spaces in Photoshop, see Lesson 20, "Producing and Printing Consistent Color."

Color management: An overview

Although all color gamuts overlap, they don't match exactly, which is why some colors on your monitor can't be reproduced in print. The colors that can't be reproduced in print are called *out-of-gamut* colors, because they are outside the spectrum of printable colors. For example, you can create a large percentage of colors in the visible spectrum using programs such as Photoshop, Illustrator, and InDesign, but you can reproduce only a subset of those colors on a desktop printer. The printer has a smaller *color space* or *gamut* (the range of colors that can be displayed or printed) than the application that created the color.

——— RGB ······· CMYK

Visible spectrum containing millions of colors (far left) compared with color gamuts of various devices and documents

To compensate for these differences and to ensure the closest match between on-screen colors and printed colors, applications use a color management system (CMS). Using a color management engine, the CMS translates colors from the color space of one device into a device-independent color space, such as CIE (Commission Internationale d'Eclairage) LAB. From the device-independent color space, the CMS fits that color information to another device's color space by a process called *color mapping*, or *gamut mapping*. The CMS makes any adjustments necessary to represent the color consistently among devices.

A CMS uses three components to map colors across devices:

• A device-independent (or reference) color space.

• ICC profiles that define the color characteristics of particular devices and documents.

• A color management engine that translates colors from one device's color space to another according to a *rendering intent*, or translation method.

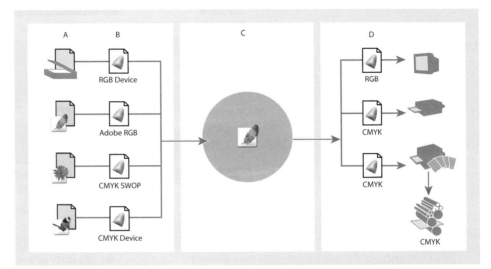

A. Scanners and software applications create color documents. Users choose document's working color space. *B.* ICC source profiles describe document color spaces. *C.* A color management engine uses ICC source profiles to map document colors to a device-independent color space through supporting applications. *D.* The color management engine maps document colors from the device-independent color space to output-device color spaces using destination profiles.

Basic color terminology

The colors that a specific device can reproduce are limited in comparison to what the human eye can see. Most obviously, this generalization applies to different kinds of printers, but it's also true of scanners, monitors, film, and digital cameras. The various ways of calculating colors also fall short of the full natural range of visible color.

color gamut (or color space) *The total range of color that a specific device can reproduce.*

color model *A dimensional coordinate system used to describe colors numerically. For example, RGB and CMYK are color models. In RGB, colors are assigned by numbers between 0 and 255 for each of the three colors: red, green, and blue. In CMYK, percentages are used to describe the levels of cyan, magenta, yellow, and black.*

About the device-independent color space

To successfully compare gamuts and make adjustments, a color management system must use a reference color space—an objective way of defining color. Most CMSs use the CIE LAB color model, which exists independently of any device and is big enough to reproduce any color visible to the human eye. For this reason, CIE LAB is considered *device-independent*.

About ICC profiles

An *ICC profile* describes how a particular device or standard reproduces color using a cross-platform standard defined by the International Color Consortium (ICC). ICC profiles ensure that images appear correctly in any ICC-compliant applications and on color devices. This is accomplished by embedding the profile information in the original file or assigning the profile in your application.

At a minimum, you must have one *source profile* for the device (scanner or digital camera, for example) or standard (SWOP or Adobe RGB, for example) used to create the color, and one *destination profile* for the device (monitor or contract proofing, for example) or standard (SWOP or TOYO, for example) that you will use to reproduce the color.

About color management engines

Sometimes called the color matching module (CMM), the color management engine interprets ICC profiles. Acting as a translator, the color management engine converts the out-of-gamut colors from the source device to the range of colors that can be produced by the destination device. The color management engine may be included with the CMS or may be a separate part of the operating system.

Translating to a gamut—particularly a smaller gamut—usually involves a compromise, so multiple translation methods are available. For example, a color translation method that preserves correct relationships among colors in a photograph will usually alter the colors in a logo. Color management engines provide a choice of translation methods, known as *rendering intents*, so that you can apply a method appropriate to the intended use of a color graphic. Examples of common rendering intents include *Perceptual (Images)* for preserving color relationships the way the eye does, *Saturation (Graphics)* for preserving vivid colors at the expense of color accuracy, and *Relative* and *Absolute Colori-metric* for preserving color accuracy at the expense of color relationships.

Color management resources

You can find additional information on color management on the Web and in print. Here are a few resources:

• On the Adobe Web site (www.adobe.com), search for **color management** or go directly to http://www.adobe.com/support/techguides/color/.

• On the Apple® Web site (www.apple.com), search for **ColorSync**.

• On the Agfa Web site (www.agfa.com/support/education.asp), search for the publication *The Secrets of Color Management*.

• On the ColorBlind Web site (www.color.com/support/education.asp), click Color Resources.

• At your local library or bookstore, look for *GATF Practical Guide to Color Management*, by Richard Adams and Joshua Weisberg (May 1998); ISBN 0883622025.

Note: Web publishers often change their Web addresses, links, and content without notice. Some addresses listed above may have changed since this writing.

For information about setting up color management in Photoshop, see Photoshop Help.

Calibrating and characterizing your monitor

The first requirement for color management is to calibrate your monitor and create an accurate ICC profile for it. Although this doesn't address your entire workflow, at least it ensures that your monitor displays colors as precisely as it can. *Calibration* is the process of setting your monitor, or any device, to known color conditions. *Characterization*, or profiling, is the process of creating an ICC profile that describes the unique color characteristics of your device or standard. Always calibrate your monitor, or any device, before creating a profile for it; otherwise, the profile is only valid for the current state of the device.

> **Using Adobe Gamma utility with LCDs**
>
> *Although the Adobe Gamma utility will adjust some features of a liquid crystal display monitor (LCD), the utility is designed primarily for calibrating and profiling cathode ray tube monitors (CRTs). If you use the Adobe Gamma utility for your LCD, skip the contrast step, because many LCSs lack a contrast control. For these, you can adjust only the intensity of the backlight. If you don't use Adobe Gamma, then either use the factory-supplied ICC profile for your LCD or consider a hardware-based product for profiling. ColorVision, ColorBlind, Gretag Macbeth, and DisplayMate are a few of the manufacturers who provide calibration and profiling solutions specifically for LCDs.*

Monitor adjustment for Mac OS

In Mac OS, use the Display Calibration Assistant in the System Preferences. The resulting ICC profile uses the calibration settings to describe precisely how your monitor reproduces color. (Photoshop CS requires OS 10.2.4 or higher for installation on Macintosh computers. Monitor adjustments on earlier versions of Mac OS are irrelevant for using Photoshop CS.)

Before you begin calibrating your monitor, be sure to remove any old Adobe Gamma control panels from your system. Then, simply follow the on-screen instructions, and you're finished with this lesson.

Monitor adjustment on Windows

Although monitor calibration and characterization are best done with specialized software and hardware, you can get reasonably accurate results with the newest version of the Adobe Gamma utility for Windows, included with your Adobe product. If you are satisfied with your existing monitor profile, you do not need to use Adobe Gamma because Adobe Gamma would overwrite those settings.

You may find it helpful to have your monitor's user guide handy while using Adobe Gamma.

Preparing to calibrate your monitor

Before you begin to make monitor adjustments, it's important that the conditions be right for the procedure and that your computer is cleared of settings or old utilities that might conflict with the process.

1 If you have any older versions of Adobe Gamma, delete them because they are obsolete. Use the latest Adobe Gamma utility instead. (Windows only): If the Monitor Setup Utility (included with PageMaker 6.x) is on your system, delete it because it, too, is now obsolete.

2 Make sure that your monitor has been turned on for at least a half hour. This gives it sufficient time to warm up for a more accurate color reading.

3 Set the room lighting to the level you plan to maintain consistently.

4 Remove colorful background patterns on your monitor desktop. Busy or bright patterns surrounding a document interfere with accurate color perception. Set your desktop to display neutral grays only, using RGB values of 128. For more information, see the manual for your operating system.

5 If your monitor has digital controls for choosing the white point of your monitor from a range of preset values, set those controls before starting. If you set them after you begin the calibration process, you'll need to begin the process again. Later, you'll set the white point to match your monitor's current setting.

6 On the Windows desktop, choose Start > Settings > Control Panel.

7 Double-click Display, and then click the Settings tab and make sure that your monitor is displaying thousands of colors or more.

Calibrating the monitor

On Windows, you'll use the Adobe Gamma utility to calibrate and characterize your monitor. The resulting ICC profile uses the calibration settings to describe precisely how your monitor reproduces color. In this section, you'll load an existing monitor profile as a starting point for calibrating your monitor.

Note: Adobe Gamma can characterize, but not calibrate, monitors used with Windows NT. Its ability to calibrate settings in Windows 98 depends on the video card and video-driver software. In such cases, some calibration options documented here may not be available. For example, if you're only characterizing your monitor, you'll choose the default white point and gamma, but not the target calibration settings.*

1 If the Control Panel is not open, choose Start > Settings > Control Panel. Then double-click Adobe Gamma.

Note: If you are running Windows XP and do not see the Adobe Gamma icon in the Control Panel, try changing the View menu selection to Classic View.

You can use either the control panel or a step-by-step wizard to make all the adjustments necessary for calibrating your monitor. In this lesson, you will use the Adobe Gamma control panel. At any time while working in the Adobe Gamma control panel, you can click the Wizard (Windows) or Assistant (Mac OS) button to switch to the wizard for instructions that guide you through the same settings as in the control panel, one option at a time.

2 In the Adobe Gamma wizard, click the Control Panel option, and click Next.

The next step is to load an ICC monitor profile that describes your monitor. This profile serves as a starting point for the calibration process by supplying some preset values. You'll adjust these values in Adobe Gamma to characterize the profile to match your monitor's particular characteristics.

3 Do one of the following:

• If your monitor is listed in the Description area at the top of the control panel, select it.

• Click the Load button for a list of other available profiles, and then locate and open the monitor ICC profile that most closely matches your monitor. To see the full name of an ICC profile at the bottom of the Open Monitor Profile dialog box, select a file. (Windows profile filenames have the .icm extension, which you may not see if the extension display is off.) Make your choice, and click Open.

- Leave the generic Adobe monitor profile selected in the Description area.

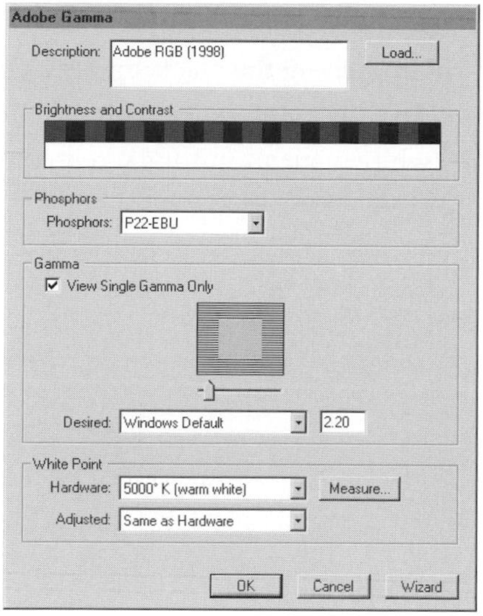

Adobe Gamma utility control panel

Setting the optimal brightness and contrast

Now you'll adjust the monitor's overall level and range of display intensity. These controls work just as they do on a television. Adjusting the monitor's brightness and contrast enables the most accurate screen representation for the gamma adjustment that follows.

1 With Adobe Gamma running, set the contrast control on your monitor to its highest setting. On many monitors, this control is shown next to a contrast icon (◑).

2 Adjust the brightness control on your monitor—located next to a brightness icon (☼) on many monitors—as you watch the alternating pattern of black and gray squares across the top half of the Brightness and Contrast rectangle in Adobe Gamma. Make the gray squares in the top bar as dark as possible without matching the black squares, while keeping the bottom area a bright white. (If you can't see a difference between the black and gray squares while keeping the bottom area white, your monitor's screen phosphors may be fading.)

A. Gray squares too light B. Gray squares too dark and white area too gray C. Gray squares and white area correctly adjusted

Do not adjust the brightness and contrast controls on your monitor again unless you are about to update the monitor profile. Adjusting the controls invalidates the monitor profile. You can tape the hardware controls in place if necessary.

Selecting phosphor data

The chemical phosphors in your monitor determine the range of colors you see on your screen.

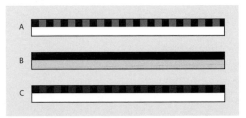

Do one of the following from the Phosphors menu:

• Choose the exact phosphor type used by the monitor you are calibrating. The two most common phosphor types are EBU/ITU and Trinitron.

• If the correct type is not listed but you were provided with chromaticity coordinates with your monitor, choose Custom, and enter the red, green, and blue chromaticity coordinates of the monitor's phosphors.

• If you're not sure which phosphors your monitor uses, see the monitor's documentation; contact the manufacturer; or use a color-measuring instrument such as a colorimeter or spectrophotometer to determine them.

Setting the midtones

The gamma setting defines midtone brightness. You can adjust the gamma based on a single combined gamma reading (the View Single Gamma Only option). Or, you can adjust the midtones individually for red, green, and blue. The second method produces a more accurate setting, so you will use that method here.

For the Gamma option in the Adobe Gamma utility, deselect the View Single Gamma Only option. Drag the slider under each box until the shape in the center blends in with the background as much as possible. It may help to squint or move back from the monitor.

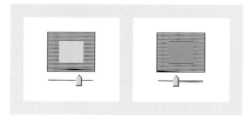

Single gamma not calibrated (left), and calibrated (right)

Make adjustments carefully and in small increments; imprecise adjustments can result in a color cast not visible until you print.

Selecting a target gamma

You may also have an option for specifying a separate gamma for viewing graphics.

Note: *This option is not available in Windows NT, due to its hardware protection shield that prevents Adobe Gamma from communicating with the computer's video card.*

If you have this option, choose one of the following from the Desired menu:

• Windows Default for Windows systems. Leave the setting at 2.2.

• Macintosh Default for Mac OS computers. Leave the setting at 1.8.

Setting the monitor's white point

Now you'll adjust the hardware *white point*, the whitest white that a monitor is capable of displaying. The white point is a measurement of color temperature in Kelvin and determines whether you are using a warm or cool white.

First, you'll make sure that the white-point setting matches the white point of your monitor. Do one of the following:

• If you know the white point of your monitor in its current state, you can select it from the Hardware menu in the White Point section. If your monitor is new, select 9300 Kelvin, the default white point of most monitors and televisions.

• If you started from a manufacturer's profile for your monitor, you can use the default value. However, the older your monitor, the less likely it is that its white point still matches the manufacturer's profile.

• If your monitor is equipped with digital controls for setting the white point, and you already set those controls before starting Adobe Gamma, make sure that the Hardware menu matches your monitor's current setting. Remember, though, that if you adjust these hardware controls at this point in the calibration process, you'll need to start over, beginning with the procedure in "Setting the optimal brightness and contrast" on page 637.

• If you don't know the white point and don't know the appropriate values, you can use the Measure option to visually estimate it. If you choose this option, continue to Step 1.

💡 *To get a precise value, you need to measure the white point with a desktop colorimeter or spectrophotometer and enter that value directly using the Custom option.*

If you were unable to choose a hardware setting as described, try the following experiment:

1 For best results, turn off all lights in the room.

2 Click Measure, and then click OK (Windows) or Next (Mac OS). Three squares appear.

The goal here is to make the center square as neutral gray as possible. You'll train your eyes to see the contrasts between the extreme cooler (blue) white and warmer (yellow) white, and then adjust the colors in the squares to find the most neutral gray between them.

3 Click the left square several times until it disappears, leaving the middle and right squares. Study the contrast between the bluish square on the right and the center square.

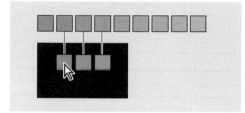

Clicking on the left square will reset all the squares a shade cooler.

4 Click the right square several times until it disappears, and study the contrast between the yellowish square on the left and the center square.

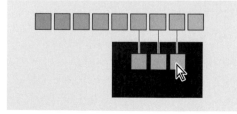

Clicking on the right square will reset all the squares a shade warmer.

5 Click the left or right square until the center square is a neutral gray. When complete, commit the changes by clicking the center square.

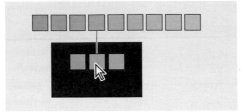

For a color illustration of adjusting the white point, see figure 19-1 of the color section.

Setting an adjusted white point

This option, when available, sets a working white point for monitor display, if that value differs from the hardware white point. For example, if your hardware white point is 6500 Kelvin (daylight), but you want to edit an image at 5000 Kelvin (warm white) because that most closely represents the environment in which the image will be viewed, you can set your adjusted white point to 5000 Kelvin. Adobe Gamma will change the monitor display accordingly.

Do one of the following to specify a separate white point for viewing graphics:

• To use the current white point of your monitor, choose Same as Hardware from the Adjusted menu.

• To specify your monitor's white point to a target value other than the Hardware value, choose the gamma setting you want from the Adjusted menu

Saving the monitor profile

Now that you have adjusted all the settings for your monitor, you will save the ICC profile you have created. Applications that support color management will use this monitor profile to display color graphics.

1 In Adobe Gamma, rename the monitor profile by editing the text in the Description text box. (We named the profile **My Monitor**.) When you name the monitor here, it appears by default when you start Adobe Gamma.

2 Click OK.

3 In the Save As dialog box, type the filename again, and save the file in the Color folder.

Adobe Gamma makes the new monitor profile the default. You can use this profile in any application that supports ICC-compliant color management.

Review questions

1 What does the color management engine do?

2 What is calibration?

3 What is characterization?

Review answers

1 The color management engine translates colors from the color space of one device to another device's color space by a process called color mapping.

2 Calibration is the process of setting a device to known color conditions.

3 Characterization, or profiling, is the process of creating an ICC profile that describes the unique color characteristics of a particular device. You should always calibrate a device before creating a profile for it.

20 | Producing and Printing Consistent Color

The document "20Start.tif" has an embedded color profile that does not match the current RGB working space.

To produce consistent color, you define the color space in which to edit and display RGB images, and in which to edit, display, and print CMYK images. This helps ensure a close match between on-screen and printed colors.

In this lesson, you'll learn how to do the following:

• Define RGB, grayscale, and CMYK color spaces for displaying, editing, and printing images.

• Prepare an image for printing on a PostScript® CMYK printer.

• Proof an image for printing.

• Create a color separation, the process by which the colors in an RGB image are distributed to the four process-ink colors: cyan, magenta, yellow, and black.

• Understand how images are prepared for printing on presses.

This lesson will take about 60 minutes to complete. The lesson is designed to be done in Adobe Photoshop.

If needed, remove the previous lesson folder from your hard drive, and copy the Lessons/Lesson20 folder onto it. As you work on this lesson, you'll overwrite the start files. If you need to restore the start files, copy them from the *Adobe Photoshop CS Classroom in a Book* CD.

Note: *Windows 2000 users need to unlock the lesson files before using them. For more information, see "Copying the Classroom in a Book files" on page 3.*

Reproducing colors

Colors on a monitor are displayed using combinations of red, green, and blue light (called RGB), while printed colors are typically created using a combination of four ink colors—cyan, magenta, yellow, and black (called CMYK). These four inks are called *process colors* because they are the standard inks used in the four-color printing process.

RGB image with red, green, and blue channels

CMYK image with cyan, magenta, yellow, and black channels

For color samples of channels in both RGB and CMYK images, see figure 20-1 and figure 20-2 in the color section.

Because the RGB and CMYK color models use very different methods to display colors, they each reproduce a different *gamut*, or range of colors. For example, because RGB uses light to produce color, its gamut includes neon colors, such as those you'd see in a neon sign. In contrast, printing inks excel at reproducing certain colors that can lie outside of the RGB gamut, such as some pastels and pure black. For an illustration of the RGB and CMYK gamuts and color models, see figure 20-3, 20-4, and 20-5 in the color section.

But not all RGB and CMYK gamuts are alike. Each model of monitor and printer is different, and so each displays a slightly different gamut. For example, one brand of monitor may produce slightly brighter blues than another. The *color space* for a device is defined by the gamut it can reproduce.

RGB model

A large percentage of the visible spectrum can be represented by mixing red, green, and blue (RGB) colored light in various proportions and intensities. Where the colors overlap, they create cyan, magenta, yellow, and white.

Because the RGB colors combine to create white, they are also called additive colors. *Adding all colors together creates white—that is, all light is transmitted back to the eye. Additive colors are used for lighting, video, and monitors. Your monitor, for example, creates color by emitting light through red, green, and blue phosphors.*

CMYK model

The CMYK model is based on the light-absorbing quality of ink printed on paper. As white light strikes translucent inks, part of the spectrum is absorbed while other parts are reflected back to your eyes.

In theory, pure cyan (C), magenta (M), and yellow (Y) pigments should combine to absorb all color and produce black. For this reason these colors are called subtractive colors. *Because all printing inks contain some impurities, these three inks actually produce a muddy brown and must be combined with black (K) ink to produce a true black. (K is used instead of B to avoid confusion with blue.) Combining these inks to reproduce color is called* four-color process printing.

An ICC profile is a description of a device's color space, such as the CMYK color space of a particular printer. In this lesson, you'll choose which RGB and CMYK ICC profiles to use. Once you specify the profiles, Photoshop can embed them into your image files. Photoshop (and any other application that can use ICC profiles) can then interpret the ICC profile in the image file to automatically manage color for that image. For general information about color management and about preparing your monitor, see Lesson 19, "Setting Up Your Monitor for Color Management".

For information on embedding ICC profiles, see Photoshop Help.

Getting started

Before beginning this lesson, restore the default application settings for Adobe Photoshop. See "Restoring default preferences" on page 4.

You will also need to make sure that you have calibrated your monitor as described in Lesson 19, "Setting Up Your Monitor for Color Management." If your monitor does not display colors accurately, the color adjustments you make to an image displayed on that monitor may be inaccurate.

Specifying color management settings

In the first part of this lesson, you'll learn how to set up a color-managed workflow. To help you with this, the Color Settings dialog box in Photoshop contains most of the color management controls you need. (This dialog box appears the first time you start Photoshop.)

For instance, Photoshop is set up for RGB as part of a Web/online workflow by default. However, if you're preparing artwork for print production, you would likely change the settings to be more appropriate for images that will be printed on paper rather than displayed on a screen.

You'll begin this lesson by starting Photoshop and creating customized color settings.

1 Start Adobe Photoshop.

If you used another application to modify and save the current color-settings file, a dialog box appears, prompting you to synchronize the common color settings when you start Photoshop or reopen the Color Settings dialog box in Photoshop.

Synchronizing the color settings helps to ensure that color is reproduced consistently among Adobe applications that use the Color Settings dialog box. You can also share custom color settings by saving and loading the settings file in the desired applications and providing the settings file to other users. For more information, see Photoshop Help.

2 Choose Edit > Color Settings (Windows) or Photoshop > Color Settings (Mac OS) to display the Color Settings dialog box.

The bottom of the dialog box contains information about the various color-management options in it, which you'll now review.

3 Move the mouse pointer over each part of the dialog box, including the names of areas (such as Working Spaces) and the options you can choose (such as the different menu options), returning the options to their defaults when you're done. As you move the mouse, view the information that appears at the bottom of the dialog box.

Now, you'll choose a general set of options that will specify the individual options for you. In this case, you'll pick one designed for a print workflow, rather than an online workflow.

4 Select a prepress default from the Settings menu at the top of the dialog box (we used U.S. Prepress Defaults) and click OK.

Proofing an image

In this part of the lesson, you'll begin working with a typical file of the kind you might scan in from a printed original. You'll open it, convert its color profile, and set it up so that you can see on-screen a close representation of what it will look like when printed. This will enable you to proof the printed image on your screen for printed output.

You'll begin by opening the file.

1 Choose File > Open, and open the 20Start.tif file from the Lessons/Lesson20 folder.

Because the 20Start.tif file contains a color profile that indicates that the image was created in a different color space than the one you set up for Photoshop, the Embedded Profile Mismatch notice appears, asking you to resolve this difference.

There are three options in the notice. Selecting Use the Embedded Profile changes the color settings from the ones you defined for Photoshop in the previous section to the ones represented by the profile in the image. Selecting Discard the Embedded Profile displays the document as though it had no profile and can result in inaccurate colors being displayed. Rather than choose either of these, you'll select another option instead.

2 Select the Convert Document's Colors to the Working Space option, and click OK.

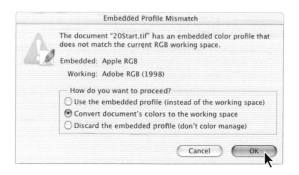

An RGB image of a scanned postcard is displayed.

The Convert Document's Color to the Working Space option makes Photoshop compare the color space in the 20Start.tif file's embedded color profile with the color space you defined in the Color Settings dialog box. Photoshop then converts the 20Start.tif file's colors as necessary to display the image on-screen as accurately as possible.

Note: Depending on what you've specified in the Color Settings dialog box, if the image did not have a color profile already, the Missing Profile notice would have appeared. This notice gives you the choice of whether to leave the image without a profile (that is, without color management); apply the current color profile that you specified in the Color Settings dialog box; or assign a profile from a list of possible profiles. Applying the current color profile is generally a good choice.

Before soft-proofing—that is, proofing on-screen—or printing this image, you'll set up a proof profile. A proof profile (also called a *proof setup*) defines how the document is going to be printed, and adds those visual properties to the on-screen version for more accurate soft-proofing. Photoshop provides a variety of settings that can help you proof images for different uses, including print and display on the Web. For this lesson, you'll create a custom proof setup. You can then save the settings for use on other images that will be output the same way.

3 Choose View > Proof Setup > Custom.

4 Make sure that the Preview check box is selected.

5 On the Profile pop-up menu in the Proof Setup dialog box, choose a profile that represents a final-output source color profile, such as that for the printer you'll use to print the image. If you don't have a specific printer, the profile Working CMYK - U.S. Web Coated (SWOP) v2 is generally a good choice.

6 Make sure that Preserve Color Numbers is not selected. Leaving this option off simulates how the image will appear if colors are converted from the document space to their nearest equivalents in the proof profile space.

Note: This option is not available on all operating systems. Continue to the next steps.

7 From the Intent menu, choose a rendering intent for the conversion (we chose Relative Colorimetric, a good choice for preserving color relationships without sacrificing color accuracy).

8 If it's available for the profile you chose, select Ink Black. Then choose Paper White.

Notice that the image appears to lose contrast. Ink Black simulates the dynamic range defined by an image's profile. Paper White simulates the specific shade of white for the print medium defined by an image's profile. That is, the whites shown in the image are now simulating the white of paper.

Normal image

Image with Ink Black and Paper White options

9 Click OK.

To turn the proof settings off and on, choose View > Proof Colors.

Identifying out-of-gamut colors

Most scanned photographs contain RGB colors within the CMYK gamut, and changing the image to CMYK mode (which you'll do later in order to print the file) converts all the colors with relatively little substitution. Images that are created or altered digitally, however, often contain RGB colors that are outside the CMYK gamut—for example, neon-colored logos and lights.

Note: Out-of-gamut colors are identified by an exclamation point next to the color swatch in the Color palette, the color picker, and the Info palette.

Before you convert an image from RGB to CMYK, you can preview the CMYK color values while still in RGB mode.

1 Choose View > Gamut Warning to see out-of-gamut colors. Adobe Photoshop builds a color-conversion table and displays a neutral gray where the colors are out-of-gamut.

Because the gray can be hard to spot in the image, you'll now convert it to a stronger gamut-warning color.

2 Choose Edit > Preferences > Transparency & Gamut (Windows, Mac OS 9) or Photoshop > Preferences > Transparency & Gamut (Mac OS 10). Then click the Color sample at the bottom of the dialog box.

3 Choose a vivid color, such as pink or a saturated clear blue, and click OK.

4 Click OK again to close the Transparency & Gamut dialog box. The gray is replaced by the new color you chose.

5 Choose View > Gamut Warning to turn off the preview of out-of-gamut colors.

Photoshop will automatically correct these out-of-gamut colors when you save the file in Photoshop EPS format later in this lesson. Photoshop EPS format changes the RGB image to CMYK, adjusting the RGB colors as needed to bring them into the CMYK color gamut.

Adjusting an image and printing a proof

The next step in preparing an image for output is to make any color and tonal adjustments to the image. In this part of the lesson, you'll add some tonal and color adjustments to correct an off-color scan of the original postcard.

So that you can compare the image before and after making corrections, you'll start by making a copy.

1 Choose Image > Duplicate and click OK to duplicate the image.

2 Arrange the two image windows in your workspace so that you can compare them as you work.

Here you'll adjust the hue and saturation of the image. There are various ways to adjust color, including using the Levels and Curves commands. In this lesson, you'll use the Hue/Saturation command to adjust the artwork.

3 Select 20Start.tif (the original image) and choose Image > Adjustments > Hue/Saturation.

4 Drag the Hue/Saturation dialog box aside so that you can still see the 20Start.tif image, and then select the following settings:

• Drag the Hue slider until the colors, especially the flesh tones, look more natural. (We used +20.)

• Drag the Saturation slider until the intensity of the colors looks normal (we used –17).

• Leave the Lightness setting at the default value (0), and click OK.

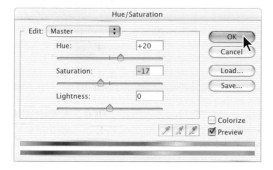

5 With 20Start.tif still selected, choose File > Print With Preview.

6 In the Print dialog box, make sure that the Show More Options check box is selected, or select it now. Then select the following options:

• In the pop-up menu immediately below the Show More Options check box, choose Color Management.

• Under Source Space, select Proof Setup.

• Under Print Space, use the Profile and the Intent pop-up menus to select the profile for the color printer on which you plan to print the image for proofing. If your specific printer isn't listed, choose Working CMYK.

- Click Done.

7 Choose File > Save to save your work.

8 Print a copy of the image to a color printer and compare it to the on-screen version.

Saving the image as a separation

In this part of the lesson, you'll learn how to save the image as a separation, so that it can print out on separate cyan, magenta, yellow, and black plates.

1 With 20Start.tif still selected, choose File > Save As.

2 In the Save As dialog box, select the following options:

• On the Format pop-up menu, select Photoshop EPS.

• Under Save Options, for Color, select the Use Proof Setup: Working CMYK check box.

Note: These settings cause the image to be automatically converted from RGB to CMYK when it is saved in the Photoshop Encapsulated PostScript (EPS) format.

3 Name the file **20Start.eps** and click Save.

4 Click OK on the EPS Options dialog box that appears.

5 Choose File > Open, and open the 20Start.eps file, located in the Lessons/Lesson20 folder.

Notice that the 20Start.eps file is now a CMYK file.

6 Choose File > Save and then close the 20Start.tif and 20Start copy.tif files.

Now only the 20Start.eps file is open in Photoshop.

Selecting print options

To select printing options, you make choices in the File Info and Print With Preview dialog boxes and then choose Options from the Print dialog box. The next sections introduce you to some of the printing options.

[?] For information on all the print options, see Photoshop Help.

Entering file information

Photoshop supports the information standard developed by the Newspaper Association of America and the International Press Telecommunications Council to identify transmitted text and images.

1 Select the 20Start.eps image and choose File > File Info. The File Info dialog box opens with Description selected in the list on the left side of the dialog box.

2 Type information in any of the options available, such as a title for the image, the author, a description of the image, and so forth.

Note: To print a description when you print an image, choose File > Print With Preview, and click the Description option.

3 In Keywords, type a keyword (such as **skating** or **winter**) in the text box. You can type and enter as many other keywords as you want.

4 In the List menu, select Origin.

5 Click the Today button to enter today's date in the Date Created text box. Then type any other information you want to enter in the other options.

6 Click OK to close the File Info dialog box, and then choose File > Save.

For complete information about the File Info dialog box panels and options, see Photoshop Help.

Printing

When you're ready to print your image, use the following guidelines for best results:

• Set the parameters for the halftone screen.

• Print a *color composite*, often called a *color comp*. A color composite is a single print that combines the red, green, and blue channels of an RGB image (or the cyan, magenta, yellow, and black channels of a CMYK image). This indicates what the final printed image will look like.

• Print separations to make sure the image separates correctly.

• Print to film.

Printing a halftone

To specify the halftone screen when you print an image, you use the Screen option in the Print With Preview dialog box. The results of using a halftone screen appear only in the printed copy; you cannot see the halftone screen on-screen.

You use one halftone screen to print a grayscale image. You use four halftone screens (one for each process color) to print color separations. In this example, you'll be adjusting the screen frequency and dot shape to produce a halftone screen for a grayscale image.

The *screen frequency* controls the density of dots on the screen. Since the dots are arranged in lines on the screen, the common measurement for screen frequency is lines per inch (lpi). The higher the screen frequency, the finer the image produced (depending on the line-screen capability of the printer). Magazines, for example, tend to use fine screens of 133 lpi and higher because they are usually printed on coated paper stock and on high-quality presses. Newspapers, which are usually printed on lower-quality paper stock, tend to use lower screen frequencies, such as 85 lpi.

The *screen angle* used to create halftones of grayscale images is generally 45°. For best results with color separations, select the Auto option in the Halftone Screens dialog box (choose Print With Preview and select Show More Options; select Output from the pop-up menu and then select the Screen button). You can also specify an angle for each of the color screens. Setting the screens at different angles ensures that the dots placed by the four screens blend to look like continuous color and do not produce moiré patterns.

Diamond-shaped dots are the most commonly used in halftone screens. In Adobe Photoshop, however, you can also choose round, elliptical, linear, square, and cross-shaped dots.

Note: By default, an image will use the halftone screen settings of the output device or of the software from which you output the image, such as a page-layout program. You usually don't need to specify halftone screen settings in the following way unless you want to override the default settings.

1 Make sure that the 20Start.eps image window is active.

2 Choose Image > Mode > Grayscale; then click OK to discard the color information.

3 Choose File > Print With Preview, and make sure that the Show More Options check box is selected.

4 Immediately under the Show More Options check box, select Output from the pop-up menu.

5 Click Screen to open the Halftone Screen dialog box, and enter the following options:

- Deselect the Use Printer's Default Screen check box.

- In Frequency, type **133**, and make sure that Lines/Inch is selected.

- For Angle, type **45°**.

- For Shape, choose Ellipse.

- Click OK to close the Halftone Screen dialog box.

6 Click Done to close the Print With Preview dialog box.

7 To print the image, choose File > Print. (If you don't have a printer, skip this step.)

8 Choose File > Close, and don't save your changes.

For more information about printing halftones, see Photoshop Help.

Printing separations

By default, a CMYK image prints as a single document. To print the file as four separations, you need to select the Separations option in the Print With Preview dialog box. Otherwise, the CMYK image prints as a single, composite image.

In this optional part of the lesson, you can print the file as separations.

1 Choose File > Open, and open the 20Start.eps file in the Lessons/Lesson20 folder on your hard drive.

2 Choose File > Print With Preview.

3 In the Print dialog box, make sure that the Show More Options check box is selected, and then set the following options:

• In the pop-up menu immediately below the Show More Options check box, select Color Management.

• For Source Space, select Document.

• On the Profile pop-up menu, select Separations.

4 Click Print. (If you don't have a printer, skip this step.)

5 Choose File > Close, and don't save the changes.

This completes your introduction to producing color separations and printing using Adobe Photoshop.

For information about all color management and printing options, see Photoshop Help.

Review questions

1 What steps should you follow to reproduce color accurately?

2 What is a gamut?

3 What is an ICC profile?

4 What is a color separation? How does a CMYK image differ from an RGB image?

5 What steps should you follow when preparing an image for color separations?

Review answers

1 Calibrate your monitor, and then use the Color Settings dialog box to specify which color spaces to use. For example, you can specify which RGB color space to use for online images and which CMYK color space to use for images that will be printed. You can then proof the image, check for out-of-gamut colors, adjust colors as needed, and—for printed images—create color separations.

2 A gamut is the range of colors that can be reproduced by a color model or device. For example, the RGB and CMYK color models have different gamuts, as do any two RGB scanners.

3 An ICC profile is a description of a device's color space, such as the CMYK color space of a particular printer. Applications such as Photoshop can interpret ICC profiles in an image to maintain consistent color across different applications, platforms, and devices.

4 A color separation is created when an image is converted to CMYK mode. The colors in the CMYK image are separated into the four process-color channels: cyan, magenta, yellow, and black. An RGB image has three color channels: red, green, and blue.

5 You prepare an image for print by following the steps for reproducing color accurately, and then converting the image from RGB mode to CMYK mode to build a color separation.

Working with Version Cue

If you own Adobe® Creative Suite Standard or Premium, you can take advantage of Adobe Version Cue™, an integrated workflow feature included in the Creative Suite. If you own Adobe Photoshop CS as a separate product, you can use Version Cue as a client when you collaborate with others who own the full version of the product.

With Version Cue, you can easily create, manage, and find different versions of your project files. If you collaborate with others, you and your team members can share project files in a multi-user environment that protects content from being accidentally overwritten. You can also maintain descriptive comments with each file version, search embedded file information to quickly locate files, and work with robust file-management features while working directly within each application.

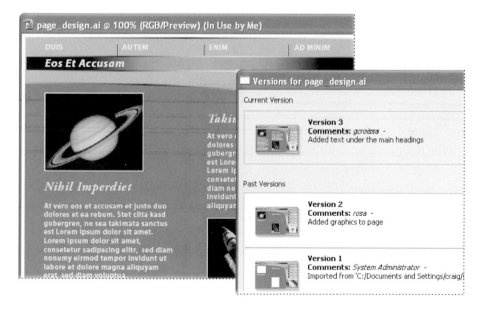

Note: The Version Cue workspace is a feature of Adobe Creative Suite. If you purchased Adobe GoLive CS, Adobe Illustrator CS, Adobe InCopy CS, Adobe InDesign CS, or Adobe Photoshop CS separately, and don't own Adobe Creative Suite, you can use the Version Cue feature in your Adobe CS application only if an owner of Adobe Creative Suite gives you network access to their Version Cue workspace.

Following are the steps you need to take before you begin working with Version Cue, and for how to use Version Cue.

1. Set up the Version Cue workspace.

You and others in your workgroup need access to a Version Cue *workspace* in order to work with the Version Cue feature. When you fully install Adobe Creative Suite, a Version Cue workspace automatically installs on your computer. Depending upon each project's needs, you may choose to work with other Version Cue workspaces located on your colleagues' computers or on a server.

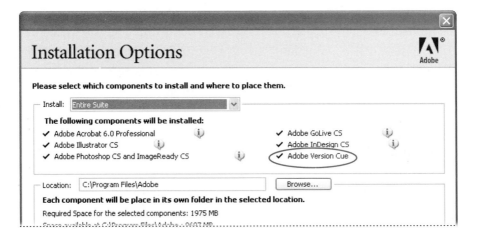

For projects and file versions that you don't need to share with others, or if you work on a laptop that isn't always connected to a network, it's easiest to use the Version Cue workspace located on your own computer. When you change your mind, Version Cue lets you immediately share any Version Cue project with other users. If you mostly intend to collaborate with others, make sure that a Version Cue workspace is located on a computer that everyone can access on a network and that the collaborative projects are kept in that workspace. For installation instructions, see "How To Install" on the Adobe Creative Suite CD.

2. Turn on the Version Cue workspace.

Before you can begin working with the Version Cue feature, you need to turn on the Version Cue workspace. Open the Adobe Version Cue preferences from Control Panel (Windows) or System Preferences (Mac OS) on the computer where the Version Cue workspace is located, and choose On from the Version Cue pop-up menu. To allow others to see and access the workspace over the network, choose This Workspace is Visible to Others from the Workspace Access menu, or, to keep it private, choose This Workspace is Private, and then click OK.

3. Enable the Version Cue preference in Adobe Photoshop CS.

In Photoshop CS, choose Edit > Preferences > File Handling (Windows) or Photoshop > Preferences > File Handling (Mac OS). Select Enable Version Cue Workgroup File Management, and click OK.

4. Create a Version Cue project for each set of related files.

Now you're ready to create a Version Cue *project*, which is used to organize related files. For example, to begin with, you can create a Version Cue project for files you want to keep private, and another project for those files you want to share with others. Choose File > Open and click the Version Cue button; the Open dialog box then switches to display tabs, buttons, and menus for working with Version Cue projects. Double-click a Version Cue workspace to open it, and then choose New Project from the Project Tools menu. Enter a project name, information about the project (optional), and select Share This Project With Others if you want to give other users access to your project. Click OK.

5. Add files to the Version Cue project.

To add an existing file or new file to the Version Cue project, choose File > Save As. Then click the Version Cue button, open your Version Cue project and its Documents folder, enter comments for this version in the Version Comments text box, and click Save.

If you have several files to add to a Version Cue project, you can add the files to the project's Documents folder inside the My Documents/Version Cue (Windows) or Documents/Version Cue (Mac OS) folder on your computer . Then choose File > Open, click the Version Cue button, open your Version Cue project, and then choose Synchronize from the Tools menu.

6. Create file versions.

After you've saved a file to a Version Cue project, you can begin creating versions of the file and adding comments to it by choosing File > Save A Version.

File versioning with Version Cue ensures that no one overwrites the work of anyone else in a Version Cue project, but also prevents users from locking out others who need to work on the same file. You can use versioning to seamlessly retain multiple states of a single file as you work on it, in case you need to restore the file to a previous version. You can also use versioning to quickly compare file versions with team members or with a client before selecting a final version.

7. Review all versions of a file.

After you've created several versions of a file, you can choose File > Versions to view thumbnails of all versions of the file, alongside comments and dates for each, and then open, manage, or delete the versions.

8. Collaborate on a Version Cue project.

When you want to work with other users on one of your Version Cue projects, you can instantly give them access to your Version Cue project. Choose File > Open, click the Version Cue button, and then open the Version Cue workspace that contains the Version Cue project you want to share. Select the project in the dialog box, and then choose Share Project from the Project Tools menu.

To access your Version Cue project, other computers need to be on the same subnetwork as the computer where the Version Cue workspace is installed. Computers outside the subnetwork can access the workspace by choosing Connect To from the Version Cue Tools menu and entering the Version Cue Client URL (IP address).

9. Locate files by searching embedded metadata.

Adobe Creative Suite lets users enter a wide variety of information in the File Info dialog box. This information gets embedded into a document as XMP metadata. For example, the metadata might contain a document's title, copyright, keywords, description, properties, author, and origin. Also, any comments you add to each file version are included in the file's metadata. With Version Cue you can quickly locate a file by searching the embedded metadata of all files in a Version Cue project, including Version Cue comments. You can also view a subset of metadata to quickly check the status of a file, its last comment, version date, and who is editing it.

Choose File > Open, click the Version Cue button, open the Version Cue workspace that contains the project you want to search, and then select the project. Select the Search tab and enter any text that may be embedded in the metadata of the file you want to locate or search by filename.

10. Perform advanced tasks with the Advanced Version Cue Workspace Administration utility.

You can choose to set up a simple collaboration where you share a Version Cue project with anyone using a Creative Suite application, or you can set up a more controlled environment in which users have to log in before accessing your project. Using the Version Cue Workgroup Administration utility, you can set up user IDs and define their project privileges, remove file locks, edit Version Cue Workspace preferences, and perform other project and workspace maintenance.

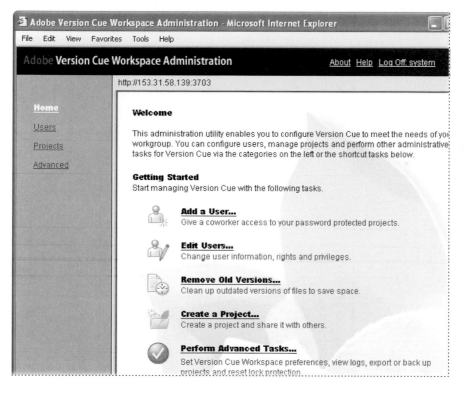

To display the Version Cue Workspace Administration utility log-in page, open the Adobe Version Cue preferences from the Control Panel (Windows) or System Preferences (Mac OS) on the computer where the Version Cue workspace is located, and click Advanced Administration.

Index